IN SEARCH OF LONDON

South Kensington Sta. for Victoria & Albert, Science, Geology & Natural History Museums, Imperial Institute and Albert Hall.
W.H.Bromage · 1951

Map to illustrate
H.V. MORTON'S
"IN SEARCH OF LONDON"
Scale
0 1/4 1/2 3/4 1 Mile
DOMINE DIRIGE NOS
The CITY GATES from West to East: 1 Ludgate, 2 Newgate, 3 Aldersgate, 4 Cripplegate
5 Moorgate
6 Bishopsgate
7 Aldgate
GRAY'S INN RD
THEOBALDS RD
Gray's Inn
Smithfield Market
CHARTERHOUSE ST
BARBICAN
ALDERSGATE ST
Moorfields
Liverpool St.
St. Bartholomew the Great
HOLBORN
HOLBORN VIADUCT
CHANCERY LANE
Lincoln's Inn
FETTER LANE
Gough Sq.
KINGSWAY
Law Courts
ALDWYCH
STRAND
FLEET ST
The Temple
NEWGATE ST
Old Bailey
LUDGATE HILL
St. Paul's Cathedral
CHEAPSIDE
Guildhall
GRESHAM ST
LONDON WALL
MOORGATE
Bank
LOTHBURY
POULTRY
Royal Exchange
CORNHILL
LEADENHALL ST
Mansion Ho.
CANNON STREET
QUEEN VICTORIA
UPPER THAMES ST
EMBANKMENT
BISHOPSGATE
HOUNDSDITCH
MIDDLESEX ST
Petticoat Lane
WHITECHAPEL HIGH ST
ALDGATE
FENCHURCH ST
MINORIES
EASTCHEAP
Monument
Billingsgate
LOWER THAMES ST
The Tower
Royal Mint
St. Katherine's Docks
Wapping
RIVER THAMES
WATERLOO BR.
BLACKFRIARS BR.
SOUTHWARK BR.
LONDON BR.
FESTIVAL of BRITAIN
STAMFORD ST
BANKSIDE
Site of Globe Theatre
SOUTHWARK ST
Southwark Cath.
TOOLEY ST
Tower Bridge
London Bridge
Bermondsey
BOROUGH HIGH ST
SOUTHWARK BRIDGE RD
BLACKFRIARS RD
YORK RD
Waterloo
Archbishop's Park
LAMBETH PALACE RD
Lambeth Palace
Old Temple Bar –
Boundary between the City & Westminster.

Books by H. V. Morton
published as Methuen Paperbacks

A Traveller in Italy
A Traveller in Southern Italy
A Stranger in Spain
A Traveller in Rome
In Search of Ireland
In Search of Scotland
In Search of England
In the Steps of the Master
In Search of Wales

IN SEARCH OF LONDON

by

H. V. MORTON

Methuen · London

A Methuen Paperback

First published in Great Britain 1951
Reprinted five times
This edition first published 1988
by Methuen London Ltd
11 New Fetter Lane, London EC4P 4EE

Printed in Great Britain by
Richard Clay Ltd, Bungay, Suffolk

British Library Cataloguing in Publication Data

Morton, H. V.
In search of London.
1. London (England)—Description—
1901–1950
I. Title
914.21'04855 DA684

ISBN 0-413-18470-6

CONTENTS

CHAPTER ONE

I go in search of London, visit the site of Roman London, see the Bank of England, the Mansion House and the Royal Exchange, take a walk up Cheapside and explore the air raid ruins that lie between Cheapside and Moorgate. Upon a Sunday morning I go down to the East End.

§ 1

AS the Skymaster came up the Thames the passengers crowded to the windows and looked down upon London. They saw a silver thread of river twisting through a landscape black with buildings. Arterial roads, railway lines, building estates, factories, hundreds of separate townships with their churches, municipal and shopping centres were all linked together by continuous masonry and seemed to stretch from horizon to horizon. The passengers looked down, some perhaps with awe, upon the evidence of so much human energy.

Suddenly it became possible to pick out a landmark here and there. The Tower of London and Tower Bridge . . . St Paul's Cathedral and Blackfriars Bridge . . . The Houses of Parliament and Westminster Bridge. . . .

Then, as the aircraft continued to roar over London, still more and more unrecognisable suburbs slid beneath its wings, more main streets, more arterial roads, more playing-fields and thousands upon thousands of little semi-detached villas, each one with a back garden.

I glanced down from my window, thinking that Shakespeare died only three hundred and thirty-five years ago—not a long time, even as men with their short lives reckon time. Yet this confusing landscape sprawling over one hundred and seventeen miles, known as the County of London, has happened since Shakespeare's time. None of it existed three hundred years ago.

Shakespeare's London was a small walled town whose gates were shut each night with the coming of darkness. His contemporaries went a-Maying and gathering primroses where now are tramcars and gasometers. A Londoner was to Shakespeare a man who was born probably within sound of Bow Bells, who worked and slept within the ancient town wall of London, and would probably die there and be buried in one of the city churchyards. London three centuries ago was a small comprehensible cathedral city standing behind its wall, and its citizens could look at it and walk all round it, as men can walk round York and Chester.

A mile or so away was the royal City of Westminster, where the King lived. There were two ways to it, one by river and the other along the strand of the Thames. To the north of the Strand were meadows and hedges, a Convent Garden, a Long Acre and more fields stretching up to a rural lane that lead to Reading and was to become known by the odd name of Piccadilly. And the Londoner from any high ground could look over fields and woodlands and see the spires of parish churches which denoted the hamlets and little market towns round about, pleasant little places like Stepney and Clerkenwell, Islington, Bethnal Green and Camberwell.

Then for three hundred years the flood of bricks and mortar spread out in every direction, turning the hedges into roadways linking village, hamlet and market town for miles around, until the old walled city on its hill stood among miles of chimney pots. To the Londoner of three hundred years ago London was one place—the City. To us London is a hundred different places. It is never easy to know exactly what we mean when we use the word. Indeed, to the question "What is London?" there is no satisfactory answer, unless it be that it is the original little walled city that still exists. It contains St Paul's Cathedral, the Mansion House, the Guildhall, the Bank of England and London Bridge. Thousands of people work there in the day-time, but no one sleeps there at night but the Lord Mayor of London and a few hundred caretakers. Yet the physical boundaries of this ancient city are still visible. It is still possible to walk along the line of the Roman Wall that centuries ago limited the size of London to one square mile. And as an administrative reality London has resisted all change. It is still ruled as it was in mediæval times, by its unique municipality.

This city, by night so ghostly and deserted, is still the one and only historic London. The hundred-odd miles of surrounding brickwork—with the exception, of course, of Westminster—are mere accretions, suburbs, bedrooms. And it is odd that the City of London has never had any territorial demands upon its colonies. It has never had any desire to fly the dagger of St Paul over Wandsworth Town Hall. The Lord Mayor of London is one of the few monarchs in history who has never wished to extend his realm.

So the enormous area of a hundred and seventeen square miles, which for administrative and sentimental reasons is known as London, is ruled by the London County Council. But in the centre is one square mile of the original London, an independent little city-state that might have come down to us from the ancient world.

The Skymaster landed us on the fringe of the Metropolitan area and it took us nearly an hour and a half to get within sight of St Paul's.

§ 2

Days of summer rain were succeeded without warning by a violent heat-wave. In the twinkling of an eye London became a changed city. The sun rose in a cloudless sky, and the buildings stood up with the post-card clarity of a Canaletto.

Because the climate of London is fickle, one never gets tired of it. A spring day can sail into the middle of winter and seem the loveliest day of the year, a week of heat can arrive between two deluges, and that too will seem exquisite, and I have even thought, during one of these meteorological transitions, that London has never looked more marvellous than beneath a white crust of snow.

It was natural that this unexpected heat-wave, coming after weeks of rain, should have cast its enchantment upon London. The sky above Regent Street and Piccadilly was the sort of sky you see in Rome. And Roman indeed London looked that morning, majestic, unselfconscious, great, and, in an age when empires are no longer fashionable, imperial.

I took an omnibus from Piccadilly to the Bank.

We ran down the Haymarket into Cockspur Street, and as we were passing the National Gallery an engineer in the control-room beneath Trafalgar Square turned on the fountains. Two jets mounted into the sunlight, and then, having reached the limit of their climb, came whispering down in two plumes of water. The pigeons, which have become as plump and pampered as the pigeons of St Mark, took panic at this daily event and, exploding upward from every corner of the square, performed a couple of turns round Nelson before they settled down again to bow on their mulberry-coloured feet to kneeling provincials with bags of dried peas.

Yes, I thought to myself, London looks marvellous this morning. . . .

We were held up by the traffic. I glanced across the square to the end of the Strand, where a herd of red omnibuses stood waiting for the lights to change. Some would soon be rushing down Whitehall to Westminster, where, between the narrow defile of the buildings, I could see the Houses of Parliament and the clock-face of Big Ben; others would dash up Lower Regent Street to Piccadilly and the regions of the west. While they vibrated, waiting to move on, a line of traffic poured itself across them into Northumberland Avenue and the Thames Embankment, down Whitehall and beneath the Admiralty Arch into the Mall, where, at the end of the straight avenue, stood Buckingham Palace with the Royal Standard upon its roof, hanging limply in the summer heat.

The sun fell upon a scene in red, white and black; for those are the colours of London: the red of omnibuses, pillar-boxes, Royal Mail vans and the Brigade of Guards, the piebald Portland Stone, bleached white on one side and stained black on the other. That is London, and could be nowhere else in the world.

The lights changed, and we moved on to pause a moment beside the paved churchyard of St Martin-in-the-Fields. I reflected that the burial registers of this church include the names of Nell Gwyn and Chippendale. Such improbable reflections explain something of the charm of London. We turned into the Strand at Charing Cross, and my thoughts sped down six and a half centuries to the Cross at Charing which used to stand where the statue of Charles I stands now, at the beginning of Whitehall. It was the last of the crosses erected by Edward I, to mark the resting-place of the coffin of his queen, Eleanor of Castile, on its way from Lincolnshire, where she died, to Westminster. Then because those two once went crusading together I thought of Acre in Palestine, and I began to wonder if she really did suck the poison from his arm. I was recalled to the present by a man in front of me who said to his companion that he was going to the bioscope. This told me that he was a South African. So Nell Gwyn, Chippendale, the Crusades—and Cape Town!

If one really put down all that flies through the mind every ten minutes in London what a remarkable record it would be.

The omnibus went on down the Strand.

§ 3

I glanced down at the people.

Those over the age of forty had lived through two wars and had survived the Blitz. Boys and girls of sixteen and seventeen remembered no other London but a city of jagged ruins, of hob grates perched in the sunlight in shattered walls, of cellars draped with willow-herb and Canadian fleabane. This London, so heart-breaking to me, and still in a sense so incredible, is to them normal and commonplace. Children of a cynical and frightened age of revolution and insecurity, they have no idea what it was like to live in the wealthy, self-confident London of 1913, or in the less confident but still wealthy, London between the two wars.

Because of the vitality which makes them great, ancient cities are always changing; indeed, throughout history there comes a time in middle-age when the Londoner, noting the changes in fashion, habits and conduct, and the disappearance of old landmarks, is heard to say that he can no longer recognise the city of his boyhood. Such changes, piling one on top of the other for a century and more, transform a city so completely that perhaps Chaucer would have had difficulty in recognising the London of Queen Elizabeth, just as Shakespeare would have been lost in the brick-and-stone London of Dr Johnson, while Dickens, well as he knew London, would have been bewildered by the steel-and-concrete London of to-day. But the natural changes of growth known as "moving with the times" are different from the violent changes of disaster. If London as it is to-day may be compared with any other period in its history, perhaps that time would be the years immediately after the Great Fire, in the reign of Charles II, when so much of the City lay in ruins, as it does now.

Yet the comparison is by no means perfect. To those who experienced it, the Blitz was a more fearful ordeal than the Great Fire. The Fire of London was an accident, and it lasted a matter of days. The Blitz was the deliberate attempt of an enemy to subdue a city whose watchword has always been Freedom. So although the outward and visible results of the Fire and the Blitz may be much the same, the effect of those two events upon the population cannot be compared. This generation of Londoners has endured more than any previous generation, except maybe that far-off population, of whose trials and anxieties we know nothing, whose fate it was to inhabit London when the Romans left Britain, after which the country sank into centuries of anarchy and pillage.

In my own lifetime, I reflected, I have seen four separate and distinct Londons. The first is a vision so dim, yet so vivid, that I sometimes wonder whether it may not be something out of Dickens that I have adopted as a personal reminiscence. Yet this cannot be, for I have documentary proof that, as a small child, I was taken on a visit to London during the last years of the reign of the great Victoria. I recollect a city of terrifying noise and movement, of mud and slush, for it was winter-time, and one of my clearest memories is that of the warm stable smell of the straw, damp and muddy with melted snow, which covered the floor of a horse omnibus as it went up Ludgate Hill. I remember distinctly the sable dome of St Paul's lifted above a roofline white with newly fallen snow.

London in those days, although it would have been astonished and indignant to know it, had reached the end of the horse age. The strange-looking motor-cars, made like carriages, and driven by men in goggles, which caused so much amusement when they broke down, were in a few years to drive the horses from London and to transform the appearance of the streets. Still, when I first saw London it was a city of horse-drawn omnibuses, four-wheelers, hansoms and private broughams, and it seemed to me that everybody in that London was either cracking a whip or shouting. The streets rang to a perpetual jingle of harness and shook to the thud of hoofs. Enormous jaunty men, bulky in greatcoats and with rugs wrapped round their knees, sat red-faced in the frosty air, with reins in their gloved hands.

A bus journey was a slow procession, with many halts and every opportunity for the exchange of pleasantries. A traveller was part of the street life of London in those days, as it is impossible to be to-day, enclosed as we are in an omnibus or a motor-car. One was carried slowly in the open air above the heads of the crowds, like a tableau in the Lord Mayor's Show. The drivers had plenty of time to toss jokes from one to the other, or to exchange irony with any member of the general public. All the drivers seemed to know each other, and in those moments when the arm of a policeman brought to a standstill hundreds of horses—many of whom, I seem to remember, tossed their heads and blew air from their nostrils—these men shouted and bellowed what to a frightened child appeared horribly ogre-like greetings and intimacies.

I now realise that I was witnessing much the same kind of London as Hogarth knew: a city with a hearty and vocal lower class, a city full of loud human and animal noises which to-day we would neither tolerate nor recognise. There were German bands, trombonists, street singers, hurdy-gurdies, shouting pedlars, butchers in striped aprons who yelled at shop-doors, and, in the background, the rumble of wagons and drays, the chink of bits, the creak of harness and the cracking of whips. Possibly the noise of London impressed itself upon me because the relative in whose house I was staying became so ill that a bed of tan was laid down outside to deaden the sound of wheels. I remember kneeling upon a chair at a window, watching the approaching traffic, listening to the sudden muffling of the sound as the tan was reached, and the resumption of the normal clump and clip-clop and rumble lower down the road.

Perhaps because I was so small, the pandemonium appeared to me to be organised by people who were larger than life-size. The Cockney is not remarkable for size, yet for years the idea persisted in my mind that he was enormous and belonged to a special race of laughing, bearded giants. I cannot imagine that a modern child, seeing for the first time the slow and orderly procession of mechanical vehicles through the streets of London, would be appalled, as I was, by that brief glimpse into the London of Queen Victoria.

§ 4

Of Edwardian London I remember nothing, because my schooldays were spent elsewhere, but, returning to the capital again in 1913, a youth just ripening for war, I saw my second London, a city from whose streets the solid-tyred motor-cars had driven the horse-drawn traffic; but you could still hire a hansom or a " growler ". It was a London in which the silk hat or topper was a symbol not only of prosperity, but also of respectability. Many barbers kept a man who did nothing else but iron these hats while their owners were having a hair cut. The silk hat of the fashionable man was ironed every day. The bowler hat was socially a lower type of hat, and the cap, except in the country, lowest of all. No one except a few eccentrics went bareheaded, as so many Londoners do to-day.

It was a rich and arrogant London. The last landaus drawn by beautifully matched horses spun through Hyde Park, footmen, in cocked hats, frock-coats and white breeches, sat with folded arms next to the drivers, and in the mellow sunshine of that dying age of wealth and privilege, Society, in the Georgian sense, still existed in the great Eighteenth Century houses and squares of the West End.

It was a dressy London. It was easy to tell at a glance, as in all former periods in history, the aristocrat from the commoner, the rich from the poor. Many men about town wore the now almost extinct eye-glass which performed no optical function at all. They were known admiringly as " toffs " or " swells ", and were in direct descent from the Beaux and Dandies of the Georgian Age, the Pretty Fellows, the Smarts, the Jenny-jessamies, the Bucks and Corinthians of the Regency, and the Johnnies, the Chappies and the Mashers of the Victorian Age. Their swan song was sung during the first War by Nelson Keys: it was called " Gilbert the Filbert, the Knut with a K ".

The Knut of 1914, who brought to an end a long line of exquisites, was fated to be crucified upon the barbed wire of the Somme. He was frequently irritating to his relatives and amusing to the onlooker, but he was a gentleman, and the world has been suffering from his death ever since.

In those days extravagancies of fashion were copied with varying success down the social scale by all except manual workers. The working-man was in 1913 as easily distinguished by his garments as a member of the House of Lords. In those days the navvy was not a gentleman with a pneumatic drill. He was a huge man who wore a heavy frieze jacket and a pair of corduroy trousers strapped at the knee, and a muffler, or " choker ", was usually round his neck. He smoked a short clay pipe. This once common and admirable type is now absent from the London streets. The costermonger—a queer word derived from costard, an apple—was a typical figure of the markets, loud-voiced, humorous, ironic. He had a dress of his own for gala occasions, sewn with hundreds of pearl buttons, and his wife and daughters went in for enormous hats decorated with ostrich feathers. The coster is still with us, but he now looks like anyone else.

In that throbbing, self-confident city just before the first War, wages were paid in silver and gold. The Treasury Note was unknown. The sovereign, or " Jimmy-o'Goblin " in Cockney slang, was a beautiful coin, heavy in the hand and of a rich golden red. It gave one a comforting sense of wealth and power which even a fat wad of paper money fails to impart in these days. On one side was the head of Victoria, or Edward VII, while on the other St George was slaying the Dragon. At a time when quite a number of articles might be bought for a penny, and even a half-penny, the sovereign went a very long way indeed.

Purses have never been popular in England, and I am still prejudiced when I see a man take one out of his pocket and carefully pick out a few coins, yet I remember with pride a little metal sovereign purse which was given to me when I was a young man. The coins were pressed into it, and released by a downward pressure of the thumb which caused the top coin to slide out between thumb and forefinger, while the one below, if one existed, was moved up into its place.

When the heart is young all the world seems gay and cheerful, so that it is difficult to say now whether the impression of London's terrific jollity and good temper in those days was indeed a fact, or whether I was gazing at the capital through the rose-coloured spectacles of youth. An enormous number of people led incredibly bestial and sordid lives. The memory of the beggars flits across my mind, the people who used to sleep on the Embankment, and the barelegged, unshod urchins. Nevertheless the superficial appearance of London was that of an immense, hearty and cheerful metropolis. Although the gap between rich and poor, privileged and unprivileged, was immense, and although there was an enormous amount of genteel misery, I fancy that there was nothing like the envy and malice which is the mark of a more socially conscious age.

The moving-picture had arrived at the time of which I am writing, but nobody thought much of it. It was shown in all kinds of extemporised cinemas, and I think it was called the bioscope, a name that has become obsolete everywhere except in the Union of South Africa, where the most sumptuous air-conditioned cinemas are still called by that archaic word. The first films I remember were mostly spotty travelogues taken in a gondola on the Grand Canal, but it was amusing and thrilling to see people moving. It would have been unbelievable in those days to have been told that in a few years time the art of moving photography would have slain the all-powerful music-hall. And I can think of no greater contrast between that age and this than the sight, then seen everywhere in London, of a music-hall audience pouring out into the lamplit streets, whistling and singing, bubbling over with mirth and good nature, having seen Vesta Tilley, Marie Lloyd, Little Titch, George Robey or Harry Tate, a very different exit from the familiar hang-dog departure of a modern crowd from a cinema, as if from some gigantic morgue.

The London I remember before the first War was black with silk hats in spring and winter, and white with straw boaters in the summer. Carried forward down the Mall upon a hot day in August, 1914, upon a sea of straw hats, I remember shouting with thousands of others for King George V; for we were at war with Germany and, although none of us at the time realised it, the rich London of private enterprise had come to an end.

Four years later I saw my third London.

This was the London of the Long Armistice, the London of Between the Wars. I was young and romantic. I was astonished to be alive. I was thrilled to be earning my living in the city which, above all places on earth, seemed to me desirable and exciting. I do not know whether young men in the provinces to-day still think of London as I did, and as many other young men of that time did, as the land of golden opportunity. We excused our inefficiency and our general ineptitude with the belief that if we could only get to London, that magic and enchanted city, all would go well with us and fortune would smile upon us as it had smiled upon Dick Whittington, Shakespeare, Garrick, Samuel Johnson, and many another poor, ambitious provincial.

It was not a vastly different city from that which I had so briefly known before the War. Its colossal confidence had been slightly shaken and the wind of a new age was blowing. The golden sovereign had disappeared, the silk hat was in decline. Outwardly, however, it was still the cheerful, hearty old London of before the War. Old men said it was different and would never be the same again, but who believes old men? There were still enormous reserves of wealth and elegance. The striped awnings were still put out in the forecourts of the great houses during the "season", and the music of orchestras came down on many a summer's evening to the crowds who watched the arrival of guests in large chauffeur-driven cars.

It was the London of Lloyd George, Bonar Law and Baldwin. It contained the Prince of Wales, Lord Beaverbrook, Lady Cunard, George Lansbury, Ramsay MacDonald, Michael Arlen, Noel Coward, Lord Lonsdale, Margot Asquith, Lady Astor, Philip Snowden, Mr and Mrs Sidney Webb, James Barrie, Joseph Conrad, John Galsworthy, Bernard Shaw, Dean Inge, and quite a lot of other people as well.

I thought it was an exciting city to work in. One day I had the sobering experience of glancing up into the eyes of a man whom I had known and admired in the Army. He was standing on the kerbstone holding out his hat for pennies while three miserable comrades patrolled the pavement with musical instruments. To him London was not an enchanted city. The inequalities of life, which a former age had accepted as the decree of fate, were now sharply challenged. I remember watching mounted police concealed near Trafalgar Square ride out with drawn sword-sticks towards a huge crowd of demonstrators. Yet life was not all strikes and demonstrations; indeed, looking up the appalling unemployment statistics of that time, it seems strange that there were not more of them.

The ordinary people cherished an Eighteenth Century interest in reigning beauties which has now been transferred to film actresses. Like the Georgian crowds who mobbed the Gunning sisters in the Park, the crowds of those days assembled to gaze in unmalicious admiration at Lady Diana Manners or the beautiful Paula Gellibrand. There was still a visible aristocracy, and people liked to see it. Lord Lonsdale in a frock coat, with a cigar in his mouth and a gardenia in his buttonhole, was a popular figure at Olympia. The whole of Eaton Square, now either derelict or in course of transformation into flats, was occupied, and so were all the great squares and terraces of Belgravia and Mayfair. Old Devonshire House still stood in Piccadilly, gloomily resisting the age from behind its long and forbidding wall, until the day came when the breakdown men swarmed over it. The lovely Adelphi Terrace fronted the Thames, and I remember many an amusing evening there in the old home of the Savage Club.

Covent Garden Opera House on a gala night was an unforgettable sight as the lights glittered upon a fashionable audience. There was no difficulty in those days about sending a dress shirt to the laundry. Any man who wore a lounge suit in the stalls of a theatre in the evening would have felt himself conspicuous, and the sight, so common now, of grown-up people eating ice-cream with cardboard spoons would have struck the social historian as most peculiar. Bond Street was still fashionable. The Burlington Arcade had a smell of its own, a mingling of all the most costly French perfumes.

In those days the *Mauretania*, the *Homeric* and the *Aquitania* brought to London crowds of rich Americans who took suites at the Savoy and travelled all over England in hired Daimlers. There were others, not so rich, who dashed through London in motor-coaches, and then left to dash in the same way through the cathedral cities before they departed to rush through Paris. Between the two wars London became one of the most popular of the world's cities.

It was a giddy, jazzy London, I suppose, almost as though people were subconsciously aware that a new war was on its way. It was certainly a London in which money was of importance. Every morning the Continental Boat Express, later to become the Golden Arrow, left Victoria Station to link up with the Blue Train to the South of France.

The emotion of the time was focussed upon the grave of the Unknown Soldier in the Abbey, and the Cenotaph in Whitehall. For many years, indeed almost until the outbreak of the next holocaust, any man who did not reverently uncover his head as he passed the Cenotaph risked having his hat removed for him by an indignant stranger. Even people sitting alone in taxi-cabs took off their hats when they passed the Cenotaph.

And so the nineteen-twenties merged into the cold war of the nineteen-thirties, all leading to that Sunday in September, 1939, when Mr Neville Chamberlain told us in a weary voice that we were at war again.

And now the years had passed, and I was looking at my fourth London.

It is this modern London of jagged ruins and hatless crowds. The well-known background is there, a trifle shabbier, but, miraculous to relate, it is still there. And the omnibus bound for the Bank took me through this London, down the Strand to Temple Bar and across the invisible boundary into the City of London. The glimpse of the great black dome on top of Ludgate Hill was the same as ever, and a lovely glimpse of London it is. But it was into the faces of the Londoners that I looked with interest. They were not apparently the same people who had laughed and smiled between the two wars. They were a graver, sadder people. They no longer exhibited that rich variety which formerly made up the pageant of the London streets. They all looked alike. It was no longer possible to distinguish a lord from a navvy, a poor man from a rich one. It was outwardly a classless London, or at least should I say a lower middle-class London? The quality that London had always possessed, elegance, or *ton* as the Eighteenth Century put it, had completely vanished. London, for the first time in my experience, looked provincial.

And, glancing at the faces in the street, I remembered with something approaching awe that those were the faces of men and women whose courage had been expended in many years of air warfare; they were the air-raid wardens, the fire-watchers, the firemen. Some of them had known two wars. The newspapers which they carried mentioned the possibility of a third. Probably that was why so few of them were smiling.

" Bank! " called the conductor.

And I found myself in the heart of London.

§ 5

In ancient times a river fed by streams from north-east London ran beneath what is now the Bank of England and the Mansion House and flowed into the Thames. It was called the Walbrook. It was wide and powerful, and it divided London into two parts: its course was a slight valley between two hills, on one of which now stands St Paul's Cathedral, and upon the other Leadenhall Market.

It was upon the banks of this stream—now I believe not even a sewer, but merely a street name—that the first London of which we know anything was built. That is why, were I a guide, I should take my charges to the Bank of England and say to them, "You are standing about twenty feet or so above the old Walbrook, on whose banks the first Roman London was built. Let us therefore begin our explorations from this place."

When I came to London after the first War to earn my living, I was bewildered by the size of the capital. I was startled and thrilled by the millions of Londoners with whom I rubbed shoulders every day of my life. I was dumbfounded by the unbroken miles of chimney-pots, and it seemed to me impossible that anyone could ever find his way about this appalling labyrinth. I was fascinated by the thought that this tremendous massing together of Humanity in one spot must have had a beginning, although it hardly seemed possible that there was ever a time when the site of London was unoccupied. Whenever I climbed to the dome of St Paul's, or when at high tide I watched the tugs pressing up and down stream beneath the bridges, I would try and imagine what the landscape had looked like before Man had claimed it as the scene of his complex activities.

Did Ancient Britons in their coracles cast their nets into the Thames, and cook their fish on fires of oak twigs where St Paul's Cathedral now stands? Did wandering tribes, finding their way along the tracks that became Watling Street and Ermine Street, seek the high ground above the Thames as night fell and camp out, with no idea that they were sleeping upon ground that was to be dedicated to so many centuries of living?

On many a Saturday afternoon and Sunday I would walk the streets of the City trying to imagine—a most difficult feat—what London looked like when there was nothing but the rise and fall of the Thames, the flight of birds in the marshes, the leap of a salmon. The Museums were not of much help. The relics of prehistoric London are so few, and so dreary to look at, that I soon gave it up and turned my thoughts to something a little more tangible: the first of the many Londons that have followed—Roman London.

And here I was indeed fortunate. At this time I met a remarkable man, the late G. F. Lawrence, who, with a delightful touch of Nineteenth Century pedantry, called himself an antiquary. Whenever I hear people say that Dickens over-drew and exaggerated his characters, I think of Lawrence, or "Stoney Jack", as he was called by every navvy who worked in the City. He might have been created by Dickens. In appearance, Lawrence was rather like a genial frog. He was small and square, and had a habit of puffing and swelling out his cheeks when he talked. He was generally dressed in blue serge, with a stiff white collar and a black tie. His eyes behind steel spectacles were wide, blue and laughing, his hair was white, his moustache was white, and he had the pink complexion of an infant. He was victimised by asthma and addicted to a powerful, slender kind of cheroot which did not help his cough. Those rancid little squibs always ultimately drove him into a shocking paroxysm of coughing, from which he emerged gallantly to resume his unfailing conversation.

To Lawrence, the past appeared to be more real, and infinitely more amusing, than the present. He had an almost clairvoyant attitude to it. He would hold a Roman sandal—for leather is marvellously preserved in the London Clay—and, half closing his eyes, his head on one side, the cheroot obstructing his diction, would speak about the cobbler who had made it ages ago, the shop in which it had been sold, the kind of Roman who had probably bought it and the streets of the long-vanished London it had known. The whole picture took life and colour as he spoke. I have never met anyone with a more affectionate attitude to the past. I suppose it was natural that in his old age he should have become a spiritualist, and so have found himself in even more intimate contact with former ages and on speaking terms with their inhabitants.

On West Hill, Wandsworth, Lawrence kept one of the strangest little shops in London. It is now a laundry, or something like that, and I can never pass it without a pang, for I spent there some of the happiest Saturday afternoons of my life. In the upper regions Lawrence lived with his wife and a daughter, who, I seem to remember, was a medium. The shop sign that swung over the door on a bracket was the ka-figure from an Ancient Egyptian tomb, an object washed to the original wood by years of wind and rain. The window was full of flint arrow-heads, stone axes, Egyptian, Greek and Roman antiquities, some of them fragmentary and all of them cheap; for Lawrence numbered no millionaires among his clients, the more ardent of whom were schoolboys, poor students, and the secretaries of school museums. The window was a feeble introduction to the shop. There, one had the impression that some mighty gale of Time had been blowing into the little room in Wandsworth all sorts of litter from Nineveh, Babylon, Thebes, the Ægean, Cyprus, Crete, Rome and Byzantium. The black hand of a mummy would be lying in a Samian bowl, and it was not surprising upon opening a cigar-box to find it full of silver Cæsars or Coptic embroidery rifled from the sand-heaps of Akhmîn.

Lawrence was to be found in his shop only on a Saturday afternoon, when he was to be seen all day long behind the counter with his cheroot. There was a special reason for this. During the week he had certain duties to perform at the London Museum, then in Lancaster House, St James's, but his real mission in life was to haunt every demolition site in the City and make friends with the navvies, so that they would bring to him on Saturday afternoons anything that had been found during excavation. To some of these men, and he knew them all, he had given a rudimentary archæological training. There was an enormous amount of demolition and rebuilding going on in the City during the nineteen-twenties, and the foundations for the new concrete offices penetrated the Roman level into the London Clay. Lawrence knew that this was the last chance to save any antiquities that might still be hidden in the soil.

The authorities of Guildhall Museum, on whose territory he was poaching, looked upon him as a dangerous pirate, and many were the bitter complaints lodged against him. I suppose the officials of the London Museum either disowned him or administered a technical rebuke, but in any case Lawrence was unmoved, and continued for years to poach and pry and whisper, and to conduct mysterious transactions behind hoardings and in the tap-rooms of City public-houses. All this led to a procession of navvies to Wandsworth on Saturday afternoons, with mysterious objects wrapped in spotted handkerchiefs.

In that extraordinary way was built up the magnificent collection of Roman Samian ware in the London Museum. It took years to assemble and it required incredible patience. The hundreds of pots came to Lawrence, sometimes a bit at a time, and often weeks separated one fragment from its fellow. But Lawrence knew them all by heart. The contents of his cupboards were like a collection of unfinished jig-saw puzzles. He waited until the London Clay had been reached before he gave up hope of completing a pot, and only then, when no further hope was possible, patched up the missing parts with red ochre and beeswax.

I cannot count the times I have been present when navvies have appeared and passed their treasure across the counter with a husky " Any good to yer, guv'nor? " I have seen handkerchiefs unknotted to reveal Roman pins, mirrors, coins, leather, mediæval pottery, Tudor relics, and every kind of object that can lie concealed in old and storied soil. I was with him one day when two navvies handed over an immense mass of clay found beneath a building in Cheapside. It was like an iron football, and they said there was a lot more of it. Sticking in the clay were bright gleams of gold. When they had gone, we went up to the bathroom and turned the water on to the clay. Out fell pearl ear-rings and pendants and all kinds of crumpled jewellery. That was how the famous hoard of Tudor jewellery, which occupied a room to itself in the London Museum, was discovered.

I believe Lawrence declared this as treasure trove and was awarded a large sum of money, I think a thousand pounds. I well remember that he gave the astounded navvies something like a hundred pounds each, and I was told that these men disappeared, and were not seen again for months!

The secret of his success with the navvies was that he was kindly, honest and sincere, and he never sent them away empty-handed. Even if they brought him something worthless, he would always give them the price of a pint of beer. His kindness was delightful. He loved nothing better than a schoolboy who was interested in the past. Many a time I have seen a lad in his shop longingly fingering some trifle that he could not afford to buy.

"Put it in your pocket," Lawrence would cry. "I want you to have it, my boy, and—*give me threepence*!"

That was the remarkable little man with whom I had the privilege of exploring London years ago, listening to him, learning from him, fascinated by his enthusiasm and his knowledge. To us, walking the river-side streets on some hushed Sunday, the Thames was alive again with galleys and triremes, men were unloading wine and olive oil and a consignment of legionary sandals upon the quaysides of Billingsgate, and behind us lay not the London of to-day, but the red-tiled London of nearly two thousand years ago, a rectangular city with the wide Walbrook in the middle and two hills on each side, upon one the Forum, and—but the other had not yet been baptised.

§ 6

Standing on the steps of the Royal Exchange, I watched the press of omnibuses at the Bank and attempted, as I have so often done, to visualise the beginning of London.

In the days when I used to collect coins, you could generally pick up at London auctions a gold coin minted by the Emperor Claudius in the year 44 A.D. to celebrate the inclusion of Britain within the boundary of the Roman Empire. It bore the head of the Emperor and a triumphal arch with "*De Britt*" inscribed above it. I always loved this coin. It was like holding the very roots of our history.

Why the Romans decided to invade Britain is obvious. Until that small island off the shores of Gaul, which was a stronghold of Druidism, had been subdued the conquest of Gaul was incomplete. Rebels could always seek refuge in

Britain and from the groves of Anglesey agitators could always find their way to the Continent. There were also commercial motives and personal ones, for we are told that Claudius desired to stage a military triumph in Rome and to appear before the populace in the unlikely guise of a conqueror.

He selected three Rhenish legions for the expeditionary force: the II Legion, *Augusta*, from Strasburg, the XIV Legion, *Gemina*, from Mainz, the XX Legion, *Valeria Victrix*, from Cologne, and from the Danubian province of Pannonia he withdrew the IX Legion, *Hispana*. The whole force with its auxiliaries probably numbered about forty thousand men. When the troops learnt that they were to fight in Britain they mutinied, refusing to serve beyond the confines of the known world. But their fears were soothed and the invasion was planned to take place in the autumn of the year 43 A.D.

As the Crucifixion is generally placed between the years 29 and 33 A.D., the Claudian invasion of Britain, and the foundation of London, occurred some ten years after the events described in the Gospels. It is strange indeed, as you stand at the Bank watching the omnibuses, to think that it is not outside the bounds of possibility that some of the Roman legionaries who helped to peg out the first boundaries of London might have served with the XII Legion in Jerusalem, and may even have been stationed round the Cross.

London's roots go back to the age of St Paul. He was just starting on his missionary journeys when London was founded, a little Roman frontier post and port on the confines of the Empire. St Peter was alive. Pilate was probably alive. Although the great Augustan Age of Latin literature was over, there were old men still alive at that time who could remember Virgil and Horace, and men not so old who would remember Ovid, Livy and Strabo. The year of the invasion was the year of Seneca's exile.

The Emperor's parting instructions to his general were that he was to bring the Britons to bay, but not to fight a conclusive battle. Instead word was to be sent back to Rome, whereupon Claudius himself would go post haste to Britain to be present in person, and thus qualify for a military triumph in Rome. And the operation worked out as planned. The legions fought two actions, one on the Medway and the other on the Thames, near some obscure ford called Lyn-din, and then the messengers sped across Europe to summon the Emperor.

Claudius set off with perhaps the most fantastic pageant that ever placed foot upon English soil. He took with him the Praetorian Guard and a phalanx of war elephants, as well as a brilliant staff of officers and senators. This entourage sailed to Marseilles and then crossed France partly by land and partly by the rivers, arriving in Boulogne three months later. Having landed in Britain, the Emperor moved up through Kent with his astonishing escort, and joined his main army near Colchester, which was the capital of Caractacus. Everything was in the bag, as more recent military men might put it, and it only remained for the Emperor to give the order.

The legions went into battle, and fought an action so decisive that all the tribes in south-east Britain were subdued, while others in Essex and Sussex paid homage in order to save their territories from fire and pillage. Claudius is said to have spent only sixteen days in Britain before he hurried back with the Praetorian Guard and the elephants to enjoy the triumph he had so cleverly organised for himself.

How interesting it would be to know what Claudius did during those sixteen days in Britain. It is tempting to imagine him in the unaccustomed gilt breastplate of a Roman general, surveying the site of London, asking the polite questions which royal personages ask on such occasions, while staff officers perhaps unrolled plans and maps of London's first streets, explaining that the Forum was to be on that hill opposite and that the harbour was going to be down there, where the men were cutting willow-trees. It is fascinating to think of the war elephants fording the Thames with their Indian mahouts perched aloft in nests of feathers—the first elephants and castles to be seen in those parts!—and it is surely not unreasonable to suppose that, with so many distinguished staff officers present, the victory was celebrated by a banquet.

Were this so—and it is likely, for Claudius was a noted

gourmet, and both mushrooms, which he loved, and oysters were in season—possibly the banquet was held behind the lines on the site of London. What wondering British fisherman or fowler prowling the marshes of the Thames may have looked up to see the imperial marquee, with the legionary standards stacked outside, upon a site where a great church would one day be built, dedicated to a man who was at that very moment tramping Asia Minor spreading the Gospel of Christ. But whether the imperial marquee was erected at London or Colchester, it is certain that two interesting guests were bidden to the feast, two men who were fated to wear the purple: Vespasian, commander of the II Legion, and his son, Titus.

What an occasion that would have been! It would be the first time that Britain was linked with the Holy Land, for it was Vespasian and Titus who, nearly thirty years afterwards, fought the Jewish War and fulfilled Christ's prophecy that " Jerusalem shall be trodden down by the Gentiles ". It was Titus who conducted the siege, and upon its conclusion levelled the walls of the Temple and left Jerusalem a ruin.

We who know their destiny like to picture those two emperors riding through the meadows and woodlands of Britain, listening no doubt to the sound of the first saws, hammers and chisels on the place which was to become London.

§ 7

London, or Londinium, was a Roman city for nearly four hundred years, a space of time as great as that which separates us from the age of Queen Elizabeth. Generations of Romans and Romanised Britons were born beside the Thames, and family history accumulated. Every fifty years or so old men no doubt said that they could no longer recognise the Londinium of their young days. " Not the same place I remember when I was a boy. Why, Marcus, when I was courting your mother, you could count the ships at Billingsgate and—now look at them! Londinium is getting too big. And young people have no manners now. The London girls aren't as pretty. No grace, Marcus, no womanliness. And as for the new temples; well, of course, no one can build now. It's a lost art. . . ."

And all the time the real work of London went on: the loading and the unloading of ships, as the galleys and merchantmen from Gaul and Italy came to the Pool, bringing with them stories from the great and dangerous world beyond the seas.

The unrecorded history of four centuries would be fascinating could we know it. Thousands of visitors must have come to Londinium, official reports must have been filed in the local archives, and in the Roman foreign office imperial secretaries must have put on record details of royal tours, yet not a single line has survived to preserve for us an eye-witness account of this first London, what it looked like, the lay-out of its public buildings, and how it lived.

Londinium must have been rebuilt more than once. But probably the main features did not change. There is believed to have been a wooden bridge across the Thames, not far from the site of the present London Bridge; there was a massive wall right round the city, built at some unknown period; the harbour was the present Pool of London; and the Forum, the heart of Roman London, lies twenty feet or so beneath Leadenhall Market. There were public baths, arenas, amphitheatres; but where these were, no one knows.

London always has been a commercial city, and there were naturally many inns and hotels. I remember when I was at Herculaneum some years ago, they were digging an hotel out of the volcanic dust. It was a building on the main street, with a balcony. No doubt many of the Roman hotels in London were like that. Guests would have stood on the balconies and looked down upon streets which must at times have been crowded with strange men from the utmost confines of the Empire, for the Roman Wall dividing Britain from the Picts and the Scots was manned by every nationality under the sun—except Romans and Britons. Strangely accoutred troops must often have passed through London on their way to the north, and the Londoners of that time would have been acquainted with the appearance, the arms and the habits of every kind of outlandish soldiery in the Empire. There were Batavians and Tungrians and Gauls, mounted Scythian archers, Spaniards, Thracians, Dalmatians and Asturians, Hamian archers, Balearic slingers, all in their distinctive dress, as well as barbaric-looking cavalrymen and artillerymen, who drew along the northern roads great catapults which hurled rock and stone for hundreds of yards.

All these strange men brought their own gods with them to Britain. How many temples there were in London we do not know, but we do know that there was at least one temple to the Egyptian Isis. Centuries ago someone in Southwark scratched three words on a water-pot—now in the London Museum—*ad fanem Isidis*, near the temple of Isis. What a strange thought it is that the sistra of Egyptian priestesses were shaken in Southwark and that a band of priests and priestesses, like those described by Apuleius in *The Golden Ass*, roamed the streets of London seeking converts and inviting Londoners to attend their mysterious rites.

It is believed that before London was converted to Christianity the prevailing religion was the worship of Diana, the goddess of the chase, and it was once widely held that her temple stood on the site of St Paul's Cathedral. In support of this, Camden's account has often been quoted of the curious stag ceremony which used to be held in St Paul's in ancient times. A stag's head, mounted on a spear and carried in procession round the church to the sound of horns, was received by the priests, who wore garlands of flowers.

Many of the houses in Roman London must have been delightful, especially perhaps those upon the banks of the Walbrook. The fountain in the atrium would have been fed by the stream, and one such house discovered in Bucklersbury possessed a little veranda overlooking the water. When you stand at the Bank, it is difficult to cast back the mind to a day when the view included a pleasant stream bordered with alder and willow and bearing upon its banks square houses roofed with red tiles, whose gardens contained flowers and fruit-trees.

All over London, fifteen to twenty feet below the modern streets, beautiful mosaic pavements have been found constructed above hot-air chambers fired by wood furnaces. The flues of these chambers sent an even current of air through the rooms, so that Londoners in Roman times enjoyed comfort in winter.

The most important monument left to us from four centuries of Roman rule is London Wall and its significance cannot be exaggerated. It enclosed a square mile of territory. It was a massive construction, with gates, bastions, and crenellated battlements, remains of which exist to-day both above and below ground. So massive are the foundations of London Wall—or the Town Wall of London, to give it its proper title—that special arrangements are made by contractors who have to excavate on the line of it.

The Roman Wall froze, so to speak, the size of London for centuries, and it also settled for ever the frontiers of that square mile known as the City of London.

Although London Wall has been repaired and strengthened, its course has never been altered, and it remains as it was plotted by the Romans. Until the time of Elizabeth every traveller approaching London saw a city surrounded by a wall. The six gates of this wall—Aldgate, Bishopsgate, Moorgate, Cripplegate, Aldersgate and Ludgate—were closed at night, and it was not until the reign of George III that, becoming an obstruction to traffic, they were pulled down and sold. Their names, however, exist to-day, and are carried all over the Metropolitan area on the indication boards of omnibuses. Thus the City of London is a square mile of territory enclosed by the Romans nearly two thousand years ago. It is the germ-cell from which the tremendous growth known as the County of London, and an even wider circle, Greater London, have developed. Yet to this day the diminutive little City lives on, surrounded by its now invisible wall, the centre of a stupendous mass of bricks and mortar.

The " Square Mile " is an unique survival. There is nothing else in England which so closely resembles a city-state of antiquity. It is ruled, not by the London County Council, but by its own chief magistrate, the Lord Mayor of London, the " King of the Square Mile ", whose state is modelled on that of a mediæval baron. The government of the City is carried out by the Common Council held at Guildhall. The City Police are a separate force, who wear a slightly differently shaped helmet from that worn by the Metropolitan Police, and their armlets are barred in red stripes instead of white. Technically, a Metropolitan policeman has no power of arrest beyond the City boundary, and vice versa, but I suppose these matters are arranged by mutual agreement. Thus in these and many other ways the ancient City of London seeks to preserve its dignity and its independence.

Perhaps the most significant of its traditions, in which may be seen the shadow of London's power in past ages, is the custom, always observed, that the King, on his way to the City, must halt at the boundary and, in theory, request the Lord Mayor's permission to enter his domain. That is really what the ceremony means. Every time the reigning monarch goes to the City, his coach, or his car, is stopped at Temple Bar, the City's boundary on the west, where the Lord Mayor, with the Sheriffs, the Sword-bearer, the Mace-bearer, and the City Marshal, are waiting. The Lord Mayor advances and tenders the City's sword to the King, who touches it and returns it. His coach then enters the City. This brief ceremony, although apparently an act of submission on the part of the City of London, also clearly implies that the King is asking permission to enter. In theory, the gates, although no longer in existence, are closed against him. The ceremony was more obvious when Temple Bar was standing. It was then the custom to close the gates upon the approach of the royal carriage, and the King's Herald knocked and asked permission to enter.

The unique status of London, well illustrated by this strange and interesting formality, was recognised by William the Conqueror, and was confirmed by later kings, with the notable exception of Charles I, many of whose woes sprang from the fact that he never understood the temper of the City. So remarkable is the status of the City that writers such as Sir Laurence Gomme have developed the theory that its municipal privileges and traditions go back to Roman London, and that throughout the Dark Ages which followed the departure of the Legions, when England became a prey to Danish and Saxon pirates, a Romanised community lived on within London Wall, carefully preserving its link with the mother city of the Empire. There are many opponents to this view, who believe that from 410 A.D., when the legions departed, until 886 A.D., when London emerges again as a Saxon town, the city was desolate and deserted, all its links with Rome severed.

But the undoubted fact remains that the shape and size of the City of London is Roman. Though it is no longer possible to see the City standing up on Ludgate Hill behind its town wall, the wall is nevertheless there, a powerful, invisible girdle, and if you would see the remains of it you must go down to the cellars of warehouses or to those few places, such as All-Hallows-on-the-Wall, and St Giles, Cripplegate, where that great relic of the Roman age may be seen in daylight.

§ 8

London possesses at least four architectural compositions which are recognised all over the world; one of these is the group composed by the Bank, the Royal Exchange and the Mansion House. The three others, I would say, are Trafalgar Square, the National Gallery and St Martin-in-the-Fields; Westminster Abbey and the Houses of Parliament; and Tower Bridge, with the Tower of London.

As I stood on the steps of the Royal Exchange, a beadle unlocked the doors, and I went, for the first time for years, into this now disused building. Strangers in London, hearing of the Royal Exchange, must often go down to the City with the idea that they are about to witness a scene of tremendous commercial activity: brokers rushing about, merchants in conclave, messengers speeding here and there, telephones ringing, tape machines chattering, and the sight of the impressive Victorian Corinthian portico, so majestically facing the western flow of 'buses, must raise their hopes. But the English are a strange people. Here in the very heart of the great City, and upon perhaps one of the most costly sites in the world, they maintain a mighty temple in which no exchange of any kind occurs unless it happens that a couple of office-boys, having their luncheon, arrange to swap a cheese sandwich for one containing potted meat.

The first Royal Exchange, built in Elizabeth's time, would have been worth a visit, and so perhaps would the second, which went up in flames in 1838, just after the bells had chimed " There's nae luck aboot the hoose "—surely a rather unfortunate tune to have in any Royal Exchange! The present Royal Exchange is interesting because Sir Thomas Gresham's grasshopper, a relic of the Elizabethan Exchange, is still its weather-vane, and because the unusual floor of Turkish hone stone is another relic of the first building. But beyond that I have never found anything of interest in the place.

The brokers who formerly met here in their thousands are now elsewhere, so a commercial need which was acute in Elizabethan times, when the merchants had no common meeting-place, has at last outlived its mission.

Quite a number of sightseers visit the Royal Exchange every day and wander round listlessly, looking at the historical frescoes, vaguely disappointed, and with the feeling that there must be something more which they have not been shown. I followed behind an earnest American, waiting eagerly for the question which I knew he would eventually ask one of the janitors. He diligently examined the frescoes—" The Phœnicians trading with the Early Britons ", " Alfred the Great repairing the Walls of the City ", and so on—until at last, finding himself near one of the officials, he asked in a polite whisper:

" Say, what goes on here? "

" Nothing, sir," said the janitor briskly, and his tone was so final that the American murmured, " Oh, I see; thanks a lot," and departed.

I have mentioned the transformation which has taken place at the Bank since Roman and mediæval times, and more recently an almost equally drastic transformation occurred when the three great buildings of this group were erected. In the course of this, a market and two churches were swept away. The erection of the Royal Exchange swept away the preposterously dedicated Wren church of St Benet Fink, Mr Fink being the Londoner who restored the church and, as a reward, found himself apparently canonised! (An even odder dedication was that of the now vanished church of St Margaret Moses.) When the Bank of England was built, the church of St Christopher-le-Stocks was demolished, and the Garden Court of the Bank, which can be seen from the vestibule, was the churchyard.

I imagine that the Bank of England is probably the most imperial and costly of London's great commercial palaces. No expense was spared when Sir Herbert Baker, the architect of the Union Buildings in Pretoria, South Africa House, and many fine buildings all over the world, skilfully and successfully added to the Bank without interfering with the classical windowless lower storey, which is a great feature of Sir John Soane's Eighteenth Century design. Sir Herbert had ample scope for his love of symbolism, and together with his sculptor exercised a mild touch of humour here and there, such as the electric light reflectors, which show eagles in pursuit of lions, a reference to the battle then in progress between the dollar and the pound. There are many buildings in London in which Latin is the language of inscriptions, but the Bank is the only one I know of in which Greek has been used. The architrave to the doorway to the Governor's House bears the words in Greek, akin to the well-known warning over Plato's Academy in Athens, "Let no one bring dishonest schemes here". Deep down in the excavations Sir Herbert Baker discovered two Roman pavements, which he relaid because, as he said, he liked the thought that they should come to life again and bear the tread of Londoners after their buried sleep of fifteen centuries.

There are naturally dozens of stories about the Bank of England, and some are even worth telling. One of the founders of the Bank in 1695, and its first deputy chairman, was Michael Godfrey, nephew of Sir Edmund Berry Godfrey, whose body, with money and jewellery intact, was discovered transfixed by his own sword on Primrose Hill one morning in 1678, a mystery that was never solved. Michael Godfrey was sent to Holland, where William III was at war, to open a branch bank to pay the British army. Arriving at

Namur, which was besieged, Godfrey was asked to dinner by the King, and after dinner accompanied the monarch on a tour of the trenches. The King suggested that as Godfrey was not a soldier, he ought not to risk his life, to which Godfrey made the courtly reply, " Not being more exposed than your Majesty, should I be excusable if I showed more concern? " The King then said, " I am in my duty and have a more reasonable claim to preservation ", which seems to have been instantly proved, because the conversation was terminated by a cannon-ball which killed Godfrey.

Another story is dated about 1740, when it is said one of the directors obtained a note for £30,000, the price of an estate he had just bought. Upon his return home he was called suddenly from his room for a moment, and he left the note on the mantelpiece. When he went back, although no one had entered the room, the note had vanished. Having carried out a thorough search, the director was convinced that it must have fallen into the fire, which was alight, and he explained the position to his fellow-directors, who issued another note on the understanding that he would return the first should it ever be found. Thirty years after, when his heirs had inherited his estate, a man presented himself at the Bank of England with a note for £30,000, which he said came to him from abroad. The Bank tried to prove that the note was null and void, and the director's heirs disclaimed all responsibility. Eventually the Bank was obliged to pay and to sustain the loss—although one cannot help feeling that this would not have happened to-day! Long afterwards it was discovered that an architect, who had bought the director's house and had pulled it down in order to build another, had discovered the note for £30,000 wedged in the crevice of a chimney.

A third story concerns poor George Morland, the artist, who, during one of his frequent flights from his creditors, took refuge in an obscure house in Hackney. There his furtive habits gave rise to the suspicion that he was a forger of bank-notes. The Bank of England sent two agents to search his lodgings. Morland, believing them to be bailiffs, escaped by the back door as they came in at the front. When Mrs Morland explained matters to the agents, and showed them some of her husband's unfinished work, the men made a report to the directors, who, in order to compensate Morland for any alarm caused to him, presented him with two bank-notes of twenty pounds each. Here again I must say that the old-time banker seems to have been much more human than his modern counterpart!

The Bank is still guarded at night by a detachment of foot guards, who march every evening from Wellington or Chelsea Barracks. This guard was posted in 1780 when the Bank was believed to be in danger during the Gordon Riots and it has never been withdrawn. The men receive an allowance for this duty, and the officer, who is provided with a pleasant suite of rooms, is allowed to entertain a male guest to dinner. In the old days he was allowed two guests and three bottles of wine. One Sunday in 1793 the two guests enjoyed themselves so completely that, rather than leave the scene of so much happiness, they fought violently with their host in the Bank yard, thus providing the only hint of battle which has ever disturbed the Bank Picquet during the hundred and seventy years of its existence.

The third building of the group, the Mansion House, stands on the site of the old Stocks Market, so named from the stocks which used to stand at the top of Walbrook. At first specialising in meat and fish, the Stocks Market later became vegetarian and floral, at which period, it has been said, it bestowed its name upon the scented stock.

During his year of office the Lord Mayor lives at the Mansion House, which, like the Doge's Palace in Venice, is a house, a court of justice and a prison. In the days when I used to prowl about London at night, I often paused in front of the Mansion House and saw lights burning—the only indication of life in what by day is one of the busiest scenes in the world. The Mansion House is the last great residential house in the City, and although sheriffs and aldermen may sleep in Bromley or Leatherhead, or wherever they like, the Lord Mayor of London must during his year of office sleep in the bosom of his deserted kingdom.

Wandering the City streets at night, pausing to exchange a word with a policeman, a caretaker or a cat, I have often thought how eerie it is that a place, which centuries ago was the most densely inhabited square mile in the country, should now, after nightfall, be the most desolate and the most empty.

§ 9

A street whose post-war aspect I deplore is Cheapside.

It has always seemed to me that this street possessed a greater mediæval dash and vitality than any other in London. It was so clearly the main street of the City. In the luncheon hour City clerks and typists would do their shopping and their window-shopping, so that the pavements were always crowded to the kerbstone. So strong is custom in London, that to-day, although Cheapside has been badly damaged by blast and fire, although so many of the shops have disappeared and there is not much to buy in those that remain, the old London habit of perambulating Cheapside in the luncheon hour still continues.

This was the market-place of Old London. If you can think of Romans at the Bank, you can think only of mediæval and Elizabethan Londoners in Cheapside. It is one of the few streets in London which are narrower to-day than in ancient times. In the old days Cheapside must have resembled one of the great Flemish market-places, perhaps Bruges or Ghent, for it was twice its present width, with five-storey houses of timber, striped black and white, each storey projecting above the lower, rising up round it like galleons. For centuries Chepe was the Piccadilly, the Bond Street and the Oxford Street of London, and those powerful organisations, the London Trade Guilds, grew up in its stalls and workshops. Until the Fifteenth Century the north side was a tournament ground on which contests took place while the King, the Queen, and their courtiers, watched from scaffolds erected on the south side. All the great land processions passed along Cheapside: monarchs on their way from the Tower to be crowned at Westminster, foreign kings and ambassadors, returning heroes, such as the Black Prince, who after Poitiers rode through Cheapside in a suit of battle-stained armour, while the crowds cheered and the London merchants with their families crowded windows decorated with hanging tapestries, with cloths of gold and silver, and with wreaths of fresh spring flowers.

It was the most public place in London, therefore the place where malefactors were punished and placed in the pillory. A baker of bad bread was condemned " to be drawn upon a hurdle from the Guildhall through the great street of Chepe ", where " the streets are most dirty, with the faulty loaf hanging to his neck ". Badly made goods and " other false and deceitful commodities " were publicly burned in Cheapside.

A feature of the street was Cheapside Cross, which stood in the middle of the road facing Wood Street. It was the last but one (Charing Cross being the last) of the twelve crosses erected by Edward I to mark the resting-place of Queen Eleanor's body on its way from Hanby, near Lincoln, where she died, to Westminster Abbey. The Great Conduit of Chepe stood in the centre of the street near the Poultry, the Little Conduit faced Foster Lane, and upon great occasions the water was cut off and wine was substituted.

The market of Cheapside was held in the centre of the roadway, like any Continental market, and it must have presented the appearance of a crowded London street market of to-day. Perhaps Petticoat Lane on a Sunday morning looks as like mediæval Cheapside as anything modern London can show.

The pride of old Cheapside was Goldsmiths Row. From the early Middle Ages down to the time of Charles I, attempts were made to confine goldsmiths to this street. One writer in 1563 called it the " Beauty of London ", while another, only sixty years later, deplored the invasion of " meaner trades " into Goldsmiths' Row, such as milliners, linen-drapers and booksellers.

What a world of London sentiment is wrapped up in St Mary-le-Bow Church, now, alas, a bare and roofless shell. Though the famous Bow Bells have gone, the steeple still remains, and so, fortunately, does the Norman crypt, which was the most interesting part of the church. I suppose that after St Paul's, Bow Church is the pride of all Londoners, even of those who have never been inside it! The fondness of the citizens for the sound of Bow Bells seems to have been responsible for the old saw that only those born within hearing of them are true Cockneys.

I wonder how many Londoners could give the origin of the word Cockney? It really means a milksop or a mother's darling, and was used in the old days in no complimentary sense, but with the intention of deriding the Londoner. The word comes from the obsolete verb, to cocker, or pamper, and a Cockney was a Londoner who had been " cockered ", or so tenderly brought up that he was good for nothing. So the Londoner, with his supposed airs and graces, found himself throughout the Sixteenth and Seventeenth Centuries the target for a lot of not always pleasant banter. Nowadays, of course, the word Cockney has completely lost its sting.

My own personal bereavement in Cheapside is the disappearance of Simpson's Fish Ordinary in Bird-in-Hand Court, a delightful backwater which is now a hideous gap of bombed and blasted masonry. Simpson's, I believe, was the last genuine " ordinary " in London. The title " physician in ordinary to His Majesty " means a doctor regularly in attendance, and " an Ambassador in ordinary " is a diplomat constantly in residence in a foreign country, two examples of the use of a word which our ancestors employed to describe anything that was habitual. Most of the London taverns in the old days specialised in " ordinaries " to suit every purse. In Queen Anne's day we read of a " Twopenny Ordinary ". It means a set everyday meal, or, as we should say to-day, *table d'hôte.*

Even before the last War I thought that Simpson's two-shilling fish ordinary was one of the cheapest meals in London, and I often wondered how they managed to make it pay. It was also a remarkable glimpse into the graceful manners of a past age. While I do not agree with so many people who say that we have become curt and rude, there is no doubt that we have lost the graciousness of good manners. Those of us who still wear hats can raise them if necessary, but none of us can make a bow.

The elegance of an age of good manners as opposed to modern politeness gave to the little upper room in Bird-in-

Hand Court an easy warmth and friendliness every Friday, when City men and strangers to London were in the habit of meeting to eat a fish luncheon and to guess the weight of a Cheshire cheese. Should this cheese be accurately assessed, champagne was given to the entire company, and the profit of the fish ordinary must immediately have evaporated. Though I was never present when anyone guessed correctly, it must have happened now and again, for one side of the room was hung with the framed certificates presented to successful candidates.

There was a long table, at the head of which were three throne-like chairs, one for the Chairman, and the others for the two most distinguished guests. Shortly before one o'clock an old gentleman with a white imperial, who was said to be nearly eighty years of age, would arrive carrying a silk hat. Having introduced himself as the Chairman to those who did not know him, the head waiter would invest him with a black apron, and he would take his place at the head of the table.

He said grace, and then served the soup. The last time I was there I clearly recollect that we had jellied eels, followed by fried plaice and *sauce tartare*, and jam roly-poly pudding. On this occasion, I also remember, the Chairman was in remarkably good form, and as the pudding-plates were being cleared away, he made a little speech and told us one or two amusing stories.

A wooden stand was placed in front of him, made, I believe, of oak from Nelson's *Victory*, and upon this two waiters lifted an enormous Cheshire cheese. Slices were sent round to each guest with slips of paper, upon which we were invited to write an estimate of the height, girth, and weight of the cheese. One man correctly guessed the height and girth, but failed us on the weight, so the Chairman's optimistic command to " put the champagne on ice " came to nothing. We broke up with laughter and handshakes, and went out into the streets of London glowing with good nature, and conscious of our importance as individuals.

Faced by the ruins which now rise up in this once happy little courtyard, I had the strangest feeling of disbelief. Was it possible that only so recently it had been the scene of so much good nature, and had I been there and taken part in it? Almost like ghosts, we pick our way about the places we once knew so well.

I walked down King Street to the Guildhall, which presents a good front to the world. I remember so often showing to friends the black marks on the columns in the great hall, where the Fire of London had scorched them; now I can show to them the marks of the second Fire of London. It is surprising to me, remembering the building on New Year's Day, 1941, when it was still smouldering, that it has been tidied up so well. It seemed to me on that grey morning that it must have gone for ever. I wrote a diary at the time, in which I find the following entry for January 1, 1941:

> In Cheapside I saw most of the streets to the north railed off by police, offering a ghastly vista of roofless broken buildings and glassless windows, with piles of rubble lying in the road in pools of water. Approaching Guildhall, I saw the Union Jack flying above the porch, which is now merely a screen. Firemen were rushing about; the fire engines stood in odd corners. I wondered how badly the Library had been injured, and went round the corner into Basinghall Street to find out. As I was about to enter the half-open door, a dusty man in overalls, whose face was as black as a chimney-sweep's, barred the way and asked irritably who I was. I told him I was a friend of the Librarian and was only anxious to know if much damage had been done.
>
> " I *am* the Librarian," he said; and I then recognised beneath the grime and the dust my old friend, J. L. Douthwaite, who at the same moment recognised me, and his distracted features relaxed into a smile that was a weary grin.
>
> " Come inside, Morton, and have a look," he said, drawing me into the building. He took me up to the Library, where I have so often seen royal and stately gatherings. The three bays at the end have vanished, together with the books in them. It was a beastly sight,

and my heart sank. Only a few yards away from this ghastly mess Douthwaite's room was absolutely untouched. His Christmas cards were still standing in rows on the mantelpiece.

He took me down to the ruins of the Bridge, where we stood on a pile of books lying in a gigantic heap on the floor and stlll gently smoking and smouldering. Lovely little pages curled up wetly from the pile; Eighteenth Century calf bindings protruded here and there.

" Part of a life's work," said Douthwaite. " Mostly collected one by one. This was a student's library, and one can never replace what has gone. It is terrible. The picture-gallery next door is untouched and—it was empty! Yet all this has gone for ever . . ."

He told me that all the books with a financial value had been removed, but in his opinion the students' books which had been destroyed were infinitely more worth while.

He led me into the ruins of Guildhall itself. What a scene! The big black timbers of the roof lay criss-crossed and charred, jet-black and wet across shapeless piles of masonry. The statues round the walls, now so strangely standing not in the light from stained-glass windows but in daylight, were chipped and damaged. Some of the figures had lost their heads. The hand of a symbolic figure—I should imagine of Grief—lay at our feet. The big windows were merely fretwork screens through which the unhappy daylight of this New Year's Day was filtering. The screen at the Minstrels' Gallery end of the hall was still standing, although badly charred.

" I'm sorry about Gog and Magog," said Douthwaite. " Not a bit left of them. It was my fault that they remained, for I could never reconcile myself to the idea that the giants who have guarded Guildhall for so long should go away and leave the place undefended. I suppose I was wrong."

He looked at the ruins.

" This fire has done to Guildhall exactly what the fire of 1666 did," he said. " The crypt and the porch remain, and the walls. Roughly speaking, that's all. Between you and me, there wasn't a thing in the Guildhall that mattered, except Gog and Magog and the Court of Aldermen. Glass and carving that some thought was mediæval was Victorian. The real tragedy is the books. And this need never have happened. Sparks from St Lawrence Jewry blew over and set the building alight. If the Church had been adequately watched, the fire could have been put out at one time with a bucket of water."

We said good-bye, and I went away. I was now inside the police barrier and could go where I liked. I walked down the ruins of Gresham Street. It looked like Ypres or Arras in the first War. It was terrible. The streets leading off were all devastated areas. Aldermanbury is burned out. Those buildings that still stand are just front walls of brick. Even the signs of business have disappeared, and you look through vacant halls and rooms piled high with refuse, and see stone columns and iron pillars leaning crazily this way and that from the appalling mess. I cannot say how far the damage extends. It seemed to me to be everywhere. All memory of the fine buildings is now wiped out. It is impossible to tell whether this blackened shell was once a great bank or that one a tea-shop. They are all reduced to a common uniformity by fire.

I saw a long queue of well-dressed men and women waiting at an A.B.C. shop. I was told that they were City folk who were lining up for a police pass to go beyond the barriers and find out if anything were left of their businesses. This was a grim and awful sight, and I wondered what these people do when they discover nothing but a ruin. How do they exist? Who pays them? How do they pay their staff?

I stepped into the ruins of one building through a great hole in the wall, and saw a man walking about amid the piles of rubble. He was wearing a bowler hat and carried an umbrella. He told me in a calm, stunned voice that he had come to see his offices, and was wondering if the safe were lying beneath the piles of brick and stone on which we were standing.

At all points in these streets the firemen were still playing their hoses, and it was the fourth day since the fire.

The place is still in ruins, for, like their ancestors after the Great Fire, the Londoners of to-day at the moment I am writing this book are prevented by building difficulties and restrictions from reconstructing their city.

§ 10

Milk Street is a little lane which used to lead to one of the most crowded portions of the City of London. Crossing it at right angles is Gresham Street, and ahead is Aldermanbury. I remember this part of London when its streets and lanes were congested with cars, lorries and trucks, and its pavements crowded with busy, hurrying people. Tucked away in this district were many splendid mahogany halls—some of them occupying the same site since the Middle Ages—in which at frequent intervals the master and wardens of Livery Companies would give a stately and sumptuous dinner.

When I reached the end of Milk Street, I looked out towards Moorfields across an area of devastation so final and complete that the memory of it will always rise in my mind whenever I hear the word Blitz. There are other parts of London as badly ravaged, but this to me will always be the most horrific. Thousands of buildings have been burned and blasted to the cellars. Here and there the side of a building rises gauntly from the rubble, a detached gateway stands by itself in the undergrowth, the towers of a few churches, or a spire, lift themselves mournfully, like tombstones in a forgotten cemetery.

It is tempting to compare this portion of blitzed London with Pompeii or Herculaneum, and of course all ruins have a certain similarity, but the ruins of Greece and Rome may be inspected without the expense of any human feeling. The people who lived in them are so far away from us. It is possible to wander round them happily and archæologically, with sketch-book, camera, or luncheon-basket. But I could not do this in Gresham Street and Aldermanbury. There is a savagery, a fury and a hideous wickedness about the ruins of London—and of Berlin also—that chills the heart.

The Corporation has erected neat brick walls round the ruins. Now and again the explorer comes across a signboard stating that such and such a tavern once occupied the site, or that a certain well-known building stood there, or that a particular firm occupied premises at that point. The names of streets well known since mediæval times might have been forgotten by many, and would certainly have been unknown to the younger generation, were they not written on notice-boards nailed to lengths of timber or fixed to the boundary walls.

I walked about this lonely place looking at acres upon acres of sunlit cellars. There are still thousands of people alive who used to work in the vanished buildings which rose above these cellars, who used to arrive there promptly in the morning, climb stairs or ascend in lifts, take down their office coats from pegs, open the post, telephone, make jokes, suffer the pangs of love or bereavement, achieve promotion or receive dismissal, and all the time they believed that this great and thriving area behind Cheapside and Moorgate was the immutable background of their lives. Then one day they came down to the office and saw the whole place, as far as they could see, smoking and smouldering, the roads high with fallen masonry, the gas-mains on fire and the pavements littered with broken glass, mangled typewriters, office furniture and with all the hideous débris created upon the earth when a youth in the sky presses a button.

There are several well-known references in literature to the ruins of London, all of them interesting to former generations because they appeared to be the height of improbability. Horace Walpole imagined a traveller from Peru visiting England to describe the ruins of St Paul's, Macaulay followed with a New Zealander who was to take his stand on London Bridge and sketch these ruins. Shelley was even more devastating. He visualised a day when " St Paul's and

Westminster Abbey shall stand, shapeless and nameless ruins in the midst of an unpeopled marsh ". It is fortunate that both these landmarks are unharmed; but how I should like to be able to guide Walpole, Shelley and Macaulay from Milk Street to Moorgate!

Sitting on a wall near the burned-out church of St Mary-the-Virgin, I tried to rebuild this district as I remember it. This churchyard still contains unharmed its bust of Shakespeare, just as Dr Johnson has been preserved in the Strand, in the act of reading a bronze book, with the shell of St Clement Danes behind him. Nearby is the destroyed church of St Albans, which smouldered so fiercely that for a week no one could approach it.

Haberdashers Hall has vanished from Gresham Street, and Wax-chandlers Hall opposite is now merely a ground floor and basement. To the left, in Foster Lane, Saddlers' Hall has gone; ahead there is only empty sky where once were the halls of the Parish Clerks and the Coachmakers. Still farther off towards St Giles, in Monkwell Street, the splendid hall of the Barber Surgeons, in which so many graceful ceremonies have been held, is no more, and St Giles itself, alas, is a ghastly ruin. Fortunately the parish registers, which contain the entries of Cromwell's marriage and Milton's burial, were not destroyed.

It is impossible now for anyone who did not know this part of London to imagine what it looked like before 1940. How can anyone reconstruct a town from its cellars? The buildings have vanished. The mountains of rubble have been removed. Only the cellars remain, where, among rank growths of grass and weeds, water-tanks lie as they crashed from roof level to basement. Sometimes you see a length of fire-hose lying in the undergrowth, or an old shoe, a bottle, a scarred and blistered radiator.

While I was sitting there, feeling like Macaulay's New Zealander, three fair-haired little boys, about ten years of age, came along, climbed over the wall near me and dropped down into the basement of a building.

They hunted busily in the willow-herb, and one of them called to the others, " Coo, lummy, look at this! " They gathered round and bent their yellow heads over the discovery, which was pocketed, and they climbed back over the wall.

"Been finding buried treasure?" I asked.

One of them shyly held out an incredibly dirty and dissolute-looking fountain pen.

"Do you ever find much in the cellars?" I asked.

"Once I found a cigarette-lighter," one of them replied. "I gave it to me dad. He cleaned it up, and it works."

I asked if they had been in London during the War. They had been, they told me, in the language of Whitehall, "evacuated". I tried to tell them that I remembered before the Blitz, when the buildings on each side of the narrow roads were so tall that you had to have the electric light on in the afternoon, sometimes all day in winter, and the streets on which they now played were crowded with horses and vans. But I could see that they did not believe me.

I walked across to Goldsmiths' Hall, which, although damaged, has fortunately survived. It is one of the grander halls, and I was glad to be shown over it and to discover that most of the fine rooms, though unfortunately not the court dining-room, are undamaged. In the strong-room in the basement I saw the splendid collection of plate, perhaps the best possessed by any of the City Companies, gleaming intact in the light of strip lamps. The Assay Office in Gutter Lane, where silver and gold are hall-marked, was completely destroyed, and this work is now done, as I saw for myself, in Goldsmiths' Hall.

In strange contrast to the comparative normality of the Hall is the little garden opposite, on the Company's property. This was a horrible fragment of bomb damage until the caretaker, or someone associated with the hall, began to tidy it up and grow flowers there. It was bright with gladioli, hollyhocks and dahlias. Quite a tall sycamore tree was growing there. A few clerks were eating an early lunch in the shade among the flowers, and upon the garden gate was framed a certificate of merit awarded by the London Gardens Society "for making a City blitzed site into a garden: Nov. 8, 1948".

I thought, as I continued my walk, that the story of London has been the steady conquest of grass, flowers and trees by bricks and mortar. There is a pleasant little rhyme:

Here Herbs did grow
And flowers sweet.
But now 'tis called
St James's Street.

From the time of Elizabeth onward London has been eating up the countryside at increasing speed, and it is indeed a strange reversal of this process which we witness to-day in the return of grass, flowers and trees to some of the most ancient and closely built-up areas of the City. The speed with which vegetation draped itself over the bomb damage surprised many people. Where did the flowers come from? they asked. Had the seeds always been blowing about, but had they been unable, in that wilderness of stone, to find anywhere to germinate and grow?

After the Great Fire of 1666, when so large a part of the City perished, the dominant plant on the devastated areas was the London Rocket—*Sisymbrium irio*. This is now so rare as to be seldom seen on bombed sites. Mr R. S. R. Fitter, in his fascinating book, *London's Natural History*, notes that in our own time the Rocket's place has been taken by the rose-bay willow-herb. This plant was noted years ago in the Strand, when the site of Bush House was vacant, and to-day it can be found on most blitzed sites. Mr Fitter says that in 1869 the rose-bay was regarded as a rare denizen of gravelly banks and woods and was given only eight stations in the whole of Middlesex, including Ken Wood and Paddington Cemetery. How, then, has this plant conquered all the vacant land in Central London? Mr Fitter says that it loves plenty of light, which it gets on bombed sites, that it likes soil which has been subjected to heat, that "a single young plant is capable of producing eighty thousand seeds in one season, each one adapted to float on the slightest breeze". It is not surprising, therefore, that Dr E. J. Salisbury, Director of the Royal Botanic Gardens at Kew, who has studied the flora of blitzed London, found rose-bay on ninety-nine per cent of his sites. This plant is also responsible for bringing into the heart of London many elephant hawk moths, which breed on its leaves.

A strange inhabitant found on nearly half of the bombed sites is the Oxford ragwort, which is really a native of Sicily, where it thrives on volcanic ash. It was first reported in 1794, at Oxford, having apparently escaped from the Botanical Gardens. It came to London, or was first noticed there, in 1867. Now it is found on nearly every other piece of blitzed land in the City.

Another invader which, as Mr Fitter puts it, has " muscled in on the blitz ", is the Canadian fleabane, first recorded in London in 1690. It was abundant on the site of the Exhibition in South Kensington in 1862, and fifteen years later was advancing on waste land and climbing railway embankments. It is such a prolific breeder that it is probably only a question of time before it is found on every bombed site in the City.

The number and variety of the plants in the ruins grow every year. Most of them are said to be windborne, others are carried by birds and some by human beings. Tomato plants and fig saplings are attributed to clerks who have had lunch in the ruins. But who brought the deadly nightshade?

I climbed over a wall in Aldermanbury and picked some flowers, whose names I did not know, to press in my notebook. As I was scrambling back, I saw above me an amused face full of typical Cockney irony. It belonged to a postman, who was on his way to St Martin's-le-Grand with an empty bag on his shoulder.

" Marvellous, isn't it? " he said, removing his pipe from his mouth and pointing with it at the ruins.

" Do you," I asked, " ever get letters addressed to this? " and I waved a hand at the cellars, the rose-bay and the fleabane.

" Every blinkin' day," he replied. " And from all parts of the world."

I have no idea how the legend of English reserve originated, for it has certainly broken down nowadays. Once the modern Londoner begins to talk it is difficult to stop him. This postman had seen a lot of the Blitz, and he told me all about it.

I was told all about the A.R.P. and the A.F.S., the lack of water, and what he and his pals did the night so and so happened. Then we got on to the subject of botany.

It appeared that he, like many of his friends, was an amateur gardener. They had run a little allotment during the War.

" As a gardener, tell me," I asked, " where you think all these plants and flowers came from? "

He nudged me in the ribs and gave a slow and villainous wink.

" Well, between you and me and the gatepost," he said, " I can tell you where some of 'em came from. Me and my mates have often bought packets of seed from Woolworths and chucked 'em over the walls, and have waited to see 'em come up. It's funny to read in the newspapers how this rare flower or that was carried by a bird! A bird, my foot! Laugh? We've had some laughs all right, me and my mates. . . . Well, so long. . . ."

And shouldering his bag, he disappeared in the direction of the General Post Office.

I walked to Moorgate across our tragic garden of weeds thinking that, while it is natural for anyone who loves London to mourn the losses suffered by the capital in the War, at the same time it is heartening to realise how infinitely worse it might have been. Who would have dared to hope at the height of the air war on London that all the chief sights would come through unscathed or only superficially damaged? These include Westminster Abbey and the Houses of Parliament, Buckingham Palace, Piccadilly, Trafalgar Square and the National Gallery, the British Museum, St Paul's Cathedral, the Bank, the Mansion House and the Royal Exchange, the Tower of London, Southwark Cathedral, the South Kensington museums, the Tate Gallery, and all the bridges.

Many of these had extremely narrow escapes, but they survive, and, seeing them as they always were, many a visitor asks, in a most irritating way, " Where is the blitz damage to be seen? "

§ 11

Sunday in London. . . .

A Puritanical hush lies upon the West End. Bond Street is as empty as a country lane. Miserable foreigners slink about, or hide in hotels and wish they were in Paris. But take a bus to Aldgate and you come to another, brighter London—the London that holds the sixth day holy and goes gay on Sunday.

Near Houndsditch about thirty men linger at a street corner. They are mostly Jews. They stand in little groups. They whisper together and they are utterly unselfconscious. If you introduce your head into the gathering, they do not mind a bit; indeed, they welcome you. It is then that you will notice that the central figure in each group cannot close his hand. Each finger is stiff with diamond rings.

There is an argument. An emphatic negative is backed by an opulent gesture and there is a five hundred pound flash, or at least it looks like that. On the opposite side of the road is another even more blinding flash, which must surely be worth at least a thousand pounds.

This street corner is the Hatton Garden of the East End. The Jews who wish to buy a diamond ring meet there on Sunday morning and spend many happy hours bargaining. The " ring men " are trusting. They will allow a customer to detach a ring from their fingers and take it to the other side of the road.

" How much? " I heard one ask.

" I gave ten pound for it—what profit will you give me? "

Then the trouble starts. Is it serious, or is it a game? The hands cast up to Jehovah, the contemptuous shrugging of shoulders, the sudden angry walk-away, the equally sudden return. It is a game as old as Jerusalem and Babylon, and the rules never seem to alter. You get as much as you can, and take as long as possible in getting it.

A few yards away is an old-clothes market. It is a wholesale market in the week and a retail market on Sunday. Half of it is given over to female garments, half to male. Old costumes and old suits have by some mysterious process been cleaned and pressed in order that they may survive for a few moments the fierce light of publicity. These clothes are pitiful. They have been knocking around the world for years. They have lived their lives. They have done their job. And now at the end of it, instead of being turned into dusters and cloths to clean motor-cars, they are smoothed out into a spurious impersonality so that an ardent young Jew may shout over them.

" Come along now . . . blue suit fit for a lord. . . . Fifteen bob . . . eighteen . . . a quid . . . one pound five. . . . Going at one pound five. It breaks my heart! Any advance on one pound five? . . . I'm *giving* it to you! See the tears in my eyes. . . ."

Women's clothes are sold in the same way. Coats, skirts, hats, costumes are knocked down for whatever they will fetch.

" Why go naked? " shouts the auctioneer. " Come along, ladies. Who says ten bob for this coat and skirt? "

The women move up and finger the cloth.

" It's a gift! " says the auctioneer.

In the roadway a young man acts as mannequin. He slips on a jacket and waistcoat and turns round slowly, shouting:

" Suit to fit a smaller guy than me . . . half a quid."

And the strange thing is that no matter how old and worn out a garment may be, there always seems someone sufficiently short-sighted to buy it.

These are streets packed with life, and they are also packed with good nature. They are overflowing with good humour. There is an Oriental vitality about them that excites admiration and envy. Each side of the road is lined with booths. Behind each booth are the ageless eyes of the Jew.

There are barrows piled with nylon stockings. Every factory girl must have nylon stockings. Someone says they have been smuggled in from America. Someone else says they are damaged goods. The girls do not know what to believe, as these commercial rivalries confuse them.

" Do you want the real thing? " whispers one huckster. " Look at these. Go on, take 'em out; look at both of them. Not a flaw anywhere, or your money back next Sunday."

He spills the stockings out of a cellophane envelope into their hands.

" If I was to tell you the film stars wot come down here to buy my nylons, strewth! you'd be surprised, ladies."

His rival opposite feels that his crowd of women is about to melt away.

" The best nylons in the world," he suddenly shouts at the top of his voice. Then, speaking out of the corner of his mouth, he adds, " Which is more than can be said for *all* the nylons in this street, I'm telling you. . . ."

You look at this street, and wonder why people go to the Zoo. Human beings are so much more interesting to watch than animals, and so much more difficult to understand.

Perhaps the most amusing sight in the street is that of a Jew trying to bargain with a Lascar. Those queer brown men drift down from the docks when a ship berths. Houndsditch is the West End of London to them. They wear blue overalls and astrakhan caps. Now and then a dandy appears in a woman's coat. The crowds roar with laughter, and receive in return a chilling and dispassionate glance, something as old, as cold and as uncompromising as the expression on the face of the Sphinx. Six Lascars surround a stall on which a Jew is selling old shoes. They stand round like cattle. They hold up trade. They try on dozens of pairs. The Jew attempts to get rid of them. They refuse to go away.

" Seven shillings," says the Jew in desperation.

" One shilling," replies a Lascar.

" Seven shillings! " shouts the Jew.

" One shilling," says the Lascar in a voice like cold milk.

The argument has all the elements of eternity. After hours of passive resistance a brown hand, slender as a monkey's, is thrust into a blue blouse. A few shillings appear, wrapped in an oily rag. The Lascar painfully selects four. He looks at both sides of each shilling as if saying farewell. He hands them to the Jew. The crowd laughs. The Lascar gazes round with the uncomprehending dignity of an animal. He bends down, puts on his new shoes and walks away without troubling to tie the laces. The Jew takes off his hat and mops his head.

" I ask you—with tears in my eyes. . . ."

Scattered about the streets are men who put a week's work into a Sunday morning. They earn whatever they can make.

" Look at me! " says one. " I'm a fit man."

He stands in an athlete's vest and a pair of flannel trousers. He gives himself a terrible smack on the chest. He works himself up into a passion. He shows his biceps. He offers to fight anyone. His audience begin to feel weaker and weaker.

" I've got vim! " he shouts. " That's what I've got—vim! I've got tons of it," he cries, giving his chest another tremendous smack. " I've got vitality! I've got pep! I'm a man! Look at my muscles! I've got a heart like a lion! I've got kidneys like steel! I've got a wonderful liver. . . ."

All the time he gives himself appalling punches in the mentioned portions of his body, and then, before the dazzled eyes of a crowd, which does not know whether he is a boxer or an acrobat, he swiftly produces a very small bottle and holds it up dramatically.

" Here is the secret of perfect health," he cries. " This will give you—Life! Who'll have a glass of Life with me? "

A dozen hands go up. A small glass is passed round. He sells every bottle of his patent medicine. What a lesson in psychology!

So for hours the crowds fill the streets of Brighter London. There is not a dull yard in them. They are charged with vitality. And one leaves them astounded by the Jew's almost amazing ability to thrive where other men would starve.

CHAPTER TWO

In which I go to the Tower of London, see the Crown Jewels and recall upon Tower Green the deaths of Anne Boleyn, Catherine Howard and Lady Jane Grey, and also the romantic tragedy of Lady Arabella Stuart. On a Sunday morning I go to church on Tower Green.

§ 1

FEW ancient buildings are able to achieve a greater air of benevolence than the Tower of London upon a fine spring morning or a summer day. At such moments it is difficult to believe in the burden of misery which this fortress has carried down the ages. But go there on a wet day or during a fog or, better still, after dark, and you will have a different impression.

As a living survival in a modern city, the Tower is a dinosaur among the institutions of London, something improbable and extinct from the remote past which somehow, in the atmosphere of England, has contrived to adapt itself to modern life. It is staffed by men who wear the dress of five centuries ago, and all kinds of memories, traditions and fictions still persist within its enormous battlements. Although London has changed from age to age, the Tower remains fundamentally the same. It would be unremarkable were it a ruin; that it is very much alive, that it is still " His Majesty's Tower ", that it is still, as it was centuries ago, the Royal jewel-safe, that it is still garrisoned by armed men, and that twice in one generation it should have become a prison again, and have visited death upon the King's enemies, is more than improbable.

Whenever I go there, I am struck by the incongruous character of the place. I have often passed through its horrible dungeons, dedicated to old cruelties and hatreds, to emerge in the sunlight before the married quarters where a soldier's wife was rocking an infant to sleep, while a cat licked its paws on a doorstep. How strange it is that normal domestic life should go on, children be born and reared, meals cooked and beds made, in that grim spot whose weight of pain and suffering, it might be thought, would have put the Tower of London out of bounds with Humanity for ever.

But no, the Tower is a pleasant residential spot, and the continuity of its domestic life is one of the most interesting things about it. There has been not a night since Norman times—a matter of something like nine centuries—when men and women have failed to seek their rest within its walls or have ceased to regard the Tower as "home". It is the most ancient inhabited dwelling-place in London, and I doubt whether any other building in the world can boast a longer history of unbroken bed-making.

The rooms in the Tower resemble nothing so much in their rocky massiveness as caves or something hewn out of a mountain. When you glance through a window, you notice that it has been cut in a wall four feet thick. If the windows were blocked up, the room, although high in a tower, would become a dungeon. Electric light, gas stoves and bathrooms have been introduced into rooms which were constructed to defy archers, pikemen and siege engines. The only thing stronger than the Tower of London is the tradition of interior decoration inherited by the wives of some of the warders! You would not think it possible for anyone to take all the drama out of the Tower, to make it entirely everyday and to bring it into line with almost any suburb. But this has been triumphantly achieved, and in this achievement it seems to me the Tower of London has been vanquished for the first time.

Most of us, if faced with the problem of furnishing a room in the Tower, would buy tapestries, oak refectory tables, wooden benches, bits of Gothic velvet and silver candlesticks. In other words, we should allow the Tower to dominate us. But not so Mrs Jones and Mrs Robinson! They dominate the Tower. It is extraordinary to mount a spiral stairway and to come to an oak door studded with nails, beyond which is an interior for whose origin you must seek the most refined streets of Balham. The scene is perfect when a warder returns home, flings his beribboned Tudor bonnet upon a chiffonier and sits down upon a piano stool.

Whether there was a Roman or a Saxon fort on the site is unknown. All we know for certain of the Tower's origin is that William the Conqueror gave a charter of independence to London with one hand, while with the other he built the Tower to show his " beloved subjects " that, in spite of their liberties, he was their master. He began to build the central keep, which we call the White Tower, eleven years after Hastings. It was only one, but the strongest, of the many royal castles constructed by the Conqueror at strategical points in England. It was the stronghold from which the King, who had confiscated all the land of England, enforced his power; and so it was for centuries the guardian of the feudal system.

While the architect Gundulf, a pious Norman monk, worked year after year at the massive walls, little Saxon London lay around him on the banks of the clear Thames. It was a town of thatched wooden houses lying within the old Roman Wall. Life was rough and uncouth. Swine rooted among the dung-hills and the refuse. Wolves descended from the heights of Hampstead in winter. Roman Londinium had been forgotten, and no doubt many a fine marble column was built into a swineherd's hut. The temples of Diana, Mithras and Isis had been overthrown, and instead small wooden churches commemorated Saxon saints: Erkenwald, Ethelburga, Osyth, Alphege, Swithin and Botolph. And upon Ludgate Hill stood the little wooden church of St Paul. We can just see for the first time the faint shadow of the London we know.

The Tower was the portent of a new age: it was the beginning of one of those transformation periods which London has seen throughout her history. The age of Norman stone was about to begin. Just as we to-day have witnessed the disappearance of Regency stucco and Victorian brick and the arrival of a new style of architecture derived from concrete, steel and glass, so the Saxons saw their humble little town of wood and thatch make way for the solid stone buildings of the Normans.

One may imagine with what mixed feelings the Londoners of that time watched the workmen swarming upon Gundulf's scaffolding, aware perhaps that a new and a greater age was being born beside the Thames.

§ 2

I passed through the wicket gate and bought tickets at a little hut near a restaurant which stands on the site of the vanished Lyon Tower. For many centuries this was one of the great sights of London, for in this place, in a semi-circular pit, the King kept his " lyons " and other strange beasts.

Henry III began the menagerie in 1235, with three leopards given to him in a fanciful and heraldic moment by the Emperor Frederick II, and in the same year he acquired a polar bear from Norway. This creature is mentioned in the State archives as the recipient of an allowance of fourpence a day from the Privy Purse. The keeper of " our white bear " was also ordered to provide a long and strong cord to hold the animal when he was fishing in the Thames. What fun the boys of Plantagenet London must have had when " our white bear " was led out to fish!

In the reign of Edward III the menagerie was increased by the gift of an elephant, the first seen in England, it is said, since the war elephants of Claudius in Roman times. A royal order is preserved commanding the erection of a house forty by twenty feet to accommodate " our elephant ". It then became the custom to keep lions in the Tower, one of which always bore the name of the reigning king, and was supposed to languish and die after the decease of the monarch whose name it bore. This zoo, which was added to from reign to reign, was naturally one of the most popular sights of the capital in days when foreign animals were rarely seen in England. The animals remained in the Tower until 1834, when they were moved to Regent's Park; and so the Zoological Society began.

I walked on towards the Byward Tower, and came to a little gate beneath the archway, which is the door to the orderly room of the Beefeaters; and that is the first and last time I shall give this name to the Yeomen Warders. They dislike it, and to some extent resent it. It is strange that London has never been able to distinguish the Tower Warders from the Yeomen of the Guard, to whom the name Beefeater might be applied if the derivation is, as some suppose, *buffetier*, for the Yeomen were on duty at the royal buffet, and they even made the royal bed, and were generally in personal attendance upon the monarch.

The Tower Warders never left the Tower. They were the porters and guardians of the fortress from Norman times onward, and they regard themselves as the oldest corps of men in the world still engaged in their original duties. In comparison with the Tower Warders, the Pope's Swiss Guard is a creation of yesterday. The confusion between the Tower Warders and the Yeomen of the Guard—a corps created by Henry VII after the Battle of Bosworth—is due to the fact that the Yeomen Warders became incorporated with the Yeomen of the Guard and were given the same uniform. The only difference is that when in full dress the Yeomen of the Guard wear a cross belt and the Yeomen Warders do not.

The duties of the junior and senior branch of this corps remain distinct. The Yeomen of the Guard, who all wear Van Dyck beards, are only in attendance upon the King. They make the periodic search for Guy Fawkes in the vaults of Westminster. The Yeomen Warders leave the Tower only on special state occasions. They have the Crown Jewels in their keeping, and it is their duty to take the Crown and other emblems to Westminster on state occasions—I regret to say in a taxi-cab!

The Yeomen Warders are retired Army sergeants, and there is always a long waiting list for any vacancy that may occur. The Chief Warder is the Governor's right-hand man, and on state occasions he carries, as a badge of office, a staff surmounted by a model of the White Tower in silver. A survival from remote times is the post of Yeoman Gaoler. This warder when in full dress carries a ceremonial axe which many people wrongly imagine to be the execution axe.

From the Byward Tower, where the Chief Warder has a pleasant flat, the curfew may be heard every evening ringing from the Bell Tower. Soon afterwards it is the task of the Chief Warder to lock His Majesty's Tower for the night. He marches to the entrance gate with an armed escort, holding a bunch of keys and, in winter, a lantern in which a candle is burning. He goes to the wicket gate, closes it, and, marching back along the route, locks and bars each of the gates in the various towers as he comes to them. When he approaches the Bloody Tower, the sentry steps out and challenges him.

"Halt, who goes there?"

"The Keys," answers the Chief Warder.

"Whose Keys?" asks the sentry.

"King George's Keys," replies the Warder.

Having satisfied himself that the Tower has not passed out of the King's possession, the sentry calls out:

"Pass King George's Keys, all's well."

The Keys and escort pass through the archway of the Bloody Tower to the terrace beyond, where the troops are drawn up on parade. They present arms. The Chief Warder steps forward and, lifting his Tudor bonnet, cries with a loud voice:

"God preserve King George."

"Amen," respond the troops.

The band plays the National Anthem, after which the Chief Warder takes the King's Keys to the King's House and lodges them with the Governor for safe custody during the night. From that moment anyone walking about the Tower is halted by the sentries from the shadow of gloomy archways and ordered to give an account of himself. Anyone approaching the main gate is asked to give the password, which is changed every night. Many are the stories of officers serving with the garrison who, returning late at night after a party in the West End, have forgotten the password and have been forced to spend the night in a taxi-cab or in the guard-room; for the Tower takes its password as seriously to-day as it did in the Middle Ages. Every quarter a list of the passwords for the next three months is sent to the King and the Lord Mayor of London.

So it is that when night falls over London, and the millions who have been filling the City during the hours of daylight have deserted it for their distant homes, the two key-stones of old London are still in position: the Lord Mayor in his Mansion House and the Governor in His Majesty's Tower of London.

§ 3

As I walked on through the Tower I came to Traitor's Gate, which is I think one of the gloomiest places in the fortress. Nothing can make it share the air of benevolence which occasionally shines over many other portions of the Tower. This spiked water-gate positively drips with melancholy and despair, in spite of the fact that the whole thing is a shocking modern sham. When the Tower was tidied up in Victorian times a senseless act of vandalism was perpetrated by the authorities. The old steps, worn thin by the feet of those who had used them for centuries, were replaced by the present neat steps of Bath stone. Traitors' Gate was also taken away and sold to a Whitechapel shopkeeper for fifteen shillings!

These gates had been pickled by centuries of tides, the Thames water had turned them green, and probably they would have been good for another few centuries. Jesse, writing in 1847 in his *Memorials of London*, wondered " whether they have been converted into fire-wood, or turned to some baser purpose ". What happened may have been more exciting than that. Barnum, of Barnum and Bailey's Circus, is said to have given £50 for them. It has been said, but never verified, that they were sent to New York, where they became one of the great side-shows in the circus. Where are they now? Did they return to England, or are they still in existence in the United States?

The water-gate is, of course, now high and dry, but in the old days the high tide lapped the steps. All the noble and distinguished prisoners of the Tower came there by water, and were sent from the Tower by barge to stand their trials in Westminster Hall. On the way back the inhabitants of the Tower gathered at vantage points to learn the verdict, for it was possible to discover it long before the barge and its prisoner came within hail of land. If the verdict were

" guilty ", the Yeoman Gaoler stood in the barge with the edge of his axe held towards the prisoner; if " innocent ", he held it away from him.

Upon the site of the present stairs stepped Anne Boleyn, Catherine Howard, Sir Thomas More, Cranmer, Somerset, Lady Jane Grey, Sir Thomas Wyatt, Robert Devereux, Earl of Essex, Sir Walter Raleigh and many more. The great Elizabeth, when princess and suspected of plotting against her half-sister Mary, was sent by barge to the Tower, and was landed at Traitor's Gate. She sank to her knees on the stairs and protested before God that she had played no part in the Wyatt Conspiracy. It is interesting to reflect that the greatest queen in English history was so sure that she was fated to die in the Tower that she discussed, as her mother, Anne Boleyn, had done, the possibility of being slain by the sword in the French fashion rather than by the cruder axe of the English headsman.

In the White Tower I saw a magnificent collection of arms and armour, beautifully kept and perfectly displayed. It has occurred to many people that as a race we have grown taller during the last few centuries, for the average man to-day would find most of the armour too small for him. This does not apply, of course, to the armour of the gigantic Henry VIII. His splendid suit of tilting armour gives one a vivid idea of his massive and overpowering appearance.

Under the steps of the White Tower, on the south side, close to the Wakefield Tower, was the burial-place of the murdered princes, Edward V and his little brother, Richard, Duke of York. The only person who knew this was the Governor of the Tower at that time, Sir Robert Brackenbury, who was killed at the Battle of Bosworth, so that the secret was kept for two centuries until, during some alterations to the Tower in the reign of Charles II, the bones of the young Princes were discovered and were, by order of the King, taken up and buried in an urn in Westminster Abbey.

Modern men gazed on the bones of these two Princes when their remains were exhumed in 1933, in the presence of a small gathering of Abbey officials. The bones filled an oblong cavity within the urn. A fairly complete skull and a portion of another lay on top. Many bones were missing, but this was accounted for by the fact that the workmen in the time of Charles II at first threw them away, and they had to be recovered from a rubbish-heap. An anatomist who examined the bones found that they were those of two children, and was able to date within a few months their age at death, which was that of the two little Princes; and he found also some evidence that they had been smothered. This exhumation, by dating the age of the Princes, cleared Henry VII from the suspicion of their murder and placed the crime upon the crooked shoulders of the traditional murderer, Richard III. After the bones had been examined, they were wrapped in the finest lawn, and the skull and jawbones of Edward V were wrapped separately. The Dean of Westminster placed the bones back in the urn with a written statement describing the exhumation. He then read part of the Burial Service, and the urn was re-sealed and re-buried.

Ascending and descending stone staircases, I came at length to the finest feature of the White Tower, the beautiful little Norman chapel of St John, which has mercifully come unscathed through the hazards of two wars. This stern but exquisite Norman church is the finest of its kind in the world. Although it is nearly nine hundred years old, it looks as though it had been built yesterday. Many an English queen and her ladies have heard Mass in the triforium of this chapel, unobserved by the guards and the courtiers below. It was before the altar that Robert Brackenbury, while at prayers, was tempted to murder the two Princes. It was in this chapel that Mary I was married by proxy to the King of Spain.

In early times the Knights of the Bath held their vigils there. Before they made their vows it was the custom for them to take a bath, which was symbolic of spiritual purification, and the wooden bath-tubs were ranged round a room in the Tower. When they had been installed in their tubs—there is an engraving which shows each tub fitted with a brocade canopy like a little tent—the King, accompanied by his great officers of state, entered the room and walked round solemnly, touching each knight upon his bare back as he sat in the water. After this the knights were put to bed by their esquires: then, habited as monks, they were conducted to the Chapel of St John, where they prayed all night beside their armour. The oaths of virtue and excellence, and the ritual of arming, were of a most elaborate character.

A delicate situation was created when Mary came to the throne and arose again in the reign of Elizabeth. It was hardly proper for a woman to enter the bathroom of the Order, therefore during these reigns a deputy was appointed to perform the act of touching in place of the Sovereign.

In the Bloody Tower I saw the spot where the Princes were murdered, and also, overlooking the river, the turreted walk where Sir Walter Raleigh paced to and fro when he was a prisoner there. Not far away, housed inadequately in a room unable to accommodate the large crowds of visitors, I saw the Crown Jewels.

In an octagonal steel and glass safe, countless diamonds, rubies and emeralds and every kind of precious stone shimmered and sparkled with the strange fiery vitality that belongs to jewels. I think the most beautiful objects are the King's three crowns. The first is the Crown of St Edward the Confessor, or the Crown of England. This is placed for a moment upon the head of the King during his Coronation. The original was a Saxon crown which vanished during the Commonwealth, and the present crown is a copy made for Charles II. In shape it is more beautiful, but in value and historical association much inferior to the Imperial State Crown which the King wears at the opening of Parliament and on other great occasions of state.

This glittering object is a mass of diamonds and pearls and other precious stones, among them some jewels of romantic interest. In the centre of the cross of diamonds on top of the crown is the large sapphire which was formerly set in the coronation ring of Edward the Confessor. The two pearls, which were once the ear-rings of Queen Elizabeth, are seen pendant where the arches of the crown meet. The enormous uncut ruby belonged to the Black Prince. The clusters of diamonds which run up the arches of the crown are formed to represent oak leaves, with pearls for acorns, an allusion to the oak-tree at Boscobel in whose branches Charles II concealed himself when he was flying from Cromwell's troopers.

The third crown is the Imperial Crown of India, which was made for King George V in 1912, when he was crowned Emperor of India at Delhi; for it is against the law for the Crown of England, or the Imperial State Crown, to leave the country.

It may seem incredible, but typically English, that on at least two occasions large and valuable objects of the Regalia have been mislaid for years, to turn up eventually as if they were a pair of spectacles or a bunch of keys! How can it be possible to lose a sceptre? If I possessed a sceptre and could not find it, I should naturally assume that someone had stolen it, which would be comprehensible, but to mislay a sceptre is surely quite fantastic. Yet for years the beautiful Sceptre with the Dove was missing, and was found by chance in 1814, hidden away in an old cupboard in the Tower. An even more remarkable disappearance was that of the great State Sword, which is used only at coronations. The hilt and scabbard of this sword are encrusted with diamonds and emeralds—hardly the kind of object which one would imagine could be lost. However, during the reign of Queen Victoria, the State Sword was missing for years, until at last someone, rummaging in a disused cupboard, saw what looked like an old gun-case, which, when opened, was found to contain the missing sword.

It is extraordinary, considering the casual way the Crown Jewels were kept in former times, that nothing has ever been stolen, if we except the almost successful attempt of Colonel Blood to steal the Crown in the reign of Charles II. Nowadays such cunning mechanical and scientific devices guard the Regalia that a thief would probably be guillotined, and most certainly electrocuted, if he smashed the plate glass which seems to be all that separates him from so much easy wealth.

§ 4

Colonel Blood was a reckless Irishman who, like many another soldier of fortune, made London his headquarters when Charles II was restored to the throne. He was a desperate ruffian, ready to take on any venture.

In the time of Charles II the Regalia was kept, without any of the precautions which safeguard it to-day, in an iron cage on the ground floor of the Martin Tower. The upper floors formed the living apartments of the Keeper in charge of the jewels, an old man of nearly eighty named Talbot Edwards. His salary had been in abeyance for some time, which was not unusual in the reign of Charles II, and he was therefore allowed to take fees from visitors who wished to see the jewels. The only precaution observed was that as soon as anyone entered the jewel-house, Edwards locked the door.

One day in April, 1671, an inoffensive country parson in bands and gown visited the Tower with his wife. They said they were strangers in London and would like to see the Crown Jewels. The " parson " was, of course, Colonel Blood, and the " wife " was a female accomplice. While old Edwards was describing the Regalia to his visitors, the " wife " was suddenly seized by " internal qualms ", and the kind-hearted old keeper invited his visitors to step upstairs, where Mrs Edwards helped the "parson's" wife to recover.

Thus Blood and his companion " established confidence " in their victim, as the modern crook would express it. In a day or so the " parson " called to thank Mrs Edwards and to give her a present of a pair of gloves. So the acquaintance grew into friendship, and the " parson " with his " wife " became frequent visitors in the Edwards household. Edwards had an unmarried daughter and also a son, who was absent in Flanders. It was suggested that a marriage might be arranged between Miss Edwards and a nephew and ward of the "parson", an idea which found favour with the Edwards' family. A day was therefore appointed on which the " parson " was to produce his " nephew " for inspection. Upon this day, just as it was growing dark, Blood, still disguised as a parson, arrived at the Tower on horseback with four companions. One man was to hold the horses at St Katherine's Gate, while Blood and the other three, one of whom was to impersonate the " nephew ", were to steal the Regalia. Blood was to steal the Crown, an old ex-Ironside, named Parrot, was to pocket the Orb, while a third rogue was to file the Sceptre into three pieces and place them in a bag. The " nephew " was to keep guard. The thieves were armed with sword-canes and a brace of pistols apiece.

Old Edwards greeted them warmly at the Martin Tower, and said that his wife and daughter would be down in a moment. Blood remarked that, as his friends were strangers to London, they would like to see the Crown Jewels. The old man at once unlocked the jewel-room door, and the thieves trooped in, except the " nephew ", who guarded the stairs with the coy remark that he would rather catch a glimpse of his bride than of any jewels! No sooner were the thieves inside than they knocked down Edwards and gagged him. Blood snatched the Crown, and smashed in the arches with a wooden mallet in order to make it easier to pocket; Parrot secured the Orb, with its enormous ruby, while the third man began to file the Sceptre. At this point there occurred one of those incredible surprises which no novelist would dare to introduce into fiction. Young Edwards, who was believed to be in Flanders, suddenly arrived home, and was startled to find a stranger on the stairs. He ran up past the watching man to see his mother and sister.

Alarmed by this unexpected development, the " nephew " lost his nerve and gave the alarm. The thieves opened the door and walked out calmly with the Crown and the Orb, leaving the half-filed Sceptre behind. Edwards, freeing himself from the gag, began to shout that the Crown had been stolen.

The alarm spread until the Tower was in confusion. Blood added to it as he ran, the Crown hidden in his parson's gown, by shouting, " Stop the rogues! " and pointing to running figures. Captain Beckenham, commanding the main guard, happened, more by luck than anything else, to spot Blood as the real thief, and he chased him out of the Tower to St Katherine's Wharf. There a rabble joined in the chase, and captured the thieves as they were actually mounting their horses. Beckenham closed with Blood, who let off a pistol in his face, but it missed fire. The next instant Blood was captured, after a struggle in which several stones fell from the Crown into the mud; a pearl was picked up by a sweeper, a diamond by an apprentice and several stones were never recovered.

Parrot was also overpowered, the Orb still in his breeches pocket. One of the rubies had worked loose, and was found afterwards in his garments. As the thieves were being led off, Captain Blood said over his shoulder to Captain Beckenham, " Ah well, it was a gallant deed, although it failed. It was to gain a Crown."

The strangest part of the story, in an age when any petty theft was punishable by death, is perhaps the sequel. In a few days time Blood was summoned to Whitehall, where Charles II received him in private audience. It would be interesting to know what was said during this interview, for Blood emerged from it the owner of an estate in Ireland which brought in £500 a year! Charles II has never been cleared of the suspicion that, in need of ready money as usual, he had hired Blood to steal his own Crown! Another rumour at the time was that the King had boasted that no man could steal the Crown and, in order to bring himself to the King's notice, Blood had attempted to do so.

Blood was eventually vanquished by a libel action brought against him by the Duke of Buckingham, who was awarded £10,000 damages. The prospect of paying such a sum killed Blood. He was buried in Westminster, but so bad was his reputation that the public believed that his death was really a trick. He was therefore exhumed and identified by a mark on the thumb. Centuries afterwards, when Victoria Street was made, Blood was again disturbed. Two unkind lines in a broadsheet in the British Museum must be his epitaph:

Thanks, ye kind fates, for your last favour shown,
For stealing Blood who lately stole the Crown.

§ 5

When the first World War broke out, London realised with considerable astonishment that overnight the Tower had suddenly sprung to life as a prison. Such a reversal to type was surprising, and when stories leaked out of captured spies and of firing parties at dawn, the word " Tower " sent into London, for the first time for many centuries, a genuine chill of horror.

During the last War the same thing happened. The Tower suddenly closed its gates to schoolchildren and became a fortress. When Rudolf Hess made his mysterious landing in this country, he was taken to the Tower and lodged in an upper room of the Yeoman Gaoler's house, overlooking Tower Green.

" During the first months of the War," a Warder told me, " all the German submarine prisoners were brought here before being sent on to prison camps. Fancy being picked up in the North Sea and finding yourself in the Tower of London! No wonder many of them were nervous. Some of them expected to be tortured first and then put up against a wall."

The Tower's record in two wars is interesting, and one fancies that it would have intrigued the Conqueror, who built that mass of stone to withstand arrows, pikes and primitive siege engines, to know that it survived two attacks from the air. In the first War, as in the second, several attempts were made to destroy Tower Bridge, and bombs fell dangerously near the Tower. During the last War fifteen direct hits from high-explosive bombs were recorded in the Tower, none of which, surprising to say, caused any serious damage. Three flying bombs fell inside the Tower, and many incendiaries. The only casualties were the ravens, and the only damage was to window-glass.

As soon as the war ended, it was decided to renew the ravens. No one can say at what period ravens became a feature of the Tower, and it may be that these sinister-looking birds nested and bred there and just lingered, protected by public sentiment, longer than elsewhere in London. Pigs, kites and ravens were the three unpaid scavengers of mediæval London. Foreign visitors remarked on the extraordinary number of kites, especially upon old London Bridge, and one observer noted how they would swoop down and take food from people, just as they do in modern Cairo. It was noted also that the English, unlike many other nations, were not superstitious about the raven, neither did they object to its ghoulish croak, but, on the contrary, they liked this bird and protected it. It was only when London developed a sense of sanitation in the late Eighteenth Century that the kites and ravens, which had performed such admirable service in earlier times, were trapped and shot and so were seen no longer in the capital. Only the Tower ravens remain, the last privileged representatives of a numerous and historic company.

One of the Yeomen Warders has charge of the ravens, and the Governor draws an allowance of one shilling and sixpence a week for each bird. The ravens have names and an attestation card like a soldier's, on which are set out their particulars and peculiarities. One who flourished between the wars was named James Crow, and his profession was entered as "thief"!

The present number of ravens is six, which is the full establishment. When it became known after the War that the Tower wished to obtain ravens, offers poured in from many parts of the country, and the six birds now on Tower Green came from Scotland, Wales and Cornwall. They were born wild, and were sent to the Tower before they were a year old. There are four males and two females, but, although the birds place a few twigs together in the spring and form a rudimentary nest, they have never been known to breed in the Tower. They live to a great age, and it is said that one raven died at the age of forty-four years.

§ 6

It is commonly believed that the site of the block on Tower Green is soaked with the blood of countless victims. The truth is that only six persons were executed there, five of them women. The usual place for executions was outside the Tower, on Tower Hill, where a railed-off space may be seen in Trinity Gardens, which marks the site of the scaffold. Royal persons and women were not executed in public, and that is why the six executions took place inside the Tower. The five women were Queen Anne Boleyn, Queen Catherine Howard, Lady Rochford, the Countess of Salisbury, and Lady Jane Grey. The only man executed there was the Earl of Essex, who died in private by the favour of Queen Elizabeth.

The monstrous charges brought against Anne Boleyn may

or may not have been true, who can say? It is significant that two months before she died ambassadors in London were writing to the courts of Europe to say that Henry VIII was flirting with Jane Seymour. Whether Anne were guilty or not, it is clear that Henry was tired of her.

She was sent to the Tower, found guilty and condemned either to be burned to death on Tower Green or to be beheaded, "as the King's pleasure shall direct". Her execution was fixed to take place three days after her so-called trial had ended. Documents in the Record Office state that as the moment of her death approached, the poor young woman—she was twenty-nine years of age—alternated between moods of hysteria and moments of remarkable composure. When hysterical she would burst into peals of laughter and feel her neck, which was unusually slender, for she could not bear the thought of the axe. Her request that she might die by the sword in the French manner was granted, but as no Englishman could be found who was able or willing to use a sword in that way, the executioner of Calais was summoned. He arrived with his sword, but without his costume. One was hurriedly made for him in London, and the bill has been preserved in our archives.

At two o'clock in the morning of May 18, 1536, Anne Boleyn awakened and entered the oratory where three priests were waiting. Before and after taking the Sacrament she swore on the damnation of her soul that she had never been unfaithful to the King.

The light of a May morning stole into the Tower as the Queen rose from her knees, comforted and ready. At seven o'clock, incredible as it may seem, she sat down to breakfast with her trembling, tear-stained women. No one had slept. Everyone was on the edge of hysteria. When the meal was over Anne rose suddenly and flew into the arms of Mrs Margaret Lee, sobbing pitifully and asking to be remembered to all the servants at Hever Castle, her father's house in Kent, remembering pet dogs and her ponies at Greenwich. The minutes dragged on, and there came no tramp of feet to summon her to death. Becoming anxious and unable to bear the suspense, she made enquiries, and learnt that the execution had been put off until noon, probably because the French executioner's garments were not ready. She called Kingston, the Constable of the Tower.

"Mr Kingston," she said, "I hear I am not to die afore noon, and I am sorry therefor, for I thought to be dead by this time and past my pain."

"It will be no pain, madam," replied Kingston. "It is so subtle."

"I have heard the executioner is very good," said Anne, "and I have a little neck."

She laughed and put her fingers to her throat, as she had so often done in moments of hysteria. But her calmness astonished Kingston, who wrote to Secretary Cromwell:

"I have seen many men and women executed, and they have been in great sorrow; but to my knowledge this ladye has much joy and pleasure in deathe."

Later in the day a shock awaited her, for they told her that the execution had been postponed until the morning—Friday, May 19—so she was faced with the agony of another night of life. Or did hope, which walks beside man even to the scaffold, whisper to her that this delay might mean that Henry's heart had softened and that she might expect to live? If so, the poor Queen did not know her husband.

Early in the morning Kingston warned the Queen that she must prepare herself. He gave her a purse containing twenty pounds to distribute according to custom between the executioner and his assistants. (Could anything be more bizarre and gruesome than the act of tipping the headsman?) Meanwhile her women had robed her for death, and shortly before nine o'clock Kingston came again to say that all was ready.

The terrible procession marched slowly through the State apartments of the Tower and out into the spring morning, towards the scaffold on Tower Green. First went two hundred Yeomen of the Guard with halberds, then the swordsman of Calais, dressed all in black, with a black mask covering the upper part of his face, and upon his head a high, horn-shaped hat. On either side of him walked the English headsmen, wearing the English costume of tight scarlet, scarlet masks hiding their faces entirely, and upon their heads the same horn-shaped hats, but of scarlet.

The officials of the Tower followed. Behind them walked Anne Boleyn, Father Thirlwall on one side of her and the faithful Mrs Margaret Lee on the other. The Queen was flushed and her eyes were red with weeping. She wore a loose robe of grey damask and a deep ermine collar. Beneath it peeped a red petticoat. Her dark hair was covered by a small black hat above a white coif. A gold chain and cross hung from her girdle, and she carried a prayer-book bound in gold. As she walked, it was noticed that she kept glancing back, as if looking for someone in the small crowd that lined the way. Did she still hope for a reprieve?

The scaffold stood five feet high, and was covered with straw. It was surrounded by a low rail. In front of it was a stand with a raised seat, on which sat her uncle, the Duke of Norfolk, with the Earl Marshal seated at his feet. Secretary Cromwell was, of course, there, and others who had brought her to death. Anne was then formally handed over to the Sheriffs, who led her to the foot of the scaffold; and it was then five minutes past nine. Before she mounted the few steps the Queen turned and passionately embraced her women, telling them to be brave for her sake.

She made a short speech praising the King. With her own hands she removed her hat and undressed her neck. A small linen cap was placed on her hair.

"Alas, poor head, in a brief space thou wilt roll in the dust on the scaffold," she said.

She knelt down on both knees and prayed silently for two minutes. As she rose she closed her eyes, while Mrs Lee bound them with a handkerchief. She was then led blindfolded to the block and knelt down. The women clung together at the far corner of the scaffold, sobbing. The French executioner removed his shoes.

"O Lord, have pity on my soul," cried the Queen.

The Frenchman, who had hidden his sword beneath the straw, softly drew it forth and advanced silently in stockinged feet. He motioned one of the English assistants to approach the Queen on the other side, a movement which caused her to move her head a little. Instantly the sword rose and fell. The Frenchman bent down and picked up the head. A cry of horror passed through the crowd, for death had been so mercifully swift that the Queen's lips were still moving in her last prayer. So the King's will was done.

Then a strange thing happened. No one had remembered a coffin. The sobbing women were left alone with the body of their mistress, looking vainly and distractedly for something in which to place it, until a kindly warder brought from a nearby armoury an old arrow chest of elm wood. " Sobbing woefully ", the women bore the dead body of Anne Boleyn a few paces into the Church of St Peter-ad-Vincula.

That was how Queen Elizabeth's mother died, and on the following day Henry VIII married Jane Seymour.

§ 7

If only Henry VIII had instructed his many spies to look into the life of young Catherine Howard, perhaps he might not have married her, and thus a lot of sorrow and tragedy would have been averted and Tower Green spared another harrowing and frightful spectacle. This young woman, whose face in the National Portrait Gallery is modest, demure, almost nun-like, was really a gay and laughing baggage who knew the facts of life at an unusually early age. Her father, the obscure and penurious Lord Edmund Howard, was one of the poorer half-brothers of the Duke of Norfolk, and his daughter was brought up under the wing of " Old Agnes ", dowager Duchess of Norfolk, a scandalous and greedy old dragon, step-mother of the Duke, who lived in a dower-house at Lambeth.

" Old Agnes " kept almost regal state—or was it a boarding-school? She was waited on by thirteen girls of good family, who were supposed to learn manners and morals from their mistress. The girls slept in one large room, and were frequently leaping out of bed to hold dormitory feasts. The State archives contain mention of pigeon pies stolen after dark from the larder.

They were sometimes joined in these feasts by certain young

men up from the country, or family dependants, who were also attached to the " court " of " Old Agnes " as pages or gentlemen-in-waiting. A certain Mr Mannock, or Manox, a music teacher, and a Mr Francis Dereham, who played the mandolin, became attracted to Catherine Howard, who at that time was about fifteen or sixteen years of age. Mannock, becoming jealous of Dereham, wrote a note to the Duchess advising her to visit the dormitory after dark. She did so and found a feast in progress, and she also discovered Dereham and Catherine Howard " in arms kissing ". The old lady boxed ears right and left, the young men fled, and no one seemed to be very upset until years afterwards. When Lord William Howard heard of it, he merely said, " What mad wenches ! " But one of these mad wenches was to become Cæsar's wife.

When Henry first met Catherine Howard, he was nearly fifty and she was about nineteen. The King was vast and horrible, diseased, afflicted by megalomania, addicted to enormous meals and potations, and he walked with the aid of a staff. In the three years which had elapsed since the execution of Anne Boleyn he had experienced a lot more domestic life. He had been married to Jane Seymour, who had died after giving birth to the prince who later became Edward VI, and he had married (platonically) the unattractive Anne of Cleves. Finding her intolerable, he had divorced her and had given her a pension together with a diploma of purity, and the title of " royal sister ".

Coming into his life at that moment, Catherine Howard was irresistible. He had never seen so sweet and demure a maid. He called her his " rose without a thorn ". He romanticised her, he sentimentalised her, and he removed her from the house in Lambeth to the palace, where everyone liked her. " She is always laughing and gay," wrote Marillac, the French Ambassador; and in Paris the French Court must have smiled cynically.

Henry married Catherine secretly in the summer of 1540. He was crazily happy with her, and found her a blaze of sunshine after his seven gloomy months with Anne of Cleves. Under Catherine's influence he almost became young again. " This King has taken a new rule of living," wrote Marillac to Francis I, " to rise between five and six, hear Mass at seven and then ride until dinner time, which is at 10 a.m."

Twelve months after the marriage Henry made a progress through the north of England, and Catherine went with him. During their absence a man named Lascelles, whom Froude, the historian, in a moment of forgetfulness, described as a gentleman, went to the Archbishop of Canterbury in London and told him that before her marriage the Queen had been familiar with Mannock and Dereham. Cranmer, who by this time must have been almost demented by the domestic revelations of the English Court, instead of kicking Lascelles downstairs, went chattering about London and told the story to the Chancellor and to others. When the King returned from his northern progress, he also was told at Hampton Court. He refused to believe such things of his " rose without a thorn "; but at the same time he ordered enquiries to be made.

Mannock and Dereham were arrested and confessed. A council meeting was called. The proof of Catherine's guilt was placed before Henry, who began quietly to cry. Then he sobbed until his huge frame was shaken by grief. Cranmer was sent to the Queen, and she, after becoming hysterical, admitted her guilt and begged the King's forgiveness. She was sent from Hampton Court to Syon House. All her ladies were examined, and a shocking story was revealed. It came out that during the northern progress the beautiful but poisonous Lady Rochford, before fixing the Queen's lodgings in the various towns, had carefully examined all the back stairs and ways of escape in order that one of the King's gentlemen, Mr Thomas Culpeper, might visit the Queen. Catherine Howard was now doomed. Lady Rochford was sent to the Tower. Thomas Culpeper was arrested and sent there also. At his trial he admitted that he and Catherine were in love before her marriage to the King.

" Do not seek to know more than that the King deprived me of the thing I love best in the world," he said at his trial. " Though you may hang me for it, she loves me as well as I love her, though up to this hour no wrong has ever passed between us."

Culpeper was hanged at Tyburn, cut down alive, split open and finally beheaded.

Henry behaved, for him, in a most extraordinary manner. He was reluctant to execute his " rose without a thorn ". He talked of banishing her to a nunnery. Now that her lover was dead, she asked only to be executed in private. Months elapsed, during which Catherine remained outwardly cheerful, wore her best clothes and said only that she was guilty and deserved to die.

Finally the King made up his mind, and she was sent to the Tower on February 10, 1542. She went by river. First went the Lord Privy Seal in a barge rowed by twenty-four oarsmen, then came the Queen in a little covered boat rowed by two men, and last came the great state barge containing the Earl of Suffolk and a hundred armed men. Darkness had fallen when the barges shot London Bridge, otherwise the Queen would have seen the head of her lover impaled on a spike above the central arch. In the darkness the Queen, dressed in black velvet, landed at Traitor's Gate and walked to her apartments.

In two days time they came to tell her that she must die on the following morning. She then made the most remarkable request that any condemned prisoner has made in the history of the Tower. She asked, as she did not know what was expected of her, if it would be possible for the block to be brought to her room so that she would know what to do? This was done. Catherine had the horrible object placed in the middle of the room, and then knelt down and placed her neck in the groove, rising with the remark that she could " go through the dread ordeal with grace and propriety ".

At seven o'clock on the next morning the same grim procession that had led Anne Boleyn to Tower Green only six years previously called for Catherine Howard. She passed through the same state apartments and was led to the same place on the Green. When she had mounted the scaffold she spoke a few words into the cold February air. She said that it was true that she loved Thomas Culpeper and that, had she only been true to her lover instead of becoming a queen, she would not then be dying. She turned to the masked man dressed in scarlet who stood near her, leaning on the axe.

"Hasten with thy office," she said.

He knelt, according to custom, and begged her forgiveness. Before the axe fell, the Queen cried, "I die a queen, but I would rather die the wife of Culpeper."

The axe descended, and the Queen's head fell into the straw. While they were covering her body, Lady Rochford was brought out to execution. An eye-witness said that she seemed "in a kind of frenzy till she died".

The French Ambassador, describing these events to his master in Paris, ended with the words: "Such are the odd customs of this very strange country."

Poor Lady Jane Grey, a child of sixteen, was hounded to death by her ambitious relatives, who, against her will, made her Queen for nine days, after which she was sent to the Tower by Mary Tudor, her doom inevitable. Fuller said that she had the birth of a princess, the learning of a clerk, the life of a saint and the death of a criminal.

On the raw and misty February morning in 1554 upon which she was condemned to leave this life, the poor girl was standing at a window in the Tower waiting to be summoned to the block. She saw some men wheeling a handcart, upon which lay the headless body of her young husband, Lord Guildford Dudley, who had just been executed on Tower Hill. Her reserves of courage deserted her, and the poor child broke into a fit of weeping. In a few moments she was summoned to the scaffold.

The dreary procession came slowly across Tower Green: the Yeomen of the Guard, the halberdiers, the Lieutenant of the Tower, then Lady Jane, small and helpless, beside her Dean Feckenham and behind her two gentlewomen, Mrs Elizabeth Tilney and Mrs Ellen, both in tears. Lady Jane was dressed in the same black gown she had worn at her trial in Guildhall. She carried a small book in her hands, and never lifted her eyes from its pages as she walked to the scaffold. The book was a prayer manual which she had borrowed from Sir John Brydges, the Lieutenant of the Tower.

When she had mounted the scaffold she made a short speech to the small crowd. She then knelt in prayer, and afterwards stood up and began to disrobe for her death. It seems that on many of these terrible occasions the headsman kept thoughtfully out of sight among the crowd until the final moments, when he appeared and knelt according to custom and begged forgiveness. But this time the headsman, no doubt well meaning, advanced and offered to help. At the sight of him the poor child burst into hysterical sobbing. She saw a masked figure nearly seven feet high, dressed in a suit of skin-tight wool.

Lady Jane flew to her women, and refused to let the headsman touch her. The women removed her black dress and her head-dress. She was given a handkerchief to bind her eyes. The headsman knelt. She forgave him and knelt down.

" Will you take it off before I lay me down? " she asked the executioner.

" No, madam," he replied.

Feeling blindly for the block, she said, " Where is it? What shall I do? "

Her head was guided to the place, and in a few seconds Jane Grey, one of the most wronged and innocent of all the Tower's victims, paid with her life for the ambition of her family.

It is interesting to read what a girl of sixteen wrote in a prayer-book while she was under sentence of death. This book, now one of the treasures of the British Museum, is the book which Lady Jane Grey borrowed from Sir John Brydges, who asked her to write something in it. These are her words:

> " For as much as you have desired so simple a woman to write in so worthy a book, good master Lieutenant, therefore I shall as a friend desire you and as a Christian require you, to call upon God to incline your heart

to His laws, to quicken you in His ways, and not to take the word of truth utterly out of your mouth. Live still to die, that by death you may purchase eternal life, and remember how the end of Methuselah, who as we read in the Scriptures was the longest liver that was of a man, died at the last; for as the preacher sayeth, there is a time to be born, and a time to die: and the day of death is better than the day of our birth."

§ 8

It is a relief to turn from such gloomy and frightful scenes and to remember a chapter of Tower history which, although tragic in the long run, did at least contain a great element of romantic comedy. This, my favourite Tower memory, is the story of the Lady Arabella Stuart.

She was the only child of Charles, Earl of Lennox, who traced his descent from Margaret, Queen of Scotland, daughter of Henry VII. She was the first cousin of James VI of Scotland and I of England, and was thus perilously near the throne. Queen Elizabeth's stubborn refusal in her old age to discuss the succession created the utmost confusion, which was happily solved by Cecil's secret correspondence with James, and the agreement reached between the two of them behind the back of the dying Queen, that the moment Elizabeth was dead, James would be proclaimed King. Next to James, however, Lady Arabella Stuart had the best claim to succeed Elizabeth. She was also on the spot, and many people indeed preferred her title to that of James, because she had been born on English soil.

Arabella was poor and dependent. She lived at Elizabeth's Court under the watchful eye of the Queen, who took up the attitude that so long as she remained unmarried she was not dangerous. The girl was therefore condemned by royal orders to a life of spinsterhood unless, defying them, she was willing to risk the Tower, and perhaps even the block. Like Jane Grey in the former reign, she was the victim of her dangerously blue blood.

Just before Elizabeth died, when Arabella Stuart was

twenty-eight years of age, a rumour was spread that she was about to be married. Elizabeth instantly caused her arrest, and the affair came to nothing. When James I succeeded to the throne, he adopted the same policy: as long as Arabella remained single she was his beloved cousin. The one thing she was not permitted to do was to marry.

But Love, it has often been noted, cannot be regulated. Unknown to James, Arabella, while living at Woodstock, had met and fallen in love with a young undergraduate of Magdalen College, Oxford, named William Seymour, who claimed descent from Edward, Duke of Somerset, and Henry Grey, Duke of Suffolk. Here was a most dangerous match. Arabella at this time was thirty-five years of age and her lover was twenty-one. They had many opportunities for meeting in the leafy woods of Oxfordshire, far away from the prying eyes and the busy tongues of London. Even so, the human gossip being what he is, their meetings were not unobserved.

There is little doubt that this poor frustrated woman was more in love than the young man. He appears to have been impressed by her regal birth and to have idealised her as the great lady with whose help he was to mount the ladder of ambition. In any case, it was doubtless his first serious love affair, and the irresistible attraction of a woman of thirty-five, who doted on him, was probably responsible for what followed.

As soon as James heard of the affair, the lovers were summoned before the Privy Council. Seymour denied in writing that they were engaged and promised that they would not marry without the King's consent. This explanation was accepted, and Arabella was taken back into favour. But the love affair continued. Somehow Arabella and her young man contrived to meet in secret for something like four months, at the end of which time they were married secretly—as they imagined—at Greenwich. But this was too much to hope! Almost at once their marriage was the talk of the town. Arabella was placed in custody, and young Seymour was sent to the Tower.

Here he made himself extremely comfortable in St Thomas's

Tower, overlooking the river. He sent out for tapestries to adorn the walls, and when he wanted furniture he asked Arabella to send it to him, which of course she was only too happy to do. She wrote love-letters to him which he sometimes answered. On more than one occasion Arabella, eluding her guardians, took a boat to the Tower, where, as Seymour's windows looked out on the Thames, she was able at least to see her darling. This indiscretion was, of course, asking for more trouble. It was known instantly in Westminster, and the King ordered her to the north of England. Here in time she became so ill that she was invalided to a cottage at East Barnet.

Being a Stuart, madly in love and a woman of thirty-five, something was now bound to happen. Arabella, with the help of a wealthy aunt, devised a wonderful scheme. She would steal her lover away from the Tower and sail off to France with him, where they would live happily ever after. Accordingly, one morning a cart drew up outside St Thomas's Tower. Wearing a black wig, a false beard and a carter's smock, Seymour slipped out of the Tower and mounted the driver's seat. He drove the cart out of the fortress and left it on the wharf. In a house nearby a friend was waiting with a change of clothes and a boat. Seymour set off in the boat for Blackwall, where he was to meet Arabella at an inn.

While this was happening in London, Lady Arabella, disguised as a man, was riding from East Barnet to Blackwall. She wore French-made hose and doublet, a black hat, brown boots with red tops and a black cloak. A rapier hung at her hip. So the woman who by the very faintest deflection of fate's finger might have been Queen of England in succession to the great Elizabeth, rode to meet her lover.

When she arrived at the inn, he was not there. She waited some time, and still he did not turn up. A ship which she had chartered was ready, and the captain said that unless he set sail at once the tide would not serve. She went aboard and sailed for Calais. Two hours later Seymour arrived at Blackwall to find that his wife had left for France. He hailed a collier and bribed the skipper to take him across to Calais, but the collier could not get there, and put in to Ostend. So the lovers were parted, and they were fated never to meet again.

The tragic end to their great adventure was caused by one of those strange and improbable happenings which, as in the story of Colonel Blood, I have said no novelist would dare to use. It appeared that the escape of Seymour by boat from the Tower was observed by many people, who noted the young man's haste and anxiety. A retired admiral named Monson happened to be there talking to the watermen. Hearing of Seymour's departure, Monson—a typical busybody—came to the conclusion that Seymour must be a fugitive from justice, and accordingly gave chase. He arrived at the inn at Blackwall which had been the trysting place, learnt of Arabella's departure in the ship, and of Seymour's flight in the collier, and, using his rank as an admiral, commandeered a warship, perfectly called H.M.S. *Adventure*, in which he crossed the Channel. He was just in time to stop Arabella's ship before it ran into Calais. The ship was boarded. Poor Lady Arabella gave herself up, a woeful cavalier by this time, and was taken to England, where she was lodged in the Tower.

From that moment the story becomes one of tragedy. Arabella lingered in the Tower for four years, poor, neglected, and heart-broken. Her mind gave way and she died insane in 1615, and was buried in the same vault in the Abbey with Mary, Queen of Scots. And what of Seymour? Learning of Arabella's capture, he remained on the Continent, and did not return to England until after her death. James, strange to say, took him back into favour and made much of him. As the Earl of Hertford, he fought valiantly for Charles I, he survived the Commonwealth and, as an old man of seventy-two, was one of those who went down to Dover to greet Charles II upon his restoration to the throne. In the same year he was created Duke of Somerset, and in that year he died. Although in his youth he appeared extremely casual, and it is perhaps easy to under-estimate his affection for Lady Arabella, the memory of his romance evidently remained with him all his days, because at the end he asked to be buried with her, a wish that was not fulfilled.

§ 9

I went to the Tower on a Sunday morning to attend the service in the church of St Peter-ad-Vincula. It was a warm summer morning, the tide was high, a Sabbath hush was upon the City, Tower Bridge, empty of traffic, spanned the Thames, and the Tower, in one of its most benevolent moods, shone white and clean in the sunlight.

I sat for a while, for I was early, upon a seat near the site of the block on Tower Green. A raven was lumbering across the grass with drooping beetle blue wings, lifting each foot deliberately, while a highly superior marmalade cat wearing a collar sat beneath a tree watching it closely and dispassionately. Some unnaturally tidy children struck the note of Sunday, a few members of the public wandered about, for they are allowed to attend church in the Tower, and in the background rose the black-and-white Tudor building, the King's House, in which the Governor lives. Many years ago a former Governor, who is now dead, told me that he could keep no servants in that house because doors opened and shut in an unusual way, and there were peculiar noises at night. The present Governor has noticed nothing uncanny in the house and gave me the impression that he was rather disappointed about it. His dressing-room is the room in which Anne Boleyn is said to have spent her last night on earth.

I must say that for a place like the Tower, steeped in human tragedy, the ghosts are unconvincing. They have been seen generally by nervous sentries on dark nights, and few of them, except perhaps the ghost who was challenged by a soldier and whose appearance was described in evidence at a court-martial, would bear discussion by daylight. Much stranger than such spectres is an incident, quoted by Sir William Barrett in *On the Threshold of the Unseen*, which occurred during a spiritualistic seance in June, 1889. The medium, who was using a planchette, found that the instrument had written (upside down) the name "John Gurwood". Then came the sentence, "I killed myself forty-four years ago next Christmas". Asked if he was in the Army, "John Gurwood" replied, "Yes, but it was the pen and not the sword that did for me." When asked where and when he was wounded, the planchette spelt out, "In the Peninsula. In the head. I was wounded in 1810."

Neither the medium nor anyone at the seance had ever heard of "John Gurwood", but on reference to the Annual Register for 1845—the date given as that of his suicide—it was discovered that Colonel John Gurwood was the Deputy-Governor of the Tower, that he had been wounded in the head at the storming of Ciudad Rodrigo, that his work of editing the Wellington Despatches had upset the balance of his mind and that he had committed suicide on Christmas Day, 1845. If it be really true that the medium knew nothing about Gurwood, that is surely a really genuine Tower ghost story. There is a memorial to him in St Peter-ad-Vincula, but it makes no reference to his suicide.

The church bell began to ring. The door of a house in Tower Green opened, and out stepped the Yeoman Gaoler, wearing a neatly pressed suit of blue serge. Several other Yeomen Warders, looking strange in civilian clothes, strolled across Tower Green with their wives and families, as if they were walking to the village church.

There was a congregation of about fifty, Warders and their families, a few officers of the garrison with their wives, a few members of the public. The choir came in, wearing scarlet cassocks, each boy's shining face rising above a white starched frill. As the service proceeded it was constantly punctuated by the loud croaking of the ravens on Tower Green outside, but so accustomed were most of the congregation to this sound that no one appeared to notice it. To me it was the one indication that we were in the Tower of London, and not in some little parish church in the country.

I am afraid my mind strayed from the service to those whose dust lies so thickly beneath the pavement of St Peter-ad-Vincula. And what a perfect dedication this is for such a mausoleum—St Peter-in-Chains. Here in this melancholy place the Prince of the Apostles, himself a prisoner bound and under sentence of death, opens his arms to receive those fellow-prisoners whose chains had been severed by the headsman's axe. It is a little Westminster Abbey of the unhappy and the unfortunate. It is the cemetery of Tower Hill, the church of the scaffold, the parish church of violent death. Beneath the pavements lie Sir Thomas More; Lord Rochford; Anne Boleyn; Thomas Cromwell; Catherine Howard; Lady Rochford; Thomas, Lord Seymour of Sudeley; Edward Seymour, Duke of Somerset; Lord Guildford Dudley; Lady Jane Grey; Thomas Howard, Duke of Norfolk; Robert Devereux, Earl of Essex; Sir Thomas Overbury; James, Duke of Monmouth; the Scottish lords executed after the 1745 Rebellion, and many more.

Some of those who lie in this church were in their time as great and as noble as those who went to their rest in the Abbey Church with pomp and circumstance and to the sound of a nation's mourning. But to this place they came headless, and often at dead of night, to be hurried out of sight by the hands of their gaolers; and those who dared to weep for them did so in secret. It is indeed, as Macaulay wrote, the saddest spot on earth.

One of the most melancholy and gruesome excavations ever undertaken took place when St Peter-ad-Vincula was restored in Victorian times. Those who had to remove and re-lay the nave saw, lying together as they had been flung there, the remains of some of the most notable men and women in English history. The Norfolk tradition that the body of Anne Boleyn was secretly removed from the Tower, and privately interred in the family burial-place at Salle, was disproved at this time, for her bones were easily identified, and were medically examined. She was no more than five feet high, or at the most five feet three inches. Catherine Howard was also an unusually small woman. All the remains discovered were carefully placed in a leaden sarcophagus and reverently re-buried.

While we sang the final hymn, the ravens, hearing us, joined in; and so we trooped out into the sunlight.

§ 10

If you wish to see the site of the scaffold where all except six of the victims of royal displeasure met their death, you must go outside the Tower and walk up Tower Hill to the shabby little park known as Trinity Gardens, opposite the Port of London Authority building.

When I went there I found the site in a shocking condition. The rails which surround it had been invaded by rubbish and rubble. An old shoe, dirty scraps of newspaper and broken tiles lay about, and one of the terminal obelisks had been thrown down. It looked as though it was nobody's job to look after it.

Lying on the site of the scaffold was a scrap of paper attached to a withered bunch of flowers, and written upon the paper I read: " In honour of St John Fisher and St Thomas More, who died on this spot for the glory of God and the Holy Catholic Faith."

CHAPTER THREE

I go to London Bridge in the early morning, pay a visit to Billingsgate Market, cross the Bridge into Southwark, where I see the splendid Cathedral and the old George Inn. I climb the Monument, look into Fishmongers' Hall and call at the College of Heralds.

§ 1

SHORTLY after eight o'clock on a silvery-grey morning I stood at the end of London Bridge. The tide was high, the tugs were passing up and down river; on one side the Tower stood as if cut in white steel in the morning mist, and Tower Bridge was a Gothic cobweb drawn across the Thames; on the other side, beyond the black roof of Cannon Street Station, rose the dome of St Paul's.

There advanced towards me a great army of Londoners, some empty-handed, some with newspapers tucked under their arms, some carrying attaché cases, all marching briskly and purposefully; and all of them going the same way. How many hundreds of thousands of men and women from the southern suburbs are discharged each morning upon the platforms of London Bridge Station I do not know, but from about eight o'clock to half-past nine they march across the bridge without ceasing: managers, clerks, typists, office-boys, messengers, every conceivable type of Londoner, every age, every size, ugly and good-looking, smart and shabby, happy and morose, a great flood of human beings directed, as if by an enormous funnel, towards the offices, the banks, the warehouses and the shops of the City of London.

There is no better place to study the type of person who works in the City to-day. At other places London fills with its daily tide of life almost imperceptibly. People arrive from all directions by bus, tube and Underground. They scatter towards their offices like rabbits bolting into a warren. You see them, not as a crowd, but as scurrying individuals. But here on London Bridge in the early morning thousands cross from the south to the north bank of the river, and you can look at them and study them as if they were an army on the march.

Of all the approaches to London this is the most inspiring and the most romantic. Those who cross the bridge see on their right the old grey Tower, apparently so innocent in the early morning, on their left St Paul's and, ahead of them, the Monument and the roof-line of the City, with its church towers and spires. Yet how few of those hurrying thousands pause to look at the river.

They cross the bridge every morning, and so most of them have given up looking. Probably the first few times they went to work it was exciting and thrilling, then it became routine. However, although they are not aware of it, the scene is etched upon their minds for ever. It is part of them. Remove them to Kenya or Brazil, and they will suddenly see that morning walk across the bridge in minute detail. They will begin to long for it and to feel homesick; although if you told them this, they would probably not believe you: they would say that they would much rather be in Kenya or Brazil than marching across London Bridge towards Associated This or Consolidated That. But at this very moment there are people in distant and lonely parts of the world who would give anything to hear, as those marchers hear, the tramp of dray-horses across London Bridge, the steady drumming of feet, the hooting of the tug coming down-river, the hammering from the wharves. And, in addition to the sound of the morning, there is that silver-greyness in the air out of which the buildings rise with such sable dignity, and in the air also is a smell, or rather a number of smells: from Billingsgate, fishy; from the river, a cold freshness; and then a sudden whiff of petrol as a warm red bus goes past. Those are the memories which tug at your heart when you are far away, yet you never think of them while they are a part of your life.

To me the sight of London Bridge in the morning is the very essence of London. It is beautiful, it is romantic and, like all beauty, it is profoundly disturbing. It is the place where countless young people must have dreamed dreams, where, maybe, ambition first touched a young man on the shoulder. I have often whiled away half an hour watching the boys who lean over London Bridge at various times of the day, when they are supposed to be delivering urgent messages. I have wondered what they think about. The majority perhaps think of nothing, but surely there must always be one lad who cannot gaze unmoved upon the Pool of London, who turns away from the ships and the swooping gulls and returns to his duty with the resolve to be a Dick Whittington or a Walter Raleigh. Or have modern boys been taught that Dick Whittington was an exploiter and Raleigh a pirate? I hope not.

In the old days this view from the bridge must have been even more tantalising. The ships were not all corralled far away down-river in the docks. The Pool held a forest of masts as thick as a fir wood in Surrey, and you could see the merchantmen lying, their sails reefed, back from the Indies, Peru and China, from the Americas and the hot green islands of the Java seas, anchored quietly side by side in the shadow of London Bridge.

Becoming tired of watching the apparently endless flow of men and women to the City, I began to think of Old London Bridge—the bridge that spanned the Thames like a street of houses, as if Cheapside were taking a walk into Surrey. They pulled this bridge down at the beginning of the last century, and built the present bridge about thirty yards upstream to the west. They sold the stone, the iron and the wood that for so many centuries had resisted the ebb and flow of the Thames. A cutler in the Strand bought fifteen tons of iron which had shod the piers of the old bridge, and declared that it made the best steel he had ever seen. No doubt thousands of knives were made about 1835 from the metal of old London Bridge. The stone went to build Ingress Abbey, near Greenhithe, which is, or was when I last saw it, a naval training college. From the ancient elm wood thousands of snuff-boxes and other objects were formed, so that, unknown to those who possess such relics, London Bridge still lives, although surprisingly transformed.

Behind the large modern Adelaide House in Lower Thames

Street you will find the church of St Magnus the Martyr. Old London Bridge came out upon the City bank exactly opposite this church; indeed, the arcaded tower was actually part of the footway.

I have sometimes thought that could I have lived in Tudor or Stuart London, I would rather have had a house on London Bridge than anywhere else; but this may be pure romanticism. Pennant, who remembered the old bridge, wrote that " nothing but use could preserve the repose of the inmates, who soon grew deaf to the noise of falling waters, the clamours of watermen, or the frequent shrieks of drowning wretches ". Still, I think the view westward must have been superb, with its uninterrupted sweep of river curving round towards the Temple and Westminster—for there was no other bridge across the Thames until 1749—and, in the other direction, the Tower, seen through the rigging of ships, must have been equally lovely. In days when the river was the main highway of London, a house on London Bridge must have been rather like one on the Grand Canal in Venice. Those who lived on the bridge occupied a watch-tower from which almost everything that happened on the Thames was clearly visible and much of it, no doubt, audible.

Imagine awakening upon a spring morning in Shakespeare's London, in a raftered room on old London Bridge. You would hear the roar of the water rushing through the arches, the clank and wheeze of the water mills and machines that obstructed the river in so many of the openings and, high in the air above, you would hear a sound long absent from London, the whistle of hovering kites. And, opening the window, what a London you would have seen! The old black-and-white houses that were to be swept away in the Great Fire crowded to the water's edge, their gardens overlooking the river; above their roof-tiles rose the towers of the churches and, highest of all, the steeple of old St Paul's.

The shopkeepers who lived on old London Bridge must have been a community on their own. They were the only landsmen who lived and earned their living on the Thames as if they were anchored there in a great ship. Holbein is said to have lived on London Bridge. Swift and Pope used to visit an old bookseller, named Crispin Tucker, who had a shop there. Hogarth lived on the bridge when he was engraving for John Bowles of Cornhill, and left a glimpse of it in one of the plates of *Marriage à la Mode*. Another painter who lived there was the marine artist, Peter Monomy. There was a haberdasher called Baldwin who was ordered country air by his doctor, but he returned to London at once because he could not sleep away from the roar and the creak of the water wheels.

Of course the bridge, which was incredibly ancient even in the times of the Tudors, changed its character from age to age. The houses were sometimes burnt down and had to be rebuilt. The shops became fashionable, or else fashion, in its well-known way, deserted them. At one time, in the reign of Elizabeth, London Bridge was a great place for booksellers and publishers. Among the bridge imprints to be found on title-pages are *The Three Bibles*, *The Angel*, and *The Looking Glass*. I wonder how often Shakespeare might have been seen turning over the books on London Bridge, flirting with a copy of North's *Plutarch* or perhaps wondering how he might justify to himself the possession of an unnecessary volume of Holinshed, or Reginald Scot's new book, *Discoverie of Witchcraft*, which would come in useful if he went on with a play about Macbeth!

The only list we have of London Bridge shopkeepers at one particular period was made in 1633, when a number of houses were destroyed by fire. Among those burned out were eight haberdashers, six hosiers, one shoemaker, five hatters, three silk mercers, one male milliner, two glovers, two mercers, one "distiller of strong waters", one girdler, one linen-draper, two woollen-drapers, one salter, two grocers, one scrivener, one pin-maker, one clerk, and the curate of St Magnus the Martyr. Later on the pin-makers increased, until Pennant says that in his time "most of the houses were tenanted by pin or needle makers and economical ladies were wont to drive from the St James's end of the town to make cheap purchases".

The bridge must have been extremely inconvenient. The footpath was not of the same width all the way. At one place it was only twelve feet wide, and at its widest only twenty. There were chains and posts to protect the foot-passengers. The overhanging houses made the bridge dark for most of its length, and frequent arches of timber from roof-top to roof-top kept the rickety old houses from toppling into the water. The traffic blocks must have been appalling when coaches became common. Pepys described a hold-up that lasted half an hour, when he was trying to get across from Southwark. Becoming tired of waiting, he slipped out of his coach and went into an inn, but when he came out his coach had been swept forward with the traffic, and he was obliged to walk. There was a hole in the roadway, in which his foot became wedged, and he might have broken his leg if someone had not come to his help.

The narrow arches of the bridge offered such obstruction to the flow of the river that the Thames above the bridge was a comparatively placid lake, and that is why there were so many frost fairs in the old days and why the river no longer froze from bank to bank when old London Bridge disappeared. The obstruction also created rapids which could be highly dangerous to the unskilled oarsman. Many Londoners lost their lives, or were at least flung into the water, during the skilful act known as " shooting the bridge ", which was the act of shipping oars and guiding the boat through the rapids. This perilous act explains the old proverb, " London Bridge was made for wise men to go over and for fools to go under ". It was usual for the prudent, on their way downstream, to leave their boats at the *Three Cranes* in Upper Thames Street and to join them again at Billingsgate, after they had shot the bridge. Pepys, going the other way, described how he got out of the boat and stood on the piers of the bridge while his boatmen hauled their craft up through the rapids.

A sight which impressed old London Bridge upon the minds of all who saw it was the heads of criminals and traitors, and so-called traitors, mounted on pikes upon the central tower. But in an age when skeletons hung in iron cages from gibbets upon lonely heaths all over the country travellers would probably not lose much sleep when greeted, upon arrival in London, by such a spectacle.

§ 2

Long before the business men begin their march across London Bridge, Billingsgate has almost ended its morning's work. The fish market used to open at four o'clock in the morning in remote times; when I knew it before the last War opening time was five o'clock, but now the later hour of seven o'clock, which was introduced during the black-out, has prevailed. Even so, Billingsgate is still the earliest of the City's morning activities. All the streets which lead downhill to the market are crowded with lorries, motor vans, horse vans, and even donkey-carts. Round them swarm fish salesmen, fish porters, fishmongers and hundreds of men in cloth caps, who stand vaguely about at street corners. This splash of vitality in a city not yet awake has an air of conspiracy. It seems that all these horses and all these men are trying to do something quickly before London wakes up and finds out about it. And it is true. They are trying to give London fish that was caught in the North Sea only the day before.

Of all the creatures which we eat, fish when dead rouse in us the least compassion. Disliking hens, as I do, I cannot pretend to feel much sympathy in Leadenhall Market, yet the sight of small wild birds, such as woodcock or snipe, and even, I would add, pheasants and partridges, must rouse in us a momentary pang as we see them lying, as birds do, so pathetically earthbound and dead. But codfish, hake, eels, soles, lobsters, crabs and plaice, perhaps because they inhabit an element strange to us, are interesting in death, but are never surely even mildly shocking, even to the most tender conscience.

It is delightful, therefore, to survey this great mortuary of the sea, and to watch the men in white overalls who have devoted their lives to it. One of London's charms is that it is a city of experts, and among them are those who, having been in the fish trade all their lives, know everything that is to be known about fish. To you and me a dead fish is just a dead fish, but to them it is an infinitely more complicated corpse. These experts are every bit as learned in their own way as the art connoisseurs who, in the sale-rooms of St James's, can tell you what is genuine and what is not.

Billingsgate is one of the few places in London from which women have been gradually excluded. Every other trade and profession has opened its doors to women in the last half-century. But the fishwife of Billingsgate no longer exists. She used to sit with her basket in front of her, sometimes smoking a clay pipe, or taking a pinch of snuff or a drink of gin, and in this position Rowlandson placed her on record in the *Microcosm of London*. But to-day you can seek everywhere in vain, not only for a fish-wife but for any woman actively associated with Billingsgate.

The distinctive note of Billingsgate is struck by some of the fish-salesmen, who often wear straw hats in winter, and by the crowd of fish porters, who wear a hide helmet, shaped rather like a pagoda, on which they balance ramparts of boxes. These hats, which are studded with hundreds of brass nails, cost over five pounds each, and upon them, once a porter's neck " sets ", he can carry sixteen stone in weight.

I have known Billingsgate for years, yet I have never heard any bad language there. The porters say that it ceased to be used when the fishwives disappeared, and Bailey's Dictionary bore this out as early as 1736, when it defined the word Billingsgate as " a scolding, impudent slut ". Although Billingsgate, like Covent Garden and Smithfield, has a public-house which opens before breakfast, I have never found anyone using it to excess. On the contrary, the Billingsgate porters like chocolate, or they did so before it was rationed. I used to think that one of the most surprising sights of a London dawn was a six-foot Billingsgate fish-porter, covered with silver scales, groping in his overalls for a penny to buy a stick of chocolate cream.

Billingsgate, in spite of its nearness to London Bridge, was not seriously smashed up during the Blitz, although there is a good deal of damage here and there, and I noticed that many of the excellent fish-shops and restaurants have disappeared. Having wandered all over the market, I asked a fish-salesman where I could have breakfast. He pointed to an Italian restaurant on the second floor of a building near the Monument.

The room was full of tobacco smoke. Salesmen in white

overalls who knew each other shouted badinage from table to table. In this surprising place I ordered what turned out to be the best breakfast in rationed London. I had a fillet steak and fried onions, coffee, toast and marmalade, and the fixed price was two shillings and threepence! A man sitting next to me followed his steak with a pêche Melba—the first time that I have seen this ice eaten at seven-thirty in the morning!

§ 3

I walked across London Bridge firmly resolved not to linger there. When I was almost at the Southwark end I saw a great crowd of boys and men leaning over the bridge, gazing downward towards the river in dead silence. Of course I had to edge my way in; and what do you think I saw? I saw a foreign ship leaving London. The captain was on the bridge, the ship was edging its way gingerly into the river, and one or two of the deck-hands, seeing the fringe of heads above on the bridge, cheerily waved to us. I am sure that not one of us did not wish he could sail away with that ship!

Then I noticed that no women were looking down at the ship. Women passed by, but it never occurred to them that something wonderful and exciting was happening on the Thames. I suppose they thought, if they thought at all, "Just a lot of men wasting their time, as usual." And it occurred to me that this famous view from London Bridge is essentially anti-domestic. It is unsettling. It appeals to all the vagrant, wandering and no doubt disreputable and regrettable instincts of the male. It makes it more difficult to go home to Streatham. And as the ship moved and left us, we shook ourselves from its spell as best we could and went on our various ways with a vision of foreign towns, blue waters and coral reefs.

On the other side of the bridge a grey church on low ground lifts its tower against the warehouses and the cranes. This is one of the least known, and one of the most interesting, churches in London. It is Southwark Cathedral. I wonder why so few ever visit it? There is no excuse for this, for it is one of the most accessible sights in London.

Southwark to-day suggests miles of dreary streets and thousands of warehouses, but ancient Southwark suggests Shakespeare, the theatre, bull-baiting, cock-fighting, taverns, murders in dark corners and the notorious Stews. It is natural that Southwark in the old days should have had a bad name, for how easy it was for anyone who had been expelled from London to remove himself from within the walls and just across the river to the opposite bank. Numbers of women, mostly Flemish, driven out of London during a purity campaign in the time of Edward I, fled to Southwark, where, as long as they refrained from wearing miniver, which is spotted ermine, or candale—which was thin silk—they were permitted to live in peace. That was the beginning of the Southwark Stews. When van den Wyngaerde drew his pictorial map in the reign of Elizabeth, Southwark was a marshy district with a wide foreshore washed by the Thames, and there were hardly any buildings upon the river-bank between Bankside, where the theatres stood, and Lambeth Palace. Southwark High Street at that time looked like the main street of Stratford-on-Avon to-day: a wide street of black-and-white half-timbered houses, with gardens leading down to the water.

The traveller coming to London from the south would have had a foretaste of the lawlessness of Southwark when he rode past a clump of trees about half a mile from the bridge. There thieves and cut-purses were executed. One ambassador in the time of Elizabeth mentions having seen twelve corpses swinging from the boughs, a gloomy introduction to London, which London Bridge itself would not dispel, with its distinguished heads rotting in iron cages on the end of pikes.

Throughout the varied centuries the grey church, which is now Southwark Cathedral, has kept watch on the sometimes hectic history of the Borough. Its foundation takes one back to a remote Saxon London when, so it is said, a rich ferryman left his fortune to a maiden daughter called Mary. This pious girl is claimed as the foundress of the church. It was called in the old days St Mary Overie, which is explained as St Mary over the Ferry or St Mary over the Rie (water). In Norman times another church rose upon the site, and parts of it are still preserved in the present building.

What a noble church it is! I entered it again for the first time for many years, and sought out the verger, who knows it stone by stone.

"If this cathedral stood within ten miles of a popular watering-place," he said, "it would be one of the most famous sights in England. Although millions of people pass it every week, they are always in a hurry, either rushing to work or else rushing home after work. It is a great pity that one of the finest churches in London should be known only to students of architecture or to Americans who have been to Harvard University. All Harvard men know it. They all come here because John Harvard, the founder of the University, was born in this parish and was baptised in this church. We sent a bit of the Norman shaft from the left of the altar to America in 1908, and they have preserved it in the porch of Appleton Chapel."

There is no church in the country with a greater interest for writers and dramatists than Southwark Cathedral. The verger took me with pride to the alabaster figure of Shakespeare. The poet may have lived in Southwark when he was writing his plays, and round him were gathered an immortal company of players and fellow-actors, a group which included Christopher Marlowe, Massinger, Beaumont and Fletcher, Ben Jonson, Philip Henslowe, and Edward Alleyn, the founder of Dulwich College. Shakespeare himself must have stood in the church on December 31, 1607, surrounded maybe by this great gathering of Elizabethans, for in the church register for that date is the following entry:

> Edmund Shakespeare, a player, buried in ye church with a forenoon knell of the great bell.

This was Shakespeare's youngest brother, who, maybe encouraged by William's success in the great city, left his home to join the band of stage players in Southwark. I asked the verger if the site of his grave were known, but all that can be said is that his bones have never been disturbed and must lie somewhere in the church.

Unknown Edmund and his immortal brother lie at the last in much the same atmosphere. There is a strong resemblance between Southwark Cathedral and Holy Trinity Church, Stratford-on-Avon; both are beautiful, tall, mediæval churches, and both are distinguished by that architectural peculiarity known as a " declination "—a slight difference in the direction of nave and choir—said by some authorities to be a symbolical representation of Christ's head drooping on the Cross.

I have no idea if many people collect epitaphs. They have always seemed to me much more worth collecting than many things. If so, I advise collectors to go to Southwark Cathedral and seek out the excellent material to be found there. There is, for instance, the grave of a man called Lockyer who is sculptured in stone in a lying position, leaning up on one arm. He wears a long Charles II wig and an enigmatic expression. This was Lionel Lockyer, a famous quack doctor in the time of James I, who lived through the reign of Charles I, and also through the Commonwealth, to expire at a ripe old age in the reign of Charles II.

His great contribution to medicine was a pill called " Radiis Solis Extractae ", which, if taken early in the morning, guarded the patient against fogs, contagious ills and, still better, against all diseases known and *unknown*! His pills not only improved personal beauty but, so the inventor claimed, made old age delightful! Lockyer was one of the first great advertisers; indeed, his pamphlets foreshadow the quack medicine advertisements of to-day, and it is tempting to assume that he wrote his own epitaph, which concludes:

His virtues and his pills are so well known
That envy can't confine them under stone,
But they'l survive his dust and not expire
Till al things else th' universal fire.
This verse is lost his PILL embalms him safe
To future times without an epitaph.

One of the most charming monuments in the church is a coloured effigy of a man and his wife, John and Mistress Trehearne. He died in 1618, and she survived him for twenty-seven years. The old couple are a perfect example of solid, middle-class Elizabethans, a type not often seen on monuments. They wrote no madrigals or plays and had no interest in navigating the earth, or such-like nonsense! They were interested in living a quiet, peaceful life and in bringing up the two sons and the four daughters who are sculptured below in attitudes of prayer. All this is clearly written on the blunt, bearded face of the man and on the careful, stern face of the woman, rather prim and hard, with a tight mouth and hair scraped back under an Elizabethan lace cap.

In spite of the placid expressions of this couple, they must have seen many interesting and exciting events, for Trehearne was for many years a servant of Queen Elizabeth, and was taken over with other members of her household when James I arrived from Scotland to occupy the throne. He is described on the monument as " Gentleman Portar to King James I ", and the epitaph, which man and wife hold in the form of a tablet, suggests in the quaintest manner that had James been able to retain his services, there would have been no question of him leaving his situation for another and a more mysterious one.

> Had Kings a power to lend their subjects breath,
> Trehearne, thou should'st not be cast down by death
> The royal master still would keep thee then
> But length of days are beyond reach of men.

There are many other epitaphs well worth copying in this church, including an extraordinary composition in Latin which might be rendered something like this.

> " These be the incinerated remains of Richard Benefield, associate of Grays Inn, to them, after they were roughly purified by the francincense of his piety, the nard of his probity, the amber of his faithfulness, and the oil of his charity, his friends, the poor, everyone, in fact, have added the sweet-scented myrrh of their commendation and the fresh balsam of their tears."

I think that this must be the most unctuous epitaph in England.

One of the finest features of Southwark Cathedral is the retro-chapel built during the Thirteenth Century. In Tudor times, when so many churches fell into disrepair, it was leased as a place of business to a baker. It was a workshop for about seventy years, and an attempt to demolish the lovely thing in 1832 was defeated by the Bishop of Winchester and a group of artists and architects.

There are also several beautiful little side-chapels which prove that Southwark Cathedral is no dead memorial to the past, but that its work and its influence are spread over the world. One chapel is dedicated to missionary work, another to the Good Samaritan, and a third to St Christopher and all the young people of Southwark.

"Let us by our prayers and work," says an inscription, "help to carry the boys and girls safely through the dangers and glories of growing up."

I left Southwark Cathedral thankful that the Great Fire, to say nothing of more recent flames, spared this noble church to gaze out across the Thames as it has gazed for so many centuries.

§ 4

The great hotels of London are found to-day everywhere except in the City. In the old days inns and taverns were grouped at both the Southwark and City ends of London Bridge. Southwark was full of inns. There was the famous *Tabard*, mentioned by Chaucer, the *King's Head*, the *Spur*, the *Queen's Head*, the *Bull*, the *White Hart*, and many more, all in the High Street.

If you arrived in Southwark after dark you would find the Bridge Gate shut, and unless you tipped the gate-keeper to let you into London, which, I imagine, might not have been too difficult, it is probable that you would decide to spend the night in the Borough. On the other side of the bridge there was an even more magnificent selection of inns to choose from: the famous *King's Head* at the bridge end, the *Three Cranes* in the Vintry, the *Emperor's Head* nearby, the *Old Swan*, the *Shades* in Thames Street, the *Buckler*, the *Three Tuns* in Billingsgate, the *Dolphin on the Hoop*, the *Swan* at Dowgate, and if these were full up, you could ride on to Cannon Street and try the *White Hart*, or you might go to the *Boar's Head* in Eastchepe; but perhaps that place was a bit noisy when Master Shakespeare and such-like riff-raff were in the bar!

These old inns have vanished, leaving nothing behind to this age but maybe a name-plate on a wall—all except the *Old George* in Southwark, the last galleried inn in London, which you will find beneath an unprepossessing archway a few hundred yards from London Bridge, on the left-hand side of the High Street. It is a great pity that three sides of the gallery have been demolished, but from the main gallery, which exists in fine condition, it is easy to imagine—even if you have not seen the *New Inn* at Gloucester—what these old coaching inns looked like.

The bedrooms of the *George* open out upon two wooden galleries, one above the other, which are railed with wooden balusters. Upon this rail guests used to lean to watch the coaches come in through the archway and to speculate about the new arrivals while the ostlers took away the steaming horses and lead out a fresh team. This is one of the last places in London which cannot fail to awaken memories of Dickens and Mr Pickwick.

Twenty years ago I remember spending a night at the *George* in a huge four-poster bed so high from the floor that a little flight of three mahogany steps was provided to help one up. There was no bathroom, and the chambermaid carried in a hip bath, which in the morning was filled with buckets of warm water. The bedside light was a candle.

I remember how strange it was to go to sleep in the authentic atmosphere of another age, and in a building consecrated by so many centuries of wayfaring; for the *George* was first heard of in 1554, ten years before Shakespeare was born.

It is the personal relationship between master and man, as between host and guest, which this age so sadly lacks; and it is surely remarkable that in a time when class distinctions were so clearly defined, this cordial relationship undoubtedly existed between noble and commoner. I remember thinking how intensely personal and friendly it was at the *George*. There were no modern comforts, no bells, no telephones, no running water, no bathrooms, and only the most rudimentary sanitation, yet the atmosphere was full of kindness and geniality. I have often thought how easy it would be to die unnoticed in a modern hotel, but at the very hint of a cold at the *George*, they would have offered to rub your chest with some old-fashioned remedy like camphorated oil. I was astonished in the morning to discover that the chambermaid, with no thought of a tip but, as I wrote at the time, " through sheer womanly kindness of heart ", had darned two pairs of my socks!

I found the old inn looking much the same as I always remembered it. The brace of pistols was still in the bar and the high pine settles still divided table from table in the coffee-room. You can still have luncheon there, but it is no longer possible to stay at the *George* and sleep in an old four-poster bed. Old Miss Murray, who owned the place when I was last there, has departed this life, and the *George*, after passing through several hands, has at last been safely gathered into the ample bosom of the National Trust.

On my way back across London Bridge I saw men working on a scaffold erected against the façade of Fishmongers' Hall, that fine classical building at the north end of the bridge. I thought it would be interesting to find out what happened to the headquarters of the Worshipful Company of Fishmongers during the Blitz. One thing that happened to it I noted even before I mounted the steps: the great hall had been turned into a British Restaurant. They were advertising, as the dishes of the day, " Corned beef pie " or " Egg salad ".

I went upstairs, and found that some unknown vandal had stuck large black pipes through the walls of the banqueting hall wherever he thought they might be useful. The place looked horrible. It was designed for large and stately gatherings, and now about fifty mean little deal tables covered with oilcloth dotted the floor. There were cards with " Ice Cream " written on them hanging on the once-splendid walls. I ordered a cup of coffee, and the waitress said " Yes, love ", and brought me a cup. But the sight of the fine place degraded in this way and reduced to such unnecessary squalor, almost as if those responsible were anxious to insult something that was noble and possessed beauty and tradition, so depressed me that I went away quickly and sought out the Clerk to the Company. While we discussed the history of the Company and the adventures of the Hall during the War, he opened a cupboard and gave me a glass of sherry and one of those fat, opulent Turkish cigarettes smoked only by princes, pashas and aldermen.

The Hall, although it looks intact from the street and the river, suffered from blast, and some of the smaller rooms have been badly damaged. We made a quick tour of the building, where I saw the encouraging sight of a great Company hall coming back to life after the War under the expert hands of English craftsmen. The men were working as men once worked when they had pride in their jobs. They whistled from their scaffolding. And the reason they were happy and proud was because they were not hammering pre-fabricated buildings together, or pulling dry rot out of Acacia Road, but they were working with mahogany, and other rare and expensive woods, and they were uncurling gold leaf and pressing it upon pilasters and capitals. This was a " high-class " job, and they loved it.

Down in the strong-room I saw the Company silver, all safe and intact. I saw the London Bridge Chair made from the oak of the old bridge and I was told that the damage it suffered during an air raid is to be made good with oak taken from the blitzed Guildhall. One of the most treasured relics is the dagger with which William Walworth, Lord Mayor of London, is said to have stabbed Wat Tyler. This came safely through the War, and is kept in a bank.

The Clerk reminded me, as we went over the building, that the Fishmongers Company has had an unbroken existence for more than seven hundred years, and that it is one of the few Companies still actively engaged in the trade out of which it was born. Every day two inspectors appointed by the Company, and known by the queer name of " fishmeters ", patrol Billingsgate Market, and have the authority to condemn any fish unfit for food. Shell-fish is regularly tested by the Company, and if it does not come up to certain standards is condemned. In many other ways connected with fish and fishing the Worshipful Company is a noteworthy example of an ancient Guild that throughout its long history has retained its original function.

It was amusing to hear the Clerk talk of distinguished Freemen of the Company.

"The Duke of Edinburgh is a Fishmonger," he said, "so that Prince Charles was born a Fishmonger, and will be entitled to take up the Freedom by patrimony when he becomes twenty-one. The Prince Consort was a Fishmonger and so, oddly enough, was Garibaldi! Then George V was a Fishmonger, so is the Duke of Gloucester."

"And the Queen?" I prompted.

"Oh no," he replied; "the Queen is a Draper, and so is Princess Elizabeth."

§ 5

When I had left Fishmongers' Hall I decided to climb the Monument and look down upon London. But as I crossed the road into Fish Street Hill I began to think of several reasons why I should not climb the Monument: it was rather misty, fairly late, and anyhow I had climbed it before on several occasions.

"But," said a still, small voice, "you are writing a book about London, and it is your duty to climb the three hundred and forty-five steps."

"Why are you so precise?" I asked Conscience. "Why mention the number of steps?"

"I hate weakness and vacillation," said Conscience, "and you are becoming self-indulgent."

"I am not!" I cried angrily. "I have been tramping the streets of this city almost since daybreak, and now you try to bully me into climbing the Monument."

"It was your idea," whispered Conscience.

"Well, I have changed my mind," I said, "not because I could not climb the steps or because I don't wish to do so, but simply because you are trying to bully me into doing it."

"All right," said Conscience, "have it your own way," and faded out, leaving me standing in Fish Street Hill gazing up at Wren's memorial to the Fire of London.

I wonder how many people who crowd the streets of London every day, and call themselves Londoners, could give an account of the base of this important monument, and it is particularly well worth studying to-day by those who have lived through the Blitz.

There are inscriptions on three sides, and on the fourth is an allegorical bas-relief which shows a female figure, representing the City of London, sitting amid ruins in a sad and languishing attitude. Her head is bowed, her hair has not been done for days, and her hand lies nervelessly upon her sword. A winged elder with a bald head, who is Time, attempts to lift her up, while another encouraging figure, a female, points hopefully to the sky, where two goddesses are enthroned. One, with a cornucopia, is Plenty; the other, with a palm frond, is Peace. At London's feet is a bee-hive, denoting Industry, and above her head are the burning streets of London with flames gushing from the windows of the houses.

The most interesting of the three inscriptions is as follows:

> " In the year of Christ, 1666, on the 2nd of September at a distance eastward of this place of 202 feet, which is the height of this column, a fire broke out in the dead of night, which, the wind blowing, devoured even distant buildings, and rushed devastating through every quarter with astonishing swiftness and noise. It consumed 89 churches, gates, the Guildhall, public edifices, hospitals, schools, libraries, a great number of blocks of buildings, 13,200 houses, 400 streets. Of the 26 wards it utterly destroyed 15 and left 8 mutilated and half burnt. The ashes of the city, covering as many as 436 acres, extended on one side from the Tower along the bank of the Thames to the church of the Templars, on the other side from the north-east gate along the walls to the head of Fleet-ditch. Merciless to the wealth and estates of the citizens, it was harmless to their lives, so as throughout to remind us of the final destruction of the world by fire. The havoc was swift. A little space of time saw the same city most prosperous and no longer in being. On the third day, when it had altogether vanquished all human counsel and resource, at the bidding, as we may well believe, of Heaven, the fatal fire stayed its course and everywhere died out."

What an interesting inscription that is to-day, when so much of London lies in ruins again. I was so fascinated by it that, forgetting my resolve, I paid sixpence to the guardian and began to mount the three hundred and forty-five black marble steps that wind up to the top of the Monument.

"If you can go up and not feel a twinge of anything," said the guardian, "then there's no need to go wasting your money on doctors."

I thanked him and began to corkscrew upward. At step two hundred I decided to give up smoking, at step two hundred and fifty I began to deplore my energy, and at step three hundred I was thinking of the return journey. But, as in climbing mountains, the moment I stepped out at the top of the Monument and found myself within the iron cage put there to prevent people from taking the quickest way back to earth, the ascent was forgotten and the superb view wiped everything else from my mind. It is, in a way, a finer view than that from the dome of St Paul's, because that great black object is one of its main features. From few places does St Paul's look grander than from the Monument. Then you can see the Tower to the east and the Thames, broad and white, running under its many bridges towards Westminster, and beneath, as far as the eye can see, is an unbroken panorama of chimneys, roofs, spires, towers and domes.

The Great Fire and the Blitz (unless we have another war) will remain the two terminal points in London history. The Great Fire lasted three days, and consumed much of the City; the Blitz lasted intermittently for years, and destroyed a large part of the same area; but in 1666 the City was residential, and thousands lost their homes and all they possessed, while the City to-day is an office and a workshop, and Londoners lost only their typewriters, their desks and their files.

The spectacle which met the eyes of Charles II, Pepys, Evelyn, and all those who lived in London at the time, was the same as that which confronts us to-day when we look out towards Moorfields. Eye-witnesses writing in 1666 describe acres of rubble and rubbish from which nothing coherent arose except the chimneys of houses and the towers of burnt-out churches.

"You may stand where Cheapside was and see the Thames," wrote Alexander Fleming to his brother; and no doubt many a modern Londoner has written to someone describing the Thames seen through gaps in the vanished buildings of Victoria Street. The most awful sight in London after the Great Fire was old St Paul's, which, as one observer put it, "retains nothing of its former shape except the open roof and the windows", a sight which, miraculous to relate, this generation has been mercifully spared.

Evelyn wrote on September 7, 1666:

> "I went this morning on foot from Whitehall as far as London Bridge, through the late Fleet St, Ludgate Hill by St Paul's, Cheapside, Exchange, Bishopsgate, Aldersgate and out to Moorfields, thence through Cornhill etc., with extraordinary difficulty, clambering over heaps of yet smouldering rubbish and frequently mistaking where I was: the ground under my feet so hot that it even burnt the soles of my shoes."

Thousands of living Londoners have had the same experience, and all of them will bear out Evelyn's remark about the ease with which it is possible to become lost in the chaos after a fire which has consumed all landmarks.

The legend that London was rebuilt within three years after the Great Fire is nonsense, and Walter G. Bell rightly exploded it in his book, *The Great Fire of London.* For years Londoners camped out in shacks and tents and other makeshift shelters and saw, as we see to-day, the site of their dwellings covered with weeds. The plant of the Great Fire was the London Rocket (*Sisymbrium irio*), as that of the Blitz is the willow-herb. A yellow clump of London Rocket was even noticed growing high up on all that was left of the tower from which sprang the steeple of old St Paul's.

London, once a city of church bells, became a silent city after the Great Fire. For years makeshift sheds—from which the term "tin tabernacle" is said to have originated—were built as temporary places of worship in London churchyards. Four years were to elapse before the problem of rebuilding the eighty-nine lost churches was tackled, and only twenty-five had been completed seventeen years after the Fire. The idea that Londoners of that time rushed with impetuous energy into the task of rebuilding, following the old lines of the mediæval city before they could be stopped, is fantastic. Just as to-day, no one could build without authority, and houses rose slowly and one by one, as the permission and the money for their rebuilding were forthcoming, until eventually several were joined together and a new street was formed.

It was easy for complacent centuries like the Nineteenth, which knew no overwhelming disasters, to say that the Great Fire was a blessing because it swept out of existence a vast conglomeration of insanitary streets and made way for the cleaner brick-and-stone London of Stuart and later times; but we of to-day, who have seen so much that we loved go up in flames, are probably in a better position to feel sympathy for those of our forebears who suffered the tragedy of the Great Fire. It should be encouraging to modern Londoners, who often criticise the delay in rebuilding the City, and cite the supposed speed with which Londoners in the time of Charles II did so, to know that the task of rebuilding London took many long years, and that before it was completed a new generation, like the young people of to-day, was brought up among the untidy and depressing ruins of the mediæval and Elizabethan City.

§ 6

One of the remarkable escapes during the air raids was that of the College of Heralds in Queen Victoria Street, a fine red Wren building which magically stands, although everything to the right of it has been shorn away as if by a mighty scythe. It is the finest building in the street, and its function as well as its staff quite the most unusual. Other buildings in Queen Victoria Street may concern themselves with newspapers, bath-tubs, typewriters and the salvation of souls, but the College lives in a world where trumpets are still sounding and where emblazoned knights are riding up to castle gates.

The staff consists of three kings of arms, Garter, Clarencieux and Norroy; six heralds, Lancaster, Somerset, Richmond,

Windsor, York and Chester; and four pursuivants, Rouge Dragon, Bluemantle, Portcullis and Rouge Croix. These appointments are in the gift of the Duke of Norfolk as hereditary Earl Marshal of England.

Whenever the need to consult some document not elsewhere available has drawn me to that red-brick building, I have mounted its steps in a strong *Alice in Wonderland* atmosphere. There is nothing quite so improbable in the whole of London. If one met the King of Hearts, the Queen and the Knave coming out, one would merely raise one's hat and think it all perfectly normal and in order.

"Good morning, sir," said the doorkeeper. "Have you an appointment with anyone?"

Struggling with a powerful feeling of unreality, I asked:

"Is Rouge Dragon in?"

"No, sir, Rouge Dragon is out. Will anyone else do?"

Rouge Dragon is out! How terrible that sounds! Somewhere in London Rouge Dragon, probably rampant, is at large, unknown to the population.

"Is Bluemantle in?" I asked.

"Yes, sir, but he is engaged."

"Well, could I see Portcullis?"

Instead of blowing a silver trumpet, or mounting a horse and galloping upstairs, the attendant picked a telephone from a hook, while I thought that it would not be surprising if Mr Debrett arrived with a unicorn, or perhaps the editor of *Landed Gentry* might appear, carrying a fine bar sinister which he had found in a box-room.

"Bluemantle is now disengaged, sir. He will see you," said the attendant, and I glanced round the panelled hall with its banners and its carved throne, in which the Earl Marshal used to sit in judgment upon those who bore false arms, before mounting the stairs into the most fantastic office in London. There have been no serious staff changes since 1480.

One can imagine Don Quixote tip-toeing round the corridors, reading with joy the titles of those inhabiting the various rooms: "Garter King of Arms", I read beneath a blaze of heraldry, "Norroy King of Arms", and "Rouge

Dragon ", his door slightly ajar in the most sinister manner. What an odd experience it is to knock at one of those doors and to hear a muffled voice say " Come in ". Anything might meet one in such a room! Perhaps its occupant will be discovered in a suit of armour, a leopard couchant in front of the fire. But when you go inside you see a man who looks like a barrister sitting at a desk, and wearing a black coat and a pair of striped trousers. Can this really be " Portcullis " or " Bluemantle "? Have the trumpets of Agincourt died down to this?

Heralds are always delighted to advise members of the public who wish to place a coat-of-arms upon their notepaper, their motor-cars, their soup tureens or their perambulators. To such a thin whistle have the drums and trumpets of chivalry dropped. This, of course, costs money. Heralds are still paid on the Tudor scale of something like sixteen pounds a year. Therefore, as even a red dragon has to live, they sit like barristers in chambers, waiting to be briefed. And they are almost as expensive. It costs the best part of a hundred pounds to take out armorial bearings, and another fifty pounds for a badge which female members of the family may embroider on cushions.

The hunting up of pedigrees is, of course, a great part of the work undertaken by the College, and this is also expensive. The searchers who ransack village registers were before the War paid a guinea a day. The most difficult people to trace are the Browns, the Joneses and the Smiths.

" There is a ridiculous belief that a pedigree is often faked for a rich man," a Herald told me. " This is absolute nonsense. A pedigree passed by the College of Heralds is a legal document, and it is passed by a council of experts before it is granted."

Many a searcher has gone to the College with a soul filled with grandeur, only to depart with the depressing knowledge that great-great-grandmother was not properly married.

The library of the College is unique. It was begun long ago by the Heralds who rode through every shire at the command of the King to make a complete list of all men who were entitled to bear arms. It contains the roots of every old family in England and Wales. There are two tragic relics in the library: the ring and the sword taken from the dead body of James IV of Scotland after the Battle of Flodden.

The room in which the heralds interview those who desire to " bear arms " is a solemn room built after the Fire of London.

" We were burnt out, you know," explains a Herald.

That is how they talk in this building. Time is nothing. If a Herald talks about the Battle of Agincourt, he would give you the impression that he was there. It is a confusing habit.

Another function of the College is to preserve state ceremonial procedure. Their last great field day was the Coronation of George VI. But it would be wrong to imagine that this building reeks of aristocracy. That is not at all true. Unlike many countries, England has recruited her aristocracy from the common people since the old families were destroyed during the Wars of the Roses, and the Library in Victoria Street contains the often extremely humble origins of British nobility. The self-made merchant, who becomes a country gentleman and bears arms, is a constant figure in English history.

CHAPTER FOUR

Describes St Paul's Cathedral and the great man, Sir Christopher Wren, who built it. I climb to the Whispering Gallery and to the Golden Gallery and go down into the crypt to see the tombs of Nelson and Wellington. I take a walk up Fleet Street, visit Dr Johnson's house, the Law Courts, the Record Office and the Temple, and catch a tramcar to Westminster.

§ 1

I MET a flock of shiny-faced girls at the west door of St Paul's Cathedral. A teacher had gathered them into a corner away from competitive flocks, much as a maternal duck assembles her young on an overcrowded pond, and I heard her say:

"Now, all of you have heard of the Great War, haven't you?"

A circle of shiny faces gazed up: there was a whispered affirmative:

"Yes-s-s," they replied.

Some of them, shoulder-high, would in a few years be married, I reflected. I began to feel incredibly old. Had I any right to be alive? To these children the War of 1914–18 was just something in the history books; in fact, they might have been talking about the Crimea. Their attitude of polite indifference seemed to place the War, and all those who took part in it, in a museum.

"Well," continued the teacher, "a great general at that time was a man called Lord Kitchener. Have you all heard of him?"

There was a distinctly doubtful affirmative this time.

"Now, Lord Kitchener was going abroad in a battleship which was sunk, and he was drowned. We are going to see his memorial. Keep to the left, children. . . ."

The girls trooped into the Kitchener Memorial Chapel, and

I followed them. They stood in a hushed circle round the white marble which depicts Kitchener lying in death. I looked at their faces. Kitchener meant absolutely nothing to them. How could he? He was merely one of those tedious people, like Alfred the Great or William the Conqueror, who did something long ago. (Only at least Alfred the Great did something interesting, he *did* burn some cakes, and William the Conqueror was decent enough to fight the Battle of Hastings on a date everyone can remember. But this man, Kitchener, only got drowned!) I could see the more thoughtful girls thinking something of that kind. One fat little girl with a naughty freckled face gazed blankly at Kitchener, while her hand stole into a pocket and moved swiftly to her mouth. With a bulging cheek she continued to gaze stolidly at the hero.

I remembered so vividly the bushy moustache—rather like an old-type N.C.O.'s—and the pointing finger of the " Kitchener wants *you* " poster, and I thought how incredible it is that in my own life-time, and in years which have fled so swiftly, one generation has grown up and has produced this new shoulder-high generation, a sample of which was now before me in blue gym dresses and straw hats. And in their eyes Kitchener stood side by side in time with Nelson and Wellington.

" I'm afraid it means very little to them," I whispered to the teacher, " You and I . . ."

I found myself gazing into a pair of attractive blue eyes, and I realised, with a hopeless sinking of the heart, that she herself was no more than twenty. I moved away, glad that at least I was not yet on crutches or in a bath chair.

Inset in the marble pavement of the nave of St Peter's in Rome are a number of marks which few visitors ever notice, giving the length of the largest churches in the world in relation to that of St Peter's. The next longest is St Paul's Cathedral, followed by the cathedrals of Florence, Rheims and Cologne.

St Paul's is different from most of the great cathedrals in

the world as the work of one man, Sir Christopher Wren, who would appear to have been placed by Providence in the London of Charles II in order to repair the ravages of the Great Fire. That an architect of such extraordinary inventiveness, and—even if half the edifices attributed to him are really his—fertility, should have been waiting and ready to rebuild London is one of the most fortunate accidents in history. No matter from what direction you look at the City, whether from Hungerford Bridge, the Surrey end of Waterloo Bridge, London Bridge or the Monument—to give only four first-class views—the character of the scene before you was stamped upon it by Christopher Wren.

His grandfather was a London mercer, and Wren was born at East Knoyle, near Tisbury, in Wiltshire, and, like so many great men, was the son of a rector.

Wren was a genius whose unusual talents were seen when he was a small boy. Under the famous Dr Busby at Westminster, he became a distinguished Latin scholar, and he gathered round himself, later on at Wadham College, Oxford, some of the keenest intellects of his time. It has been said that had Wren devoted his life to mathematics and astronomy—and until the age of thirty it seemed probable that he would do so—he might have rivalled Isaac Newton. While he was still at Oxford he was—far ahead of his period in history—experimenting with blood transfusion from one animal to another, and with a system of fumigating and purifying sick-rooms. He originated a number of inventions, but thought nothing of them once they were completed, and it has been suspected that an admiring friend was in the habit of communicating these to inventors in Germany, who passed them off as their own.

Wren was only thirty-four when the Fire of London took place, but for several years he had been surveyor-general to His Majesty's Works, so that the awful scene of devastation had a professional interest for him. The Fire had been dead only four days when he appeared with a complete plan for the rebuilding of the City. It has always been considered the best of the plans prepared at the time, and some have said that had it been adopted London would be a much finer-looking city to-day. But all kinds of private interests conflicted with the plan, which was shelved.

So Christopher Wren had to be content with the rebuilding of St Paul's Cathedral, more than fifty London churches, thirty-six company halls, the Custom House, Temple Bar, numerous private and official buildings, and the Monument. Such enormous buildings as Greenwich Hospital he apparently built in his spare time. There has surely never been a more prolific architect nor one who exemplified in his career the old maxim that genius boils down to hard work. He was the least avaricious and self-seeking of men. For the rebuilding of St Paul's and the parish churches of London the only salary he asked was a miserable two hundred pounds a year. He accepted his task in a spirit of piety, not counting the reward in personal gain. There is a well-known story of Sarah, Duchess of Marlborough, who, annoyed by a bill connected with Blenheim Palace, reminded her architect that the great Christopher Wren was content to be dragged up in a basket to the top of St Paul's three or four times a week for years, at the risk of his life, for a salary of two hundred pounds a year!

The architect was forty-three years of age when the first stone of the new cathedral was laid, he was sixty-five when the choir was opened for use, and he was an old man of seventy-seven when the last stone was set upon the cathedral. All his life, from the forties onward into old age, he watched his mighty creation growing higher against the London sky, and they point out upon the Surrey bank of the Thames a narrow house tucked away between warehouses in which it is said he lived and watched.

His inspiration in the designing of St Paul's was obviously St Peter's in Rome. He designed surroundings very much after the style of Bernini's magnificent colonnade, but the land was too valuable, and this was never carried out. Wren thought so highly of Bernini that he went to Paris the year before the Great Fire to discuss architecture with him. But every man, no matter how much a genius, and no matter how far in advance of his times, is in reality a child of his own age. I was reading recently in the laconic diary of that brilliant friend of Wren's, Robert Hooke, that the scientific and mathematical genius, who created St Paul's, and so many other grand and splendid things, cured Lady Wren of what was evidently tonsilitis by " hanging a bag of live boglice about her neck ".

The great genius died quietly of old age. One day his servant entered his room to find him dead in his chair, aged ninety-one. What an astonishing sweep of history was commanded by his long life! When he was born there were men alive who had spoken to Shakespeare and Queen Elizabeth; when he died there were infants living who were fated to see the beginning of the century that saw the invention of steam locomotion. Only thirteen years elapsed between his death and the birth of James Watt, and could Wren have lived so long this old man and the young one just born would have been links, one with the age of Elizabeth, the other with that of Victoria.

§ 2

As I climbed up to the Whispering Gallery I thought that the fatigue of this ascent is generally much exaggerated. Although there are three hundred and seventy-five steps to the Stone Gallery, and another two hundred and fifty-two to the Ball below the Cross—a region to which few visitors penetrate—the climb is easy because the spiral tunnel is wide and the steps are low.

Arrived in the Whispering Gallery, the verger on duty asked me in his patient, automatic voice—for how many times a day must he say it?—to walk round the narrow railed enclosure to a point opposite and then to sit down and listen. In time I heard his voice coming to me a yard or so away—out of the stone, it seemed—telling me practical details of the building of the church, with dates and figures. It is an extraordinary sound freak, and would have been invaluable to the Oracle at Delphi.

The downward view from this gallery into the distant church, where men and women, reduced to the size of ants, move in a slow noiselessness, is as fine as the view upwards to the Pauline frescoes of James Thornhill. The cleaning of the frescoes some years ago made it possible to see them properly for the first time in our generation. The view of London from the gallery—the gallery at the base of the Dome—although magnificent, is not as fine as that from the Golden Gallery, another hundred and seventy-five steps upward. And the climb is worth it. On the way I examined the remarkable cone of brick and the outer dome which Wren built to support the stone lantern with the Cross and the Ball. The dome that is visible inside the cathedral is not the same as that which is seen from the street.

From the Golden Gallery—a small, narrow space, and often windy—there is an unforgettable view of London. You see how London lies in a broad, shallow valley, and how the green heights of Sydenham, on the south, and Hampstead, on the north, enclose it. You see the often narrow, winding streets of the old City, while to the west the towers of the Abbey Church of Westminster rise up above the white ribbon of the Thames; in the streets below, omnibuses no bigger than flies crawl into the dark cavern of Ludgate Hill.

What a miracle it was that St Paul's was not burnt down in the last War. No building in the whole of London was in greater peril, as one can see when glancing down at the ruins of buildings round about, whose destruction ringed the cathedral with flame. It is a privilege to be able to pay a tribute to the gallantry of the clergy, the vergers and other members of the staff, who for years guarded St Paul's every night, sleeping there, and ready, when the fire-bombs were falling, to tackle them with rakes, sand-buckets and pumps. Had it not been for their splendid efforts this great church, whose dome is a symbol of London all over the earth, would doubtless have suffered, like its predecessor, in the second Fire of London.

I remember one Christmas time during the War, when Ludgate Hill and the little streets leading from it had been turned into hell overnight, walking towards St Paul's, stepping over fire-hoses and picking my way through piles of broken plate-glass. There was a hideous smell of burning in the air, and the great fire of Paternoster Row, in which four million books perished, was still acridly smouldering. At the sight of St Paul's standing unharmed on Ludgate Hill I lifted up my heart in praise and thankfulness, and tears came to my eyes when I saw framed against the darkness of the façade, at the top of the steps, a Christmas tree full of coloured lights. I went into the cathedral, where another tree was standing, loaded with gifts for London children and for men of the minesweepers, and far off, isolated in the great space of the church, a few people were kneeling, while a clergyman was praying. I joined them, grateful for the peace of a place which, it seemed, God had not deserted. And while the sound of the prayers echoed round the dome, they were joined by harsh sounds from outside: the urgent note of a fire-bell, the shouts of the weary firemen as they dragged their hoses like dripping pythons across the street, and the sudden crash of plate-glass as a window collapsed. How much longer, I wondered, can this great target remain unharmed? Is it possible, I asked myself, that I am looking at St Paul's for the last time?

How narrow were its escapes from destruction perhaps only those who were on duty at the time really know. A delayed-action bomb fell near the clock tower one night and made a hole twenty-seven feet deep. It was dug out and taken to Hackney Marsh to be exploded where it blew a crater a hundred feet in diameter. Upon another occasion a land-mine came floating down on its parachute and fell a few feet from the eastern wall. Instead of the appalling explosion which was expected there was silence, for the fuse was out of order. This also was safely removed. St Paul's suffered two direct hits. One bomb, in October, 1940, fell through the roof of the choir and destroyed the high altar; another, in April, 1941, fell through the north transept and exploded inside the cathedral, shattering stained glass, twisting iron-work and destroying the portico inside the north door.

As I stood on the Golden Gallery and looked down at the air-raid damage, I marvelled, as I shall always marvel, that St Paul's came safely through the War.

§ 3

From the winds that blow round the dome of St Paul's to the silence and the darkness of the crypt is a sudden transition. To me the crypt has always been the most interesting portion of the church, for here, between the massive arches, are the actual graves of those great men whose memorials may be seen above.

" I slept down here for four years," said an elderly verger. " Four years is a long time, sir, isn't it? But it was worth it, for we managed to save St Paul's. It all seems like a dream. . . ."

I looked at him with admiration. Until now the history of verging has been distinguished by no battle honours. In fact and in fiction the verger is often an obsequious individual, either tip-toeing officiously with his wand to lead the Dean to his place, or else lingering behind at a church door, with an expression something between that of a bishop and a butler, while doubtful visitors from overseas, catching a grave ecclesiastical reflection in his countenance, wonder whether they might dare to tip him. But in the late War the vergers of London, hitherto mice, became lions, and every one of them who remained at his post during the air raids deserves a Distinguished Service Medal. If future ages continue to gaze upon St Paul's and Westminster Abbey, let them remember with gratitude the humble and unknown individuals who preserved those great buildings during the Blitz on London.

There are three outstanding tombs in the crypt. The first, and the most simple, is that of the architect, Christopher Wren. Above it may be seen his wonderful epitaph, *Lector, si monumentum requiris, circumspice*—" Reader, if you seek his monument, look around you."

Flaxman's memorial to Nelson, typical of its period, looks as if it has strayed into St Paul's from Westminster Abbey. It shows Nelson standing beside an anchor and a coil of rope while Britannia, helmeted but temporarily without her trident, points towards him, and is evidently saying to two extremely young sailors, " Go thou and do likewise." The great sailor lies beneath the dome in a fine sarcophagus of marble which was originally designed to hold the remains of Cardinal Wolsey, a strange fate after it had been lying neglected for centuries in a chapel at St George's, Windsor.

The innermost coffin, in which Nelson's body lies, was made by a ship's carpenter out of the mainmast of *L'Orient*, Admiral de Brueys flagship at the Battle of the Nile, and presented to Nelson years before his death—surely a grim gift—by Captain Ben Hallowell. But Nelson did not think it grim. He carried it round with him at sea and transferred it from one ship to another. On one of these occasions, when it was lying on the quarterdeck, Nelson emerged from his cabin and, walking up to a group of officers who were gazing at it, one imagines with surprise, remarked cheerfully, "You may look at it, gentlemen, as long as you please; but, depend upon it, none of you shall have it." It was noticed uneasily by some who dined with Nelson at sea that his coffin stood in his cabin behind his Windsor chair. Much to the relief of the ward-room, I should think, Nelson eventually stored this mournful relic in London, and it is said that during his last leave, upon the eve of Trafalgar, he paid it a visit and said prophetically to its keeper that he might have need of it on his return.

There has probably never been a funeral in the history of England which aroused deeper popular emotion than that of Nelson on January 9, 1806, eleven weeks and a few days after his death at Trafalgar. Like some hero of antiquity, he had expired at the moment of victory, and his countrymen, swept by grief, gratitude and admiration, eventually erected to him a greater mass of stone than the memory of any other Englishman in history has quarried: Trafalgar Square, in London, the Nelson Monument in Edinburgh, the Nelson Pillar in Dublin, to say nothing of other monuments and busts in various parts of the country.

Nelson's body, like that of many another naval casualty of the period, was brought home preserved in rum. Before the lying-in-state at Greenwich, while the *Victory* was sailing from Spithead to the Downs, Sir William Beatty, Chief Surgeon in the flagship, conducted an autopsy and extracted the fatal musket-ball. In the course of this examination he came to the conclusion that, frail as Nelson was, he might have lived to extreme old age, because his vital organs were more like those of a youth than a man of forty-eight.

Upon the morning of the funeral a brilliant January sun melted a morning frost, and the great bell of St Paul's began to toll at eight-thirty, by which time the cathedral was full. The streets were packed with silent crowds. The sound of guns firing a salute told London that the funeral car, which was made to resemble, so far as a wheeled vehicle could do so, a man-of-war with a lantern and stern windows, had left the Admiralty. The muffled drums and the fifes wailed the Dead March from *Saul* as the immense procession began to move.

"The procession was so long," wrote Carola Oman in *Nelson*, "that the Scots Greys, leading it, had reached the cathedral before the officers of both services, bringing up the rear, had left the Admiralty, but it was remarked that the only general sound made by an unusually orderly mob was one resembling a murmur of the sea, caused by a spontaneous movement to uncover as the funeral car came in sight."

It was two o'clock in the afternoon before it reached St Paul's, where twelve seamen of the *Victory* lifted the coffin, while six admirals advanced towards it bearing a canopy. Someone, foreseeing that the service would be appallingly long, had provided torches, and as the January light died away the congregation saw the yellow torchlight flickering upon the central space beneath the dome where Nelson's coffin, surrounded by sailors, stood in a ring kept by kilted Highlanders.

When the moment came for the lowering of the coffin into the crypt, the men of the *Victory*, who were to place the ship's ensign upon it, tore the flag to shreds instead and stuffed the pieces into the necks of their blouses, determined to possess some relic of their great commander. It was a touch of ill discipline which Nelson might perhaps have frowned upon, but not one of those who saw it could ever have forgotten it. A touch of raw human feeling and passion had invaded a state ceremony, an incident fit to close the life of one who was no stranger to emotion. It was past nine at night when the last members of the congregation descended the steps of St Paul's Cathedral in the darkness.

Another great outburst of popular feeling was observed when the Duke of Wellington, in extreme old age and covered with honours, was carried to his last resting-place in St Paul's. Forty-six years had passed since his great contemporary had been buried. Standing gloomily beneath the arches of the crypt may be seen the remarkable funeral car of gun-metal upon which his coffin was carried. Philip Guedalla called it " twenty-seven feet of assorted allegory ". Genuine muskets, bayonets and swords sprout from it, in addition to those engraved upon it, and it looks as gloomy to-day, covered with dust and cobwebs, as it must have done when it was drawn through the dampness of a November morning by twelve powerful dray-horses decked out with mourning plumes. Carlyle thought the funeral car " of all the objects I ever saw the abominably ugliest, or nearly so. . . . An incoherent huddle of expensive palls, flags, sheets and gilt emblems and cross-poles, more like one of the street carts that hawk door-mats than a bier for a hero." The crowds waited in the rain throughout a pouring wet night to see the Iron Duke carried to his grave. So thickly were they packed upon the London pavements that the lamplighters could not get to the lamps in the morning to turn them out, and they burned all day long.

Soldiers and, oddly enough, painters come to rest in St Paul's Cathedral. Reynolds, Lawrence, Opie, Holman Hunt, Landseer, Millais, Alma Tadema, and many others lie there. Among the few famous women commemorated in the cathedral is Florence Nightingale.

As I left St Paul's, a well-known story came to mind. When Wren stood among the ruins of the old cathedral, he asked a workman to bring a stone to mark the centre of the new church. The man brought to him the fragment of a gravestone on which was readable the word " Resurgam "— " I shall rise again."

§ 4

I walked down Ludgate Hill one afternoon, trying to remember the shops which now expose their cellars to the sun. Which one sold watches, which one books, and which one carpets? How easy it is to forget these things? A queer invasion on Ludgate Hill is a garden amid the ruins in which you can buy rustic seats and garden ornaments, and there is another like it near London Bridge.

And so I came to Fleet Street just at that hour of the afternoon when all the evening papers are looking for a new lead story. It may be my fancy, or is it true, that Fleet Street is not quite as exciting as it once was? Has it as much character as it once had? It is difficult to say when you are no longer part of it.

To me, Fleet Street will always seem like a village; and it actually boasts a village pump, which you can see protruding from the wall of St Bride's churchyard. Like all villages, it is full of gossip, scandal, slander and rumour, and it is therefore fit and proper that, with the growth of London, it should have developed into a super-village which deals in gossip and news from every part of the world. Still it remains essentially a village whose inhabitants are well known to one another, and each one of whom knows where the others are to be found at various times of the day; for Fleet Street's habits of eating, and especially of drinking, are extraordinarily regular.

Like the mediæval Strand when the great barons and nobles had their town houses there, Fleet Street is full of the retainers of the Press barons who, although they wear no visible livery, are to themselves as clearly marked as though they wore the badge of Norfolk or John of Gaunt. I have always said you could tell a *News Chronicle* man at sight, and *Chronicle* men have told me that they can spot an *Express* or a *Mail* man almost before the door opens. You become like that when you live in a small, highly competitive community.

It is a short street, but it is a concentrated one. To the man on an evening paper it is a slightly different street from that seen by the man on a morning paper. The evening-paper man sees it when the sun is on the Bouverie Street side, when the Griffin and the dome of St Paul's are gilded by the morning light, whereas the morning-paper man, arriving much later, finds the sun on the Shoe Lane side, and afternoon is already leaning towards evening. Both these men live on each other's efforts to an extraordinary degree. The first thing the evening-paper men do is to read the morning papers, and the first thing the morning-paper men do is to read the evening papers. Fleet Street is like a python that is always trying to swallow its own tail.

Having been the slave of both evening and morning papers, I can tell you that Fleet Street only reveals itself to you in that pathetic moment of the small hours when it is empty of life, when the traffic no longer pours down to Ludgate Circus, when the large cat population is on the prowl, when the pavements shake to the sound of rotary presses which is the pulse of Fleet Street. It is then as touching to look at Fleet Street as it is to gaze upon the face of someone asleep. Being a romantic young man, although ever conscious of the cruelty of Fleet Street and always slightly afraid of it, especially in moments of apparent triumph, I was also aware of its dangerous attractiveness. It is not possible to be neutral about it: you either love or hate it, and sometimes these emotions are hardly distinguishable. It can be such a generous street, and the next moment—if not to you, to someone else—brutal, cruel and heartless. And sometimes, as I left it in the early hours of the morning, it seemed that the gutters were strewn with the hopes and the aspirations of so many men better than myself.

When I look at Fleet Street to-day, and then at prints of the Sixteenth and Seventeenth Centuries, it seems hardly possible that it could ever have been a street of tall wooden houses with decorative, over-sailing storeys such as Izaak Walton knew, and it is only when you explore the many courts and alleys that you discover with delight that the picturesqueness of a former age still lingers, if only in a name, such as Plum Tree Court or Hanging Sword Alley. I have often thought that Neville's Court, in Fetter Lane—now, alas, bombed flat—with its few fine old houses with front gardens, should have been turned from tenements and restored in order to give us an idea what this part of London looked like when men lived in it. One of the few houses left which gives an idea of Fleet Street when it was a residential street is Dr Johnson's house in Gough Square, which fortunately has come unscathed through the Blitz. Like all vital and living parts of London, Fleet Street is always changing. When I first knew it, you could have your bumps read by a phrenologist at Ludgate Circus, and a palace of glass and steel has swept away a number of interesting old shops near Shoe Lane, including a little cook shop where the most delicious sausages were fried in the window in sizzling pans of fat; and the smell at noon reached almost to that regrettable monument, the Griffin. There was also Anderton's Hotel, where I once spent a night, conscious that one of London's mediæval hostelries—the *Horn Tavern*, as it once was—had become commonplace in its old age. But one thing has not altered, and that is the superb view of St Paul's framed by Fleet Street as you walk down on the north side.

It would be tedious to mention all the great names associated with this crowded street, for one overtops them all—that of Samuel Johnson, its presiding deity.

When all of those who have laboured in Fleet Street have been forgotten, the massive shade of the old doctor, thanks to Boswell, will still pass beneath the ghost of Temple Bar, touching the posts as he goes, and counting the lines between the paving-stones. I went to the pretty red-brick Queen Anne house in Gough Square where Jonhson spent about ten years of his life, half expecting to find it closed, for I remembered hearing that it had almost been destroyed during the air raids.

There was nothing to indicate that it had even been in danger, although all round, towards Fetter Lane, extended a scene of the utmost devastation. Johnson's house was intact, and a fig-tree was growing on the right of the door, while in a little paved garden to the side were French marigolds, fuchsia and geraniums in green tubs. The door was answered by the caretaker, Mrs Rowel, who told me that the house had been repaired and was now open again to the public.

" Did you live here all through the War? " I asked.

" Oh yes, or there wouldn't be a thing left," said Mrs Rowel.

She then unfolded a chapter in the history of Gough Square that would have startled Boswell and the Doctor. She was living there as caretaker with her daughter, Betty, and her mother, an old lady who died from shock after the first raid. On December 29, 1940, when the bombs began to fall, an oil-drum from a neighbouring printer's-ink factory was hurled through the air and lodged itself on the roof. No one had any time to think how appropriate it was, or how ironic, if you like, that a printer's-ink factory might have been the means of destroying the house of Dr Johnson, for the roof-beams were crackling and blazing and the tiles were falling into the room below. This fire was put out by the firemen and the caretakers, and in the morning it was seen that the beams, though charred, were still sound. The house was in grave peril on five subsequent occasions. It was, of course, closed to the public, and, as the Blitz on London developed, it became a rendezvous for the Auxiliary Fire Service. How Dr Johnson, that irrepressible clubman, would have loved that! It is almost too perfect to be true.

" You see, the firemen used to get so tired night after night," said Mrs Rowel, " and there was nowhere for them to get any rest or refreshment, so we had tea, coffee and cocoa ready for them whenever they wanted it, and anything else we could scrape together. We had some good times here during the War. We even had musical evenings during the Blitz! "

If ever the ghost of old Sam Johnson came back to London, it must surely have been during this time, though, oddly enough, no fireman is reported to have encountered a bulky figure on the stairs, or to have been addressed as " sir " by someone who offered to relieve him at his post.

" Of course Dr Johnson was physically courageous," I said, " and he would not have been scared by anything you went through here."

" My dear old man scared? " echoed Mrs Rowel indignantly. " Not him! It would take more than a land mine to scare Dr Samuel Johnson "; and I knew then that I was in the presence of a true Johnsonian.

We wandered together over the attractive house. Mrs Elizabeth Carter's mahogany secretaire bookcase is in a downstairs room, and it contains some nasty pieces of shrapnel. In another room is a lock of Johnson's hair, very silky and fine, in colour whitish, but with a trace of red or auburn. "My dear old man," said Mrs Rowel again. Then we saw Mrs Thrales "tea equipage", her gift to Johnson, consisting of two cups, a tea-pot, a sugar-basin and a milk-jug. I believe it has never been used since Johnson's death in 1784.

There is an interesting picture, attributed to Reynolds, of Johnson's black servant, Frank Barber. He was a Jamaican slave who received his freedom in 1752, became Johnson's man-servant and, apart for a short period, served him faithfully until his master died thirty-two years later.

The view from Dr Johnson's drawing-room windows was appalling. The old houses in Fetter Lane have all vanished. Upon the uneven mounds of rubble, covered with weeds and tall privet trees, steps descend to cellars which, for the first time for centuries in many instances, are open to the light of day. Immediately opposite the house is a stationary water-tank, drained of its water, but in which a good supply of rain-water had collected. Mrs. Rowel told me that two ducks had nested there year after year and had brought up families in the heart of London. Johnson, who used to buy oysters for his cat, would surely have expended his monumental kindness upon these birds.

People come from every part of the world to see Johnson's house. Some of them know more about Johnson than probably he knew about himself; others just go there because it is one of the sights.

Of all Johnson's many London homes, the house in Gough Square is, I think, the one most of us would prefer to see, for here it was that, as an impoverished scribbler of thirty-nine, he started the great Dictionary which brought him fame. In the upstairs attic his six clerks were for years engaged in filing words and copying references, while in the rooms downstairs Johnson lived with his wife, Lucy, the widow of a Midland draper, who was twenty years his senior. Outwardly, this was a preposterous alliance, the Doctor with his huge convulsive frame, his twitchings, writhings and mutterings, and his elderly spouse, described cruelly by Garrick as " very fat with a bosom of more than ordinary protuberance, with swelled cheeks of florid red, produced by thick painting and increased by liberal use of cordials ", and by Anna Seward as the possessor of " an unbecoming excess of girlish levity and disgusting affectation ". From Mrs Thrale we learn that Lucy was a blonde with hair " like that of a baby ", which she threatened to dye black, but was restrained from doing so by her adoring Samuel. Robert Levett, Johnson's broken-down doctor friend, said that Mrs Johnson was always drunk, and addicted to opium, which people in the Eighteenth Century took as lightheartedly as this age takes aspirin. Be this as it may—and one suspects more than malice in Levett's description—Johnson loved Lucy with pious adoration, and when he was forty-three, and she sixty-three, her death left him temporarily broken, and he never ceased to mourn for " dear Tetty " to his dying day.

In this house he wrote *Irene*, which was produced by Garrick at Drury Lane. Normally Johnson was hideously untidy, covered with dust, with sagging stockings and with a bushy old-fashioned wig singed to the network by bedside candles, but upon this occasion, thinking that a dramatist ought to look fashionable, he dressed himself up in a scarlet waistcoat with gold braid and sat in a box with a gold laced hat before him; the only concession he ever made to appearance, apart from the struggle of the Thrales in later life to clean him up a bit for dinner-parties.

In Gough Square he began the *Rambler*, and wrote it twice a week for two years, and it was in this house that he wrote his famous letter to Lord Chesterfield. Here " dear Tetty " may have died and have plunged him into despair.*

Johnson left Gough Square four years before he and Boswell struck up their fruitful friendship. At the time of their meeting Johnson was fifty-four, now the celebrated Great Cham of Literature, and Boswell was a young man of twenty-three. Both of them were remarkable neurotics, Boswell perhaps a

* Mrs Johnson may have died at Bromley. She was buried in Bromley churchyard, where her tombstone remains, though cracked by bombs.

more easily understandable dipsomaniac, but Johnson a more complex mass of still unexplored and unknown complexes and neuroses. Some people imagine that Boswell and Johnson were never apart, but the truth is that, in the twenty-one years they knew one another, they were rarely together. Boswell was generally on his estate in Scotland and his London appearances were holidays or " jaunts ", as he called them. Croker estimated that, apart from the Hebridean tour, Boswell met Johnson only on one hundred and eighty days. How well he used his time.

Although so vast a mass of literature has been built up around Johnson and Boswell, there still remains one more book about them, and I think it might be written by a competent doctor. It might throw some light on Johnson's love for " dear Tetty ", and his later devotion to the brittle Mrs Thrale. Although Boswell wrote the best biography in the language, and one of the most entertaining books ever written, there were large areas of Johnson which, of course, he never saw or comprehended.

§ 5

I found that the Record Office in Chancery Lane has opened again after the War, and that it is offering the student of history, the collector of autographs, and the calligraphist, what is undoubtedly the finest museum of its kind in the world. The first thing they told me when I went there is that the Domesday Book did not spend the War years in the United States, as most people believe, but in Shepton Mallet Gaol.

The tons of manuscripts came safely through the perils, and are all now stored away again in the fireproof vaults. The ground on which the Record Office stands was occupied in 1232 by an institution called the House of the Converts. It was founded by Henry III for converted Jews. When the Jews were expelled from England by Edward I, the post of Keeper to the House of Converts was merged in that of the Clerk to Chancery, whose duty it was to look after the parchment rolls and other State papers. These were kept in all kinds of places, from the Tower of London to the Palace of Westminster, and no one knew where anything was to be found. It was not until about a century ago that all these records were brought together and a competent tame Tudor building erected to house them.

The museum is open to the public, and the Search Room to students, and others interested in ancient documents. The polite young man in charge of this room cannot be surprised. You can ask him for almost anything, and he will disappear, or send one of his minions, down to the vaults and produce for you a letter written to Queen Elizabeth, or the bill for one of Nell Gwyn's dress lengths, or an I.O.U. of Charles II. Whether in moments of inactivity he ever pauses to reflect upon the peculiarity of his clients, I have no means of knowing, but I should think this must be almost inevitable, for some strange people go to the Record Office.

The people who probe about among the dry parchment bones of English history are either elderly men with a vague vacant expression, the men who leave suit-cases, hats and umbrellas in tramcars, or baffling young women, often of considerable beauty, who spend months poring over mediæval Latin documents. Then there are teams of Americans who will go like a swarm of locusts through manuscripts in the hope of finding a stray reference to Shakespeare. All these people know the subtle joys of research, and years of effort are, in their minds, well spent and rewarded if they can establish the fact that it was raining when John signed the Magna Carta, or that Bloody Mary was left-handed. No detective who has caught his man knows half the excitement enjoyed by searchers in the Record Office when some dusty little scrawl gives them what they have been wanting.

This is where the material is gathered for those sound but unreadable historical works which the general public never buys. The old man in the corner, who is reading a mediæval manuscript with the aid of a watchmaker's glass, is writing the classic book on feudal tenures. It will live longer than a thousand best sellers, but few will ever read it. He will never make any money from it, and he does not care. The girl in the horn-rimmed glasses is " hunting " for a famous historian. She has a list of cues, and she methodically plods through the centuries. Women are marvellous at plodding through the centuries. They are exact, accurate and tireless. If you ever wish to discover some minute fact, buried away at the bottom of a bin of forgotten parchments, find a girl with horn-rimmed spectacles and straight hair and ask her to do it for you.

One type of visitor to the Record Office has, I am disappointed to learn, almost completely vanished. He was the man with a bee in his bonnet. Most of such searchers were trying to establish the fact that they were the rightful Earl of Brixton, or the lost Marquis of Shepherd's Bush. I remember these old men perfectly well years ago, when their number was beginning to fall off slightly. They were all alike. They all suggested a dingy background of boarding-houses and back rooms in Bloomsbury. They all brought little packets of sandwiches with them. And thus supported by who knows what delirious visions of cheering villagers and obsequious tenants, they would spend sometimes a life-time poring over brown parchments in search of their nobility. But there is to-day a great slump in would-be peers. The aged delusionists now know that a title is not worth having.

In the Museum you can see the Domesday Book, whose real title, by the way, is *Liber de Wintonia*; or you can read the Log of the *Victory*; Wellington's despatches; the Muster Book of the *Bellerophon*, which shows Napoleon and his staff on the ration strength; the original secret letter which warned Lord Mounteagle of the Gunpowder Plot; the signatures of every English king from Richard II to George V, and of many queens; and also a letter, which I enjoyed reading very much, in which the Sultan Amurath III addressed Queen Elizabeth as "refulgent with splendour and glory, most sapient princess of the magnanimous followers of Jesus, most serene controller of all the affairs and business of the people and family of the Nazarines, most grateful rain-cloud, sweetest fount of splendour and honour".

When I was looking at these treasures, I was introduced to the only cat which is officially a civil servant. The Record Office cat receives a penny a day from the State, and the terms of her contract are that she must keep herself clean, catch rats and mice, and bring up her children.

§ 6

It must sometimes seem strange to the intelligent foreigner that, while the City's chief church should be lucidly classical in style, the Law Courts in the Strand should be tortuously and confusedly Gothic. I often used to wonder why one should have to be divorced or sued for libel in a building which, more than any other recent addition to the metropolis, suggests an inconvenient mediæval stronghold.

Closer contact with the Law, however, has convinced me that those who, in the latter part of the last century, chose the design of an ecclesiastical architect, G. E. Street, from among many others, were right: they have housed the Law in an admirably suitable building, full of little loopholes and twisting passages, nooks and crannies and badly ventilated corridors.

" What is it? " ask visitors to London.

" Those are the Royal Courts of Justice," reply pedantic guides, and then sometimes have to explain—this is difficult to believe, but it is true—that the Law Courts are not a genuine relic of old London!

I dislike the building, for it is associated in my mind with so many dreary days spent there as a young reporter, listening to long and tedious law-suits. However, I went there recently and, hunting about through the day's programme, thought that I would look into the Divorce Court.

This, I think, is the most cynical room in London. It is the room in which Love so often finds itself when it has taken the wrong turning; and I have more than once suspected that the quill pens occasionally seen lying about have been dropped, or perhaps been plucked, from a certain person's wing. The room is in a remote part of the stronghold. It is panelled in fumed oak. The President's chair, or throne, is set against a Gothic screen that would look effective in a vestry. By some glorious stroke of irony, there hangs above the chair an immense anchor attached to a sculptured rope, which is clearly twisted into a true lover's knot. That tactless symbol of stability broods over the court and adds to the general air of cynicism.

The witness-box, at the end of a narrow passage in the court, has been designed, so it would seem, in order that wives and the other woman, or husbands and the other man, should be obliged to crush past each other on their way to it. An usher enters the court. The strange assembly of men and women—erring wives and husbands, here and there a co-respondent, a chambermaid, and a man nursing an hotel register—rises to its feet. The President enters and takes his seat. (It would probably be contempt of court to wonder —daring thought—whether he himself has ever been in love.)

A barrister rises with a sheaf of papers.

" Brown *versus* Brown . . . if it please, your lordship."

And the Divorce Court is opened for the day.

The only other court which deals with human nature in the raw is the Bankruptcy Court, which is round the corner in Carey Street, at the back of the Law Courts. It has been my experience that there are only two addresses in London which rouse a faint look of interest in the face of a taxi-driver. One of them is Buckingham Palace, and the other is Carey Street. When you ask to be driven to the Bankruptcy Court, you can see the driver wondering how deeply you are in debt, for human nature being what it is, no driver would ever believe you to be the creditor.

When you visit the Bankruptcy Court, even as a spectator, you are aware that life is essentially a financial problem. There is a chilling doorway through which no man or woman has ever wished to pass. Many, it is true, have passed through in financial flight as criminals, and others in the old days rushed into sanctuary; but no one, I imagine, has ever enjoyed the experience.

Once inside, people look different. The icy air of bankruptcy blows round them. There is a large element of doubt about everybody. You look at debtors and wonder if they are creditors, at creditors and wonder if they are debtors. And people look at you in the same way. Their eyes say:

" I wonder how much he hopes to save from the wreck! "

Only two kinds of men are recognised in this place: the hunter and the hunted.

The court in which " the first public examination in bankruptcy " is held is a stuffy, dull place that reeks of failure, inquiry and dispute. The Registrar, gowned and in a brindle wig, sits writing diligently at a desk, while the Official Receiver, or his minions, recite the stories of men's misfortunes. There is a polite absence of police. It has not quite got to that yet. While the Bankruptcy Court has the appearance of a criminal court, its atmosphere is that of a rather dreary debating society or a mock trial.

No brazen voices shout names down corridors. No counsel ever rises maliciously, lifts an admonitory forefinger, and leans forward horribly before he tears a reputation to bits. The Bankruptcy Court is as well mannered and polite as a court can be. Bankrupts are known not as " cases ", but more delicately as " matters ".

" And now the matter of Jones," says the Registrar in a conversational voice, glancing from his writing to give the court an almost benevolent glance from behind his tortoise-shell glasses. And Mr Jones, who a few weeks before was a milliner and is now merely a " matter ", rises uneasily and walks to the witness-box.

You think of a bankrupt—at least, I do—as a rich man brought to the earth by folly or misfortune. That is because bankruptcy, like war and theft, becomes interesting only when it is on a sufficiently large scale. But the real drama of Carey Street is not that of the ruined millionaire, but of the poor little men and women driven mad by debts of a hundred and fifty pounds. They turn up, looking dazed and bewildered, with their hungry creditors at their heels. There are thousands of them, some of them unfortunate, some stupid, some hopeless.

" And now the matter of Jones . . ."

The Official Receiver outlines the trouble. A solicitor rises and makes a remark. The Registrar leans forward and says something inaudible to the Official Receiver. It is all very conversational. There is no drama of words, no rhetoric, as in a criminal court. There are no twelve good men and true to impress. It is perhaps the dreariest oratory outside the London County Council or the Dail in Eire.

"And what was the cause of the trouble?" asks the Registrar, like a benevolent uncle.

Then comes one of those intimate flashes which humanise the woes of Carey Street.

"Well, my mother-in-law . . . You see, my wife and I lived with her for a year, and I owed her twenty pounds. Then . . ."

A woman rises in court and says in a loud voice:

"I would like to know if there is any hope of being paid the money I had to borrow to . . ."

In an ordinary court an usher would cry "Silence!" and an official would edge up, but in the polite Bankruptcy Court someone goes to the angry mother-in-law and soothes her.

Other "matters" follow each other at full speed. A woman has been trying to keep a sick husband on the profits of a small shop. Unfortunately there were no profits. Next "matter". A young foreman explains that he decided to set up as a road contractor with a capital of one hundred pounds. The experienced eyes of the Registrar leave his desk and gaze at the witness without surprise, much as a doctor might survey a patient.

"A very small capital," he says quietly.

"Yes, sir," agrees the road contractor.

Smash!

The next "matter". A Polish Jew puts on a bowler hat and takes the oath. He describes how he became a jeweller, then, thinking that a little versatility might improve trade, how he took the shop next door and became a tobacconist as well. Things were going splendidly—in fact, the jeweller-tobacconist was making the grade, when, suddenly in the night, thieves broke into the jewellery shop and went off with two thousand pounds worth of uninsured goods.

"Uninsured?"

A sigh, not of surprise, for that would be impossible in Carey Street, but almost of weariness hangs for a moment in the sad and dreary air.

"Yes, uninsured," says the Jew apologetically.

Smash!

In the course of the next " matter " it appears that a woman who had inherited fifteen hundred pounds under the will of her deceased husband had been having a commercial flirtation with Bond Street. The hat shop she had opened was not a success. But she continued buying more and better hats, hoping that the tide would turn. She described her failure to get the right hats, even in Paris. One felt that one knew this hat shop quite well. How often, walking down Bond Street, has one heard women say, as they look into a shop window:

" My dear, what perfectly revolting hats! Who on earth buys them, I wonder? "

" Oh, don't you think that little black one is rather sweet, darling? "

" It's perfectly nauseating. It was absolutely made for Cynthia. I must tell her about it. . . ."

All this flashed across the mind as the woman told her story of sinking deeper and deeper into debt.

" But why," asked the Registrar kindly, for she was not only beautiful, but pathetic, " did you do so and so? "

" I was acting under my solicitor's instructions."

The perfect answer—if true! Those staunchest of trade unionists, lawyers and doctors, would never follow up such a reply.

Smash!

So Carey Street lays bare the financial secrets of men and women as the Divorce Court round the corner exposes their emotional crashes. When heroism and ambition enter the witness-box and prove that they have taken the wrong turning, you feel sorry; when greed, stupidity, folly, extravagance and pig-headedness stand there, you smile a little sadly and wonder if you would have been able to do any better yourself. And so you go out into the streets of London, where people no longer all look like debtors or creditors—but who knows? You examine the faces in the crowd, wondering how many are fighting against bankruptcy, dreading every day the thought of that awful doorway dedicated to people who can't pay.

§ 7

Walking through the Inner Temple Gateway, down the slight hill past the Temple Church, I came to a scene which I regard as perhaps the saddest in London to-day.

The Temple has been loved by generations of Londoners, and by others from all countries in the world, because it brings into the heart of a great city the peace of some ancient university town and the dignity of a past age. It is a place of green lawns, of Queen Anne and Georgian houses, of paved courts, of subtle little architectural glimpses, court leading to mulberry-coloured court, a colonnade here, a fountain or a sun-dial there; and all these things taken together form a complete whole in which nothing is offensive or vulgar. The terrible punishment inflicted upon the Temple during the air raids has shattered this unity, and it will be years—how many I would not care to say—before the Temple recovers its air of solemn and seasoned tranquillity.

For many centuries Londoners have slipped away from the turmoil of the City, taking with them to this ancient sanctuary the burden of their sorrows and their perplexities. While the Temple belongs officially to the Law, whose minions may be seen hurrying about carrying beneath their arms sheafs of papers tied with red tape, it belongs equally to all the men and women who have taken to it the personal problems of life. I am not thinking of those problems placed upon the desk of "my learned friend", but of the things of which lonely individuals think when they seek the solitude of the Temple in odd moments stolen from a lunch hour, as they sit listening to the shrillness of the sparrows and the sound of feet upon the worn pavements. We who live in an ancient country hallowed by many centuries of living rarely consider the effect upon us of this background of experience. It is only when we go to live in a new country, where the fathers of living men were pioneers, that we sense a spiritual vacuum and miss, sometimes, in the most poignant and heart-aching way, the background of England, or of London, which, whether we consciously know it or not, tells us that in the long catalogue of human woes no sorrow or perplexity is new.

Like the City churches whose parishioners are all those who "labour and are heavy laden", the ancient Temple offers stability and courage. The contrast between this quiet place and the foaming flood of life at its gates is that between a church and a market-place. And no one will ever know how many people have received guidance and been given renewed strength by that little cluster of buildings and lawns.

Bombs fell on the Temple intermittently for four years. I well remember the first raids, the hideous landslide of damage, old well-loved buildings sliced in two, hob-grates revealed to daylight four storeys up, the litter of books and paper unhappily blowing about the courts, the fragments of stained glass. One morning, the day after the Inner Temple Hall and Library were gutted, I remember looking at the chaos and thinking that the Temple was doomed and that it could never again be restored.

But bomb damage often looks worse than it is. Who could have believed, when fifty thousand books were blown from their shelves and eight thousand damaged when the Middle Temple Library was hit, that only one book would be beyond repair? This was *Decisions of the Court of Southern Rhodesia*, and it has now been replaced by another copy, the gift of a South African judge.

It was different with the library of the Inner Temple. Like the Inner Temple Hall, which was gutted so completely that to-day the sky gleams bleakly through its windows, the adjoining Library caught fire, with a loss of forty thousand law books. I suppose law books can be replaced, but who can replace Wren's cloisters, or the south side of Pump Court, or the two old buildings in Brick Court, in one of which Goldsmith spent the last six years of his life? Crown Office Row, where Lamb was born, may be rebuilt, so may the house of the Master of the Temple, of which not a vestige remains, but it will not be quite the same thing.

Infinitely worse than any destruction in the Temple is the savage shambles into which the lovely old Round Church has been flung. As I passed it, I saw workmen wheeling trucks along a railway beneath the elaborate Norman gateway, which fortunately is unharmed. But inside, what a scene of chaos! The pillars of Purbeck marble which support the triforium have been split by fire and blasted by high explosives. The Crusaders, who once lay so peacefully at rest, have been shattered, their swords, their armour and their mailed, pointed toes blown to fragments.

The one blessing is that Middle Temple Hall has not proved to be in such a perilous condition as it first appeared to those who saw it after it had been hit for the fifth time. Except for the Round Church, this is the greatest feature of the Temple. In this lovely place, and beneath the same superb roof, *Twelfth Night* was produced, possibly with Shakespeare in the cast, and many a time Queen Elizabeth dined there, and left, as a token of her visits, the high table of Windsor oak. This, with the famous " Drake " table made from the wood of the *Golden Hind*, is unharmed.

The magnificent roof has been repaired, and many long months of affectionate skill have been expended on finding sorting and reassembling the hundreds of pieces into which the beautiful carved oak screen was shattered.

But I find it hard to reconcile myself to the odd stumps of masonry, the drums of columns and the other odds and ends of the bomb damage, now so richly covered with vegetation, which already look as ancient as Herculaneum.

No place in London has a more romantic origin than the Temple. The name commemorates the Temple of Solomon in Jerusalem, and came to Thames-side with the crusading Order of the Knights Templars in the Twelfth Century. It is interesting to sit, as I have done so often in this place, and to try to project the mind back into the distant days when such seeds were sown.

When the Crusaders had captured Jerusalem and had created, so far from the feudal system, an exact copy of a European kingdom, some of them banded together to guard the roads so that pilgrims might in safety visit the sepulchre of Christ. Those knights were vowed to poverty and chastity. As a symbol of purity they wore a white surcoat with a red cross on the shoulder. They swore to avoid feminine kisses, whether from widow, virgin, mother, sister, aunt or any other woman, and at night they had to keep a light burning, " lest the dark enemy, from whom God preserve us, should find some opportunity ".

Those austere knights were accommodated on the large space in Jerusalem which had once held the Temple of Solomon and now holds the mosque of el-Aksa. They therefore took the name of " the Poor Knights of Jesus Christ and of the Temple of Solomon "; and it was as the Knights Templars that Europe grew to know them. Houses of the Order were soon established in every Christian country. The first London settlement was in Holborn, then the knights, acquiring the strip of riverside land where the Temple still stands, moved there and made it their permanent headquarters in London. They built the Round Church on the model of the Church of the Holy Sepulchre, and it was ready for consecration in 1185, in the reign of Henry II.

This was the time when the Crusaders were being expelled from the Holy Land by Saladin. The completion of the Temple Church coincided with the arrival in England of Heraclius, the Patriarch of Jerusalem, who, hoping that Henry was still smarting for the murder of Thomas à Becket, actually offered the King absolution if he would fit out an army and go to the rescue of the Christians. Henry listened with tears, and—promised to bring the matter before Parliament at the earliest opportunity; and that is where the matter ended!

But the Templars took Heraclius to their river-side home and asked him to dedicate their new church. This he did and, perhaps to show there should be no ill feeling among the soldiers of Christ, also dedicated the church of the rival Order, the Knights of St John, at Clerkenwell.

As time went on the Knights Templars became so rich and powerful that they roused the envy of their monarchs. Their treasures were plundered, and at length the Order was suppressed. The Temple then came into the possession of the Knights of St John, who leased it about 1338 to certain professors of the common law; and so the lawyers remained in possession as tenants until the reign of James I, who granted the property to them. Few memories of the crusading knights now remain in the Temple except the title, Master of the Temple, which was once held by the head of the Order. It might be imagined that he is the head of the two Inns of Court, a kind of chief Bencher, but in reality he is not a lawyer at all, but the clergyman who officiates at the Temple Church.

The Middle and Inner Temples seem always to have been separate societies. The device of the Inner Temple is a winged horse, and of the Middle Temple a lamb bearing a flag. These law societies are two of the four which by royal grant have the exclusive right to maintain a course of legal instruction, to hold examinations, and to admit persons to practise as barristers. It is the duty of all law students to dine a requisite number of times in Hall, and no one can be called to the Bar unless he has done so.

I am not sure in my own mind whether it is true, as some writers claim, that the extra-territorial status of the Temple is a relic of the independence it enjoyed under the Knights Templars, or whether it is not merely a piece of shrewd legal dealing. But the fact remains that it has not only resisted inclusion under the Union of Parishes Act, but it also assesses its own rates. Although part of it is within the City boundary, it is the one place in the City which the Lord Mayor of London cannot enter in state, because the lawyers have never admitted his jurisdiction. If the Lord Mayor were invited to dine in the Temple, or to attend some ceremony there, and appeared, as he does on official occasions, accompanied by his Sword- and Mace-bearers, he would be refused admission. As recently as 1911 the Benchers declined to admit the City Coroner, who wished to hold an inquest there.

No doubt to-day such delicate matters would be handled with the utmost politeness, and it is highly improbable that a modern Lord Mayor would behave as Sir William Turner did in 1668, when he was invited to dinner and asked not to come in state. He replied that he would go with his sword, and see who would dare to take it down.

When he arrived, a crowd of barristers and students wearing rapiers beneath their gowns met him and told him that unless he lowered the City's sword he would not be admitted to the hall. As he defied them, there was a rush for the sword, the Sword-bearer was injured, the City Marshal's men were hustled out and the Lord Mayor had to take refuge in friendly chambers. Meantime the drums were beaten to call out the trained bands, and messengers were sent to Whitehall to tell Charles II that a first-class riot was about to begin.

His Majesty, wise as usual, advised the Lord Mayor to go home.

§ 8

I walked through the Temple to the Victoria Embankment, where I took a tramcar to Westminster. It was a fine morning and the tide was high. The Thames was giving slapping kisses to the Embankment as the tugs and the barges went past, and ahead of me was the clock face of Big Ben, and behind me the dome of St Paul's.

If anyone desires a pleasant and interesting walk in London I would like to recommend the walk I have taken so often from Westminster Bridge to Blackfriars along the Embankment, with excursions into the Embankment Gardens on the way. Here you will find a remarkable collection of celebrities commemorated by statues, busts, bronze plaques and medallions, people who have evidently been assembled in a kind of second-class pantheon; for these are the most modest and retiring of all London memorials. Nevertheless it is a charming spot in which to be tucked away and forgotten; indeed, could a man choose the site of his bust or medallion, surely the Thames Embankment beneath the plane trees, or in the Embankment Gardens within a few yards of the great river, is the most perfect of all places.

The statues begin at Westminster Bridge with Boadicea in her chariot and end at Blackfriars with Queen Victoria. But in between are the oddest assortment of celebrities that could possibly have been brought together. In the first section of the Embankment Gardens at the foot of Villiers Street you will find William Tyndale, who translated the New Testament in 1525, Sir Bartle Frere, the Indian administrator who later on had a frightful time during the Zulu War as Governor at the Cape, and General Sir James Outram, whose gallant conduct during the Indian Mutiny earned him a baronetcy, the thanks of Parliament and the Freedom of the City of London.

Upon the wall of the Embankment, opposite Northumberland Avenue, is a bronze bust of Sir Joseph Bazalgette, the engineer whose great work was the wall on which he is commemorated. A little farther on, also upon the wall of the Embankment, opposite Charing Cross Underground station, is a bronze medallion of W. S. Gilbert; and if you are looking for Sullivan you will find him in the next stretch of the Gardens together with Robert Burns, Sir Wilfred Lawson, the temperance advocate, and Henry Fawcett, the remarkable Liberal statesman who, although blinded when a young man, became Postmaster-General in 1880 and inaugurated the parcels post and carried out schemes which have ripened into post office savings.

Sir Walter Besant, the writer, is commemorated on the Embankment parapet, opposite the end of Savoy Street, and opposite Strand Lane is a memorial to Sir Isambard Brunel, a French refugee who, after becoming a distinguished engineer in New York, made his home in England and built the tunnel beneath the Thames from Wapping to Rotherhithe. In another section of the Gardens, near the Temple Underground station, are to be found memorials to W. E. Forster, the Victorian statesman and Quaker, John Stuart Mill and Lady Henry Somerset, the temperance reformer, and the only woman to be discovered in the whole galaxy of good will, bravery, literary and mechanical talent and political probity. The parade of near greatness is concluded, on the parapet of the Embankment opposite the end of the Gardens, with a memorial to W. T. Stead, the journalist and spiritualist, who lost his life when the *Titanic* went down.

Of course the great sight of the Thames Embankment is the absurdly named "Cleopatra's Needle", for the obelisk was in existence fourteen hundred years before Cleopatra was born. It is the only one of the many obelisks removed from

Egypt which has not been erected in a great park or square. Rome's finest obelisk stands in front of St Peter's, the Paris obelisk is in the Place de la Concorde and the New York obelisk in Central Park. What a debt of thanks we owe to those in 1878 who resisted the temptation to erect "Cleopatra's Needle" in Hyde Park or Kensington Gardens.

It is now so much a part of the London background that few of us, I imagine, ever think how unexpected and original is "Cleopatra's Needle" upon the very brink of the Thames. I wonder if those who had the imagination to place it there felt that this ancient monolith linked the Thames with the Nile over a great gap of three thousand years. I know that it had this association for me when I was a young man, and I could never see it standing in the grey light of a London afternoon without thinking of its great age and of the sunny land with its blue river from which it came. It is the most ancient monument in London, and it is almost certain that Moses must have seen it, together with its companion now in America, when they stood in front of the Temple of the Sun at Heliopolis.

Both these obelisks were dedicated to the sun god by the Pharaoh Thothmes III about 1500 B.C. They stood in Heliopolis until Roman times when they were removed to Alexandria in 12 B.C. The London obelisk fell down, apparently in the Fourteenth Century, and became partially buried in the sand. The New York obelisk stood upright as re-erected by the Roman engineers, and in this position they remained until they were removed in 1877, one to London, the other across the Atlantic. Both Londoners and New Yorkers call their obelisks "Cleopatra's Needle", but few probably know that in doing so they are perpetuating the nickname given to these obelisks probably in the Middle Ages, by the native Egyptians. "Pharaoh's great needles"—*misallatî Fir'ûn*—was the common name given to obelisks by the fellahin as noted by Arab writers in the Twelfth Century. But the pair of obelisks at Alexandria were, for some unknown reason, called "Cleopatra's Needles".

In order to transport the obelisk to London a special ship was built to take it. It was a steel shell fitted with a deck and a mast and it was naturally called the *Cleopatra*. Her steering-gear was not good and she was towed out of Alexandria by a steamship, the *Olga*. In a storm near Cape St Vincent the *Olga* found the *Cleopatra* too much for her and cut her adrift. Six seamen lost their lives during this operation. Imagining that the *Cleopatra* had gone to the bottom of the sea, the *Olga* continued her voyage. But the *Cleopatra* remained afloat and was later salvaged by a ship called the *Fitzmaurice* who took her in tow, and put in a claim for £5,000, which the Admiralty Courts reduced to £2,000.

So " Cleopatra's Needle " arrived safely in the Thames and was towed up to the place near the Embankment where it stands to-day. The steel shell was cut away and the obelisk was lifted at low tide by hydraulic jacks. Before the monument was erected someone had the romantic idea that ordinary commonplace objects ought to be buried beneath it, apparently with the idea that if Macaulay's New Zealander ever visited the ruins of London he might like to see the sort of things people used in 1878. Accordingly sealed jars were buried under the plinth containing a man's suit, a woman's dress and accessories, illustrated newspapers, children's toys, a razor, cigars, photographs of reigning beauties and a complete set of the coinage. The day after " Cleopatra's Needle " had been unveiled, the following lines by an unknown hand were found attached to it.

This monument, as some supposes,
Was looked on in old days by Moses ;
It passed in time to Greeks and Turks,
And was stuck up here by the Board of Works.

The obelisk is now probably over three thousand five hundred years old. It has seen the rise, decline and fall of empires and the movement of power from the Nile to the Tiber and from the Tiber to the Thames. Of all its many experiences, probably the most unusual was that of a September night in 1917 when something fell out of the sky and caused the chips and gashes in the granite plinth which can still be seen.

That " the Thames is London and London is the Thames " is an old saw which is as true to-day as it always was. It is said that once when a monarch, angered by the City, threatened to move Parliament to Oxford, a blunt Alderman asked if the Thames were also to be moved. Upon being told that this was not contemplated, he replied, " then, by God's grace, we shall do well enough at London whatsoever become of the Parliament."

It was as a port and a mart for shipping that London grew up in the Roman era, and that is still her main function in life. In earlier times, when all the shipping in the Thames was clearly visible below London Bridge, the evidence of this fundamental fact was clear for all to see. But for the last hundred years or so ships have been hidden away in docks lower down the river, and the Londoner need never know that his city is the greatest port in the world. Dockland has become a world of its own, one of those many Londons within London, a strange and, to some, dreary district of long roads and grim-looking warehouses.

The presiding deity of dockland is the Port of London Authority—known as the P.L.A.—which is one of the most triumphant and efficient administrative innovations of the past half-century. This trust, or public utility service, for it is not a profit-making concern, is responsible for the administration of the Port of London and has jurisdiction over the river from Teddington to a point beyond the Nore Lightship. It was created by Parliament in order to take over and re-organise all the innumerable conflicting private interests which had grown up in the course of centuries.

The P.L.A. looks after all the cargoes that come into London. It stores them, keeps them in good condition and also offers merchants and shippers the advice of a large staff of specialists. One of the charms of London to me is the knowledge that if I wanted to find the one man in the world who knows more than anyone else about bananas, tortoise-shell, wool, Persian rugs, cigars, rhum or nutmeg, I would only have to go down to the Port of London Authority's fine building near the Tower to discover him.

Three times a week the P.L.A. lifts the iron curtain on the

mystery of dockland when a smart little steamer, the *Crested Eagle*, leaves Tower Pier in the afternoon for a cruise round the docks. It is a voyage which every Londoner, and every visitor to London, should make, for only in this way is it possible to guess the importance of shipping to the life of London and of the whole country.

The first docks to be visited are the older ones near London which have now become too small for the large modern merchant ship. But their warehouses, or those that survived the War, are as useful as ever. The climax of the cruise occurs when the bascules over the King George V Lock are raised and the *Crested Eagle* steams into this enormous and magnificent dock. The size, number and nationality of the ships generally to be seen there, and the variety of their cargoes and the countries of their origin, give one an idea of the wonderful things that go on, unknown to and unseen by most Londoners, every day of the week.

The docks suffered fearful punishment during the War, for they were an easy and first-rate target. If the enemy could have put the Port of London out of action we might not have been defeated but we should have been perilously near starvation. Every kind of explosive that could be dropped upon the docks was dropped: incendiaries, high explosives, land and sea mines and the V.1 and the V.2. The vanished warehouses and the gutted storerooms still tell the tale of those frightful years. But the P.L.A. was as efficient in war as in peace and, thanks to the bravery and devotion of its staff, and to the Civil Defence organisations and the Royal Navy, the Port of London continued to function throughout the War and the Thames was closed to shipping only now and then when the river was being swept for mines.

Interesting as the cruise of the *Crested Eagle* is, it is merely, as it is intended to be, a brief glimpse into the complex activities of the Port of London. A similar expedition on foot through the warehouses of the various docks could occupy weeks. I have seen vaults rather like the crypt of a Norman cathedral, where enormous barrels of wine mature slowly in a darkness lit only by rows of gas jets, which keep the wine at the correct temperature, and I have been to frozen meat warehouses full of New Zealand mutton and Argentine beef where I was assured by a Scotsman, who was incapable of flippancy, that the rats grow extra thick coats of fur.

§ 9

Sometimes in the height of a London summer I have found myself longing quite absurdly for the first fog or the first snow. When I no longer feel any excitement for these things, I shall know that I am getting old.

The thick pea-souper which tastes like iron filings at the back of your throat, which reduces visibility to a yard, which turns every lamp into a downward V of haze and gives to every encounter a nightmare quality almost of terror, is one of the most exciting acts of God. A whole city, it seems, has been translated in a moment into some fantastic region between heaven and hell. Nothing is as it was or as it ought to be. Anything could happen; apocalyptic voices might be heard crying in the darkness. Instead, voices cry, "Where do you think you're going?"; and two taxis in collision look in the gloom like a couple of prehistoric monsters locked in clumsy conflict. Two yellow moon eyes bear down, and a bus grinds past like a scarlet dragon. Men, seen for a second in the fog, appear unique, isolated from the rest of humanity; women are like pale ghosts looking for their lovers.

The strangest thing that ever happened to me in a London fog took place in Trafalgar Square. The fog was so thick that I found myself suddenly faced by a dark mass which resolved itself into one of Nelson's lions; which one I did not know. As I walked on, not knowing whether I was going towards the Haymarket or the Strand, I became aware of an odd shuffling sound and realised that I was walking behind something tall and moving. As it passed into a thin funnel of light from one of the lamps, I saw that I was following the hindquarters of an elephant.

Once I knew what it was, it seemed quite in keeping with the general fantasy of a London pea-souper. The man who was leading the elephant told me that he was trying to get to the Christmas circus at Olympia, but he was late. So when we arrived at the Haymarket, I offered to hold the elephant while he went into a telephone box to ring up and say he was on the way. I wonder how many people can claim to have held an elephant in the Haymarket? But anything might happen in a London fog. And London snow. As soon as you awaken in the morning you can tell by the more than Sunday stillness that snow has fallen in the night. The light coming between the curtains is brighter. But it is the silence, or rather the fact that normal sounds are all muffled, that tells you that snow has fallen.

When you part the curtains or pull up the blinds, you see a world magically transformed. Roofs normally black are white, and an inch of whiteness lies on every railing and on every twig. The smooth, unbroken surface of the snow is exquisite, and the milkman or the postman, as they make the first marks upon it, walk up to doors like explorers.

The dome of St Paul's rises above a harlequin roofline, and the sky is dove colour with unshed snow; the Thames is a river of ink between its whitened banks, and the gulls on the Embankment are no longer white, but a shade of yellowish-grey. But the beauty of snow, like all outward beauty, is an evanescent thing. It may be only a few hours before London is a hideous mass of coffee-coloured sludge that creams and corrugates under the wheels of the omnibuses, and in the morning all the old colours have returned, and perhaps only a patch of pure whiteness, the size of a handkerchief, may be found hiding in the square to prove that for a few moments London had been as lovely as a Christmas card.

CHAPTER FIVE

A walk along the Strand from Temple Bar to Charing Cross, with some remarks on the coffee-houses of the Eighteenth Century and the past gaieties of Covent Garden. I buy my birth certificate at Somerset House, visit the Soane Museum and take a trip down the Thames to Cherry Garden Pier where I cross the river and glance briefly at Limehouse.

§ 1

THE Strand's first function in history was to link the City of London, by way of the village of Charing, with the Abbey and Palace of Westminster. It was the royal road to London, and London's road to royalty.

It is a street which holds a singularly distinguished position among the streets of London, although perhaps its grandest days are now over. Its two great periods were the mediæval, when the strand of the river was lined with the town houses of bishop and baron, and the Victorian, when the Strand was the most famous and in many ways the gayest street in London. Here were the theatres, the restaurants and most of the best shops. When the men of that time went out to administer the Empire, or to wage frontier wars with the aid of hampers from Fortnum and Mason, they bought their pith helmets, their camp beds, and all the impedimenta of an imperial race in the Strand. No doubt Sherlock Holmes also found in the Strand his Inverness capes and those peculiar deerstalker caps with ear-flaps and a button on the top. The first cycling knickers were probably sold in the Strand, and also the first motoring goggles. It was a purely masculine street until after the first War, when there unexpectedly appeared, between the Adelphi and the Savoy, a shop which sold feminine underwear and stockings.

The Strand is richly evocative of Victorian London, of the hansom cab, Romano's, Gatti's and the Gaiety. It was to gas-lit London what Piccadilly has become to the London of electric light. Whenever Victorians thought of London from their places of exile in distant parts of the earth, it was of the Strand they dreamed in moments of homesickness, remembering the cosy plush alcoves and the shaded lights of the restaurants, and hearing in imagination the restless whirr and clatter of the hansoms and the horse buses which in those days packed the roadway from kerb to kerb as tightly as gondolas at some Venetian carnival.

In our time the Strand has lost its gaiety and also its air of richness. Theatres have drifted westward to Shaftesbury Avenue, restaurants and shops to Piccadilly, Regent Street and beyond; all part of that steady westward flow of London life that has been in progress since the Seventeenth Century. So the Strand is left, a slightly shabby street now, but still distinguished by a pre-multiple store individuality. Even to-day the Strand is peculiarly rich in those remarkable shops which have no shop windows. You find these modest little establishments up a flight of rickety early Victorian stairs. They are small, old-established family businesses which specialise in all sorts of odd things. For instance, a world authority on moths and butterflies, who knows precisely the right kind of nets to use in Brazil or Nigeria and the sort of collecting-boxes to send out to entomologists in the Andes, is to be found on an upper floor of the Strand; and all kinds of recondite experts have similar quarters there.

One of the charms of London is its great supply of unassuming expertness. I know that the term has been degraded, and that when we hear over the radio the words "Government experts", our spirits sink and we see in the mind's eye a number of self-confident graduates of the London School of Economics. But the real experts are the unassuming little men in black coats, whose fathers and grandfathers have carried on small, unusual businesses, and have been dealing for a century or more in one little commodity about which they know everything. You are never sure in London whether you may be sitting in the Underground next to the world's greatest authority on the tree frog, or a man who has devoted his life to a study of mediæval pigments.

These are real experts and, as I say, the Strand is the sort of place in which you will find them in untidy old rooms, submerged by the litter of their trade, answering letters from Yale University or from a collector of ikons in Alexandria.

A foreigner who has heard that every Englishman loves a lord might think, as he walks up the Strand noticing the street names, that an obsequious nation has more than paid homage to the great landed families of England. Between Temple Bar and Charing Cross is a whole dukery of historic names: Norfolk, Bedford, Northumberland, Somerset and Buckingham, to say nothing of such names as Howard, Devereux, Arundel, Surrey, Villiers, Chandos, and so on. These names are all that is now left of the Strand's aristocratic connections.

In the Middle Ages, when the strand of the river was a pleasant green lane running towards Charing, which means a turning or a bend, the bishops and the great nobles built their town houses there in order to be near the King and his palace at Westminster. What could have been more delightful than a house in the Strand, with orchards and gardens running down to the Thames, which in those days was a good salmon stream?

The great houses, which are seen in old maps and plans of London, were more like small villages, and consisted of dozens of separate buildings grouped round courtyards. Once a year or so noblemen would come up to London with baggage-trains and hundreds of horses and retainers, and his house in the Strand would be thrown open for a few months while His Grace attended Court and Parliament.

When the City began to spread to the west in Stuart times the ancient mansions of the Strand were not as pleasant as in the old days, also land values had increased, and the nobles gradually sold their Strand houses and moved fashionably towards the new West End. In the Middle Ages anyone seeking the Duke of Norfolk in London would have gone to the Strand; in the late Seventeenth Century he would have found him in St James's Square. The day had arrived of the piazza, the square and the lonely mansion amid the green fields of Piccadilly.

It is generally the fate of aristocratic houses overwhelmed by a city's development to become slums, and this happened in the Strand. The lordly mansions were split up and subdivided, roads were driven through them, and in a generation or so they were almost unrecognisable. The only one that has survived as a great mansion is Somerset House.

During a walk along the Strand from Temple Bar, which marks the boundary of the Freedom of London and the beginning of the Liberty of Westminster, to Charing Cross, where the Strand ends, the ghosts of eight centuries pull at the sleeve, and the Strand at its busiest moment of the day is not more crowded with living men than it is with the spectres of those whose names are associated with its past. To attempt to mention them all would be to write a full-length book.

The old name of Temple Bar persists, although the gateway which used to stand there was pulled down in 1877 when the Law Courts were being built, and the Griffin now occupies the centre of the road to mark the spot. Why a griffin should have been considered an appropriate introduction to the City of London, I have never been able to understand, indeed I cannot think of a less suitable, or perhaps more questionable, guardian of the boundary. In classical mythology the griffin was a rapacious monster which was supposed to keep watch over gold mines and buried treasure. When human beings approached, the griffin swooped down upon them and tore them to pieces, thus punishing greed and avarice. How did it happen that the Victorians, who might have been more sensitive than ourselves upon this matter, allowed such a sardonic jest at the gates of the City? However, there it is for all to see, and you can walk up to it and note that among the decorations on the plinth is a bronze representation of the last occasion that royalty passed in state beneath the old gate in February, 1872, when Queen Victoria and the Prince of Wales, afterwards Edward VII, went to St Paul's.

Old Temple Bar was built by Wren after the Fire of London. It was a gateway with a wide central arch for traffic and two smaller ones on either side for foot passengers. On the Westminster side were statues of Charles I and Charles II; on the City side were Queen Elizabeth and James I. People in the old days used to say that Elizabeth was pointing a white finger at Child's Bank, and that James I was saying to her, " Suppose we go to Whitehall and sit down a bit." There was a central room over the main arch which was rented by Child's Bank as a store-room for its old account-books, including one that must have been well worth inspection: the private account of Charles II. In Stuart times and during the Jacobite troubles of the next period the heads of traitors, mounted on spikes, were set up on Temple Bar, as in earlier days they had been displayed upon London Bridge. People who lived well into the Nineteenth Century remembered having seen them there.

When the King visited the City in the old days, the gates of Temple Bar were shut, and His Majesty halted in front of it and ordered one of the heralds to knock. The City Marshal, who, together with the Lord Mayor of London, the sheriffs and other City dignitaries, were waiting on the other side of the gate, would ride up and shout, " Who's there? " Upon being officially informed that it was the King, the Lord Mayor would appear, offer the keys of London to the monarch, and tender the City Sword in token of submission, after which Temple Bar was opened, and the honour and dignity of the centuries had been satisfied. To-day the same scene takes place in the open air at the Griffin. The spectacle of the King of England asking permission to enter the City of London is a ceremony well worth watching.

The fate of old Temple Bar is more fortunate than that of many other relics of old London. If you go to Theobald's Park, near Cheshunt, in Hertfordshire, you will see it in rural retirement as one of the entrances to the park. Its Portland stone is blackened by centuries of London life, the iron-studded gates are shut, as if waiting for some ghostly monarch to knock upon them, and the old relic looks extraordinarily wise and full of metropolitan experience as it stands among trees and grass. When I paid a visit to it some years ago, I had the eerie feeling that had I gone there by moonlight, or perhaps upon

All Souls' night, the old gate might have opened to admit a great company of those whose shadows in life had passed across it: Charles II, Pepys, Wren and Nell Gwyn, Anne and Marlborough, George I and Walpole, Boswell and Johnson, Reynolds and Garrick, and many another.

If the idea, expressed since the War, to bring Temple Bar back to London, is ever carried out, the capital would be enriched by a fascinating memorial of its past, and there should be no difficulty at all in finding a suitable place for it.

At its very beginning the Strand is packed with memories. Essex Street, where this book was published, was the site of Essex House, in which Elizabeth's headstrong favourite, Robert Devereux, Earl of Essex, hatched the stupid plot that led him to Tower Green. The old gate, now so badly damaged, at the end of this street is said to have been the water-gate of old Essex House, or perhaps it was an entrance gate to a water-gate nearer tide level. Like all the ancient Strand mansions, Essex House was a huge rambling structure with courtyards, a mass of confused roofs, and gables and battlements overlooking the river. An antiquary who visited all that was left of the old place late in the Eighteenth Century —Lord Cholmondeley, who died in 1770—said that upon a window-pane, scratched apparently with a diamond, he traced the following letters: I.C.U.S.X. & E.R., which he interpreted as " I see you, Essex, and Elizabeth Regina ", a cipher evidently scratched by someone who from that window had seen the Queen with her favourite.

At the *Essex Head* in Essex Street—there is still a public-house of this name—Johnson, dreading solitude and fearing to be alone, founded a club that met three times a week. It was when proposing Boswell as a member that he coined the delightful phrase, " a clubable man ", also a perfect description of Boswell. Devereux Court, which is at right-angles to Essex Street, leads to the Strand, and it was there that one of London's first and most famous coffee-houses—the *Grecian*—was opened in 1652.

It seems that coffee was introduced into England by Greeks early in the Seventeenth Century, and I think probably the first reference to it is Evelyn's note in his *Diary* for 1637 that a fellow undergraduate at Balliol College, Oxford, a Greek called Nathaniel Conopios, " was the first I ever saw drink coffee, which custom came not into England till thirty years after ".

The actual date was 1652, when a coffee-house was opened in Cornhill by a man called Rosa Pasquee, and though this is usually said to be the first of London's coffee-houses, the same year saw the arrival of the *Grecian* in Devereux Court, its name a reference not to the classics, but to the proprietor, a Greek named Constantine. Addison, Steele and Isaac Newton all visited the *Grecian*, which had a remarkable lease of life, remaining there until 1843. The smell of coffee, which we think so delightful and appetising, was at first considered a public nuisance, and a Fleet Street coffee-house owner named James Farr, whose establishment was on the site of the present *Rainbow Tavern*, was summoned for making " a sort of liquor called coffee " to " the great nuisance and prejudice of the neighbourhood ".

There were soon hundreds of coffee-houses all over London, and it is not perhaps generally known that they also sold wine and spirits, so that their effect upon the habits of a drunken age was not what might have been expected. The barmaid's first appearance in history was in the coffee-houses of Stuart and Georgian London. The counter near the fire, where the coffee-, tea- and chocolate-pots were kept warm, was known as " the bar ", and most coffee-house proprietors, as a lure to custom, engaged the best-looking girls they could find. " At the bar ", says a writer of the time, " the good man always places a Charming Phillis or two who invite you by their amorous glances into the smoky territories, to the loss of your sight." Steele said of the barmaids, " These Idols sit and receive all day long the admiration of the Youth ". Lloyds, now housed in a gigantic building, is the most extraordinary metamorphosis, for it began its career humbly as the coffee-house of Edward Lloyd, where those interested in shipping were in the habit of meeting.

Coffee, tea and chocolate fluctuated in public esteem with the import duty levelled upon them. Chocolate was never really popular, and chocolate-houses, such as White's and the

Cocoa Tree, which now exist as clubs, could be counted on the fingers of both hands, while coffee-houses were numbered by hundreds. Perhaps the greatest function performed by tea and coffee was to pave the way to a decent breakfast. Before these beverages arrived most of our ancestors began the day horribly with a draught of porter or gin, and the working-classes continued this habit until 1808, when the duty on coffee was reduced so that, for a time, it became the drink of the London artisan. A journeyman tailor named Place told a commission on education in 1835 that before cheap coffee-houses were available, about 1815, his usual breakfast was a pot of porter and a penny roll at a public-house. When the cheaper coffee-shops were opened he used to go there for breakfast and for supper, and for a fee of sixpence a month could see all the newspapers and reviews. Tea, which appealed to women more than to men, ultimately became more popular than coffee with the mass of the population.

§ 2

Whenever I have passed the ruins of St Clement Dane's since the War, I have been delighted to see how Dr Johnson stood up to the bombing. His statue, backed by the shell of the church in which he worshipped, survived many a fearful night, and the Doctor did not even move on his plinth, or take his eyes from the pages of the book he is reading, as the land-mines and the bombs came thundering down. Johnsonians the world over will agree that this is as it should be. The Doctor was a man of physical courage and would have made an unflinching air-raid warden.

A short walk along the Strand towards Charing Cross brings you to a narrow little alley called Strand Lane, which used to go down to the river. A few doors along this alley on the left, and down some steps, is an oblong of clear cold water, about sixteen feet long by six feet wide, known as the Roman Bath. It used to be on the tourist's map of London years ago, but when I tried to see the place recently I knocked in vain for a long time, and was told by a woman, who put her head out of an upper window, that the key was with the London County Council.

I had never heard that anyone ever bathed in it—except David Copperfield—until in *London Echoing*, by James Bone, I read that many years ago a draper in Oxford Street, who then owned the bath, offered to open it to subscribers for two guineas a year. And two men actually subscribed. " Out of the millions of Londoners only those two went down that obscure little lane to the dingy house with its rusty little front railing and opened the door with their keys and entered the dim, arched room," writes Mr Bone. " I liked to think of one of them all alone taking his plunge into the clear cold water that wells up from the bottom just as it did when there may have been togas on the stone where he had put his boots. Then out again, the old door slammed, and up under the archway and away among the buses. Nobody bathes there now and its ownership—even its Roman origin—is in dispute."

It was at the bottom of Strand Lane that Addison, as he described in the *Spectator*, landed at six o'clock one morning with a fleet of gardeners, including ten sail of apricot boats that had called in at Nine Elms for melons. They were, of course, on their way to Covent Garden. " Chimney sweepers passed us as we made up to the market, and some raillery happened between one of the fruit-wenches and those black men, about the Devil and Eve, with allusion to their several professions." I think the time of Queen Anne has left few more charming little pictures of London in the early morning.

Somerset House is the only old building in the Strand that gives one an idea of the scale and magnificence of the princely palaces of the past. Although it was rebuilt as recently as a hundred and seventy years ago, it still has the open courtyard which was a feature of all the noble Strand inns in former days.

The old Palace of the Savoy was the next great palace to the west. The hotel stands on only a small part of its site. This palace rose sheer from the river, with thick stone turreted walls and bastions, and its outbuildings and additions straggled northward to the Strand. When Eleanor of Provence—the most unpopular queen in English history—

arrived to marry Henry III, she brought with her a pack of rapacious relatives, whose fortunes she had no difficulty in wheedling out of her generous but weak consort. To her wise and powerful uncle, Count Peter of Savoy, fell the great old palace on the river-side to which he gave his name. In this way an Italian name known to the Romans, and included in the empire of Charlemagne, came to London, and now suggests to the modern mind film stars and visiting Americans.

I always think it strange to descend the Savoy steps and see, amid the tall modern buildings all around, the sad-looking little strip of churchyard in which the Savoy Chapel stands, the only part of the old Savoy that remains. It was restored in Victorian times, and all one can say is that it occupies the same site as its ancient predecessor. Nearby, in Savoy Hill, the British Broadcasting Corporation began its career in the nineteen twenties, in a modest building known to the first wireless fans as 2LO. Those were the pioneering days of radio, long before the wireless valve had appeared in the receiving set, and when fans made their own crystal sets and carried about with them, in match-boxes, their favourite crystal, a small uneven lump of silvery ore, which, in order to receive 2LO, was touched with a thin wire known as a " cat's whisker ". Some particular facet of some particular crystals were believed by their owners to have exceptional qualities of reception, and every night they would be brought out of their match-boxes and clamped into the primitive little receiving sets while the owner sat with his head-phones on, probing the surface of the crystal with the " cat's whisker ".

I remember broadcasting on several occasions from 2LO, an organisation as delightfully informal and Bohemian in its atmosphere as that of the B.B.C. is now solemn and impressive. I always had the delightful impression, which could never occur nowadays in Portland Place, that no matter what I said, it would not be heard outside the studio, which made microphone nerves impossible! But I sometimes received letters from people in Inverness or the Shetlands to say that they had heard me quite distinctly—letters which astonished me as much as the experience had astonished the writers.

In those days broadcasting, if not actually a joke, was taken very much in one's stride. Someone would ring up in the afternoon—probably because someone else had failed to materialise—and ask one to drop in and give a talk that evening.

" But what shall I talk about? "

" Anything you like, dear old boy," would reply the careless predecessor of the B.B.C. voice.

So with a hasty script, I would climb the narrow stairs to 2LO, where the grandfather of all microphones hung suspended from the ceiling. Sometimes if I entered a little noisily, fingers would be placed on lips, and someone would point dramatically to the red light which, even in those antediluvian days, indicated that we were on the air. It was all very friendly and casual, and no one had any idea that it was going to become a profession. No one could have foreseen the days to come when London would speak day after day for years to the resistance movements of a conquered Europe.

Another site of considerable interest is that on which the Strand Palace Hotel stands. Here once stood Exeter Hall, famous as the headquarters of the Philanthropists of the early Nineteenth Century, who, led by the fiery zeal of Clarkson and Wilberforce, brought about the abolition of slavery. There are several pictures in existence which show the great hall packed with a rapt audience, which included enormous numbers of women, as they listened to the story of some native chief or converted negro from Africa, America or the West Indies.

A little higher up the Strand, and on the Savoy side, is the Adelphi, the name of a single architectural composition, but now applied to the group of Georgian streets behind the Strand. I remember the Adelphi, which vanished in the nineteen thirties, after a long and helpless scream of pain had sounded from the Press when its demolition, and the erection of the present skyscraper, were contemplated.

The terrace of houses which brought the Adam brothers so much fame, and so much financial anxiety, is said to have been erected to the sound of bagpipes by Scottish labourers imported for the purpose. But when the Scots realised that they were being paid less than the London rates they downed tools, and imported Irishmen with fiddlers took their place. The terrace was a fine and noble sight even during its last years. But when it was new, and when it rose straight from the river before the Embankment was built, as it was intended to do, it must have looked magnificent.

One of the first tenants was Garrick, who spent the last seven years of his life in Adelphi Terrace, and died there. In my time the Savage Club was there, and moved to its present quarters, Lord Curzon's fine house in Carlton House Terrace, some months before the breakdown men appeared. But Mr James Bone, in the book I have quoted, says amusingly —and I can well believe it—that some of the staunchest members continued to haunt the old premises "until the housebreaker's men, they say, removed most of them". Although I was never a member of the Savage Club, I remember many cheerful nights there, and it even fell to my lot after one of these occasions to guide to his home in the Charterhouse the ghostly Odell, a frail, silvery old man in a long black cloak, if not the oldest Savage, certainly the most ancient one.

Another feature of the Adelphi which I remember well was the Adelphi Hotel, which stood at the corner of John Street and Adam Street. Dickens may have stayed there when it was known as Osborne's. It was the scene of Mr Pickwick's decision to live in Dulwich, and it was also the scene of Mr Wardle's dinner-party. The old Adelphi lived up to these associations without the slightest effort. The whole place was completely and genuinely Dickensian, even in 1936, when the bar closed for the last time and the old mahogany doors were bolted, never again to admit an actor, a journalist or an inquisitive American. I have the pleasantest memories of the Adelphi Hotel. You could stroll in at any time, have a cheerful conversation with anybody who happened to be in the office, hear all the news from the hall porter and the head waiter, and go into the bar, where you would always find some unlikely acquaintance.

There was a certain air of ancient grandeur about the place.

I remember once going there to meet a friend who had been living in Paris for years and who had unexpectedly arrived in London. I was shown up to his bedroom, which, to my surprise, was a magnificent apartment with an Adam ceiling and painted panels, and in the centre of this splendour my friend lay in a large four-poster bed with a bottle of champagne beside him on a little table. It is quite possible that one might go to any modern hotel in London and discover a friend in precisely similar circumstances, but the memory of the scene would not remain, neither would it seem at all interesting. But the Adelphi Hotel, rooted as it was in an age of individualism and soaked in character and atmosphere, gave most people who stayed there a certain air, either of comedy, of romance, or eccentricity.

§ 3

It occurred to me as I was walking up the Strand that I had not been inside Somerset House for years. Although thousands pass this building every day, it is not a place we visit unless driven there by business or by architectural curiosity. Also, it is the headquarters of the Inland Revenue, not the portion of it that sends abrupt buff forms to the taxpayer, but an infinitely higher department that uses typewriters; and, as such, is a place most people would prefer to forget.

Somerset House has had an extraordinarily exciting life, with more than its share of feminine interest, and it would now appear to be paying for it in a dreary statistical present. It is a huge, late-Eighteenth Century Palladian building, erected on the site of the great mansion which the Lord Protector Somerset might have completed had he not been executed in 1552. He intended to make this a palace which would rival Whitehall and Hampton Court. His architect was John of Padua—Henry V's architect—who built Longleat, in Wiltshire, and also the gates of Caius College, Cambridge. Somerset pulled down a number of London buildings, including a chapel in St Paul's churchyard, to get stone; and London never forgave him for it.

The palace passed to the Crown when Somerset was beheaded, and then became linked with the Queens of England. The first woman to occupy it was the young Princess Elizabeth before she became queen, and after her time it was the custom to hand this property as a dower-house to the queen or the queen dowager of the time. Here Anne of Denmark, the wife of James I, took part in masques, here Henrietta Maria held her Catholic Court in the time of Charles I, here Catherine of Braganza sought a little peace away from the gay doings of Charles II at Whitehall. But apparently nothing was ever thrown away in this palace, neither was anything repaired. Its story is one of progressive dilapidation. It was judged so inconvenient and old-fashioned in the time of George III that it was decided to pull it down and accommodate Queen Charlotte elsewhere. She was given in exchange a charming red-brick Queen Anne house in St James's Park, a house which has developed into Buckingham Palace.

When the old palace was demolished in the late Eighteenth Century an astonishing sight confronted the architects and others, for the rambling old place was seen to be a museum of mostly broken furniture, tattered silk curtains, worn tapestries, and frayed velvets and brocades. Incredible as it may seem, furniture dating from the reign of Edward IV was discovered in attics and storerooms, where it had been rotting and mouldering for three centuries.

The present Somerset House is, of course, best seen from the Thames; now that the Adelphi has gone, it is the most notable sight between the Abbey and St Paul's. When it was built, the Thames Embankment was not there, and the river washed its outer walls. The massive gateway, which is now the underground link between the tramway systems of north and south London, was originally designed as a water-gate. The Strand entrance, which is much finer than most of us realise when we dash past it on a bus, leads to a splendid inner courtyard round which rise the majestic headquarters of the Inland Revenue, the Probate Registry, and the department of the Registrar-General.

While I was wondering whom I should go and see—for you are not encouraged to idle about in Somerset House—

it occurred to me that I would buy my own birth certificate. I was shown into an ante-room to the Search Room, where I found tables furnished with three kinds of forms, edged with colour, red for births, green for marriages, and black for deaths. The room was full of people who were prying into these three supreme moments of life.

Having filled in a red form and presented it at a counter, I was charged a "search fee" and admitted to the Search Room, where all the births, marriages and deaths in England and Wales since 1837 are indexed in fat folio volumes bound in tin.

I found myself at once. Under my birthday in the quarterly volume for the year of my birth, I was suddenly confronted with myself. And I discovered that I was the only Henry Morton born during that quarter in the whole of England and Wales. One man ran me very closely, but they christened him Harry. There were three Alfreds, two James's, four Annies, three Ediths and three Marys born to Mortons in that quarter.

While the clerk was making out my birth certificate, I watched the other people who were hunting up births, marriages and deaths. Some were obviously private detectives, or so I dramatically imagined, some were possibly solicitors' clerks, some were in search of fortune, some of legitimacy; many were in search of old age pensions. There are so many men and women round about the age of sixty who cannot find their birth certificates that the Registrar-General has grouped together all the index volumes likely to be of help to them. And there they sit, turning the pages, looking for the official intimation of their arrival upon this planet.

§ 4

If you go to Covent Garden early in the morning you will see one of the greatest traffic congestions in London. On a sunny spring morning, when the light falls upon banks of daffodils and narcissi, the sight is a lovely one, and throughout the day, as the market unwinds itself and thousands of carts, lorries, vans and handcarts emerge from the central congestion and bear their loads of fruit, flowers and vegetables all over London, you are amazed by the order that long usage can bring out of apparent chaos.

I think Covent Garden Market is probably the most accessible glimpse that remains to us of Hogarth's London. Imagine the hearty, husky, shouting mob that gathers there every morning clothed in the dress of two centuries ago, and you have a living survival of the Eighteenth Century. I have often seen faces in Covent Garden which Hogarth might have drawn.

The Market is also a superb example of the vitality of markets. The spectator, watching the incredible crowd of men and vehicles pressed together in a space too small for it, must wonder how such a congestion began and how it was allowed to continue. It began in the simplest way imaginable. When houses invaded this part of London in the time of Charles I, the market-gardeners from villages round about set up stalls, and sold their cabbages, radishes and lettuces to the inhabitants. As the resident population grew, so the street market grew, until now the cabbages have long since expelled the residents, and a mountain of fruit, flowers and vegetables, some of it from remote corners of the earth, piles into Covent Garden every day.

I have often thought that on a cold winter's night Covent Garden and the neighbouring streets can appear as sinister as any part of London west of Aldgate. There are little alleys off Long Acre, within a stone's throw of the lights of Leicester Square, as forbidding as anything in Limehouse.

Covent Garden is important in the story of London as the birthplace of that architectural feature so characteristic of London, the Square. All the residential squares may be said to have originated with the Covent Garden Piazza in the reign of Charles I. The great West End squares are much older than perhaps many people imagine. The Covent Garden Piazza was built in 1630, Leicester Square in 1635, Bloomsbury Square in 1665, Soho Square in 1681, Red Lion Square and St James's Square in 1684, Grosvenor Square in 1695, and Berkeley Square in 1698. So that all the main squares were built in the time of the Stuarts.

It may seem odd and improbable, but I think it may be true, to claim the Roman forum as the parent of the London square. Inigo Jones, who inspired the lay-out of Covent Garden, had travelled in Italy and was soaked in the feeling of the Italian Renaissance. His contemporary, Evelyn, says that his inspiration for Covent Garden was the piazza at Leghorn, and it is obvious that, from the first, Covent Garden Piazza, a word most absurdly transferred in time to the colonnade itself, was an attempt to plant a bit of Italy in London. Although the plant flourished exceedingly and sent out many a famous shoot, these did not develop along Italian precedents, for nothing could be less like an Italian piazza than a London square. Even in Covent Garden the essential difference between a piazza and a square became evident about 1666, when trees were planted in the centre.

So even though the London square may have begun with the idea that it should be an open space consecrated to human activities and surrounded by houses, it was not long before, in a characteristically English way, it became a piece of open country enclosed by bricks and mortar. The piazza is open to all and sundry, the square is private, and even those who live in it rarely tread the central turf or sit beneath the trees.

Charles I took a keen interest in the building of the piazza. He often went there to watch the enrichment of his capital by what to contemporary eyes must have looked like the scenery of a Whitehall masque. And it is interesting to wonder what London might have looked like had this King been fated to enjoy a placid and prosperous reign, for he had in him the making of a great art patron and builder. Charles and Inigo Jones, given the opportunity and the money, might well have brought about more spectacular changes in the appearance of London than even the Prince Regent and Nash were able to do at a later time. But, as it happened, Renaissance architecture in early Stuart times was largely confined by force of circumstances to the plywood scenery of Court masques.

It is almost impossible for anyone nowadays to get a clear idea of the appearance of Covent Garden as people saw it in the time of Charles I. Nothing remains of the original houses or the colonnade, and even the majestic church of St Paul has been rebuilt. The remaining arcades give perhaps a fair idea of the massive strength and imposing scale of the original. And here it may truly be said the West End of London began. Covent Garden was the most fashionable address for more than a hundred years.

Fashion and vice lived at close quarters in Covent Garden, for the streets round about soon became notorious for the amount of drinking and gaming housed in a small area. People of rank and fashion shared the district with the proprietors of taverns, gaming houses, Turkish baths, coffee-houses and the euphemistically termed bagnios. It is strange, as one looks at the blameless exterior of Covent Garden, King Street, Henrietta Street and Bow Street to-day, to realise that for a hundred and fifty years it was the scene of nightly brawls, drunken revels and assignations. At a slightly later time a certain Mr Harris used to publish his *Lists of Covent Garden Ladies*, which appeared regularly every year for something like forty years.

London was never more flagrantly vicious than during the Stuart and Georgian periods. Every night the rakes would sit in their coaches and watch the parade under the arcades. One writer of the time compared the scene to that of a splendid Venetian carnival. A life-like glimpse into the underworld of this distant London is Defoe's novel, *Moll Flanders*. Hogarth's prints are also an immortal commentary on it. This artist knew Covent Garden well, for he studied there in the studio of Sir James Thornhill. The first of his four prints, *The Four Times of a Day*, shows a prim spinster walking on a cold winter's morning to St Paul's Church, while the scene round about suggests that the piazza has hardly yet recovered from its nightly debauch. No doubt the types Hogarth knew well in Covent Garden inspired his famous *Harlot's Progress*.

The early chapters of William Hickey's diary contain one of the frankest and most appallingly unashamed contemporary accounts in existence of the Covent Garden night haunts; and this was written after the great nursery of vice had been in existence for nearly a hundred and fifty years. The cheerful and admiring indulgence with which an inebriated mob observed the pranks of an intoxicated aristocracy is perhaps the most remarkable aspect of this side of London life several centuries ago. Reading Hickey, it is not difficult to understand the origin of the phrase " Drunk as a lord ".

§ 5

More than once, especially upon wet days, the gloomy desire to explore Covent Garden Opera House has come over me. I have often thought that hidden away in its basements must be some startling relic of the Victorian Age. No other public building still in use in London seems to cling so tenaciously to a vanished past, or to be enduring a more depressing present. The Opera House gazes across at Bow Street Police Station with half-shut eyes, remembering footmen in powdered wigs and red-plush breeches. Even the thunder of printing-presses in Long Acre cannot shake it from thoughts of old forgotten things. At night, before the supply of the day's cabbages has rolled into Covent Garden, the cold portals of the Opera House look as if they are waiting for the ghost of Edward VII to step from a spectral brougham.

I found a number of young men and women dancing vigorously upon the vast polished expanse of the floor. The Opera House, as opera-goers know it, had vanished. The floor had been built up to stage level. Stalls, stage and the mysterious region beyond had been turned into one gigantic dance-hall. Two dance-bands were stationed on the stage upon the precise spot—the footlight line—where so many tenors have sobbed out their hearts. The grand tier of boxes gazed down upon the scene as if anxious to be dissociated from it. In a corner where for over eighty years the rank and fashion of Europe have inspected one another, I discovered a soda-fountain.

" When does the opera season begin? "

" We don't know."

One of the bands suddenly crashed into a fox-trot, and I left the ballroom with the feeling that in spite of the bright lights and the soda-fountain, Covent Garden was still dreaming of dowagers. It is pathetic that it should be obliged to earn its living as a dance-hall. It reminded me of a poor old Russian aristocrat whom I used to know years ago. He ran a humble little restaurant in a London suburb, but on occasions he could suddenly leap back into the past and appear at an official function blazing with orders and decorations. And Covent Garden is the same. At the very whisper of grand opera, the floor sinks back to its normal position, the soda-fountain is hurried away, and all the young men and women and the dance bands depart.

A caretaker took me on a tour of the building. It is the third theatre to stand on the site. The first was built by John Rich, a famous harlequin, in 1732. There years later he founded the Beefsteak Club, which is now to be discovered in Irving Street. On the morning of September 30, 1808, the theatre was burned down. Thirty-three firemen were killed by an unexpected fall of masonry; the famous organ played by Handel when he produced the *Messiah*, and also the wine cellar of the Beefsteak Club, perished in the flames.

John Kemble, whose savings were invested in the theatre, was badly hit, but his friends rallied round him. The Prince of Wales, afterwards George IV, gave him a thousand pounds, and a more lavish gift was ten thousand pounds from the Duke of Northumberland. Kemble refused to accept this as a gift, and insisted upon giving the Duke his bond for the amount. When the foundation stone of the new theatre was laid, the Duke returned the document to Kemble with a letter, saying that as the day was one of rejoicing there would probably be a bonfire, and suggested that Kemble should fling the bond for ten thousand pounds into it to " heighten the flames ". Those were indeed the good old days! This second theatre was destroyed by fire in 1847, and the present building rose from its ashes as the Royal Italian Opera House.

My guide and I explored gloomy passages. We climbed to the " flies ", which look like a gigantic weaving-loom. We entered the largest studio in London, where Egyptian temples for *Aïda*, mountains for *Lohengrin*, and other immense and ambitious canvases have been painted on frames as big as a parade-ground.

We then met a man who for forty years has been dressing tenors and sopranos, and fitting out crowds of villagers, soldiers, Rhine maidens, Egyptian priests and an occasional Valkyrie. He presides over perhaps the most varied and costly theatrical wardrobe in the world, and he never listens to a rumour that an opera season will not be held. He goes round oiling Parsifal's sword and polishing the helmet of Rhadames; for you never can tell.

He thinks of opera in terms not of music but of tights. At a moment's notice he could turn a hundred choristers into Japanese geishas, Wagnerian warriors, mediæval peasants or Georgian courtiers. Just as a conductor has his operatic library, so this man has his more bulky one: room after room full of locked cupboards labelled *Pelleas and Melisande*, *Salome*, *La Bohème* and *Tannhäuser*. Covent Garden's wardrobe has taken eighty years to assemble.

" Down in the armoury," said the wardrobe master, " I've got pikes and swords that must have come from the old theatre."

In the basements and cellars of the Opera House, my dream of the Opera House came true. There was jazz above my head where the floor creaked to the movements of the dancers; down below were the ghosts which haunt all empty theatres. In the silence of a place built for song and music, among the folded backcloths and a crazy assembly of pasteboard trees, gold couches, imperial litters and imitation flowers, are the memories of nearly a century of opera. Forgotten names like Grisi and Mario, Albani, Sontag, Bosio, Signor Ronconi, came to mind in the depth of this theatre. They sang their way into the heart of London long ago, at a time when nearly every opera house in Europe was turning down the work of Wagner.

" Best dressing-rooms," I was told as a man flung open a door.

Ghosts of Patti, Tetrazzini, Caruso. . . .

And this part of the Opera House which the public never sees has inherited something from the Covent Garden of the Eighteenth Century. The whitewashed arches might belong to the Covent Garden that Sheridan knew. Here glides the ghost of lovely Elizabeth Farren, who became Lady Derby. One night Lord Derby appeared and demanded the arrears of Lady Derby's salary. He refused to leave the building until the money was paid.

"My dear lord," said Sheridan, "this is too bad: you have taken from us the brightest star in our little world, and now you quarrel with us for a little dust that she has left behind her."

Horace Walpole's cynical ghost haunts these operatic vaults. It was he who told the story of Lord Chesterfield's arrival at the opera when it was the custom of George III and his Queen to visit the less fashionable Haymarket Opera House, known as the King's Theatre. Lord Chesterfield was asked if he had been at the other house.

"Yes," he replied, "but there was no one there but the King and Queen, and as I thought they might be talking business, I came straight away."

Such are the spectres, elegant, witty, famous, that haunt Covent Garden while the dance bands play above. The whole place seems trying to regain its past. It seems to be waiting in a coma that looks almost like death for the minute and exciting sound of a conductor's baton tapping a music-stand.

The story of Drury Lane is that of the English stage for three centuries. The theatre was the scene of the triumphs of Garrick, Mrs Siddons and John Kemble, among many others. Sheridan became financially interested in it, and was in his seat in the House of Commons in 1809 when news was brought that Drury Lane was on fire. He opposed the extraordinary motion that the House should adjourn in sympathy with him, and then hurried out to see the flames. He retired with a friend to a coffee-house opposite, where he drank a glass of port saying, "It was hard if a man could not drink a glass of wine by his own fire." The present building, the fifth theatre on the site, was opened in 1812 with a prologue written by Byron.

The street which has given its name to the theatre is now as dingy as it is famous. The old Georgian houses, almost black with the soot and grime of centuries, have been turned into little shops and flats. Pepys mentions passing along this street on May Day in 1667, when he "saw pretty Nelly standing at her lodgings in Drury Lane in her smock-sleeves and bodice looking upon one: she seemed a mighty pretty creature".

§ 6

Nearly everyone collects something these days, but we do not often collect the things which were eagerly sought after two hundred years ago. In order to see what an Eighteenth Century man collected you must go to 13, Lincoln's Inn Fields, and look at the Soane Museum, the collection of Sir John Soane, the architect of the Bank of England. Your first impression may be that a mason's yard has invaded a private house. Enormous portions of the ancient world, the bases and capitals of marble columns, an Egyptian sarcophagus, a Roman cinerary urn, antique statues, whole or in part, and other heavy objects, many of them intended for the open air, are encountered in basement, sitting-room and drawing-room.

How Lady Soane managed to run a house which might at any moment be invaded by a crane and a breakdown gang, ready to smash a way through a wall to admit a couple of columns from Hadrian's Villa at Tivoli, I cannot imagine. Yet, it is said, she loved this collection almost as much as her husband did. I wonder! Was she not perhaps just clever and tactful? All wives know that if they are married to a man who is determined to collect pieces of ancient architecture the only thing to do is to put a good face on it.

Unlike most large collections which come under the hammer when their owner dies, the Soane Collection has been preserved by a private Act of Parliament whereby Sir John, before his death in 1837, endowed the collection and appointed trustees to look after it and to house it in the place where he had assembled it. That is what makes the Soane Museum so interesting. The house to-day is more or less as it was when old Sir John, then aged eighty-four, departed this life in the year that Queen Victoria ascended the throne.

When the front door of No 13 is opened by the " man-servant ", as he is called in the Soane Museum " Regulations ", you slip back for a century and more. No motor-cars are spinning round Lincoln's Inn Fields, there is no electric light, there are no such fantasies as radio, and no movies absorb the leisure of mankind. The cultivated world, of which this London house is a tiny preserved fragment, is still enchanted by the glory that was Greece and the grandeur that was Rome. Mr Wood had recently explored Palmyra and Baalbec, and his weighty tomes were to inspire the architects of banks and town halls for generations to come; Stuart and Revett's *Athens* was practically a new book, and so was the description of Diocletian's Palace by the Adam Brothers.

And in this pleasant house, so full of the cultured enthusiasm of that time, where the twittering of the London sparrows sounds now just as it did when Sir John came down to breakfast amid his intaglios, his bustos, his bas-reliefs, we seem to have strayed into a more comfortable world than ours. Sir John's interest in ruined cities and dead civilisations was purely academic; ours, unfortunately, is not. How interesting it would be to take Sir John down Cheapside to Milk Street and to point out the ruins of London.

It is fascinating to wander upstairs and down and to note what a mass of things an intelligent, curious man who lives to be eighty-four can accumulate in his time. At what point collecting becomes a mania, I do not know, perhaps from the first moment you begin to collect; but I do know that there comes a time when many a collector suddenly loses faith and asks himself if it is really worth it. But this could never have happened to Sir John! No man of to-day, and certainly no woman, would tolerate the invasion of a home by so many disturbing objects, but in the days of the cognoscenti and the dilettanti it was the thing to do.

Sir John, of course, assembled together a number of things which were of more interest to his generation than to ours, but one thing he collected cannot fail to delight us. In a special room you will find the eight original canvases of Hogarth's *Rake's Progress*. These pictures alone are worth a visit to No 13. The well-known engravings of this celebrated drama give no idea of Hogarth's superb skill as a painter, and to examine the originals, with their fresh and lovely colouring, is to see this work for the first time.

I suppose if this series of eight pictures were to be put up to auction to-day they would fetch a fabulous sum of money, yet in his lifetime, although he could sell his prints, Hogarth was embittered by his difficulty in finding purchasers for his magnificent originals. But perhaps it was only natural that his age should have shrunk from seeing itself through such penetrating eyes. What habitué, for instance, of the *Rose Tavern* in Covent Garden would have cared to contemplate plate four of this series, which shows the Rake at his worst? Distance had to lend a little archæological enchantment before Hogarth could be considered as a painter and not as a critic.

The *Rake's Progress* was ultimately bought by William Beckford and taken by him to his fantastic Gothic pile, Fonthill Abbey, and Soane bought the pictures for four hundred and seventy guineas at Christie's in 1802. Another fine Hogarth series is to be seen in this room—*The Election.*

These four pictures, for which Hogarth wanted two hundred pounds that no one would give, were raffled by the artist, and among those who took a ticket was Garrick. As he was walking away, Garrick began to think what an injustice he had done a great artist and, returning, gave him two hundred pounds for them. When Mrs Garrick's possessions were sold in 1823, Soane gave one thousand, six hundred and fifty guineas for the four pictures.

Over the mantelpiece in the north drawing-room is a portrait of two good-looking young men, John and George, the architect's two sons. John, the elder, died at the age of thirty-six, having written a great number of novels and plays which no one to-day has ever heard of, and with his surviving son Soane maintained a savage and implacable feud, even declining a baronetcy, it is said, and accepting a knighthood so that his son should not inherit the title. So, successful as Sir John appeared to his contemporaries, and opulent as he obviously was, the old house in Lincoln's Inn Fields, in spite of all its treasures, relics and curiosities, could not have been as happy as we imagine it ought to have been, when we stray into it for a moment to enjoy the peace of another age.

§ 7

After one of those blazing weeks which swoop out of the Atlantic in summer and turn London into an inferno which flattens out all the visitors from the tropics, I thought I would spend a day on the Thames. Many other people had had the same idea, with the result that long queues were waiting at Westminster Pier, in the shadow of the Houses of Parliament.

I asked at the ticket office if they could put me down at Cherry Garden Pier, Bermondsey, and an obliging young skipper said that, although he was going to Greenwich, he would turn aside and do this for me.

The boat was loaded with provincial and other visitors, the men in shirt sleeves, the women fanning themselves with newspapers, and off we went down the Thames, admiring the sweep of the Embankment and the distant dome of St Paul's, which we could see riding above the City in the sunlight. The criticism, so often heard, that we do not make sufficient use of the Thames seemed hardly justified that morning, for the river was alive with motor-boats, all of them loaded to capacity. Though the Thames may have been London's chief highway in past centuries, it was much less visible to Londoners then than it is to us to-day. Instead of the Thames Embankment, which now gives us an uninterrupted view of the river from Westminster to Blackfriars, the crowded streets of old London ended in water-steps, and the river was not visible until one was almost in it.

One of the first impressions of the French traveller, Peter John Grosley, when he visited London in 1765, was the difficulty of getting a clear view of the Thames " unless I entered the houses and manufactories which stand close to the river ". Grosley, some of whose criticisms were amusing, gave as his reason for London's reluctance to open up the river, " the natural bent of the English, and in particular of the people of London, to suicide," which he attributed to

" the melancholy which predominates in their constitutions ". We know, of course, that the invisibility of the Thames in former times was due to the congestion of buildings on the water's edge, many of them ancient wharves which had a definite function in life. The Southwark bank from Waterloo Bridge onwards is very like the opposite bank before the Thames Embankment was made.

As we went on, passing beneath Blackfriars, Southwark, and London bridges, we sat back and picked out the landmarks, and noted how many warehouses, gloomy and shattered, turned their glassless windows to the river, as they have done since the night they were bombed.

As the Thames became wider and the buildings upon its banks more grim and gloomy, we came to Cherry Garden Pier. If you imagine that this place looks as delightful as it sounds, you would be wrong, for it is no longer a pretty orchard as it was in the time of Pepys, but a floating pier enclosed by tall brick warehouses.

The Borough of Bermondsey, which lies at the back, and its companion Rotherhithe, are almost splendid in their uniform and massive air of gloom and squalor. Yet of all the riverside boroughs I know, I like Bermondsey the best, and if I had to live in one, I would choose Bermondsey, as long as I could find somewhere within sight of the Thames. Bermondsey has a queer attractiveness which some people have claimed to discover in Limehouse, and this is so in spite of the miles of shabby little streets, the warrens of small, smoke-stained houses, the hideous little prison-like blocks of flats, and the long roads on which the buses speed, bearing brighter names upon their indication boards. I may feel like this because the memory of old Bermondsey and its Abbey comes between me and reality, perhaps because I have met such nice people in Bermondsey, some of whom, no doubt, in escape from the present, are enthralled by the history of their borough.

All the beauty of Bermondsey is now confined to a few street names, such as Cherry Garden, Crucifix Lane, which commemorates the Holy Rood of the vanished Abbey, and Jamaica Road, which reminds one of the place of entertainment which Pepys used to visit. Spa Road might seem to strike a note of the highest improbability in such surroundings, but it really does commemorate a little spa, with a chalybeate spring in the centre, which was opened about 1770 by Thomas Keyse, the artist. It was so popular for a short time that people used to go down by boat from London to drink tea there and watch the fireworks. It hardly seems possible that a district once so lovely should have become so grim and so pointlessly ugly.

There is, however, one place in Bermondsey which is still entirely satisfactory. This is the *Angel Inn*, to which I was going. I know no better place in London for luncheon on a hot day, but it is a good idea first to make sure that the tide will be high. The *Angel* is said to be the oldest inn on this bank of the Thames, and I should not be surprised to know that it welcomed visitors to the Abbey in mediæval and Tudor times. I also have an idea that the adequate cellars must have seen many a cargo that never paid duty.

Behind the bar there is a small room overlooking the river where Mrs Reeve, the proprietress, gives luncheon to a few people who work in the neighbourhood. It is very cheerful and pleasant, and after lunch you can carry a cup of coffee to a little wooden balcony that overhangs the river. When you look towards London you see Tower Bridge, and, behind it, the roofs and spires of the City. They say that Turner came to the *Angel* and sat on this balcony when he was painting the *Fighting Téméraire*, which was broken up at a nearby yard; and I was told that he painted another picture on the balcony, which is now in Boston, Mass.

I sat watching the tugs with their barges come up on the tide like ducks escorting their ducklings. Now and then a queerly shaped coal-boat swept past with a cargo for the Gas, Light and Coke Company, to be followed by a Danish cargo-boat; then, with the tide rising, came a variety of craft, all making for the Pool of London, and putting up a wash that set the motor-boats dancing, and ended in a series of playful smacks against the walls of the *Angel*.

Seeing a police boat shoot out from the opposite bank, I realised that I was looking at Wapping Police Station, the headquarters of that admirable force, the River Police.

I remembered the many exciting nights I had spent in past years with the river patrols of this force. On many an autumn night I have gone down to Wapping while a river mist wreathed itself over the Thames, and have seen a side of London life of which we who live on the banks of the river know nothing. The river folk have a London of their own, with its own traditions and even its own vocabulary.

All Londoners may not know that the River Police are the senior branch of the Metropolitan Police and were at work more than thirty years before the Metropolitan Police Force was formed. Their founder was a Scot from Dumbarton, on the Clyde, a man named Patrick Colquhoun, who came to London in 1789 and became a magistrate. In those days it was estimated that of thirty-seven thousand men employed on the Thames, eleven thousand were either thieves or receivers of stolen property. The West India merchants considered themselves fortunate if only half their cargoes saw the inside of a warehouse.

This shocking state of affairs interested Colquhoun, who studied the methods of the river gangs and wrote a treatise which so impressed the West India merchants that they asked him to form a police force. This he did by recruiting old sailors and watermen who knew the Thames and its personalities inside out. They were given long-oared gigs and were armed with cutlasses and blunderbuses. Within a year they had broken up the gangs.

The modern Thames policeman has the last word in equipment. His patrol-boat is the fastest motor-boat on the Thames. It is fitted with a two-way radio telephone set, and on the roof is a searchlight which can suddenly be switched on with terrifying success late at night if any suspicious movement is seen on barge or lighter. They also carry rocket rescue gear, stretchers and a first-aid kit.

The Thames police saw the Blitz from the river, and a fearful sight it was when rows of warehouses were on fire. Their nights were spent in putting out fires, in chasing blazing barges, which were sometimes swept out to sea on the tide, to return, still blazing, on the next one; and in rescuing people who were trapped on the river banks by the flames.

I thought I would go over and look at Limehouse, which I had not seen since the War. There was a young man with a motor-boat at the pier who said he would take me across the river, and we were soon exploding over to the Wapping bank. The Tunnel Pier at Wapping marks the site of Execution Dock, where pirates were hanged in the old days. After they had been cut down from the gallows, their bodies were hung in an iron cage, which was placed in the river where it had to remain until three tides had covered it.

Captain Kidd met this horrible end after an unsuccessful attempt had been made to hang him with a faulty rope. The editors of the *Newgate Calendar* added a pained footnote to their account of his death. " In cases of this distressing nature," they wrote, " and which hath often happened to the miserable sufferer, the sheriff ought to be punished. It is his duty to carry the sentence of law into execution, and there can be no plea for not providing a rope of sufficient strength."

We entered Shadwell Basin, and I saw the narrow and always rather tempting entrance to the Regent's Canal, then the river straightened out towards Limehouse Reach and I stepped ashore at the pier.

Walking towards the Causeway, I saw at a glance that Limehouse has had its full share of bombs. Hundreds of terrible little houses had been swept away and an energetic local authority, or perhaps the London County Council, had already erected several large and shining blocks of flats, every flat apparently occupied.

I met at a street corner two tough old salts, and I told them what a great difference I noticed since I was last there, and how glad I was to see such fine blocks of flats. One of the men gave me a glance of the deepest contempt, and the other removed the pipe from his mouth, spat angrily, and said they weren't a patch on the good old houses with their back gardens where the kids could play.

" And stairs," he said angrily, " always blinkin' stairs ! "

I tried to put in a good word for the flats, but he told me they might be all right for some folks, but as far as he was concerned anybody could have the flats and their baths and their " ruddy little window-boxes ".

"No place for the kids to play, yer see," put in the other man.

I again defended the flats.

"T'ain't the same, guv'nor, t'ain't the same," he said.

And I went on feeling that the reformer must have a difficult task in Limehouse. I passed many dreadful little early Nineteenth Century houses, the lowest form of Regency, where front doors opened to a staircase and a Hogarthian vista of kitchens draped with drying clothes. There was a pleasant-looking woman standing on a doorstep.

"You must be longing for them to pull down this old place and give you one of the nice new flats," I said.

She inspected me cautiously.

"No, I'm not from the Council," I said.

"Me want a flat?" she echoed. "Not 'arf, I don't think. And pull down this 'ouse? What's the matter with it? There's been too much pullin' down, if you ask me."

And, with superb Cockney irony, she nodded over to a great gash of blitz damage.

I walked on towards Pennyfields. I was interested in this street once, and knew several Chinamen who lived there, all well-mannered, rather fastidious men, who, if they had to stick a knife in you, would have taken care to apologise beforehand. Those were the days when fan-tan was played in most of the ground floors of Pennyfields, but upstairs there were extraordinary contrasts. It was always surprising to climb up a creaking, uncarpeted stair in pitch darkness and to enter a well-lit, over-furnished and over-heated room, dotted with every kind of knick-knack, where some blowsy little Cockney woman was sitting on a couch like an Eastern beauty, eating chocolates or smoking a cigarette. Many of the Chinamen were married to Englishwomen and some, I was told, lavished all their money on them.

As I walked on, I saw that Pennyfields has changed since those times. I saw only two Chinamen, and they looked like birds of passage.

"What has happened to Chinatown?" I asked a woman who was coming out of a house lower down Pennyfields.

"They've all gone to Liverpool," she replied.

She then told me that she had lived in Limehouse for forty years, that Limehouse never was what it had been cracked up to be, that it had always been a pretty ordinary sort of place, that when she was a little girl all the houses in Pennyfields were occupied by sea-captains and people who had something to do with the docks. Then the Chinamen came. And now the Chinamen had gone.

I walked back up the East India Dock Road and caught a bus back to London. But then what, I asked myself, is London? To me, London is one thing; but to the inhabitants of Bermondsey, Wapping, Stepney and Poplar it is quite another. There are hundreds of Londons, all of them equally real to those who live in them.

§ 8

London is really only a series of submerged villages. Buried away beneath the flood of bricks and mortar are still many clearly defined village streets. Marylebone High Street is a good example. Chelsea retains many obvious village characteristics, and you could probably discover them in Hammersmith, and certainly in Chiswick. After all, it is not a long time since hundreds of places now on the General Omnibus routes were approached by green lanes and afforded pleasant country rambles to the citizens of the Eighteenth Century.

The great flood which has caused London to become a huge, incoherent, sprawling mass of streets and buildings took place only in the Nineteenth Century; but it is still going on. The red buses are spinning farther and farther into the country, the Tube and the Underground throw out a new, remote tentacle from time to time, and gradually a far-off village grows into a suburb.

The village mentality of so many Londoners was encountered by those whose task it was to send people into safe areas during the last War, and some officials were surprised by the strength of local association and by the fact that to thousands of people London means only a few familiar streets and shops, a cinema and a public-house. Camberwell has no sense of kinship with Highgate, or Lambeth with Hoxton.

And at the core of these boroughs is a village-like tradition and prejudice and a dislike of outside things.

The speed with which, during a lull in the bombing, people rushed back to " dear old London ", leaving without regret infinitely more pleasant surroundings, proved how strong is the pull of even the less attractive portions of London upon those familiar with them.

Whenever I think of these villagers I remember Elsie. She is a small, elderly charwoman or daily help. Before the War she used to delight me with her unfailingly gloomy view of life. She was not exactly a pessimist, but rather a sardonic philosopher, which, I think, is not an unusual Cockney attitude. Her little world was a street or two off the King's Road, Chelsea, and everything that happened in these few hundred yards came to Elsie's ears.

" You mark my words, sir, no good'll come of it," she used to say about events and actions which I thought held every prospect of hope and optimism. I used to wonder whether she might not be an extreme throw-back to the Puritan period. Her sense of evil lurking everywhere, even in the most innocent places, amounted to an obsession.

When the War came, I thought that Elsie would turn into a latter-day Solomon Eagle and go crying doom through the streets of London. But, extraordinary to relate, the worse things became the brighter became Elsie. She was convinced that Hitler felt a personal animosity for those who lived in the King's Road. When the house next door was gutted and an evacuation officer tried to persuade her to go into Hampshire, Elsie was curt to him. " What's good enough for the King is good enough for yours truly," she said sharply. " I'm not leavin' London for you, Hitler, nor nobody. . . ."

And she didn't. But she was nearly killed on several occasions, each one of which I am convinced she thoroughly enjoyed. The bliss of martyrdom had been added to the satisfaction of the successful prophet.

After the War, Elsie, now rather battered, was persuaded to go and spend a fortnight with her daughter, Muriel, who was nanny to a family in the country. It then transpired that Elsie had never before left Chelsea, except for one brief moment in an improbable youth, when she claimed to have spent a week-end at Margate. But, strange to say, she was looking forward to her visit to Sussex, and the day came when she said good-bye to all her friends and departed as if she were bound for the Great Wall of China. In three days she was back in the King's Road.

"I couldn't abide it," she said. "It was awful! I might have known that no good would come of it. I couldn't stick that there silence, and the darkness. It was 'orrible, that's what it was. An' there were owls 'ootin'. One 'ooted right under my bedroom window and give me the shivers. An' there was bats too—just imagine it! Bats! So I says to my Muriel, I says, 'Muriel, it's me that's goin' bats unless I can 'ear the traffic in the dear old King's Road again. I can't stick it a day more.' An' 'ere I am . . ."

And deep down in that sombre old heart, Elsie, moving about Chelsea again, going home at night to one room and a kitchen, both blasted by bombs, was happy. She was also typical of many thousands of Londoners. And I have often thought, when looking at the tunic of a general, that Elsie deserves one of those little strips of coloured ribbon.

CHAPTER SIX

I turn on the Fountains in Trafalgar Square, take a walk down Whitehall, see the skeleton of Napoleon's charger, Marengo, contemplate the site of the execution of Charles I and consider the problems associated with his death and burial, see the Changing of the King's Guard, remember George Downing of Downing Street and come to the site of Whitehall Palace.

§ 1

I LIKE nothing better than to meet the men who attend to London, who sweep the streets, patrol the sewers, turn the lights on and off, and perform the hundred and one acts which we accept as a matter of course. Consider Trafalgar Square. At ten o'clock every morning in summer you will see the fountains suddenly lift themselves into the air, and at four in the afternoon you will see the jets collapse and fall. This is not an act of Nature, as many Londoners may imagine: it is an act performed by a man who is paid for doing it, who probably enjoys doing it—for who doesn't love to switch on a fountain?—and to him probably the fountains in Trafalgar Square have personal peculiarities unknown to anyone else in the metropolis.

Shortly before ten o'clock I met an official of the Ministry of Works, who took me to the underground room beneath Trafalgar Square from which the fountains are controlled. You get down to it as if you were going to the Tube. The iron door was opened by a man in dungarees who was bustling about in what looked like a miniature engine-room in a liner. There were white pipes all round it, electrical switches and control-boards, dials and valves. "Cascade West Basin", I read over one of the valves.

I was told all sorts of technical details. The main pump that drives the two chief jets is a hundred-horse-power motor, another, of eighty-two horse-power, drives the bronze groups of statuary, and a third, of seventy-one horse-power, drives the basin overflow.

The pumps are so powerful that they can never be driven flat out.

" At a hundred and twenty feet," I was told, " the jets are nearly as high as the dome of the National Gallery. Even at forty feet, if a wind is blowing, the square is drenched in spray, and we get complaints from the public, the police and the London County Council."

The engineer looked at the clock. It was a minute to ten.

" Would you like to turn on one of the fountains? "

" Me? I should be thrilled."

I took a wheel and revolved it.

" Easy, not too hard over, or you'll drench the square! "

The control-room began to roar with sound, just like the noise of a liner's turbines. I longed to dash out and see what I had done to London that morning! The pigeons would be flying in alarm round Nelson's Column, children would be saying, " Oh, Mummy, look at the fountains! ", and all kinds of people on foot, on buses, in taxis, would be admiring the lovely column of water I had put up for them.

Eventually we went up and had a look at the square. It was just as I had imagined. The pigeons were settling down again, the crowds were admiring the fountains, a slight wind was blowing the spray back, wetting the pavement.

" Five feet lower! " muttered the engineer, and disappeared.

The addition of the two bronze groups at each end of the two fountains is a post-war improvement. These groups were cast before the War and were stored. The group on the right, as you face the National Gallery, is the work of Mr William Macmillan, who designed the Great War Medal and the Victory Medal, and shows a mermaid and a merman mounted on a dolphin, holding sharks from whose mouths pour powerful jets of water. The other group is the work of Mr Charles Wheeler, and also shows a mermaid and a merman, a mer-child, and sharks.

England is not a land of fountains, and the sound of falling water rarely rouses much enthusiasm in the British heart, but the fountains in Trafalgar Square, and their beautiful bronze groups—quite the finest works of their kind in the capital—have a place in the affections of Londoners, and compose a picture which is known all over the world.

Few London improvements have been so acidly criticised as Trafalgar Square. Some of our Victorian ancestors could see nothing right about it. Sir Robert Peel called the square the " finest site in Europe " (which is not true), but this was almost the only generous remark made about it in its youth. The National Gallery, which to-day we think is such a charming and dignified background, was called the " National Pepper-pot ", and was considered a piece of unworthy and effeminate architecture. Then the idea of hoisting Nelson aloft on the top of a column struck the critics as ridiculous and fantastic. The statue of Nelson was called a " hideous caricature ", which those who have taken the trouble to examine him with the help of field-glasses must think a trifle unjust. It is, as a matter of fact, an admirable likeness of Nelson. I wonder how many of the millions who see the statue in the course of a week could tell you the name of the man who carved it. He was Edward Hodges Baily, a poor Bristol boy whose father carved figure-heads for ships. The lad inherited a talent for sculpture, and worked for a time with Flaxman. He became one of the best sculptors of the Nineteenth Century, and lived so long that, although he was nearly fifty when he carved Nelson, he lived for thirty years after Trafalgar Square was completed.

The huge bronze capital on which Nelson stands is made from the guns of the *Royal George*, and the four bronze reliefs round the base of the column are the metal of French cannon captured during Nelson's sea battles. But I think the most interesting objects in the square are two octagonal lanterns mounted on masonry columns at the corners. They are old oil-lanterns from the *Victory*. Few people in London, except, presumably, the lamplighters, who call them the " Battle Lamps " and get extra pay for cleaning them, know what they are. It was a romantic thought to place in Trafalgar Square two lanterns by whose light Nelson must often have walked the deck of his flagship at night.

Another feature of Trafalgar Square which few people notice are the strips of brass let into the granite on the National Gallery side of the square. These are the official imperial measures from an inch to a hundred feet. If you are ever in doubt about the precise measurement of a yard or a foot, you can go to Trafalgar Square and check up in an instant. On the many occasions when I have wandered about the Square, I have never observed anyone doing this. I always look, in the hope of finding some anxious draper making sure that his yard-stick is in order.

The creation of Trafalgar Square removed from the face of London a mass of old buildings, including one of great interest, the Royal Mews. The word " mews " has nothing to do with horses. It is a word that was applied in ancient times to the cages in which hawks were kept when they were moulting or mewing. The Kings of England kept their hawks at Charing from Plantagenet times onward, and few of us who use the royal parks to-day realise that the mediæval passion for falconry is one of the reasons why London has so much real country in her centre. In the reign of Henry VIII there was a fire in the royal stables at Bloomsbury, the hawks were removed and the horses stabled in the Royal Mews. They continued to be kept there and, in some extraordinary way, the word properly associated only with falconry became applied to stables.

Hawks are not the only birds associated with Trafalgar Square. It seemed to me, as I watched the crowds of visitors who were feeding the pigeons and the numerous men who find it worth while to go there day after day and sell bags of dried peas, that the Trafalgar Square pigeons are now not only more numerous but also more popular than the pigeons of St Paul's.

I had never given a thought to the origin of the London pigeon until I read in R. S. R. Fitter's *Natural History of London* that they are probably descended from birds which escaped from mediæval dovecotes. Mr Fitter says that semi-wild pigeons were noted as building their nests in London as early as 1385. Their modern descendants " treat the towering buildings of modern London as cliffs, thereby giving an additional indication of their descent from the wild rock-doves (*Columba livia*) that stlll frequent our north-western coasts ".

Mr Fitter thinks that the pigeon has been unfairly treated by most writers on the birds of London, who have either ignored it or denied it full status as a Londoner. " While it may well be that the stock is constantly being reinforced by fresh escapes from pigeon-lofts round London, there can be no doubt at all," he writes, " that for more than five centuries pigeons have been living in London in as near a feral condition as is possible for any bird living in a great city."

The London pigeon, he notes, has not yet established its type, but is a hotch-potch of various domestic strains, and he thinks that the amount of white in the plumage is decreasing, and that the whole pigeon population is gradually reverting to something like the original rock-dove colouring.

On autumn evenings, as twilight is falling, the twittering of thousands of starlings sounds above the roar of the traffic in Trafalgar Square. Hearing this sound, I have stopped many a time to watch the extraordinary sight of these birds arriving back in London after a day's foraging in the country. They sweep in sometimes in enormous flocks, sometimes a few hundred at a time, and scatter over the Nelson Column, the National Gallery and St Martin-in-the-Fields—wherever they can find a nook or cranny or a convenient acanthus capital. They chatter brightly and restlessly, and take a long time to settle down. Sometimes one will detach itself and go elsewhere, which seems to infect its companions with restlessness, for they peel off the National Gallery and fly to the trees, to the Nelson Column, to St Martin's, apparently without any discoverable purpose unless it may be to impart a final scrap of shrill scandal to some bedfellow before darkness falls. Their vitality is appalling. You would never think that these birds have done a hard day's hunting perhaps twenty miles away in the outer suburbs. Gradually, as darkness falls, silence and immobility are at length achieved, and, glancing up, it is difficult to believe that thousands of glossy, talkative birds are hiding in the very centre of London.

Unlike the pigeons, which have a long London ancestry, the starlings are new arrivals. Until the first War their roosts were in the parks, then, at some period which has not been recorded—certainly by 1917—they began to invade London buildings, notably St Paul's, the British Museum and the National Gallery. Now the starling is everywhere. He has become part of London's twilight. His bright chatter is so much a part of Trafalgar Square that it is difficult to imagine that he was not always there.

§ 2

A visit to a picture gallery is to many people a solemn act of penance. You can see them painfully working their way from old master to old master, catalogue in hand, their feet becoming wearier from room to room; and why is it, I wonder, that a visit to a picture gallery can be more physically exhausting than a ten-mile walk? You may imagine that I am not fond of picture galleries, which is not so. I love pictures, but I prefer to see them singly or in ones and two's, and then only when I have an overwhelming desire to see them as one might wish to look at the face of an old friend.

I have spent hours of happiness in the National Gallery, hours which I shall never forget; and I regard as one of the delights of life in London the knowledge that the great treasury of the world's masterpieces in Trafalgar Square is always there ready to be visited.

I may not go there for months, but sure enough one day the memory of a picture will sail suddenly and unexpectedly into my mind, probably in that delightful moment of the day between sleeping and awaking. At first it will be a hazy memory, then it will become clear in line and colour, but there will always be something missing, something that has escaped me. Is the colour blue or grey? Is the woman wearing a black skirt with white fur or a white skirt with black fur. Is it a cat or a dog that is coming round the corner? I must go and find out.

Someday I may say to myself, "I must go and see the 'Rokeby' *Venus*", or it may be Botticelli's *Madonna*, Vermeer's *Lady with a Spinet*, Hobbema's *Avenue* or Hogarth's wonderful *Shrimp Girl*. It may be a Velazquez, a Titian, a Turner or a Rembrandt.

This appointment with a picture fills the day with excitement, and at last the moment comes when I mount the steps of the National Gallery and make straight for the room in which it hangs. That is the way I like to look at pictures. Sometimes a Sargent has taken me to the Tate Gallery, or Gainsborough's " Perdita " Robinson to the Wallace Collection, and I must admit that such assignations have often been more satisfying than an appointment with a living person.

Our beautifully chosen and displayed National Gallery began in a casual way a little over a century ago. At the age of fourteen a boy called John Julius Angerstein, of German–Russian parentage, came to this country and worked in the City. At twenty-one he was an underwriter at Lloyds, which was still a coffee-house, and it was largely due to his influence and foresight that the modern Lloyds was established. Angerstein made a large fortune. He was not only a business genius but also an honest and cultivated man. His hobby was the collection of pictures, in which he was assisted by Sir Thomas Lawrence and Benjamin West. When he died at an advanced age in 1803 his will directed the sale of his collection. For some time the idea of a national gallery of art had been in the air and the Government bought the Angerstein pictures for £57,000. There were thirty-eight of them including the *Raising of Lazarus* by Sebastian del Piombo, the *Venus and Adonis* by Titian, the delightful little *Bacchus and Silenus* by Carrachi, the *Woman taken in Adultery* and the *Adoration of the Shepherds*, both by Rembrandt. There was also Hogarth's *Marriage-à-la-Mode*, which is now to be seen in the Tate Gallery.

It was a humble beginning. The pictures were first shown in Pall Mall and then in the present building. It is a curious commentary upon the change in London during the past century that the early reports of the Trustees stress that the dirt and grime that collected upon the canvases was due to the amount of mud and filth brought into the building by visitors, by the enormous number of unwashed loungers who sought refuge in the Gallery on the first sign of rain, and to the amount of coal smoke in the atmosphere.

The first National Gallery storm was caused by the cleaning of the pictures in 1846, a storm that was repeated during another clean-up in 1853. It is interesting to compare the violent press attack upon the cleaners, in which Ruskin joined, with the criticisms recently directed at those who since the War have restored and cleaned the old masters.

During the first cleaning Ruskin wrote of " dust an inch thick accumulated upon the frames in the course of the day " (surely a slight exaggeration, even in an age of coal fires?) and of " darkness closing over the canvas like a curtain ", which he attributed to " the influence on floor and air of the ' mutable rank-scented many ' ". Like many modern critics, Ruskin asked whether the process of cleaning " had not been carried perilously far, and whether in future simpler and safer means may not be adopted to remove the coat of dust and smoke?"

At the back of the National Gallery, in St Martin's Place, is the National Portrait Gallery, a collection of over three thousand portraits of the great men and women of British history. It is arranged in chronological order and the thing to do is to go straight up to the top floor, where the earliest portraits are arranged, and work one's way down through the centuries.

Eminence in any walk of life, and death, are the only qualifications for inclusion in this gallery. No living person, except members of the Royal Family, are allowed a place in it. Artistic merit does not matter either. The portrait must be a good likeness, and from the point of view of the National Portrait Gallery an amateur water-colour may be as valuable as a Gainsborough or a Van Dyck. The earliest portraits are of the Tudor period. There is a revealing picture of Henry VII, who has the expression of a money-lender, and another of Henry VIII with his slanting eyes and his little self-indulgent and self-willed mouth. Anne Boleyn has not been flattered by the only portrait of her in the gallery, neither has Catherine of Aragon. Bloody Mary, on the other hand, looks charming.

There is a grand portrait of Charles II, and a delightful one of Nell Gwyn. Boswell and Johnson are both seen as they appeared to their friend Sir Joshua Reynolds. Nelson's portrait by Abbott, and Emma Hamilton by Romney, are two of the treasures. There is a drawing of Florence Nightingale and a photograph of Mrs Beeton, who wrote the cookery book, the only photograph, I think, in the gallery.

§ 3

Most Londoners will probably agree that unless you are going to enlist in the Army, or unless you are a Government official, or a soldier on leave, or are on your way to show a provincial relative the Horse Guards and the Cenotaph, you do not often walk down Whitehall. You may rush down it in a bus on your way to Waterloo or Victoria, or you may flash past in a taxi-cab, but you do not often stroll along it.

But the other morning I was quietly walking down Whitehall, and in a few minutes I found myself looking at the skeleton of Napoleon's charger, Marengo. That is the fantastic sort of thing that can happen to you in London. I had no idea that I was going to do this. It just happened.

In Whitehall, on the left going towards Westminster, is the most surprisingly housed museum in the world. It is called the Royal United Service Museum. It is the only museum I can recollect which puts samples of its wares in the window. Each window contains one exhibit in the best Bond Street manner: a shark's head, a full-dress foreign uniform, two or three realistic little battle-scenes cut from cardboard; and beside the entrance leans the painted figure-head of a ship of the line.

The museum is housed in all that now remains of the ancient Palace of Whitehall—the great Banqueting Hall which James I built for happy occasions, with no idea that his son, Charles, would step from one of the windows to the scaffold. It is, after Westminster Hall, the most splendid building of its kind in London. It is so magnificent that one resents the mass of things which congest and crowd it: the glass cases, the models, and especially the innumerable flags which obscure the noble proportions of the building.

Rubens painted for it a superb ceiling showing James I being received among the gods of pagan antiquity. It is all so splendidly painted and so full of movement and vigour that it does not occur to one at the time to wonder what Minerva, for instance, or Hercules, would have made of James I. It is pathetic, in view of the later history of this hall, that young Prince Charles should be shown on this ceiling as a little naked boy supported by various mighty allegorical figures, while his father, throned, points to him approvingly.

It is difficult in such a room to give your attention to glass cases, but it should be done, for the museum is full of interesting relics. It is a museum which every schoolboy in England should know. Here are souvenirs picked up on the battlefields from Crecy to Alamein. Here are to be seen hasty pencil-scrawls ordering cavalry divisions to advance. Here are bullets that killed heroes. Here are fragments from ships whose names come gloriously to us out of the smoke of ancient battles. Here are swords and pistols and scalping-knives, helmets, sabretaches and epaulettes, saddles, spurs, drums, lances, despatch boxes, trumpets, bugles, scimitars—all the rough material of romance.

The museum is a complete record of military and naval events from ancient times until "D" Day in 1944. There is even a case of 1939–45 War Relics, and a series of beautifully painted dioramas arranged in historical sequence, showing battles beginning with Norman times and ending in the landing of British and Allied troops on the Normandy beaches, and a dramatic and realistic air battle.

I walked round with the feeling that the American is not really, as most of us imagine, the perfect souvenir-hunter. For centuries the British soldier and sailor have ever been on the look-out for relics. One has a vision of enterprising soldiers going round after every battle, determined to pick up something to send home to mother. After Waterloo, Surgeon-Major Sir William Whymper set an exceedingly high standard by annexing the chain of the garden gate of Hougomont! There is a certain pathos in these military relics, possibly because the lustre fades so swiftly from the reputation of a soldier.

This passionate instinct to preserve anything that may be connected with a national hero almost reaches its limit with "Bottle of Port, being a portion of Lord Nelson's cellar in H.M.S. *Victory* during the Battle of Trafalgar". So this perishable thing, this bottle of port, survived Trafalgar, and poor Nelson did not! Then we have "some of the spirit in which Lord Nelson's body was preserved on board H.M.S. *Victory* during her voyage home"; or this: "Umbrella used by the Duke of Wellington".

As I was wandering round this queer, fascinating and entirely absorbing museum I came face to face with Marengo. Now, Marengo was a light-grey barb, fourteen hands and one inch high, which Napoleon bought in Egypt after the Battle of Aboukir. He became his favourite charger. Napoleon rode this horse at the Battle of Marengo, which explains his name. Marengo carried his master at Jena, Wagram and during the retreat from Moscow. We have all seen Vernet's picture of Napoleon crossing the Alps on this horse.

But, alas, Marengo, who in his time trotted so importantly across the map of Europe, is now a skeleton. He stands on horrid tip-toe in a glass case. You look at his skull and his brown ribs, and at the little bits of metal which hold him together, and feel sorry that he could not have been decently buried; for he is a distressing sight. No matter what future generations may say of a soldier, surely his horse is always above criticism.

Marengo was wounded at Waterloo, and after Napoleon's capture became the property of Lord Petre. He was then sold to General Angerstein, who kept him at Ely and bred from him. Marengo was carefully tended in his old age, and when he died snuff-boxes were made from two of his hoofs—one of them is used to-day in the guard-room at St James's Palace—and his skeleton was unfortunately preserved.

Looking at poor Marengo now, there galloped through my mind a number of horses famous in legend, literature and history, who still remain beautiful because they were never seen as bones. There was El Borak, the horse which took the

Prophet into the Seventh Heaven, and Bucephalus, the horse which only Alexander the Great could mount; Pegasus, the winged steed of Apollo; Zanthus, the steed of Achilles; Incitatus, the horse that the mad Caligula made a consul; Lamri and Spumador, King Arthur's steeds; Grani, the horse of Siegfried; Rosabelle, the favourite palfrey of Mary Stuart, and Jenny Geddes, the horse of Robbie Burns. Among the funny, lovable horses, I remembered Rosinante, Don Quixote's charger, and poor scraggy Grizzle, who took Dr Syntax in search of the Picturesque.

They are all real, vivid, alive and beautiful. And so to me, until that moment, was Marengo. Even when some white cab-horse stood stolidly among the fireworks, with an actor on his broad back, during *A Royal Divorce*, the real Marengo could not be injured. His hoofs were too firmly planted in immortal pastures.

I wish they would take his wretched framework to the cellars, and show it only to veterinary surgeons.

§ 4

The scaffold upon which Charles I was beheaded was erected at the sill level of the two lower-floor windows of the Banqueting Hall, near the present entrance to the Museum. At that time—the year 1649—the hall did not stand as it does to-day, in an open street: it was part of a rambling, haphazard jumble of courtyards and buildings of all periods known as Whitehall Palace.

Jutting out from the end of the hall at right angles and closing the view towards Westminster, was an old house with four gables, and next to it was the turreted red-brick gate-house, the Holbein Gate, which was not unlike the gate which can be seen to-day at the bottom of St James's Street. Opposite were more houses. So the scene of the King's execution was that of a cul-de-sac, or a large courtyard.

The deed which took place there sent a shiver of horror through every civilised country in the world, much as the murder of the Czar did in our own time; but the Czar's murder was at least an honest one, and was not hypocritically wrapped up in the farce of a mock trial. In the long record of English tragedy and fortitude there is no nobler death than that of King Charles I. His behaviour during the so-called trial, his courage during his last few days on earth, and his saintly death, converted many around him, who had been his most violent enemies, into friends and partisans.

He was taken under sentence of death to St James's Palace on January 28, 1649, and his execution took place on the 30th. It was a cold January with blue skies and the threat of impending snow. The King was calm and resigned. His wife, Henrietta Maria, whom he loved devotedly, was in France and at that time besieged by the Frondists in the Louvre; she did not hear of his death until a month later. On the 29th, the day before the execution, his two children, Princess Elizabeth, aged fourteen, and Henry, Duke of Gloucester, aged nine, who had fallen into the hands of the Parliamentarians, were allowed to say good-bye to him.

The Princess, who wrote an account of this meeting, burst into tears at the sight of her father. His hair had become almost grey, his beard was untrimmed and his clothes looked neglected. He took the child in his arms and, seating her on his knee, soothed her and calmed her and told her to pay particular attention to what he had to say to her. He asked her not to grieve for him, he commended certain religious books to her, he said that he had forgiven his enemies, he asked her to tell her mother that his thoughts had never strayed from her, he said that he died a martyr and that he did not doubt that God would bestow the throne upon his son, Charles.

"Sweetheart, you'll forget this," said the King.

"No," replied the weeping girl. "I shall never forget this while I live"; and she promised to write down all he had said as soon as possible.

Charles then took his little son upon his knee and said:

"Sweetheart, now they will cut off thy father's head."

The child looked "very steadfastly on him".

"Mark, child, what I say. They will cut off my head, and perhaps make thee a king; but mark what I say: you must not be a king, so long as your brothers Charles and James do live."

The little boy replied, " I will be torn in pieces first."

The King then divided between them the cabinet of jewels he had with him, consisting mostly of broken Garters and Georges, valuable only for the jewels in them; but he said it was all he had to give. He then embraced the weeping children and, anxious to make the parting scene as short as possible, was going into his bedroom when a wail of anguish from Princess Elizabeth brought him back to fold her in his arms and to kiss her wet cheeks. The children were then taken to Syon House.

On the following morning Charles was awake before dawn. Sir Thomas Herbert slept beside him on a pallet, and has left a minute account of these last hours.

" I will now rise," said the King; " I have a great work to do this day."

Herbert dressed the King's hair, and was told to make it trim. Charles asked for an extra shirt, because the weather was so bitterly cold that he might shiver, and, seeing him, his enemies would attribute it to fear.

" Death is not terrible to me," he added.

Old Bishop Juxon arrived with daylight, and he and the King went apart and prayed. Some say at eight o'clock, some ten, the King left St James's for Whitehall. He said a brisk walk across the park would warm him and help to circulate his blood. He wore a long black cloak, a waistcoat of red striped silk, and grey stockings. He wore upon his breast the Star of the Order of the Garter. The route was lined by troops, and a company of halberdiers went in front and followed behind, with banners and drums beating, so that it was difficult to talk. On the King's right walked Bishop Juxon, and on the left, bareheaded, a Cromwellian soldier named Colonel Tomlinson. As they were passing through the park at a quick pace set by the King, Charles pointed to a certain tree and said that it had been planted by his brother Henry.

Upon arriving at Whitehall, the King was taken to his usual bedchamber. Even at this last hour, although Charles was unaware of it, the warrant to the executioner for his execution had not been signed. While Charles was taking Holy

Communion, Cromwell, with jests and horseplay, was trying to cajole two of his commanders to sign it; one of them, a Colonel Huncks, had changed his whole point of view after having been in personal contact with the King. Eventually substitutes were found and, with the ink not yet dry upon the warrant, King Charles was summoned to death. It was then about one o'clock.

The King had been persuaded by the Bishop to eat some bread and drink a glass of claret. When the summons came, Charles walked with calm dignity through the palace galleries, between a line of soldiers who held back a silent crowd come to witness what Herbert, who was there, called " the saddest sight that England ever saw ".

The way led across the floor of the Banqueting Hall—that hall where to-day people gaze earnestly into glass cases—and to the northern end, where a lean-to building occupied the site of the modern entrance door. Through a window of this building, or an embrasure made in its wall, Charles stepped into the cold air of a January afternoon and to a scaffold draped all in black.

Among the large and horrified crowds who packed the roadway towards Charing Cross, and stood wherever possible behind the soldiers round about the scaffold, was a boy of fifteen, who was to live to tell us what life was like in the reign of Charles II—Samuel Pepys. Believing that the King might refuse to bow his head to the block, the executioners had fixed two iron rings to the foot of the scaffold, through which a cord was passed, to be placed round the King's neck and to hold it down by force. But this was not necessary.

Upon reaching the scaffold, Charles put on a white satin cap. His executioners were a horrible sight. Brandon, the State headsman—if it were Brandon—was dressed in tight-fitting black wool and with a mask formed like a human face. His assistant wore a mask and a false beard. The King asked them if his hair were in the way, and was requested to brush it back, which he did with his hand, remarking to Bishop Juxon, " I have a good cause and a gracious God on my side."

He said to the Bishop:

" I go from a corruptible to an uncorruptible crown where

no disturbance can be—no disturbance in the world!" He then again asked the executioner if his hair were in the way. Taking off his black cloak, and giving his Garter Star to the Bishop, he uttered the word "Remember", about which so much has been written. He then turned to the executioner and said:

"I shall say but short prayers, and then thrust out my hands." He repeated this, and asked them to make certain that the block, which seems to have been a very low one, did not move.

His Majesty then removed his doublet, put on his cloak again and made a speech and a declaration of his faith. He knelt down, and was about to place his head upon the block when one of the executioners, stooping down to arrange his hair under his satin cap, caused him to believe that the blow was about to be struck, and he ordered him to wait for the signal. There was a short pause. The King then lowered his head to the block, and it was instantly severed. The second executioner—the mysterious man in the mask and the grey beard—lifted the head and cried, "Behold the head of a traitor."

In a few moments two bodies of cavalry, approaching from different directions, began to drive the crowd towards Charing Cross. Horrified and stunned by what they had seen, the people dispersed, and it is said that London was quiet and empty all that day and night, many people making the excuse that the cold was so severe that they did not wish to leave their firesides.

The body was taken to a room in Whitehall, where Dr Topham, surgeon to General Fairfax, embalmed it, first sewing the head to the trunk. When this had been done, the public were admitted so that they might see for themselves that the King was dead. About a week after, a hearse drawn by six horses, and covered with a valvet pall, took the road to Windsor. It was followed by four coaches containing the few men, not more than twelve, headed by Thomas Herbert, who remained faithful to the King to the end, and after it.

Having arrived at Windsor, Herbert showed the Governor of the Castle Parliamentary authority to bury the King's body at any suitable place within the walls of the castle. It was therefore decided to explore the vaults of St George's Chapel. While this was being done, one of those present happened to tap with his stick upon the pavement of the choir, and, hearing a hollow sound, it was decided to remove the pavement at that place. The entrance to a vault was revealed in which stood two coffins, one large and one small, and both covered with velvet palls which, although they had been in position for more than a century, appeared to the onlookers to be quite fresh. The large coffin proved to be that of Henry VIII, and the small one that of his third wife, Jane Seymour. It was decided to lay King Charles to rest with these improbable companions.

While Herbert and his friends went to the castle to bring the coffin of the King, which was lying in his old bedroom there, strict orders were given to the sexton to lock the doors of the chapel, and to allow no one inside under any pretext. This was done, but no one knew that a soldier had secreted himself in the chapel, and as soon as the doors were locked he stole out of his hiding-place and went down into the newly opened vault. Seeking for plunder, he cut away a portion of the pall from the large coffin and bored a hole, from which he drew out one of Henry VIII's bones. When, later, he was caught and arrested, he stated that he had hoped to make this bone into a handle for a knife.

Meanwhile the body of the King was reverently carried from his bedchamber to the chapel. It was lowered into the vault beside the coffins of Henry and Jane Seymour; and the Bishop of London, who was ready to read the burial service, was forbidden to do so by the Governor. So the body of the King was committed to the grave in silence.

Charles I rested side by side with a monarch separated from him by more than a century and by profound differences of temperament, but one with whose absolutism he might have had much sympathy, and he lay undisturbed for a hundred and forty-four years. In 1813 workmen carrying out some alterations to the chapel accidentally knocked a hole in the wall of the vault, and reported the sight of three coffins lying side by side.

It seems that at this time, even despite such eye-witness accounts of the burial as that of Herbert's, all manner of doubt had been cast on the last resting-place of King Charles. The Prince Regent, hearing of the discovery, decided to open the tomb and to see if the third coffin were really that of Charles I. Therefore, on April 1, 1813, with his brother, the Duke of Cumberland, the Dean of Windsor, and Sir Henry Halford, the King's chief physician, the Prince Regent had the vault opened and a square opening made in the lead coffin, which simply bore the name "King Charles" and the date of his death.

Sir Henry Halford has left an account of the gruesome proceedings. Having disentangled the cere-cloth in which the head of King Charles was wrapped, they discovered that the head had parted from the body to which it had been sewn after the execution. They removed it, held it up and examined it, and clearly recognised the features of Charles I, as painted by Van Dyck. His hair and beard were in good condition, the beard brownish-red in colour, and the neck showed clear signs of the blow from the executioner's axe. Sir Henry, probably for the purposes of his medical report, took away with him a portion of the King's cervical vertebra, a cutting of his beard and a tooth. The coffin was then soldered and the vault re-sealed.

The relics of Charles I were carefully preserved by Sir Henry Halford and placed in a small ebony box, which contained a description of them upon an engraved plate inside the lid. When he died he bequeathed them to his son, who, in his turn, left them to his son. He, thinking that they should be returned to the vault in Windsor, presented them to the Prince of Wales, afterwards Edward VII.

Queen Victoria's permission was then obtained for the reopening of the vault, and, after the evening service on December 13, 1888, the Dean, with two canons and three workmen, superintended the removal of the pavement and the unbricking of the arch of the vault beneath. A hole about eighteen inches square was made immediately above the centre of King Charles's coffin. The Prince of Wales came alone to the chapel and lowered the box through the aperture, placing it carefully upon the coffin. The workmen then replaced the bricks and the paving-tiles; and all this was done behind locked doors.

Although the death of King Charles I is so well documented by the narratives of eye-witnesses, there are certain debatable points about it which historians and others are never tired of bringing up generation after generation. One of the most interesting of these problems is: who struck the blow that killed the King?

The public executioner at that time was a man called Brandon, who lived in Rosemary Lane, Whitechapel. Contemporary accounts say that he refused to behead the King, and that someone else had to be found who was willing to do the deed. For instance, in the *Journal of the Earl of Leicester*, in the Sydney Papers, it is written: " This I heard for certain that Gregory Brandon, the common hangman, refused absolutely to do it, and professed that he would be shott or otherways killed rather than do it."

All accounts agree that the executioner and his assistant were so fantastically disguised, one with a mask and the other with a mask and a false beard, that no one could recognise them. The Earl of Leicester's *Journal* says that they were disguised as sailors. If this is true, then it would appear highly improbable that the public executioner had any part in it, for, had he agreed to execute the King, why should he consider a disguise necessary? All his friends in Rosemary Lane would know, apart from the fact that he must have been an easily identified figure.

It is clear also that those with every opportunity of sifting the truth in the reign of Charles II did not believe that Brandon killed the King, for repeated attempts were made to discover the two masked men. A great number of men were suspected. Henry Porter, who was imprisoned in Dublin, was one, yet the request of the Duke of Ormonde and the Council of Ireland that he should stand his trial in England

" as the person by whose hand the head of our late Sovereign King Charles was cut off" was apparently ignored. Another suspect was a certain William Walker, who died near Sheffield in 1700. Colonel Hacker, who summoned the King to the scaffold, when asked who struck the fatal blow, replied that he did not know, but thought it was " the Major ". He said he would find out, but there is no record that he ever did so, and the identity of " the Major " remains a mystery.

Is it possible that during the Commonwealth various bad characters boasted in their cups that they had killed the King?

The mystery might appear, to some, to be cleared up by the confession of Brandon, the public executioner, who seems to have languished and died some months after the execution, and to have been buried in St Mary's Church, Whitechapel. A note below the entry in the register states, " This Richard Brandon is supposed to have cut off the head of Charles the First ". It is surely curious that whoever wrote this must have been familiar with Brandon's alleged confession, yet he regarded Brandon's part in the execution as a supposition.

Brandon's confession was that within an hour after he had struck the blow he received thirty pounds, all paid in half-crowns, that he took from the King's pockets an orange stuck full of cloves and a handkerchief. He was offered twenty shillings for the orange by a gentleman in Whitehall and, though he refused it, took ten shillings for it later in Rosemary Lane.

As soon as Brandon was dead a tract was printed, which may be found among the Civil War tracts in the British Museum, entitled *The Confession of Richard Brandon, the hangman, upon his deathbed, concerning the beheading of his late Majesty.* In this Brandon is supposed to have said that he " returned home after beheading the King, gave the thirty pounds to his wife, and told her it was the ' deerest money that ever he earn'd in his life, for it would cost him his life ', which prophetical words were soon made manifest, for it appeared that ever since he hath been in a most sad condition, and upon the Almighties first scurging of him with the rod of sicknesse, and the friendly admonition of divers friends for the calling of him to repentance, yet he persisted on in his vicious vices, and would not hearken thereunto, but lay raging and swearing, and still pointing at one thing or another, which he conceived to appear visible to him.

"About three days before he dy'd he lay speechless, uttering many a sigh and heavy groan, and so in a most desperate manner departed from his bed of sorrow."

It is apparent that his neighbours had no doubt that he was the executioner, for his funeral was interrupted by crowds of angry people crying, "Bury him in the dunghill", even threatening to "quarter the corpse". It seems to me extraordinary that while the people of Whitechapel at the time were sure that he had done the deed, the Government of Charles II, eleven years later, should have made a search for the man who struck the fatal blow.

Another point about which so much has been written is the meaning of the word "Remember", repeated so solemnly by the King to Bishop Juxon as he removed the George from his breast and gave it to him. What was the understanding between Juxon and the King? It is believed that Juxon was officially questioned about this at the time, but never revealed the secret, if secret it were.

Some have believed that it concerned a message to the Queen in France. The George was a beautiful one, made of onyx and surrounded by twenty-one diamonds. On one side was a picture of St George and the Dragon, and on the reverse a little spring revealed a miniature of Henrietta Maria. It has been suggested that Charles was bidding Juxon to remember to tell the Queen that only at the last moment of his life did he relinquish her portrait.

Another supposition is that he was asking Juxon to be sure to remember to see that the George was faithfully delivered to his eldest son, Charles. This seems a reasonable explanation, if it is true, as some have claimed, that the same George is seen in the large portrait of Charles I by Van Dyck at Hampton Court, and also is the same as that worn by James II and the Old Pretender, and seen in their portraits in the National Portrait Gallery. This jewel is said to have been worn continually by Bonnie Prince Charlie, and after his death is believed to have come into the possession of the

Duke of Wellington, and then, by some process of fate, to have arrived back at Windsor, where presumably it remains to-day among the Stuart relics.

A third point which has caused endless controversy—but why, I cannot imagine—is that of the position in which King Charles died. Did he kneel and stretch his head forward to a block which was at least two feet in height, or did he lie full length upon the ground? There is abundant evidence that he did this.

"The block was so low the King was forced to lie on the ground," wrote Warburton in his *History of Prince Rupert and the Cavaliers*. "I have seen two prints of the time," he states, "in which the King is thus represented."

During a debate in *The Times* on this subject in 1890, Lord Rosebery said that he had in his possession a contemporary painting of the execution by an eye-witness, a Dutchman, who left England immediately because he refused to live in a country that could kill its King. In this painting the King is seen lying full length on the ground. Additional evidence that this was the position is provided by Richard Davey in *The Pageant of London*, who says that he possessed a contemporary account of the execution in French in which it is clearly stated that Charles lay flat on his stomach—"*couché sur son ventre*"—and this also was undoubtedly the position in which six weeks later the Duke of Hamilton and Lord Capel met their deaths in Old Palace Yard, Westminster.

There are other aspects of the execution—such as, what became of the axe?—but it would be tedious to go into them. It is sometimes easier to believe a simple story than the doubt and conjecture with which time so often obscures it.

§ 5

One of the great moments of a London morning is that time, sharp on the stroke of eleven, when the King's Guard comes clattering under the arch of the Horse Guards. It comes jingling and glittering from Knightsbridge, down Constitution Hill and along the Mall, the wind tossing helmet plumes, the sun on drawn swords. Everyone knows the charger that performs an effective little dance on his hind legs while his rider sits gripping him with white buckskin thighs.

The two sentries at the Horse Guards are so much a part of London's casual pageantry that they might be the guardian deities of the metropolis. No small boy believes he has really seen London until he has been taken to stand awefully before them. They sit so still, their swords at the slope, the peaks of their brass helmets almost on the bridge of their noses, their gigantic spurred boots thrust into stirrup-irons, the pommels of their saddles rising from black fur rugs. Now and again they move their eyes, and the wind sometimes blows thin streamers of white or red horsehair over the brass of their helmets.

It would be interesting to know how many miles of film they have occupied in their time, and in how many albums in remote and unlikely corners of the world they have an honoured place.

Sometimes one is lucky enough to see the sentries changed. Two new sentries ride up and sit facing the rear of the sentry-boxes. The gates at the back of the boxes are opened and, as the two old sentries ride out, the two new ones ride in, so that for one second the box contains the tail of the departing charger and the head of its successor.

The daily changing of the guard in Whitehall, although so heavily filled with anti-climax, never seems to weary the crowds that from May onwards gather to watch it. The old guard sits its black horses facing the new guard, which also sits its black horses. And nothing happens. No trumpets blow. There is nothing to hold the attention but the splendid pageantry of shining breastplates, plumes, drawn swords, backed by the seasoned beauty of the archway. Then the clock strikes, and suddenly the pageant, without any heroics, breaks up and disappears to stables.

One morning, in an enquiring mood, I asked a man who was watching the King's Guard:

" What are they guarding? "

" War Office," he said, removing his pipe and pointing to the Horse Guards.

" But I thought the War Office was there," I said, pointing over the way.

" Ah, but this is the War Office as well," he said dogmatically, and closed the conversation.

Of course, the truth is that the King's Life Guard, to give it the right name, is guarding a tradition. The Holbein Gate to Whitehall Palace and the Tilt Yard in which the Life Guard was first quartered used to stand nearby, and a guard has been posted there since the time of Charles II, and probably before. The gate and the barracks were pulled down ages ago, but the guard is still present and correct.

There are a number of things about the King's Life Guard which are perhaps not known to its many admirers. The numbers and formation of the Guard are ruled by one fact: the presence of the King and Queen in London. If both their Majesties are in London, a full, or " long ", guard is mounted. This consists of one officer, one corporal-major, one corporal of horse, two corporals, one trumpeter and sixteen troopers. If the King and Queen are out of London, a " short " guard is mounted, consisting of one corporal of horse, one corporal, and twelve troopers.

But, by ancient custom, the change-over from a " long " to a " short " guard must occur at the precise moment when the King and Queen leave the capital. If, for instance, their Majesties leave Paddington by a train departing at 10.47 in the morning, the guard is reduced to a " short " guard at that precise moment. The exact time when the King and Queen leave London is always communicated to the King's Life Guard, in order that these changes may be made according to regulations.

The explanation of this remarkable procedure is an interesting one. In the old days the Sovereign never left London by coach without an escort of Life Guards. It used to ride beside the coach of Charles II to Newmarket, and it accompanied the Georges to Windsor and on many private journeys as well. Nowadays the Sovereign's escort is provided only upon State occasions; nevertheless the tradition persists that when the King leaves London he must be accompanied by an escort, even though it may be invisible of Life Guards!

When the brief morning pageant at the Horse Guards is

over, the crowds disperse, the spell ended, some to Charing Cross and others towards Westminster, where few nowadays pause to examine the Cenotaph, that memorial to battles long ago; but all stop to gaze at Downing Street. It is singularly English that a street so famous should be such an under-statement of a street, a little cul-de-sac with a few old houses on one side and Government buildings on the other. The austere and ordinary façade of No. 10 gives no idea of the impressive Cabinet Room beyond, where so many fateful conferences have been held in our time. It was in the little paved garden at the back of No. 10—the usual little London back garden—that Mr Winston Churchill conceived and discussed the possibility in 1940 of making a secret journey across the Atlantic to meet President Roosevelt.

Sir George Downing, who gave his name to the street, was a slick political opportunist who became a republican under Cromwell and then, when Charles II returned to the throne, turned his coat and became an ardent royalist. This man, strange to say, was the second graduate of Harvard. When he was fifteen his family emigrated to New England at the invitation of John Winthrop, the first Governor of Massachusetts. But America was evidently too small a field for Downing's ambition, and he returned to England as a young man of twenty-two, unimpeded by any principles save those of self-interest.

The Commonwealth period was a wonderful time for such adventurers. In the early thirties he was already well established, and took a leading part in the movement to offer the Crown to Cromwell. He was sent by Cromwell as British resident to the Hague, where he displayed his capacity for intrigue and double dealing, and during this time he had a melodramatic meeting with Charles, then an exile in Brussels. The King had made a secret visit to the Hague to see his sister, the Princess of Orange. Downing's spies must have told him, and Downing, although he might have made the success of his career by handing Charles over to Cromwell, decided upon an entirely different line of action. Accordingly, one night after Charles had arrived, " an old reverend-like man, with a long grey beard and ordinary grey clothes " appeared at the inn and craved an interview. He fell on his knees and, pulling off his disguise, was revealed as George Downing, Cromwell's emissary in Holland. He warned Charles that the Dutch Government had promised to deliver him to the English Parliament should he set foot in Holland. This warning probably saved the King's life, for had he been arrested and sent to Cromwell, he would probably have shared the fate of his father.

Despite this deed, Downing, when Charles was restored to the throne, might have been imprisoned. But his genius for survival was equal to the danger. He possessed documents incriminating the Howard family, and he persuaded Thomas Howard, brother of the Earl of Suffolk, to intercede with the King on his behalf. The reason he gave for his sudden political conversion is fascinating. He declared that he had "sucked in" republicanism during his youth while in America, but, having reached years of discretion, he now realised the error of his ways; and this was nearly a century and a half before the "Boston Tea-party"! The disloyal sentiments of the English settlers in New England were so well known in the reign of Charles II that Downing easily got away with this explanation. There is an interesting proof of this in Evelyn's *Diary* for May 26, 1671, when a solemn council meeting, at which Evelyn was present, discussed Colonial affairs, and it was said that the condition of the American colonies was such that "there was fear of them breaking from all dependence on this nation". It is obviously erroneous to imagine, as many do in this country, that American republicanism had its roots in the Georgian Age.

Downing, under Charles II, divided his time between lucrative posts at home and difficult foreign missions abroad. Samuel Pepys was his clerk at the Exchequer in 1660, when he began the *Diary*, and Downing once boasted to him that his Dutch spies were so good "that he hath had the keys taken out of De Witt's pocket when he was a-bed, and his closet opened, and papers brought to him, and left in his hands for an hour, and carried back and laid in the place again, and keys put into his pocket again". De Witt was, of course, the head of the Dutch State.

Perhaps Downing's dirtiest exploit was the hunting down of his former friends, the regicides, in Holland. He arrested three of them and sent them home in a warship. Pepys, while rejoicing at the deed, called Downing a " perfidious rogue ". He was also, says Pepys, incredibly mean and niggardly, and Evelyn, who had an equally low opinion of him, says that, rising from nothing, he had become excessively rich.

I suppose the truth is that a well-spoken and utterly unscrupulous rogue was occasionally indispensable in the diplomatic service, and Charles found it worth while to cherish Downing and, no matter what he thought of him in private, to give him a baronetcy and a grant of land in Whitehall. It was upon this land that Downing, as a speculation, built Downing Street.

It is ironic that the name of this rogue should have gone out all over the world and have become synonymous with the greatness of British statesmanship.

§ 6

It is a grand feeling to walk along Whitehall in the early morning, the sun shining, the Home Office geraniums flowering in the window-boxes, the Cenotaph flags hanging limply, a milkman delivering the milk at No. 10, the red omnibuses swinging down from Charing Cross, some bound for Waterloo Bridge, some for Victoria, some for Chelsea.

If the association of nations now known as the Commonwealth may be said to have a heart, it is surely here in Whitehall that you can feel the beat of it. In these days when everybody looks alike, you never know whom you may meet and pass by in Whitehall; a famous soldier in a blue suit and a black hat, a distinguished governor, administrators of every degree, ancient pro-consuls who have represented the Monarch in distant lands, men who have made roads and bridges and laws in all sorts of out-of-the-way places. Whitehall is visited at some time by everyone who has a job to do in the world. There must be few of us who have not at some time been summoned to Whitehall, or who have not called on Whitehall, and, having filled in a buff form, have sat patiently in one of its many waiting-rooms.

It was just off Whitehall, in the Old Colonial Office in Downing Street, that Nelson and Wellington met in a waiting-room for the first and last time. Nelson, strange to say, did not know Wellington by sight, but Wellington instantly recognised the sad-eyed little man with an empty sleeve pinned to the breast of his coat. What an encounter! And what incompatibility. Nelson began talking, as Wellington remembered icily, " all about himself, and in, really, a style so vain and so silly as to surprise and almost disgust me ". Then Nelson left the room, and when he returned, having learnt the identity of the thin, frosty man in the waiting-room, his manner was transformed. " He talked," said Wellington, " like an officer and a statesman."

Such encounters, but maybe not on such a high level, still take place every day in the waiting-rooms of Whitehall.

What, I have often asked myself, really constitutes the charm of London, that something about London which satisfies you as only Rome does, that queer, disturbing vision of bridges, spires, towers and crowded streets which comes to you at moments when you are far away and brings with it as much pain as pleasure? The answer is to be found in history. Behind everything in London is something else, and, behind that, is something else still; and so on through the centuries, so that London as we see her is only the latest manifestation of other Londons, and to love her is to plunge into ancestor-worship. London is a place where millions of people have been living and dying for a very long time on the same plot of earth, drenching it with their blood, glorifying it with their nobility or degrading it with their villainy, pulling it down and building it up, generation after generation, yet never destroying the vision of an earlier day.

In Whitehall we have a London street that is soaked in memories and haunted by ghosts. Its great memory, of course, is the old Palace of Whitehall, which was the principal seat of the Tudor and Stuart kings. It was probably there that Henry VIII married Anne Boleyn; that Elizabeth, blazing with jewels, received many an embassy; that Charles

II gazed sardonically at his mistresses. The scene has completely vanished, the huge, rambling, complicated structure of the palace has been swept away, and it is difficult now, as you walk the streets between Whitehall and the Thames, to imagine the gleam of candle-light on tapestry or to catch the echo of lute or viol.

Yet it is a direct and living inheritance from old Whitehall Palace that Whitehall should be full of Government offices and Civil Servants. This part of London was not suddenly captured by the Civil Service: the Civil Service had taken control of it centuries ago. We of to-day have no idea what "the Court" meant to people in ancient times. It was not, as it is to-day, simply the place where the Royal Family live more or less like private individuals: it was the administrative centre of the realm. Round the Court gathered all the Government departments, and every kind of administrative activity that has now gone its own way and become what we know as the Civil Service.

The Court in the old days was a tremendous organisation, a huge collection of aristocrats and administrators, with their staffs, whose presence brought prosperity to the neighbourhood and whose absence reduced it to penury and despair. The Law, it is true, which was once so closely connected with the royal palace, has branched off and is to be found in the Strand, but the modern equivalents of the old departments of State remain, as they have done for centuries, in the neighbourhood of the Palace of Whitehall.

It is impossible for anyone who has not studied maps and plans of old London to imagine what Whitehall looked like before the broad road was driven from Charing Cross through the Palace grounds to Parliament Square. There is a scale model of Whitehall in Stuart times in the Royal United Service Museum, which is well worth study.

The Palace covered acres of ground between the Thames and St James's Park. It was an enormous quadrangle, its centre the huge open space of the Privy Garden, and grouped round it, like a village round its green, was a mass of separate buildings, some of stone, some of brick, and some of half-timber. It was a picturesque place, as picturesque as any cathedral close. It was not planned, but was built from time to time, as necessity decreed. Some of the buildings were fine Tudor stone halls, some were Italian palaces, and next to the most splendid of the buildings might be standing some cottage like the black-and-white dwellings you can find in any English country town to-day. It was, as I say, more like a large village built round its village green than the contemporary idea of a royal palace; and indeed throughout history it has been a constant wonder to visiting foreigners that the kings of England should be so casually housed. It may be that the English inability to erect a Louvre or an Escorial has been a fortunate thing for the monarchy.

The traveller in the time of Charles II who wished to go from Charing Cross to Westminster Abbey would have to pass through the Palace, for that was the way the public road went. When he reached the Banqueting Hall, the only part of the Palace now left, he would see to his right the stables and barracks of the Life Guard, more or less where the Horse Guards are to-day, and behind them was the Tilt Yard, a huge open space where tournaments were formerly held, and now the parade ground behind the Horse Guards.

Facing him would be the Holbein Gate, a beautiful red-brick Tudor structure, which was the north gate of the Palace. When he had passed through this gate he would see a cluster of buildings on his right, the covered tennis-courts, the cock-pit and so on; and on his left would be the long garden wall of the Privy Garden. If he were able to look over this wall he would see across an expanse of grass a row of sedate buildings like those in any cathedral close, and behind them, rising above the roofs and chimneys, higher and more impressive buildings overlooking the Thames; and in these lived the King and Queen. A short walk beside the wall of the Privy Garden would bring him to the King Street Gate, or the south gate, of the Palace; passing through this, he would find himself again outside the precincts and in the open street, with the Abbey in front of him.

This regal village was the principal home of the English Court from the time of Henry VIII to that of William and Mary. But it was fated to vanish in a night. In 1693 a careless laundress started a fire that destroyed the whole Palace, with the exception of the Banqueting Hall and a few adjoining buildings. It was another Fire of London in miniature. About a hundred and fifty houses were gutted and a thousand apartments destroyed; another twenty houses were blown up to prevent the spread of the flames. Dutch William did not care, for he disliked Whitehall Palace, and was living at Kensington when the fire occurred. From the melancholy moment when that royal quarter of London, which had seen so much history, was laid in ashes, the Court migrated to St James's Palace, where it is still seated.

What shall we think about as we explore those streets behind Whitehall, between Horse Guards Avenue and Richmond Terrace, where the Palace buildings, the State apartments, the houses of the nobility, of royal dependants and favourites, as well as those of the chief officers of State, most thickly clustered? We may remember, perhaps, Cardinal Wolsey, who first glorified York House, as the Palace was originally called, or of Henry VIII, who acquired it and made it even more beautiful.

We may remember that night during a great banquet when a roll of drums announced the arrival of Henry with a band of revellers disguised as shepherds, in costumes of cloth-of-gold and crimson satin and beards of gold and silver wire. They pretended to be foreigners, and said that, having heard that the English ladies were the most beautiful in the world, they had come to see for themselves and to pay court to them. After the banquet, their disguises cast aside, the King and his courtiers danced the night through. Or we may remember the death of Henry VIII and the fear that made itself felt through all the labyrinthine corridors of Whitehall when it was whispered that the mighty oak was about to fall. Although only fifty-six, Henry was a bloated mass of flesh and disease, and a white beard stretched nearly to his waist. At first no one was brave enough to tell him that death was approaching, and it was eventually his favourite, Sir Anthony Denny, who did so. He found the King groaning with pain and rage. Henry asked what judges had pronounced such a sentence upon him. "Your physicians," replied Denny. When the frightened doctors gathered round the bed again, Henry, with a return to his old temper, cried, " After the judges have once passed sentence on a criminal, they have no more to do with him; therefore begone!" By the time the Archbishop of Canterbury arrived he was in a coma, and the last act of one who had brought so much sorrow and grief into the world was to wring his hands.

We may remember Elizabeth at Whitehall, in youth when her celebrated virginity was England's foreign policy, or in old age when it had become a diplomatic convention. In those days she was best described by a German traveller called Paul Hentzner.

" Next came the Queen," he wrote " (in the sixty-fifth year of her age, as we are told), very majestic; her face oblong, fair, but wrinkled; her eyes small, yet black and pleasant; her nose a little hooked, her lips narrow, and her teeth black; she had in her ears two pearls, with very rich drops; she wore false hair, and that red; upon her head she had a small crown, reported to be made of some of the gold of the Luneburg Table; her bosom was uncovered, as all the English ladies have it till they marry; and she had on a necklace of exceeding fine jewels; her hands were slender, her fingers rather long, and her stature neither tall nor low; her air was stately, her manner of speaking mild and obliging. That day she was dressed in white silk, bordered with pearls of the size of beans, and over it a mantle of black silk shot with silver threads; her train was very long, the end of it borne by a marchioness; instead of a chain she had an oblong collar of gold and jewels. As she went along in this state and magnificence, she spoke very graciously, first to one, then to another. . . . Whoever speaks to her, it is kneeling; now and then she raises some with her hand. Wherever she turned her face as she was going along, everybody fell down on their knees."

We may remember that charming and costly form of drama which never became public, but remained an exotic and aristocratic diversion within the walls of Whitehall. The Masque began with Henry as a rich and boisterous charade, became lovely with Anne of Denmark, the wife of

James I, and beautiful in the time of Charles II. The amount of labour and money expended on these poetic operettas is almost unbelievable. Some of them must have been as spectacular as any transformation scene staged at Drury Lane. Imagine a production written by Ben Jonson and staged by Inigo Jones! While James I preferred acrobats and fools, Anne of Denmark loved to produce a masque, and she and her ladies were as devoted to this precious flower of the theatre as some modern enthusiasts are to the Russian Ballet. Perhaps her most famous production was Ben Jonson's *Masque of Blacknesse*, in which the Queen and eleven of the reigning beauties appeared seated in a huge golden shell, their faces and hands blackened to resemble negresses. "Their apparel was rich but, some said, too light and courtezan-like for such great ones." The cost of this masque was three thousand pounds. In the time of Charles and Henrietta Maria the masque continued. Ben Jonson, Milton, Fletcher, Carew and Seldon wrote the verse, Lanière and Ferabosco composed the music, and Inigo Jones devised the "machines" and the scenery. So many lights were used during these productions that Charles, dreading their effect upon his collection of pictures, built a temporary structure of weather-boarding which was called the Masqueing House. But the Civil War put an end to masqueing for a time and this fragile and aristocratic flower perished with the Stuarts.

Or we may remember the domestic scenes in Whitehall when Charles I expelled the Catholic entourage of the Queen and ordered them back to France, and how in her rage Henrietta Maria broke a window-pane with her fists. But it is good to know that, in later life, Charles and his consort made up for such scenes when they became perhaps the most truly devoted royal couple in English history. Then we may remember Charles II at Whitehall, surrounded like a sultan by his beautiful mistresses, the candlelight shining on card-tables, two thousand pounds in gold in the bank—as described by Evelyn—laughter, jests, French love-songs from a minstrels gallery, the opening of doors in the night. We may think of the bevy of vain and lovely ladies, described by Pepys, chattering gaily in the corridors, talking, laughing, and trying on each other's hats. " The finest sight to me," says Pepys, " considering their great beauty and dress, that ever I did see in my life." We may remember the February morning beside the Thames when the master of so much gaiety lay dying at the age of fifty-five, saying that he was tired of life and apologising for the time he was taking in leaving it.

Three years later, on a December night in 1688, a strange scene occurred in Whitehall. The rain was beating against the Palace windows and the wind howled round London. James II and his Queen, Mary of Modena, had retired to rest as usual at ten o'clock. They sat listening to the sounds of the Palace, waiting for silence to come to the dark corridors. Shortly before midnight the Queen dressed herself as a washerwoman. Two women dressed in rough clothes entered on tip-toe carrying what appeared to be a bundle of linen. Parting the folds, the Queen saw her six-months-old son, James, Prince of Wales, who became the Old Chevalier.

The King gave his orders to two trusted friends, M. St Victor and Count de Lauzun, who were dressed as sailors.

" I confide my Queen and son to your care," he said, with deep emotion. " All must be hazarded to convey them with the utmost speed to France."

He said good-bye to his wife, stole a glance at the sleeping Prince, then the strange company went out into the silent Palace, crossed the great gallery and tip-toed down backstairs to a postern gate.

James turned to the window and listened to the fury of the storm. William of Orange had landed as the Protestant champion of Britain. The tragedy of the Stuarts was working itself out.

The Queen, with her two women and the two Frenchmen, crossed the Thames in a rowing-boat. She took shelter from the rain under the wall of Lambeth Church, where she remained, waiting for the arrival of a coach-and-six, and watching the dark mass of chimneys and roofs on the other bank which she was never to see again. In a few days the King stole away from Whitehall Palace to join her in France. As he was crossing the Thames his hand moved to the side of the boat, and the Great Seal of England went down into the water.

That was really the last event in the life of Whitehall Palace. From that moment, deserted by the Stuarts, whose virtues and whose follies had been its story for so long, the old place lingered, neglected and unloved, until Fate in the form of a laundress put a torch to it. "Whitehall burnt, nothing but walls and ruins left," is all that Evelyn says of the Palace which he had known in the days when it was filled with beauty, pride and power. Five or six victims perished in the fire, but it is cheering to know, as a contemporary said, that among them were "no persons of any note".

CHAPTER SEVEN

In which I go to Westminster Abbey and tell the story of its rebuilding by Edward the Confessor and, later, by Henry III. I describe the Royal Tombs, the Coronation Chair and the Royal Vaults beneath the Chapel of Henry VII. Ends with a description of London's great Byzantine basilica at Victoria.

§ 1

THE late Dean of Westminster, Dr P. F. D. de Labillière, will go down in the history of the Abbey Church as the dean who refused to leave London during the air raids. He could easily have gone; indeed, when the Deanery was blown to pieces he was urged to do so. But he was absolutely immovable: he said that as long as the Abbey stood it must have a resident dean.

He should also be remembered with gratitude by those who visit the Abbey for his decision to open the west doors and to make them, as they ought to be, the main entrance to the church. Before his time the Abbey was miserably entered by the north transept, where the visitor who had not been there before, confused by the mass of sepulchral monuments, found himself undecided which way to go; indeed, in those days I think thousands of people probably never even found their way to the nave of the Abbey.

But what an unforgettable experience it is when you enter by the west door to-day and see at a glance the slender nave, the columns and arches repeating themselves like recurring chords of music, and, eastward, like a final note of grandeur, the distant apse of the Sanctuary bathed in a light from the Lantern and the transepts.

I have always found it difficult to pass Westminster Abbey, and have spent more time there idling about, or just sitting and looking at the old building, than I care to admit. The other day when I was in the Abbey, I tried to remember how many great occasions I have attended since the end of the 1914 War. The first was, I well remember, the burial of the Unknown Soldier. It was a ceremony of extraordinary poignancy and dignity. All those who had lost a son or a husband in the hideous shambles of that conflict felt that, if the Unknown Soldier were not their own son or husband, at least some part of him was there in the middle of London, preserved for ever in the Pantheon of our race and nation. To me the service appealed particularly because I had just come from Dover, where I had seen a destroyer steam into harbour with the coffin of the Unknown Soldier upon her deck draped in the Union Jack. It was a profoundly moving experience to be present in the Abbey and to see King George V, in his field-marshal's khaki, standing there as chief mourner as the remains of this ordinary British Tommy—did one know him? had one ever met him?—were laid to rest among the immortals.

I remember the funeral service of Queen Alexandra. She lived on at Marlborough House, becoming frailer, thinner and smaller, a little old lady, a survival from a past age. As the brown candles burned round her catafalque I thought I had seen the last glimmer of an age not unlike that of Charles II, a brief Restoration period, during which wealth and privilege performed their last measure.

I remember the marriage of the present King and Queen, and I was in the Abbey when they were crowned. Suspended, as it were, above the Sanctuary, with an almost baroque disregard for the law of gravity, I gazed down a precipice of stone and saw, in a blaze of light in the centre of the church, an almost incredible blossoming of the past. The moment I shall never forget was the disrobing of the King for the ceremony of anointing. In ancient times he was stripped to the waist, and a relic of this was the canopy of cloth-of-gold which was held over him by four Knights of the Garter to conceal him from view. I remember how the Archbishop of Canterbury approached with the Dean of Westminster, who held the ampulla containing the Holy Oil and the spoon. I saw the Dean pour the oil into the spoon, and I watched the Archbishop dip his finger into the double groove and touch the King, first on the palms of both hands, then on his bared breast, and lastly upon the crown of his head. And from beneath the canopy stepped the newly anointed monarch, dressed only in white satin knee-breeches, white silk stockings, and a white silk shirt. Innocent of all emblems of kingship, he knelt in prayer while the Archbishop blessed him. Then began the intricate ceremony of the crowning, when, seated in the Coronation Chair, the slim white figure was ultimately vested with regal garments until he sat there like a Byzantine emperor, holding the sceptres, the ruby ring that is called " the wedding ring of England " upon his finger, waiting for the Crown. It was a profound spiritual experience, and I could well understand how God's anointed could believe, and how a nation could believe, that a King had been granted the power of healing and could " touch " for the King's Evil.

What was so notable about the Coronation was its air of authenticity. Although all those who took part in it were fantastically attired, no one appeared to be dressed up. At a fancy-dress ball, no matter how authentic the costumes, no one looks really genuine (except maybe in Italy, where people somehow manage to resemble their ancestors), but at the Coronation even the most unlikely peers looked at least plausible, while most of them were genuine period pieces. As the sudden springing of the past into the present, I shall always think the Coronation was the most remarkable scene I have ever witnessed.

The last ceremony I attended in the Abbey was the marriage of Princess Elizabeth to the Duke of Edinburgh, but, between such royal occasions, I have been to dozens of services of various kinds. I think the most melancholy event I can remember in the Abbey was the memorial service to Mr Neville Chamberlain during the War. The windows of the Abbey had been blasted by bombs, the church was unheated, and the members of the Cabinet, headed by Mr Churchill, stood in their overcoats, cold, miserable-looking, and a prey, it seemed, to overwhelming anxiety. The final touch was delivered by the air-raid siren.

But of all my memories of Westminster Abbey none remains more firmly in my memory than a visit I paid one night during the War, before the air raids had begun. It was a bitterly cold night at the end of January, 1940. I happened to be passing the Abbey in the black-out, and stood for a moment impressed by the enormous Gothic silhouette against the sky. I had heard that the Abbey authorities, clergy and vergers and others, had banded themselves into a complete defence unit to preserve the church in the event of air raids, and I thought it would be interesting to go in and see what was happening. I was delighted to find that my old friend, Mr T. Hebron, the Registrar, was the chief warden. He had twenty-seven wardens under him, thirty-six fire-fighters, and a first-aid party of fourteen. About a hundred people live in or about the Abbey precincts and spend their lives in attendance on the church: Dean and Chapter, choir, vergers, the Registrar and his staff, the Clerk of Works and his. All these people, some of them unknown to each other in times of peace, were now drawn by the danger in which the Abbey stood into a close community, as if the Abbey were once again a self-contained walled monastery ruled by its abbot. It was obvious that if the Abbey were bombed or set on fire the only persons to defend it were those who were intimately acquainted with the intricacies of the building. No outside firemen or wardens would have been much use there.

While Hebron was explaining his organisation, a message came from the Dean to say that he would like to see me. I went by the light of an electric torch—for it was impossible to black-out the Abbey—through the Jerusalem Chamber and into the Deanery, a lovely old building which used to be the abbot's lodgings, where I found Dr de Labillière sitting at his desk in a room full of books. We talked of many things, including the danger which now faced the Abbey. I told him that I would like to make a tour of the Abbey during the black-out and see it in its war-time state.

He took me through several doors and passages, and led the way into a cold, empty darkness. I had no idea where I was, but I could feel the chill of the great church all round.

"We are in Bishop Islip's pew," said the Dean. "Queen Victoria often used it."

Down below in the pitch darkness something moved. "The firemen," explained the Dean. I knew that we were above the nave, and I asked where the Unknown Soldier's grave was. He called down towards the shuffle in the darkness. " Shine your torches on the Unknown Soldier's grave." And two figures switched on their hand-torches and walked forward a step or two. The two beams of light lost themselves for a moment among the black pillars of the nave and petered out near the triforium, then they converged and met on a red mass of poppies.

I went down into the church, where Hebron took me on a tour of the building. Few people except those connected with the Abbey have ever been there after dark, and it was eerie beyond words to walk by the light of torches, the beams straying over well-known tombs and monuments, some of them concealed by brown hills of sandbags. There were six firemen on duty all night. One of them, evidently new to the job, said to me, " It's the chairs that make you jump. They go off like pistols now and then, or it sounds like that when everything is quiet." At intervals during the night two of the firemen climbed a stone spiral stair into the triforium and telephoned down to the nave to say that all was well. In order that access might be quickly obtained to the upper portions of the Abbey, a bridge had been erected over the west door, joining the north side of the triforium to the south.

We climbed through a spiral tube of stone into the triforium, where we tip-toed gingerly, like people on the edge of a precipice, and shone our torches downward into the inky pool of the nave. The white asbestos fire-suits which were hanging up there looked like spectres, with their huge, skull-like black goggles. They are not fond of ghost stories in the Abbey, but a persistent enquirer can generally learn something of the strange sights occasionally seen by level-headed engineers and plumbers. The last time the Abbey ghost was seen was on the eve of the marriage of the present King and Queen. It was kneeling in a brown habit at the high altar, which was already prepared for the wedding next morning. He was such a solid-looking apparition that the closed church was searched in the belief that a stranger must have been locked in. But no one was discovered.

Returning to ground level, we made our way to the crypt,

where I saw an unusual sight. This small stone chamber has a single squat pillar of red sandstone, from the centre of which spring the sixteen ribs that support the floor of the Chapter House above. The vestments for the next day's services were carefully laid out—beautiful shimmering brocades sewn with threads of gold and silver—and next to them, on four kitchen chairs, were laid out, with military precision, four firemen's kits with gum boots, gas-proof clothing, gas masks and shrapnel helmets. A more incongruous juxtaposition was surely never before seen, even in Westminster Abbey! We saw more firemen's kits in the Chapel of the Pyx, and when we entered the Norman Undercroft we found it laid out as a hospital, with rows of beds waiting for air-raid casualties. Those chiefly responsible for this strange revival of what appeared to be a monk's dormitory were the wife of one of the canons and the organist's wife. With tender thoughtfulness the ladies had removed from the Undercroft a hideous gargoyle and a huge stone coffin: two objects which they rightly felt air-raid casualties should not be required to contemplate. A visit to an air-raid shelter, fitted with its own filter plant, completed my tour of the Abbey in war-time.

As I groped my way to an almost invisible omnibus, I thought how many strange things nine centuries have shown to Westminster Abbey. It has seen dead kings lying stripped to the waist in the glow of unbleached tapers; it has seen a Queen of England, Elizabeth Woodville, sitting " alone on the rushes all desolate and amazed ", seeking sanctuary from her enemies; it has seen pomp and pride and piety go marching down the centuries in company with greed and envy and treachery: it has even known one murder.

During the War something entirely new happened to it, something that neither king nor abbot could have imagined. We called it A.R.P. or our own unhappy gift to history.

The next time I visited the Abbey was on May 17, 1941, a few days after it had been damaged and the Deanery completely destroyed. I made this note in my diary at the time.

"I went to Westminster Abbey to see the damage, and was most embarassed to meet the Dean. I knew he had lost everything, and I found it difficult to express my sorrow. However, he was bright and sprightly and said, 'Come along and see what's left of the Deanery', and we went up the stairs from the Registrar's office through the Jerusalem Chamber, which is unharmed, and then, passing into what once was the lovely panelled Deanery, we paused at the edge of an abyss open to the sky and filled with charred beams. He told me that he had lost everything but the clothes he was wearing—he was in the shelter at the time. The only portions of the Deanery saved were two spare bedrooms and their contents. We entered one of these, where the Dean's wife was sitting, wearing a fur coat, while a young man, the Dean's son, was standing holding a soldier's webbing equipment and a rifle without a bolt. They told me that he had been on leave, and had lost his uniform when the house was destroyed. Like a good soldier, he had carefully removed the bolt of his rifle and put it in the Deanery safe. It had been burned into an impossible shape. The Dean pointed to a bookshelf with eight books on it.

"'All that is left of my library,'" he said. 'I think I am the only Dean of Westminster who did not possess a Bible and a Prayer Book.' He took out a little brown book and said, 'This was among the saved.' It was my *Heart of London*. I said I wished that something more worthy had escaped in its place. The sight of a scholar who has lost his library is terrible. One can find no words of consolation.

"With great courage the Dean and his wife intend to continue to live in the two rooms left to them. When the King and Queen visited the Abbey the other day, they urged the Dean and his wife to leave London and go to Windsor; but the Dean won't hear of it. He says that as long as Westminster Abbey stands it must have a resident dean. . . .

"Afterwards Hebron took me through the Abbey. The only damage to the church itself is to the roof of the building. Incendiaries set it on fire, and the melted lead and debris fell from the Lantern upon the spot where the King and Queen were crowned. But the damage is, most fortunately, quite negligible, and they were sweeping it up and arranging a temporary altar at the end of the nave so that the Abbey may soon be opened again. Hebron pointed to the frightful statues in stucco of Gladstone and Disraeli, and several others, who formed a shocked and indignant group all gazing portentously at the damage, and remarked, 'Of course, nothing could have harmed those, could it?' And how right he was! They seemed to be armed with the invulnerable righteousness of the Victorians. 'I wonder what kind of an air-raid warden Gladstone would have made?' I asked. Hebron smiled. 'So do I,' he said."

§ 2

The mental journey into the remote past which visitors are expected to take who visit such a shrine as Westminster Abbey is exhausting; and I often wonder, as I watch the crowds listening to the mass of dates and names given to them by guides, how much is really absorbed or understood. History can be the most boring or the most exciting of all topics, and, having been so bored by it in childhood, I have had to make it interesting to myself in later life. I wish there were some magic formula to make a place like Westminster Abbey immediately thrilling and exciting to its visitors, most of whom are drawn there by a kind of spell; but there is no such formula.

The history of the Abbey is really a simple one, but it is a long story involving thirteen centuries. It begins before history, in the age of legend, when monks seeking a lonely spot in which to worship God penetrated the brambles of a little island on the banks of the Thames called Thorney. There they built a church, which has grown into Westminster Abbey.

At this time Saxon London was visible to them on its hill, sitting behind its Roman wall. England was half Pagan and half Christian. Shaggy kings were being converted by

Roman missionaries beneath oak-trees, and baptised in the water of holy wells. Sometimes they remained Christian, sometimes they strayed back into paganism. Mentally they were on the level of child-like tribes everywhere. An early Bishop of London, Mellitus, a Roman missionary, was driven out of London by the sons of a former chieftain, who had reverted to paganism, because they wanted the white bread of the Eucharist, yet refused to become converted. But they were furious with the Bishop for giving this nice white bread to ordinary common folk and not to them. And so they drove him out. I suppose the incident could be paralleled by any African missionary to-day.

The monks of Thorney, either then or at a later period, put forward one of those valuable stories which in an age of innocence acted as protective magic. We read such legends to-day and think how charming they are, but there was probably another side to them which is likely to escape us. The story was that, on the night before the church on Thorney Isle was to be consecrated, a fisherman called Edric was putting out his salmon-nets in the Thames. As he approached what is now the Lambeth bank, he saw a stranger in foreign garments, who asked to be ferried across the river. When the stranger got to the other side he approached the new church, which became illuminated, and the awe-struck fisherman sat in his boat and saw choirs of angels ascending and descending. The stranger confessed upon his return that he was St Peter, and that with his own hands he had consecrated the church. In the morning the Bishop of London arrived to perform the ceremony, but, seeing the dedication crosses and hearing the story, he realised that the act had been performed by one greater than he.

The new church was therefore surrounded by an atmosphere of supernatural approval and sanctity. The monks sought to remove it from the jurisdiction of the See of London and to achieve for it a peculiar status of independence. And the church of St Peter achieved this from its earliest moments. It has never been subject to the Bishop of London. No Archbishop or Bishop, except at a Coronation, has been able to bring his crozier into the Abbey without the permission of the Abbot or the Dean. Abbot, and Dean after him, have been supreme under the Crown, and Westminster Abbey to this day is therefore like a small independent ecclesiastical island.

If the legend of St Peter really belongs to the first church on Thorney Isle, and not, as some think, to a later date, then the founder monks were well acquainted with the art of self-preservation, and if it be true that God helps those who help themselves, their future was assured.

The monastery of Westminster first clearly steps into history with Edward the Confessor about the year 1042. This monarch was destined to be its real founder, and his bones were to rival the story of St Peter and the fisherman as the Abbey's most treasured possession. Edward was almost certainly an albino. His snow-white hair and beard and his long, thin, transparent fingers, which were said to be able to heal, seemed to his contemporaries to place him in a category apart from ordinary men. He was godly and pious, and was subject to long fits of abstraction and to sudden bursts of disconcerting laughter. The other side of his character was violent, spiteful and cruel.

Before he came to the throne he took a vow to make a pilgrimage to Rome; when he became king he found it impossible to fulfil this vow, and sent a deputation to the Pope asking for absolution. The Pope agreed to absolve him if he would rebuild the monastery of St Peter. This great task became the main object of his later years. He was half English and half Norman, and his sympathies seem to have been entirely Continental. He surrounded himself with Norman favourites and appointed Normans to positions of chief importance, thus softening up the country conveniently for the arrival of William the Conqueror. It was therefore natural that when he decided to build a great church, he should have introduced for the first time into England the massive and splendid Romanesque architecture which was fashionable on the other side of the Channel.

If we wish to imagine what Edward the Confessor's Abbey looked like we must remember Durham Cathedral, the Chapel of St John, in the Tower, and St Bartholomew's,

Smithfield. It was almost as large as the present Abbey, and at that time was the mightiest building in the country. It took twenty years to build, and was intended to last for ever. The Saxons, whose churches were mostly small stone barns with thatched roofs, after the style of the Celtic churches of Scotland and Ireland, must have looked at the new abbey with amazement and have seen in it something colossal and alien.

The great church was to be dedicated at Christmastide in the year 1065. Edward was ill. For some days he lingered, rallied and finally sank, and in the consternation which spread through England when his death was known may we not see the first glimmer of that awe and reverence which was to grow into the cult of St Edward the Confessor?

From London and from all the villages around crowds packed the new white Abbey Church of St Peter to see the Confessor lying in a blaze of candlelight before the high altar, his crown upon his head, his royal vestments upon his body, a golden crucifix round his neck and a pilgrim's ring upon his long, transparent hand. While the Confessor lay dead in Westminster, his successor, Harold, was hastily crowned, either at St Paul's or the Abbey; and when Christmas came round again Harold lay dead, and William the Conqueror was crowned in the Abbey on the tomb of its founder.

From that moment every King of England, except Edward V and Edward VIII, who were never crowned at all, has been anointed and crowned in Westminster Abbey. Many lie buried there. Although the Abbey was built to glorify St Peter, it is Edward the Confessor that, quite early in its history, it began to glorify, and his tomb became the heart and centre of the church, as indeed it is to this day. It is also the only miracle-working shrine of the Middle Ages still to be seen in this country.

It is one of the most significant objects in England, and few of us should be able to stand before it unmoved. In life eccentric, unreliable, childish and inept, in death the Confessor became the symbol of England. Probably at first the Saxons, suffering under foreign rule, began to glance back to the days of the saintly Edward and to think of them as " the good old times ", bestowing upon them that golden halo of perfection which is the compliment an unhappy age pays to its predecessor. And the Normans, instead of stamping out the legend of Edward, encouraged it for dynastic reasons, so that conqueror and conquered joined hands in Westminster Abbey at the tomb of the Confessor.

It has been the object of all Kings of England to establish some contact with the far-off Saxon. At the solemn moment of their lives, when they were anointed and sanctified, they assumed for a few ritualistic moments the carefully preserved and treasured relics of his wardrobe. His ancient mantle was placed upon their shoulders. Plantagenet monarchs, standing barefoot in the great church, drew on antique garments which were said to be the buskins, or trousers, of the Confessor, and placed their feet in his shoes. If their hair were ruffled by the anointing, it was with Edward's comb that they smoothed it into place. And the final moment came when upon their brows was placed the gold circle of his ancient crown.

Thus dressed in ancient garments that had come down from Saxon days, the Sovereigns of another age and time, completely Byzantine in appearance, went to the shrine of St Edward after the ceremony and were solemnly divested of their clothing, which they left upon the altar. Then, wearing new and modern dress, and carrying only the sceptres (which had to be returned to the Abbot of Westminster after the coronation feast), they went on their way, having kept a strange appointment with the past.

The cult of Edward the Confessor was something national and dynastic in which we can perceive the roots of our future history. That Edward should have rivalled St Peter in St Peter's church is fantastic enough, but the time came during the blazing midday of the Middle Ages when, solemnly translated and canonised, he took his place as a national saint beside St George. His legend is so powerful that few people to-day, even though they think little of such matters, would not admit, if obliged to do so, that the picture created in their minds by Edward the Confessor, a kindly, bearded, patriarchal and essentially English figure, is infinitely more appealing than that of the official national saint who slew the dragon.

Edward's body was seen at least three times after his burial, and his bones were disturbed twice. He was first seen in 1098, about thirty years after his funeral, when Henry I, in order to prove the story that the body was uncorrupt, ordered the tomb to be opened. It is said that the Confessor was seen lying, as if in life, and Gundulf, the Bishop, plucked from his colourless beard a long, pale hair. The second time was after Edward's canonisation in 1161, nearly a century after his death. This time the tomb was opened in the presence of Henry II and Thomas à Becket. The ceremony was performed at midnight in October, when, in a blaze of candlelight and torches, the King and the assembled clerics gazed with awe upon the features of the Confessor. He was lying crowned and vested, as he had been buried, and they took the Coronation ring from his finger and, removing his vestments, replaced them with others. He was seen again in a hundred and six years time, or two hundred years after his burial, and in vastly different surroundings. The massive Norman Abbey that he had built had vanished. It had been rebuilt by Henry III, and was the Abbey we know to-day. In this different scene, and before the gaze of men as remote from him as we from the Battle of Culloden, the Saxon king was again exposed to the light and was deposited in the place where his bones rest to-day.

During the Reformation, in the time of Henry VIII, they were again removed, but when Mary ascended the throne she replaced them in the shrine. The last occasion on which the tomb was disturbed was the most extraordinary of all. The story was told by James II to John Evelyn, and is to be found in his *Diary*, under September 16, 1685. The King said that, when they were taking down the stands after his Coronation in the Abbey, a member of the choir saw a hole in the Confessor's tomb, into which he thrust his arm. He could feel bones there and among them something hard and metallic. He pulled out of the tomb a jewelled gold crucifix attached to a chain.

Realising that he was holding a precious and sacred relic,

the man became afraid, and put the crucifix back in the tomb. Then, later, when it occurred to him that someone else might go there and steal it, he returned and took it out again, and, at the earliest opportunity, showed it to the Archbishop of York. The crucifix found its way to James II at Whitehall, and the King kept it.

From a description printed in 1688 it is obvious that the crucifix was an enamelled and jewelled reliquary of Byzantine design. The cross was about four inches long, upon one side, in enamel, a picture of the Passion, and upon the other a picture of a Benedictine monk in his habit. The chain was twenty-four inches long, the links oblong, and where it joined the cross was a solid circular knob of gold round which hung six gold beads.

It was evidently the loss of this precious object which upset James II so much when he was robbed at Faversham during his first attempt at flight from England. What happened to this relic of St Edward? Did the thieves melt it down or destroy it, or did it fall into the hands of someone who preserved it, and, if so, does it still exist to-day? No wonder it is difficult to pass an old curiosity shop! Is it beyond the bounds of possibility that someone might still find a crucifix that had been buried in Saxon England with the Confessor and stolen from a King of England in a Faversham inn six hundred years after?

§ 3

Henry III, who pulled down the vast Norman abbey of the Confessor and built the Westminster Abbey of to-day, was one of the most extravagant of our monarchs. He was ably assisted by an equally extravagant, but charming and elegant queen, Eleanor of Provence, who was almost more accomplished than he in the art of extortion. Henry was also highly intelligent and was the greatest builder, and perhaps the greatest lover of the arts, who has ever occupied the throne.

He was of average height, muscular, and had a drooping eyelid which partly concealed one of his eyes, a curious defect which he handed on to his eldest son, the great Edward I. He was uxorious to a degree that embraced all his wife's rapacious relatives, and his piety was such that when he visited the King of France he stopped so long and so often to hear Mass on the way that even St Louis, in a desperate attempt to speed him up, ordered all the churches to be shut.

The age in which he lived was a tremendous one. It was the age of Dante, St Francis, St Dominic, Roger Bacon, Buonaventura and Duns Scotus. Architecture, casting aside its solid Norman anchors, had found wings. It was the age of exquisite churches. The greater part of the talent, skill and inventiveness now scattered among a thousand professions and trades was concentrated within the Church. When people look at a church such as Westminster Abbey and say, as they so often do, " How on earth did men do this in those days? ", they should reflect that a large part of the total genius of a nation went into these buildings.

The age was also one in which men were thinking of their own homes and their own countries. The crusading fires were dying down. The energies of Europe were no longer scattering towards Palestine. A new class was beginning to rise. There are said to have been fifteen thousand scholars at Oxford in Henry's reign, who lived how and where they could. It was Henry's Chancellor who established Merton College, in which they could live and be disciplined, and so founded the true collegiate system of the English Universities.

It was clearly an age of transition. A new world was being born in which, in England, the Abbey of Westminster was to be a significant landmark. It is curious that Henry III—the son of the evil, excommunicate John—should have been the pious instrument of fate. His greatest sin in contemporary eyes was his excessive fondness for foreigners, yet, so inscrutable are the workings of destiny, he was the king who erected the national shrine of England. Although he did not know it, Henry was the first truly English king. His devotion to the Confessor was such that he named his eldest son after him, and so began the long run of eight royal Edwards. He was the first king who, apart from reasons of state, was genuinely proud to trace his descent back to the days of the Saxon saint. All this was a sign, so obvious now, so hazy then, that England was ready to be born. Indeed, it almost seems that Edward the Confessor had himself appointed the hour and the man. When the Confessor lay dying in the year before the Conquest, he had spoken of the "branch engrafted in the green tree", words which, to those around him, seemed to be delirium, but were probably a reference to the future union of Saxon and Norman, a union whose splendid child was England.

It is an interesting indication of the state of England from the Norman Conquest to the time of Henry III that when the Norman Abbey of Westminster was pulled down, it did not contain the tomb of one so-called English king, although it had been standing for two hundred years. William the Conqueror was buried at Caen in Normandy, William Rufus at Winchester, Henry I at Reading, Stephen at Faversham, Henry II and Richard I at Fontevrault, in France, and John at Worcester.

When Henry III began to pull down the Confessor's massive abbey in 1245 he was thirty-eight years of age, and twenty-four years later he had the satisfaction, when he was sixty-two, of seeing his splendid new church complete, except for the western part of the nave. During the twenty-four years the King personally supervised the building. He mounted the scaffolding and discussed the plans with Master Henry, the architect, and with John of Gloucester and Robert of Beverley, who succeeded him. So he created what he intended to be a worthy shrine for the Confessor, whom in so many ways he closely resembled, and also a royal mausoleum for the House of Plantagenet. What would Henry III have said could he have foreseen a day when not only Plantagenets, but Tudors, Stuarts and Hanoverians would be grouped round the Confessor's shrine, when Englishmen of genius and worth, poets, artists, musicians, writers, statesmen and inventors, would be admitted to the church; a day when pilgrims would come from all parts of the world to stand for a moment in the one place above all others which enshrines the genius of the British race?

Borne aloft upon the shoulders of the King, his brother and his sons, the body of the Confessor in a new coffin was carried to its exquisite resting-place in October, 1269. Three years later Henry died, and his body, in the old coffin of the Confessor, was buried before the high altar. So the two founders of Westminster Abbey lay for a little time alone together in the great church.

§ 4

It fell to my lot recently to take a friend from overseas to Westminster Abbey. I soon discovered that this man knew nothing about English history. He was a South African. He knew quite a lot about numerous unimportant administrators in the Cape and Natal during the Nineteenth Century, but of the great movements of the world and the men who made them he knew practically nothing.

It was therefore difficult to know how to show the Abbey to him without confusing him. I thought the best thing was to explain the foundation of the monastery, first by St Edward and then by Henry III, which I did as well as I could. When we arrived at the Abbey we looked at the Unknown Soldier's grave and at the nearby chapel which commemorates the tragedy of our times—the death in war of a million young Britons; and then we stood for a long time admiring the glorious view up the nave to the east end of the church. He delighted me by saying that it was one of the most beautiful buildings he had ever seen.

I asked him to look at something which few people notice. It is that the west end of the nave, in which we were standing, was built two centuries later than the east end of it, yet so perfectly was the earlier style of architecture copied that few people could tell where the work of Henry III left off and that of Richard II and Henry V begins. The extraordinary thing is that the later builders did not carry on the work in the style then fashionable, but copied deliberately that of an earlier day.

We then made straight for the tomb of St Edward. Here I asked my friend to note how the Confessor lies in the centre of his chapel, surrounded by all the Plantagenet kings since the time of Henry III, except two, who are buried elsewhere. Then I asked him to notice the extraordinary design of the tomb. There is nothing like it anywhere else in the Abbey, or in England. It is as foreign in appearance as if it were the tomb of a Byzantine emperor or a Saladin, and the Eastern look is accentuated by the Oriental carpet slung above the tomb to conceal the wooden super-structure. Tombs not unlike that of the Confessor are to be seen in ancient mosques in Turkey.

While we were looking at this, a young man with an over-educated voice came up with two women and, to my amazement, said: " Now do look at the Confessor's tomb, which is too enchanting for words. Don't you think the Anglo-Saxon work . . ."

Yet, I said to myself, how reasonable it is to mistake this piece of mediæval Byzantinism as Anglo-Saxon; for the art of the Saxons was Byzantine. How right and at the same time how wrong the young man was.

There is naturally a reason why this Byzantine jewel came to be placed out of its real setting, which is mediæval Rome or Constantinople. Abbot Ware, who was in Rome when the church was nearing completion, returned to England with Italian workmen, including Peter of the Cosmati family, a worker in mosaics. Whether Henry III had asked the Abbot to look out for some foreign artist capable of designing the Confessor's tomb, or whether the Abbot, visiting such churches as St Clemente, St Prassede and St Pudenziana, became enthusiastic about mosaics and determined to persuade the King to employ the Italians, we shall never know. But the strange fact remains that, after spending twenty years or so extracting the essence of what was best in contemporary French church architecture, Henry III decided to place the central jewel, for whose glorification the whole edifice was intended, within a casket as striking as a single cry of *Kyrie Eleison* in a Latin service.

The shrine of the Confessor became one of the great miracle-working shrines of the Middle Ages, as it was in Norman times. Anticipating that it would continue to be visited by pilgrims, those who designed the tomb provided recesses, three on each side and one at each end, in which those might kneel who had come to be healed by proximity to St Edward's body.

Having explained this to my friend, and finding him still interested, I was faced by the problem of introducing the

Plantagenets, by whom we were surrounded, to one in whose mind their names evoked no answering echo.

"Well," I suggested, "let us take these kings and queens in the order in which they were buried round the Confessor's tomb. First, of course, is Henry III himself. Let us walk over and look at his tomb."

So we stood at the tomb of Henry III, and saw that noble spendthrift lying above us in bronze, two elegant pointed toes protruding from the hem of his bronze coronation robes.

"Those feet," I said, "walked shoeless from St Paul's to the Abbey Church of St Peter when the King, habited as a monk, held above his head a crystal phial containing a drop of the Saviour's blood sent to him from Jerusalem. He walked beneath a canopy, while two bishops, one on each side, supported his arms all the way. So he passed through awed and silent crowds, who dropped upon their knees as he went past, noting that 'he kept his eyes ever fixed upon the Blood of Christ and wept many tears'. Such was the man who built this church."

We then passed to the tomb next to Henry's, where Queen Eleanor of Castile lies, who was laid to rest in the Abbey, eighteen years after the funeral of her father-in-law. She was the wife of Henry's eldest son, Edward I. Her effigy shows a grave and lovely lady whose hair falls on each side of her face from beneath a foliated crown. Her left hand, at the level of her breast, grasps the end of a chain that encircles her neck.

"Did you ever hear of a queen who went on a crusade to the Holy Land with her husband and sucked the poison from an arrow wound?" I asked.

A faint look of recognition lit his face.

"I think I have," he said.

"Well, this is the queen, Eleanor of Castile. She is also the queen for whom Charing Cross was made. When she died in Lincolnshire her sorrowful Edward erected twelve memorial crosses, one on each place where her body rested on its way to London. Charing Cross was the last of them. And note the exquisite iron gate which encloses her, its top a succession of three-pronged spikes which look like flames, or a bed of crocuses. Upon St Andrew's Eve, the anniversary of her death, two hundred wax tapers impaled upon those spikes burned round her every year for two hundred years."

The next royal burial was that of Edward I, her husband. He lies on the other side of Henry III. Seventeen years passed before he followed her to the grave. He warred against the infidel, the Welsh and the Scots. He drove the Jews out of England, and he carried on the Englishing of the country that had begun under his father. He was so often away at war that, in order to see anything of him at all, Eleanor had to spend much of her life as a camp follower. Her children were consequently born in all sorts of unlikely places, one of them at Acre, in Palestine. During the war in Wales, when they were at the great castle of Carnarvon, Edward met the Welsh chieftains, who offered homage if he would give them a prince who could speak neither English nor French, expecting that he would appoint one of themselves. But Eleanor had already provided the answer, and Edward, producing his three-days-old son to them, demanded and received their homage, and so created the first Prince of Wales.

When the old warrior lay dying, hearing that Robert the Bruce was on the war-path, he roused himself and commanded his sons to boil the flesh from his body and carry his bones across the Border at the head of an English army. Edward also ordered that his heart was to be taken to the Holy Land. Neither of these commands was fulfilled.

In 1774 his tomb was opened in the presence of members of the Society of Antiquaries. Edward—Longshanks, as he was called—was found to be six feet and two inches in height. He was lying in royal robes, his legs concealed by cloth of gold. Horace Walpole was indignant to learn that the Dean and Chapter had reburied the crown, robes and ornaments which were found in the tomb. "There would surely have been as much piety in preserving them in their treasury," he wrote, "as in consigning them again to decay." Dr Johnson apparently regarded the whole proceedings as sacrilege.

"Now," I said, "we must leave the royal tombs and look at the Coronation Chair. Beneath the seat is the awesome Stone of Scone which Edward I brought back from Scotland.

The Chair itself is the one that Edward made for the Stone."

We examined as much as we could see of the much-battered chunk of sandstone.* It is of the kind which is found on the north-west coast of Scotland, and a less likely sacred relic can hardly be imagined; indeed, dare I say that if anyone saw it lying on his rockery he would hardly give it a thought? Yet national sentiment has caused this stone to be one of the most hallowed objects in the world. Legend said that it was the stone pillow on which Jacob rested before Bethel, that it was taken to Ireland and became the Stone of Destiny at Tara, which rumbled as with thunder if a pretender to the throne came near, that it migrated to Scotland and became the coronation seat of the Kings of Scotland. In removing it to England, Edward intended to show that he had crushed monarchy in the north, and century after century Scotland attempted by treaty to regain possession of it. Even if later kings had been willing to part with it, their subjects would not have allowed them to do so. It became, and still is, the palladium of the English race. Scots feeling in the matter was not pacified until a Scottish king, James I, was crowned King of England upon it.

There can be little doubt that had Hitler won the War he would have taken the Stone of Scone to Germany, just as Edward took it from Scotland, and with the same object. But he would have had some difficulty in finding it. During the Battle of Britain, the Dean of Westminster, with the Surveyor to the Abbey and the Clerk of Works, so that as few as possible should know where it was hidden, went down to the vault of the Islip Chapel and themselves buried the stone. They concealed all trace of their act afterwards. A chart showing its hiding-place was sent for safe keeping to Canada, and as soon as it had been acknowledged, the Westminster copy of it was destroyed, so that no one in England, apart from the three men who had concealed the Stone of Scone, could have found it. Only four men in Canada shared the secret: Sir Gerald Campbell, the High Commissioner, the

* The stone was stolen on Christmas Day 1950, and taken from the Abbey by thieves who were believed to be Scottish Nationalists,

Prime Minister, the late Mr Mackenzie King, Mr. Graham E. Towers, Governor of the Bank of Canada, and Mr H. P. J. Roy, the Secretary of the Bank, in whose vaults the chart was kept. When this romantic story was printed in Canada after the War, the Toronto *Globe and Mail* printed an article describing the Islip Chapel as " in Oxfordshire, about six miles from Oxford, in an area free of bombing throughout the War ". It is, of course, in the Abbey, and only a few yards north of the place where the Coronation Chair usually stands. " If Hitler had got here he would never have found it," the Registrar wrote to me in 1946.

We then returned to the royal tombs and came, on the south side, to the place where Philippa of Hainault, the Queen of Edward III, is buried. Her effigy, obviously a candid portrait, shows a plump Flemish woman with a round, humorous face and a good-tempered mouth. She is wearing a peculiar headdress, fashionable in the Fourteenth Century, called the *crespine*. She was the mother of the Black Prince.

" Have you ever heard of the Burghers of Calais? " I asked my friend.

He guiltily said, " No."

I told him that he would find a statuary group of the Burghers, by Rodin, which, possibly because it is the best thing of its kind in London, has been concealed behind the House of Lords in the Victoria Tower Gardens where no one ever sees it.

" This was the Queen," I told him, " who, when her husband had reduced the garrison of Calais by siege, went down upon her knees and begged the lives of the six burghers who, in sackcloth and in chains, came to him with the keys of the town."

Although her mighty monarch was not always a model of fidelity, Philippa on her deathbed, as recorded by Froissart, asked him to promise " that you will rest by my side in the cloisters of Westminster Abbey ".

This was not strictly observed, for Philippa and Edward do not lie side by side—an impossible position in that restricted space—but he is as near to her as he can be. He was one of the greatest of the Plantagenets, a great king in a great age. Chaucer, Gower, Mandeville and Wycliffe were his contemporaries. Among the heraldic shields on the side of his tomb is one upon which the lions of England are seen quartered with the lilies of France, a shield which epitomises his life. His ambition was to wear the crown of France as well as of England, and he launched upon the Continent the armies that had been trained, and whose fathers had been trained, in mountain and border warfare in Wales and Scotland. The result was the defeat of the feudal chivalry of France at Crecy and Poitiers. Every schoolboy who stands at this tomb must remember the story of the King hearing, as he was watching the battle of Crecy from a little hill, that his son, the Black Prince, then a boy of fifteen, was hard pressed in the front of the fray. "Let the boy win his spurs," said Edward III, refusing to send him reinforcements.

And the death, thirty years later, of this son who won his spurs at Crecy, broke the old King's heart. He turned his face to the wall and paid his debt to nature. His end was perhaps more pitiful than that of any king who did not die violently or on the field of battle. In his later years he was completely under the spell of one of the Queen's ladies, Alice Perrers. This woman, whose influence over Edward was attributed to witchcraft, was described by a hostile contemporary as having no beauty of face or person, but the blandishment of her tongue is said to have compensated for any such defects. The mighty paladin died at Sheen, deserted by all his friends, and the story goes that Alice Perrers slipped the rings from his dead fingers before she fled through the rifled palace.

The effigy of Edward III is extremely interesting, for it is said to have been taken from his death-mask. It shows a sad old man, his face lined with care. There is nothing about it in its pathetic loneliness to suggest the mighty conqueror of Crecy and Poitiers.

One more tomb completes the royal burials grouped round the Confessor. It is that of Anne of Bohemia, who died in 1394, and her husband, Richard II, who followed her five years after. The tragic King and his young wife are seen together in effigy, and before their figures were mutilated during the Commonwealth, they were holding hands.

Richard, who adored Anne, was half mad with grief when, at the age of twenty-eight, she died, probably of the plague. He ordered that her funeral effigy should include his own figure, and this was done during his life-time, so that he must often have seen this strange tomb in which he lay, as if dead, grasping the hand of his beloved queen.

So unbounded was his sorrow that he solemnly cursed the palace of Sheen in which she died, and ordered the rooms associated with her brief illness to be razed to the ground. Half crazy with grief during her funeral, he snatched a rod from the hand of an attendant and so violently struck Richard, Earl of Arundel, who had offended him, that the Earl fell to the ground and polluted the sanctuary with his blood. The requiem High Mass was interrupted, and was not resumed until late that summer's night, after the Abbey had been purified. With Anne, Richard's happiness began and ended. She controlled his temper, and had advised him, and without her he made mistake after constitutional mistake until, when Bolingbroke landed to claim the crown, Richard's abdication, and possibly his murder, were already written in the stars.

No one knows how he died in his cell in Pontefract Castle. Some say he was starved to death, some that he was slain with an axe, some that only a long piercing cry in the night indicated that his end was violent. Acres of print have been occupied with theories, but no one knows and no one ever will know.

So many rumours existed, however, that he had escaped to Scotland, that Bolingbroke ordered his body, with the face exposed to view, to be carried from Pontefract to London. A weird procession came southward through the night, knights and friars grasping torches whose light wavered over a bier drawn by four horses in black trappings, upon which lay the dead body of the deposed King. Startled townsfolk and villagers must have looked from their windows with awe and fear as they heard it go past. For hours the body lay exposed in Cheapside, when twenty thousand Londoners filed past it to see with their own eyes that Richard II was dead.

He was buried at Friar's Langley, and was removed to the

Abbey about fourteen years later by Henry V. Was it really he, and not some other man, who—terrible thought—was placed in the tomb with Richard's beloved Anne? How fervently one hopes it was Richard, but Dean Stanley, who was present when the tomb was opened in 1871, wrote, "Whether the King himself really reposes in the sepulchre is open to grave doubt". The investigators found in the tomb two almost complete skeletons of a man and a woman, but two crowns, which were known to have been there, were missing. The staff, a sceptre, part of the ball, two pairs of royal gloves, and fragments of pointed shoes remained. A strange extraneous object was a pair of plumber's shears marked with a fleur-de-lis, evidently left there by a forgetful workman when the tomb was resealed in the time of Henry V.

It must occur sometimes to some who read accounts of the opening of tombs in the Abbey to wonder how it is that so many bones are missing from skeletons. Perhaps the following letter, which was sent to Dean Stanley, explains this.

Wouldham Rectory, Rochester.
30 *June* 1873.

It may be interesting to you to know that my grandfather, Gerrard Andrewes, afterwards Dean of Canterbury, saw a Westminster scholar poke his hand into the tomb of Richard II, in the year 1766, and fish out the lower jaw-bone of the king. My grandfather received the jaw-bone from the boy, and it is now in my possession. I have often shown it to medical men, who say it is the jaw-bone of a man in the prime of life. There are two teeth remaining in the jaw. On a card attached to the bone is written (the handwriting is my grandfather's, Gerrard Andrewes), "The jaw-bone of King Richard the Second, taken out of his coffin by a Westminster scholar, 1766." My grandfather was himself a Westminster scholar, at that time sixteen years of age, having been born in 1750.

CHARLES GERRARD ANDREWES.

It was also through the same holes, and no doubt by the same agencies, that such objects as Jews' harps, broken glass and tobacco pipes and many other curious things have been found in the royal tombs. Fortunately the tombs are all sealed to-day and every detail about them is known. Now and again the owners of such relics as that described in the letter have the decency to feel that these things should return to the Abbey. When the genuineness of a relic has been established, royal permission is requested to open the tomb and replace it. Just before he died, Bishop de Labillière told me that he hoped to gain permission to open the tomb of Queen Eleanor of Castile and replace a bone that had come into his possession during the War.

§ 5

There is a place in Westminster Abbey in which a man may stand, as if upon a slight hill, and look backward to the past and forward to the future. This place is the beautiful Chantry Chapel of King Henry V. When you mount the steps from the shrine of the Confessor, you find the victor of Agincourt lying in a tomb raised several feet above the level of the church. Looking back, you see the Plantagenets lying in a half-circle round the Confessor, like a family round its chief, and ahead are steps that lead down to the Chapel of Henry VII, where the Tudors and the Stuarts are buried.

Upon this raised mound of stone lies Henry V, a link between the age of chivalry and the modern world: on one side are men who dreamed of a Latin Kingdom of Jerusalem; on the other are men who helped to finance the discovery of America. I know no spot in the Abbey where one who loves the story of his own country may more profitably pause a moment.

Here also is an interruption in royal burials. After Henry's funeral in 1422 the long procession of dead kings ceased for eighty-seven years. It was the time of the Wars of the Roses. Henry VI and Edward IV were buried at Windsor, Richard III at Leicester, and the next king after Henry V to lie in the Abbey was the first Tudor, Henry VII, the founder of a new dynasty, the herald of a new age.

The Will of Henry V, made in the third year of his reign,

proves that he had carefully studied the crowded mortuary chapels round the Confessor's tomb and had realised the difficulty of occupying even a few feet of earth there without disturbing the bones of former kings and queens. The problem was solved by moving the sacred relics from the eastern end of the Confessor's tomb and, in the space thus gained, erecting his Chantry. Henry was only thirty-four when he died at Bois de Vincennes, either of pleurisy or dysentery. His position was greater than that of any other former English monarch, for he was King of France and England. The cities of Paris, Rouen and London contested for the honour and glory of enshrining his body, and it is said that the French offered great sums of money if the King were buried in France. But even if his wishes had not been known, his Will made it clear that Westminster Abbey must be his resting place.

A funeral procession two miles in length travelled across France to Calais. Katherine of Valois, the Queen, after less than two years of married life and when she was barely twenty-one years of age, brought the body of her husband back to an England that was stunned by grief. The slow procession moved up through Kent and across London Bridge. Four horses in funeral trappings drew a chariot upon which rested the royal coffin, and upon the coffin lay a crowned image of the King made of boiled leather, painted and dressed to resemble life. The effigy was clothed in a purple robe bordered with ermine, in its right hand it grasped a sceptre, and it lay upon a bed of crimson silk. This was the first time that a funeral effigy was seen at a royal funeral. Nearly a thousand torchbearers dressed in white surrounded it, and after came the nobility of England and France. As the two miles of pompous grief passed through the streets of London, every citizen stood at his doorway holding a lighted taper.

The body rested before the high altar of St Paul's Cathedral, where a Requiem Mass was sung in the presence of Parliament. When it resumed its journey to Westminster, the body was guarded by five hundred men-at-arms mounted on black chargers, and in black accoutrements, with spears reversed;

behind the King's hearse were led three of his favourite chargers. Then came the nobility of England bearing the royal standard, banners, bannerets and pennons.

The long cortège wound its way up Fleet Street and along the Strand to Charing Cross, then to Westminster, where the Abbot and the monks of the Abbey Church were waiting to receive it. The King's coffin was placed before the shrine of the Confessor, his three chargers, led by three knights in armour, were brought up into the choir. He was laid to rest in a temporary tomb while the Chapel described in his Will was constructed.

The exquisite carving round the chapel was something new in the Abbey. It tells the story of the King's life: we see him at his Coronation, and, again, surrounded by his nobles, and charging in full armour, mounted on his war-horse, upon the fields of France. It is a biography in stone. It was, and still is, the most personal of all the royal tombs. Above it still hang Henry's helmet, his saddle and his shield, now, alas, much battered and denuded of the paint, gilding and velvet which once decorated them; but surely it is wonderful that they should still be there. The final touch to all this splendour was the tomb effigy of the King. It was made of silver beaten out upon a core of oak. The head was of solid silver, the teeth were of gold. All that now remains is the shapeless trunk of oak lying on top of the sarcophagus; for the figure was plundered during the Dissolution of the Monasteries.

The object of this beautiful and ingenious chapel was to provide a place where constant prayer might ascend to Heaven to intercede with God for the soul of the King. This was planned by Henry at the beginning of his reign as carefully as he planned the Battle of Agincourt. To-day we see a beautiful shrine, but there was a time before it was built when it existed only on paper, the well-thought-out plan of a great practical organiser. In order to serve the chapel and to sing the thousands of Masses decreed by Henry for his soul's comfort, additional monks must have been necessary to form a special body to do nothing else but attend on his Chantry. It is reasonable to suppose that while his body lay in its temporary tomb, the construction of the chapel was supervised by his widow, Katherine of Valois, the " sweet Kate " of Shakespeare's play.

What, I wonder, is the truth about this woman? Henry loved her so well—" the Fair One with the Golden Locks "—during their brief married life of two years, yet posterity was cruel to her, and even visited its contempt upon her helpless body, which lay in the Abbey for centuries exposed from the waist upwards, a poor half mummy and half skeleton for every vulgar eye to see and for some to insult, like Pepys, who, in an access of unfeeling coarseness, kissed its lips and boasted in his *Diary* that he had " kissed a queen ". It was not decently buried until the reign of Victoria.

The cause of Katherine's fall from grace is as mysterious as it was romantic. Some five or six years after Henry's death—she was then perhaps not quite thirty—she fell madly in love with a handsome, penniless young Welshman much beneath her in station. He was Owen Tudor, the Master of her Wardrobe. Little is known of this romance, but it is surely a matter for wonder that such a spectacular scandal was apparently confined to Court circles during the six years Katherine and Owen Tudor lived together.

During this time the Queen Dowager bore her lover three sons and two daughters, whether in or out of wedlock is unknown. The sons were Edmund Tudor, Jasper Tudor, and a third who became a monk and lived and died in Westminster Abbey. It was natural that this love affair should have been violently opposed by the Court. Eventually Katherine retired to Bermondsey Abbey, where she very soon died, leaving a pathetic Will addressed to her son, Henry VI, then a boy of fifteen. Tudor was sent to Newgate Prison, from which he managed to escape. His enemies trapped him and sent him back to Newgate, from which he escaped a second time, on this occasion sensibly seeking the fastnesses of his native mountains.

When Henry VI came of age he did everything in his power to help his mother's lover and to show favour to his two half-brothers. He created Edmund Tudor, Earl of Richmond, and Jasper, Earl of Pembroke. Edmund was married by the King's influence to Margaret Beaufort, daughter of the Duke of Somerset. They had one son, Henry, the first of the Tudor Sovereigns, who became Henry VII, the father of Henry VIII, and the grandfather of Elizabeth.

Poor Katherine de Valois may have offended the susceptibilities of her time, but no one then living could have foreseen that from her union with her handsome Welshman would spring the bright noonday of English history. What would those men have said who hunted Owen Tudor from the Sanctuary at Westminster, tried to trap him in a Westminster tavern and eventually locked him up in prison, could they have known that all Europe would one day kneel in reverence and awe before the splendour of his great-granddaughter, Elizabeth?

Tudor's end was consistent with his sudden violent eruption into English history. Living quietly on his land in Wales, the day came, during the Wars of the Roses, when he joined a Welsh contingent of Royalists and fought in the opening battles of that unhappy conflict. He was captured at Mortimer's Cross, and his head was struck off in Hereford market-place. It is said that a mad woman rescued it, combed the hair, washed the face and ringed it around with lighted candles.

§ 6

Eastward of the Chapel of Henry V, and down steps to the ordinary level of the church, is the Chapel of Henry VII. This is in many ways the climax of Westminster Abbey. It should be saved up for the last, and, if it is inadvertently seen before the rest of the church, eyes should be closed, for it is the culmination of seven hundred years of building.

This chapel is one of the most lovely examples of Tudor Gothic in the world. As you stand at the door of this chapel and look forward to the altar and upward at a ceiling which is like a cave of stalactites in Paradise, you appear to be looking at a place in which stone has been released from obedience to the law of gravity. Stone, which can be so ugly and so intractable, is here carved into a thousand aerial lightnesses so that the whole building seems to float in the air rather than to stand upon the earth. Like the Parthenon, which seems like a bird getting ready to lift itself into the sky, the Chapel of Henry VII gives precisely the same impression of imminent flight.

Here the startled air of levity produced in some minds by solemn places is stilled as if a ghostly hand had been placed upon the mouth. I have yet to hear the would-be humorist, who haunts the flanks of sight-seeing parties, who would dare to try to raise a laugh in the Chapel of Henry VII. It seems at one moment, as you look at the emblazoned banners of the Knights of the Bath hanging above the fretted stalls, that a trumpet note has been sounded; then, as you look at the solemn sweep of the arches, at the network of the windows, at the stone lace of the roof, at the saints and martyrs standing in their niches, it may occur to you that a Gregorian chant has been turned into stone. It is one of the last beauties of the Age of Faith.

The story of the foundation of this chapel is as singular and as interesting as most things in the Abbey. It is linked logically, like everything else in the church, with something that went before, another step forward in the ceaseless march of history and in the deeds and aspirations of men.

Go to the east end and look through the gates of the tomb effigy of King Henry VII, who is lying there side by side with his Queen, Elizabeth of York. The stern, mean and worldly King who founded the fortunes of the Tudor Dynasty looks more like a bishop, or even a Protestant dean, than the man, as one pictures him, who won the Battle of Bosworth and snatched the crown from a hawthorn-bush. He lies in priest-like gown, a biretta upon his head. He looks in death the least royal of all the great kings, yet he was as great, or greater, than most.

Unless you agree that might is always right, this grandson of Owen Tudor and Katherine de Valois had an extremely slender claim to the throne. Many men with much better titles had been swept away during the Wars of the Roses. Henry based his claim as the great-great-grandson of John of Gaunt, and, in order to strengthen it, he married Elizabeth of York, the eldest sister of the Princes who were murdered in the Tower. So in him the popular fancy may have seen a mingling of the white and red roses and the final end to the horrible civil war that had torn England to pieces for so long.

Menaced for many years by pretenders to the throne, it was Henry's policy to link himself in every possible way with the Lancastrians. Some twenty years before, his uncle, the unhappy Henry VI, son of the great Henry V and Katherine, had been murdered in the Tower. He was a kindly, meek man who suffered from melancholia that verged on insanity. It is a pity that his father could not have handled his reign and the Wars of the Roses! However, Henry, once dead, became beatified, and miracles were said to occur at his tomb at Chertsey. He became infinitely more famous and beloved dead than ever the poor man had been in his miserable life. His body was moved to Windsor, where the miracles continued to occur.

It was this poor, unhappy, murdered King for whose glory, and, incidentally, his own, Henry VII decided to erect the chapel. His idea was to translate the remains from Windsor to the Abbey and erect a shrine which should rival that of the Confessor. In the centre of it would lie his " uncle of blessed memorie ", and round him would come in the fulness of time the royal House of Tudor. The Pope was asked to authorise the canonisation of Henry VI, and there can be little doubt that, had Henry VII been willing to accept the financial obligations, " St Henry " would have been introduced into the Abbey.

But nothing was done. Poor Henry, who wished to be buried in the Abbey, who had spent so much time measuring the available space in the neighbourhood of the Confessor in an attempt to find room for himself, gently tapping the pavement with a staff and meekly refusing to disturb the remains of former Sovereigns, was left at Windsor. And in the place originally intended for " St Henry VI " came, in course of time, the founder of the chapel.

The sculptor who made the superb tomb effigy of Henry VII and Elizabeth of York, the most magnificent effigy in the Abbey, was Pietro Torrigiano. In youth, with other young geniuses, he had studied art in the Florence of Lorenzo the Magnificent. Benvenuto Cellini, who was a friend of his, says that it was Torrigiano, who, when young, had hit Michael Angelo so hard upon the nose that he inflicted the injury which remained visible throughout the artist's life. Torrigiano lived for many years in England working for Henry VII, and, after him, for Henry VIII; and it is said that he lodged on old London Bridge. In addition to enriching this country with some exquisite works of genius, Torrigiano also apparently decorated many an English face in moments of rage, for he once referred to the English as "bears". During one of his visits to Florence he tried to persuade Benvenuto Cellini to return with him and work for Henry VIII, but Cellini, who was certainly no weakling and never shirked a fight, evidently found his swaggering friend too much, for he made the excuse that he did not wish to live among "such beasts as the English". In one of Torrigiano's coffins, made for Cardinal Wolsey, Nelson lies in St Paul's.

A feature of the Henry VII Chapel which distinguishes it from the earlier royal tombs is its system of underground vaults. St Edward, the Plantagenets and the earlier kings and queens, are all buried above ground in their raised sarcophagi; but here for the first time they lie beneath the ground. And what an assembly it is: Tudors, Stuarts and one Hanoverian.

The most interesting memorials, after that of Henry and Elizabeth of York, are those of Queen Elizabeth, on the north of the chapel, and Mary, Queen of Scots, on the south. Both bear portrait effigies of the queens who lie beneath. Elizabeth is seen as her contemporaries knew her in later life, high-nosed, imperious, her wig well-dressed and curly, huge pearls about her neck, a ruff standing stiffly up, her body tightly corseted, a rich gown upon her, in her left hand the orb and in her right a sceptre which time and again has been stolen by visitors and patiently renewed by the Abbey authorities. In the dark vault below, Elizabeth, the daughter of Anne Boleyn, lies side by side with Mary, the daughter of Katherine of Aragon.

Mary Stuart's memorial on the other side of the chapel is perhaps more magnificent than Elizabeth's, as James I intended it should be. He moved his mother's body by torchlight from Peterborough, where she was buried after her execution at Fotheringhay, and interred her royally in the Abbey.

Until her tomb was ready, her body was given a temporary resting-place next to the vault in which Elizabeth lies, only a brick wall separating the two queens who never met in life. Mary Stuart's effigy suggests a tall woman—she was just six feet high—and she lies with hands folded in prayer, wearing a French lace cap, a ruff, a stomacher, her body wrapped in a fur-lined cloak and her feet stretched out to a crowned and upright lion.

In the vaults of the chapel lie also James I and Anne of Denmark, Charles II, Queen Anne and Prince George of Denmark, William and Mary, and George II and Queen Caroline. And so the story of this astonishing necropolis, beginning with the Saxon saint buried so long ago, comes down into modern times.

The royal vaults have been entered on several occasions either deliberately to solve some problem, or accidentally, during repairs and alterations to the church. A most interesting, but highly gruesome, account of them is to be found in Dean Stanley's *Memorials of Westminster Abbey*. During the installation of a heating system beneath the chapel in 1867, five steps were seen leading to a low vault which was almost filled by five coffins so close together that they touched. They were seen to be those of Charles II, Mary II, William III, Prince George of Denmark and Queen Anne.

In the following year it was decided to find the coffin of James I, whose burial-place was unknown. Several unsuccessful attempts were made. One vault in which it was considered he might lie was found to be occupied by Elizabeth Claypole, the favourite daughter of Oliver Cromwell! Another contained an immense leaden chest, six feet seven inches long, which was the coffin of Queen Anne, visible proof that the stories of her unusual height are true. The investigators, baffled by James in death as many were baffled by him in life, at last, thinking that he might have decided to lie beside his mother, decided to explore the vault of Mary, Queen of Scots.

Directly beneath the monument is a large brick vault

twelve and a half feet long, seven feet wide and six feet high. " A startling, it may almost be said an awful scene presented itself," wrote Dean Stanley. " A vast pile of leaden coffins rose from the floor: some of full stature, the larger number varying in form from that of the full-grown child to the merest infant, confusedly heaped upon the others, whilst several urns of various shapes were tossed about in irregular positions throughout the vault. . . .

" The first distinct object that arrested the attention was a coffin in the north-west corner, roughly moulded according to the human form and face. It could not be doubted to be that of Henry Frederick, Prince of Wales, the eldest son of James I, who died of typhoid fever, aged eighteen. The lead of the head was shaped into rude features, the legs and arms indicated, even to the forms of the fingers and toes. On the breast was soldered a leaden case evidently containing the heart, and below were his initials, with the Prince of Wales's feathers, and the date of his death, 1612. In spite of the grim and deformed aspect occasioned by the irregular collapsing of the lead, there was a life-like appearance which seemed like an endeavour to recall the lamented heir of so much hope.

" Next along the north wall were two coffins, much compressed and distorted by the superincumbent weight of four or five lesser coffins heaped upon them. According to Crull's account, the upper one of these two was that of Mary, Queen of Scots, the lower that of Arabella Stuart. But subsequent investigation led to the reversal of this conclusion. No plate could be found on either. But the upper one was much broken, and the bones, especially the skull, turned on one side, were distinctly visible—thus agreeing with Crull's account of the coffin of Arabella Stuart. The lower one was saturated with pitch and was deeply compressed by the weight above, but the lead had not given way. It was of a more solid and stately character, and was shaped to meet the form of the body like another presently to be noticed, which would exactly agree with the age and rank of Mary Stuart."

The tragedy of the Stuarts was heaped up round the remains of Mary, Queen of Scots. They found the ten infants of James II and Mary of Modena, " infant after infant fading away which might else have preserved the race", and the eighteen tiny coffins of the children of Queen Anne, "of whom one alone required the receptacle of a full-grown child". Before they left the vault they tidied up the confusion and placed the "little waifs and strays of royalty" in a cleared space near the steps.

They next looked vainly for James I in the tomb of Elizabeth, where they saw the great Queen and her half-sister, Mary, lying alone in the darkness. They opened the tomb of the young Edward VI and, finally as a last resort, the central tomb of the founder, Henry VII, where instead of the two coffins, which they expected to find, they saw three lying side by side. This third coffin was that of James I. How it happened that the first of the Stuarts should, after a lapse of a hundred and sixteen years, come to lie beside the first of the Tudors is, and always will be, unknown.

With an exquisite sense of fitness, the central chapel of the apse, which was intended for, but was never occupied by, the miracle-working remains of the saintly Henry VI, is to-day devoted to a modern miracle—the Battle of Britain.

The chapel, which was itself damaged during the air bombardment, commemorates the 1,497 pilots and air crew who perished at that time. The Roll of Honour contains the names of 1,300 British and Colonial airmen, 47 Canadians, 47 New Zealanders, 24 Australians, 17 South Africans, 35 Poles, 20 Czechoslovakians, 6 Belgians and 1 American. The great feature of the chapel is the superb stained glass window. It shows celestial beings welcoming the souls of the fallen into Paradise. Four lights show a Squadron Leader adoring the infant Christ, a Flying Officer kneeling before the Virgin as she supports the body of the dead Christ, a Sergeant Pilot adoring the crucified Saviour and a Pilot Officer receiving a vision of the Resurrection.

The rest of this gorgeous window is occupied with the Royal Banner of England, the Badge of the R.A.F., the flags of the Allied nations and the badges of the 63 Fighter Squadrons of the R.A.F. which took part in the Battle.

So a chapel designed for a king, who died nearly five centuries ago, is devoted to the heroism of the young airmen who saved Britain in the moment of her greatest peril.

§ 7

I walked about the Abbey visiting the graves of great and famous men from the time of Chaucer to our own day. I visited Poets' Corner, which is perhaps the most popular place of the Abbey, and I visited the tombs where statesmen, soldiers, inventors and explorers lie crowded together. I came to the grave where Tompion, the clockmaker, and the equally great clock- and watch-maker, George Graham, his partner, lie in the same grave. And I mention this because I happened to have in my pocket, as I often do, a lovely gold watch which keeps perfect time, if I remember to wind it every twenty-four hours, made by Graham in the year 1735.

I took it from my pocket, and listened as it ticked off the flying seconds, and below lay the man who had made it so faithfully and so beautifully more than two centuries ago. How extraordinary that, while empires have crashed and generations have vanished, this little arrangement of delicate wheels and springs should, by some accident of fate, have been preserved intact for a man of another age to use for the purpose it was first intended, and that after all this time it should be ticking above the grave of its maker.

I thought, as I went on, what a curious text-book on grief and public emotion might be written about the memorials of Westminster Abbey. Have you ever considered the subject of conventional grief, and how narrow is the boundary between pathos and bathos? Grief in early times was cold, dignified and austere: the dead lie in prayer, confident of resurrection. The conception is simple and sincere. This habit of portraying the dead lasted for centuries and then—they began to sit up! It was the vigorous, life-loving material and Protestant Elizabethan age that liked to think of its dead in the attitudes of life, a strange denial of an indisputable fact.

This resurrection in marble is curiously uncomfortable.

The awakening began with Elizabethan matrons dressed in ruffs and wide skirts who lie in stiff, painful attitudes, leaning up on one elbow, a hand supporting a head. A little later we see the Elizabethans in a slightly easier attitude, as if they were having an afternoon nap. Then comes the period when we see them kneeling in prayer, not dead, as the Plantagenets prayed, but just as they were in life: the man facing his wife, their children sculptured below, the boys on one side, the girls on the other.

In Stuart times, however, there was a fancy to return to the earlier convention. The dead were now shown lying flat on their backs in prayer, but this simplicity was counteracted by the erection of vast Renaissance temples and shrines above them. This burst of funeral architecture seems to lead naturally to the positively reckless and enthusiastic tomb-masonry of the Georgian Age.

No great man in the Age of Reason was allowed to appear dead. He had to be shown, if a peer, in full dress, making a speech or standing with one foot forward and holding in his hands a scroll or a book. But this was not enough. He had to be attended by a bodyguard of weeping Britannias or allegorical maidens, either shading their eyes in sorrow or embracing his plinth in an ecstasy of grief, or even, so it seems, attempting to scale the pyramid of his fame and draw him back to life.

William Pitt's memorial is an example of this. The statesman stands in an attitude which is intended to be one of calm dignity, but owing to the architectural features of his memorial and the presence of Britannia and the Spirit of Anarchy, one feels that he is in reality worried by the possibility that a careless movement on their part might upset the elaborate edifice and bring him crashing to the pavement.

These Eighteenth Century sculptures are fascinating as an insight into the frightened, agnostic mind faced by the terror of the unknown and trying in every possible way to blink the fact. And they get larger and more flamboyant as time goes on, until one arrives at the immense and weighty memorial to James Watt, which would seem far more suitable to Paddington Station than to Westminster Abbey.

People with practical and mechanical minds have often wondered how this immense structure was introduced into the Abbey through doors obviously too small to admit it. It has even been suggested by the ingenious that a tunnel was made through which it was drawn from outside. But I have read the much simpler explanation that it was brought in sections and built up inside the church, but, even so, it was so heavy that the vaults below gave way and, as Dean Stanley wrote, " well might the Standard-bearer of Agincourt, and the worthies of the Courts of Elizabeth and James have started from their tombs in St Paul's Chapel, if they could have seen this colossal champion of a new plebeian art enter their aristocratic resting-place ". Still, there is something exquisitely appropriate in the noisy and weighty arrival of one who perfected the steam engine!

Perhaps the fear of death, which is so keenly expressed in the later memorials, reaches its highest point in Roubiliac's memorial to Lady Elizabeth Nightingale. It shows the dead lady mounted upon the roof of a vault accompanied by her husband who, with an expression of the utmost horror, is attemping to ward off a spear pointed by a skeleton on ground level. The idea is clearly taken from Bernini's almost exactly similar memorial to Pope Alexander VII in St Peter's, which Roubiliac must have seen, and carefully noted, when he was in Rome.

As I was leaving, I reflected—and this thought I commend to all who visit the Abbey—that while there have been many royal mausoleums in the world, there has never been one like this where the kings and queens of a country lie surrounded by a great concourse of their subjects. The opening of the doors of Westminster Abbey from the earliest times to all great Englishmen, poets, writers, statesmen, inventors, men of all creeds and men of lowly birth, makes this church the true shrine and sanctuary of the British race.

§ 8

I entered the beautiful octagonal Chapter House in the centre of which springs a single shafted column of Purbeck marble. Nothing mars the perfect proportion of this building. The only objects in it are the show-cases in which are to be seen the early charters of the Abbey.

In this place the House of Commons was born. Here it met for something like three hundred years. The first Members shared the Chapter House with the monks, and, if the Abbot needed urgently to chastise a difficult brother, perhaps the House was obliged to adjourn. There is a story, and why should it not be true ?, that the monks of Westminster complained that their devotions were often disturbed by the noise made by the first members of the House of Commons. In the year 1547—the first year of Edward VI's reign—the Commons left their ancient meeting-place and migrated to another ecclesiastical building across the road, the Chapel of St Stephen, in the Palace of Westminster; and upon the same site they meet to-day.

Somewhere, not far off in the Abbey precincts, Caxton established his printing-press where, in the year 1474, he set up and printed the first book to be produced in English. I do not know where his printing-press was situated, but some people believe that it was in the Almonry. But wherever it was, the site was sufficiently ecclesiastical for it to have bestowed upon the printing trade for ever the name of " Chapel ", which is still given to any association of printers. The head of a printer's chapel is never, as one might think, called the master, but always the " Father of the Chapel ", which is possibly another link with the monastery.

I paid a sad visit to my favourite part of the Abbey precincts, Little, or Farmery, Cloister, which was hideously bombed during the War. It was once the loveliest little backwater in Westminster—far more beautiful, I used to think, than any court in the Temple. A fountain was generally playing in the centre of the quadrangle, and round it, lifted on a series of arches, were delightful small Seventeenth Century houses of mellow red brick. Inside, they were beautiful, with their lovely old staircases, pine-panelled rooms and moulded ceilings. It was refreshing, in moments of worry or trouble, just to go there and to stand at the gate and watch the fountain playing and the sunlight on the old red bricks.

§ 9

The most splendid church to be built in England since Wren's St Paul's is the Roman Catholic Cathedral of Westminster. Its red brick walls and its tall campanile can be seen towering above the roofline of Victoria. This superb Byzantine basilica, whose nave is the widest in England, is still unfinished, but one day it will glow with precious marbles and with mosaics.

It is extraordinary to think that John Francis Bentley, the architect, had never seen St Sophia in Constantinople. When Cardinal Vaughan asked him to design this cathedral in 1894, Bentley, then fifty-five years of age and not in robust health, set out to study Byzantine architecture upon the Continent. The only great church he saw comparable in scale with that which he was to design was St Mark's in Venice, for an outbreak of cholera prevented him from going to Constantinople.

Bentley has given to London one of the most glorious Byzantine churches in the world. It is a triumph in massive simplicity and in the avoidance of the trivial. It is unlike the English conception of a Roman Catholic church, but it is essentially and truly Roman. It is a great basilica of early Christianity, a modern version of St Mark's and St Sophia.

In one of the side chapels a reliquary is to be seen which contains the body of a priest, John Southworth, who was born at Salmesbury, in Lancashire, in 1592. During the persecution of the priesthood he fled to France, but returned to England in the reign of James I when priests were still being hunted from pillar to post. Somehow he managed to minister to the poor Catholics of Westminster for something like twenty-five years. Eventually he was found out and arrested, and he paid the penalty at Tyburn in 1654 where he was drawn, hanged, cut down and quartered.

The history of his poor tortured body is a strange one. It was bought by the Howards of Norfolk, who embalmed it and sent it secretly across the Channel to Douay, which was the headquarters at that time of exiled English Catholics. The body remained in the College chapel until the French Revolution, when it was secretly buried in the garden. A hundred and thirty-four years passed and it was unearthed, brought to England and deposited in St Edmund's College at Ware, Hertfordshire. That was in 1927. Two years later John Southworth was solemnly beatified and his body was translated to Westminster Cathedral. On certain feast days the outer covering of the reliquary is opened and it is possible to see the body of the Blessed John Southworth clothed in red vestments and lying in a casket of bronze and glass.

The visitor to Westminster Cathedral should not fail, if the day is clear, to ascend in the lift to the top of the campanile, where he will be rewarded by one of the finest panoramas it is possible to see of the City and the West End.

CHAPTER EIGHT

I visit the Houses of Parliament and see the new House of Commons, I look at Westminster Hall, see the Changing of the Guard at Buckingham Palace, recall the history of this building and witness the Trooping the Colour on the Horse Guards Parade. I go to Chelsea, see the Pensioners, visit Carlyle's House and the Tate Gallery.

§ 1

DURING an air raid on the night of May 10, 1941, the House of Commons was destroyed by fire. Four people were killed that night—the Resident Superintendent, two policemen and a custodian—and in the morning it was seen that the Mother of Parliaments would have to be, in the strange words of the time, " evacuated ".

So for the first time for centuries the House of Commons abandoned the site of the old Palace of Westminster and migrated back to the place of its origin in the Abbey precincts, where, for the next four months or so, it met in Church House, Dean's Yard. At the end of that time the House moved back again, and occupied the House of Lords, while the peers met in the King's Robing Room. This arrangement lasted throughout the War and until October 26, 1950, when the new Chamber was opened by the King.

No sooner had the House of Commons been destroyed than plans were drawn up for its rebuilding. In 1948 the Speaker laid the foundation-stone with a mallet used when the present Houses of Parliament were built a century ago, and a trowel whose handle was made of oak salvaged from the timbers of the old House of Commons.

I remember visiting the Houses of Parliament early in the War, before the air raids had begun. Like Westminster Abbey, I found it to be a self-contained civil defence unit, and I made these notes at the time:

" As a topographical puzzle there can hardly be a building in England to equal the Houses of Parliament. A member of the custodian staff, who has worked there for fourteen years, said to me :

" ' I still don't consider I know every part of the Houses of Parliament. I'm always coming across something new.'

" As I explored the immense building, I saw that all the rooms which look out on the Terrace and the Thames have been darkened by ramparts of sandbags, so that, like the workers in blacked-out factories, Parliamentary officials know the discomfort of working all day long in artificial light. As I walked along the Peers' Library Corridor I came across picks, shovels, and incendiary-bomb rakes stacked at neat intervals near bookshelves filled with thousands of volumes of Hansard bound in full calf.

" ' In the event of an air raid ', I was told, ' the Lords would come down here, and the Commons would go to similar rooms and galleries on their side of the building. We have established Red Cross first-aid posts in several of the rooms so that any members injured in an air raid can be treated on the premises. We can do almost anything here but decontaminate a Member.'

" ' Without wishing to be flippant, how is a Member of Parliament decontaminated? ' I asked.

" ' By the Office of Works. They have a gas decontamination unit in King Charles Street.'

" I was told that the thirty air-raid wardens who guard the Houses of Parliament every night are clerks and other workers employed on the premises. There is a fire brigade manned by the regular staff of custodians. There are ninety-eight hydrants in the building and an adequate supply of fire-fighting appliances. Fire is, of course, the great danger. The intricate series of sloping roofs might have been designed to afford a secure resting-place for incendiary bombs.

" As I continued my inspection, I was introduced to the Red Cross commandant, who told me that nurses have been on duty in the Houses of Parliament day and night since War was declared. They are unpaid volunteers, and they have not weakened in their long and intensely boring vigil. Eight nurses are always on duty in charge of six first-aid posts when both Houses are sitting. The Lord Great Chamberlain has given up his office to them, and other high functionaries have offered their quarters as a dormitory and a rest-room for those on night duty. The girls, said the commandant, have been wonderful. Many of them are business girls who, when on night duty, come straight to the Houses of Parliament from their places of business. Two come from a draper's shop near Victoria. They bring their supper with them, and cook it over a gas-ring in the House of Lords! In the morning they cook their breakfasts, and then go off to work.

" Often, in order to relieve the tedium of their lives, the Serjeant-at-Arms gives them tickets for debates. They are becoming keen students of Parliamentary procedure. So, if their romantic dreams of bandaging the Lord Chancellor's brow or leading a bloodstained Speaker to safety have not yet come true, there are, it seems, other compensations. Camping out in the House of Lords and frying eggs and sausages there must in itself be an unforgettable experience.

" Entering the House of Commons, I saw that the war-time arrangements are the same as those laid down for the Lords. If the House is sitting during an air raid and it is considered necessary to suspend proceedings, Members are to make their way to the Library and to other recognised shelters. I was shown the Prime Minister's shelter, if it can be called by such an ambitious name. It is just one of the ministerial rooms which overlook the Speaker's Court. It is not even completely sand-bagged, and the fanlight is unprotected. I should hate to be in it during an air raid. There are two knee-hole desks in it, a few chairs, and a coloured reproduction of George Clausen's mural painting *Wycliffe's Bible read in secret*.

" My tour concluded, appropriately enough, with a walk through those vaults beneath the Houses of Parliament which the Yeomen of the Guard search each November in memory of Guy Fawkes. These apparently perfect air-raid shelters have been put to no use, because they are below water level.

" Several of the older members of the staff remember the excitement caused in the House by the first Zeppelin raid on London during the War of 1914–18. At about 9.30 on a dark night in October, 1915, two loud explosions were heard during the debate on the second reading of the Finance Bill. The House was full, but in an instant it became empty, as Members rushed outside into New Palace Yard to see if they could spot the airship. Only three men were left in the House: the Speaker, the Chancellor of the Exchequer, and the Member who happened to be speaking at the time.

" When the House filled again with flushed and excited members (for they had seen the 'cigar-shaped' object in the sky—the usual opulent description in those days of a raiding Zeppelin) the first words they heard were:

" 'As I was saying, Mr Speaker, when our debate was interrupted by the Zeppelin raid . . .'

" Although several bombs fell close to the Houses of Parliament during the first War, the only damage was caused by a small piece of shrapnel which came through a window in the Royal Gallery and flattened itself against a painting of *The Death of Nelson*, leaving a white mark. Both the hole in the window and the mark on the wall have been preserved as mementos of the war that was fought to end war."

§ 2

There was a different story to tell in May, 1941, when a scene familiar to the whole world was reduced in the space of a few hours to a mass of unmeaning chaos.

I went to see the House of Commons after the fire. Dark streams of water were still oozing down stairways, gaps which had once been doors framed hideous vistas of fallen ceilings, twisted ironwork, the metal-work of vanished chairs, the skeletons of telephone boxes, charred panelling and a tangle of twisted wires. It was the new barbarism, or rather the same thing in a new guise. And, to make it all seem crazier, here and there an unimportant and fragile object had been preserved, while the whole House of Commons had gone. I bent down and picked up a perfectly good lead pencil from a pool of water on the floor.

But how quickly, given courage and determination, can man reverse the blows of fate! Only a few years separate a horrible scene of destruction from the new House of Commons, which is a finer and more up-to-date version of the old Chamber.

I went there during the rebuilding and climbed over it, watching with pleasure stone-masons chiselling the stone as it lay in position on column and archway, just as masons did when the cathedrals were built centuries ago. I watched one man carving leaves on the crown of an arch, standing on a scaffold in his white apron, lifting his chisel, giving it just the right blow, pausing to consult a sketch of the design and continuing to create it. I had no idea that this work was done *in situ.* I had imagined that it would be done in a mason's yard.

Stone-masons have been gathered from all parts of England, not from Italy, as I have somewhere read, for we can still cut, lay and carve stone as cunningly as did our forefathers. Two hundred men were at work on the new House of Commons, skilfully handling the light brown Rutland stone.

I climbed up and walked gingerly on a scaffolding erected above the floor of the House. Above me was a superb panelled roof of English oak. Behind the carpenters who made it were centuries of tradition, and I gazed with admiration at them, ordinary-looking men, most of them the sort of men who sit next to you in the Tube and eagerly seek the winner of the three-thirty—yet in their brains and hands reposes the great tradition of British craftsmanship.

The new House of Commons is a replica, with improvements, of the old. It is the same size and it is air-conditioned. I saw the elaborate machinery reposing in the basement for this purpose. Hot air, which was formerly provided by the Members themselves, will now be readily available on the turning of a switch. Cool air, as chilling maybe as any post-war Chancellor's Budget speech, will be as easily obtainable. I think the most interesting feature of the new House is the "Churchill Arch" which, upon the suggestion of Mr Winston Churchill, incorporates the splintered and fire-scarred stones of the old entrance to the Chamber. It was a difficult job. It had to be taken down stone by stone and rebuilt.

I climbed open stairways, still without their balustrades, and gained the new roof of the House of Commons, which is of entirely different construction from that of the old House. The destroyed roof was a pitched one; the new roof is flat, and Members who find their way up there can enjoy one of the grandest views in London. Above them the Clock Tower lifts itself, sending down its sonorous chimes every fifteen minutes. On one side are the towers of the Abbey, on the other a glorious vista of the Thames, an exquisite curve of river and bridges, stretching eastward to Tower Bridge. The visibility was so good when I was there that I could see to the south the heights of Sydenham upon which the two candlesticks of the Crystal Palace once so clearly stood.

§ 3

There were once old civil servants in Whitehall who were in the habit of correcting you if you happened to mention the Houses of Parliament.

"The Palace of Westminster," they would say, with a reproving cough, giving it the correct title. And as "the Palace of Westminster", or "New Westminster Palace", this building is known in all official transactions, and its status is still that of a royal palace. I suppose if the King wished to live there he would have a perfectly legal right to do so.

When the Palace of Westminster, which had been the Court of England from the time of Edward the Confessor until the reign of Henry VIII, was abandoned for the Palace of Whitehall, two of its most important lodgers remained on the premises—Parliament and the Law. The Law occupied Westminster Hall, and Parliament managed to exist, the

Commons in St Stephen's Chapel and the Lords in the old Court of Requests. It must have been an inconvenient arrangement, but Parliament was so accustomed to it that attempts to improve matters were steadily resisted. Prints and paintings of the period—the Eighteenth and early Nineteenth Centuries—show St Stephen's Chapel near the river-side, among trees, its walls washed by the high tide, a delightfully rural setting.

From the end of the Eighteenth Century until the reign of William IV there was a great deal of talk about building a new Parliament House, and Sir John Soane, who built the Bank of England, was one of those who prepared drawings; but nothing was done. Then one night in 1834 the problem was solved in a few hours. Someone who had been burning wooden exchequer tallies overheated a flue, and a fire spread which, aided by a brisk October wind, soon took hold of the ancient buildings and reduced them to ruins. Inadequate fire engines were rushed to the scene, but the flames were too much for them. Posterity, however, owes an immense debt of gratitude to the firemen who worked that night for the valiant and successful efforts made by them to preserve Westminster Hall.

The fire was watched, of course, by a large and enthusiastic concourse of Londoners. In the previous session of Parliament, Joseph Hume had proposed, unsuccessfully, to the House that a larger House of Commons should be built. As the flames took complete hold of the buildings a humorist in the crowd is said to have cried: "There is Mr Hume's motion carried without an amendment!"

When the young Victoria came to the throne there was no home for her Parliament, and several years were spent in clearing the site and in holding a competition for the new building, the only stipulation being that the style must be Gothic or Elizabethan. How different Westminster would have been with an Elizabethan Parliament House. There could have been no Clock Tower and no Big Ben. It would presumably have been a larger Liberty's on the banks of the Thames. However, of the ninety-seven designs examined, the one chosen was that of Charles Barry.

It is the largest and grandest building erected in England since St Paul's Cathedral, and its long river front, with the beautiful Victoria Tower rising above the main building at one end and the Clock Tower at the other, is an architectural triumph which the world over is instantly recognised as—London. No other view of London, including that of St Paul's Cathedral, has been so often painted by foreign artists.

It is interesting to know something about the man who conceived this new and splendid landmark. He was the son of a prosperous London stationer and was born, strange as it may seem, in the last years of the Eighteenth Century. He was educated at the usual mercantile schools, where the only sign of his future brilliance was the excellence of his drawings. When a youth he was articled to a firm of London surveyors, and all the time, while he was studying architecture, he was longing to travel and see the world. His chance came at the age of twenty-two with an inheritance of a few hundred pounds. He travelled all over the Continent, Egypt and the Near East, returning to London in two years time, having seen all the best, and some of the worst, buildings in the world.

Barry was not only brilliant, but he was also propelled by vitality and ambition, lacking which, brilliance is generally destined for the family circle. Before he was middle-aged he had built St Peter's Church, Brighton, the Royal Institute of Fine Arts in Manchester, King Edward's Grammar School, Birmingham, which, before it was demolished, was one of the few buildings worth a second glance in that city. Two clubs in Pall Mall brought him recognition in London, the Travellers' and the Reform Club, this last a wonderful Renaissance palace.

When he tackled the immense problem of the Houses of Parliament he was forty years of age. He had the gift, which some great organisers possess, of picking the right men to serve under him, and, with a good team of supporters, he set out to translate his vast idea into the reality of stone. It took from 1840 to 1852, and I think it wonderful that it should have been done so quickly. Those of us who recognise the less angelic aspects of human nature will not be surprised to know that during this time Barry endured professional jealousy, ignorant criticism, and the malice of enemies. Whether the building of his masterpiece shortened his life I do not know, but he died of heart failure at the age of sixty-five, eight years after the Houses of Parliament were opened.

His stupendous home for the Mother of Parliaments has always been one of the chief sights of London, although I was surprised to be told by one of the bookstall managers that sometimes as many as fourteen to twenty thousand people file through the building on a Saturday, the only day upon which the public is admitted.

I went there one Saturday in company with a party of French day trippers. A young man wearing a beret and an aggressive suit of plus fours told me they had left Boulogne the previous night and, after a whole day in London, would return in the evening. He had already seen Westminster Abbey and the changing of the guard at Buckingham Palace, and after his visit to the Houses of Parliament he hoped to see the British Museum, the National Gallery, St Paul's Cathedral, and the Tower of London!

I concluded, from the assortment of warm and waterproof garments carried by these visitors, that the French Press had not been printing much about the English heat wave, or else our habit of running down our climate has bred such distrust in the Continental mind that the trippers expected, upon landing at Folkestone, to step immediately into fog and Arctic winds or blinding rain. Behind us trooped a bevy of English schoolgirls, followed by a crowd of provincial visitors, notably a number of countrymen in their best clothes.

These Saturday crowds are not shown over the Houses of Parliament: they are allowed to roam about to their heart's content as long as they follow a definite route. The visitor discovers, as he walks through a series of dim Gothic halls, that the nine apartments from the Royal Galleries to the House of Commons lie in a straight line, and that the doors open from one apartment into the other. If all the doors were opened during a State opening of Parliament, the King from his Throne in the House of Lords could see the Speaker in his chair in the far-off House of Commons.

If visitors wish to stand on the site of the old House of Commons, in which Pitt and Fox made their speeches, they must go to St Stephen's Hall, the long corridor which leads from the entrance into the Central Hall. When the new Houses of Parliament were designed in 1840, it was decided to preserve, if possible, the outline and area of the old House which is represented by this hall; and it is surprising to realise that the old House was slightly longer—by fifteen feet—than the modern House.

Unfortunately, visitors are not allowed in the Clock Tower, which is an interesting feature of the building, and affords, especially in the evening just as the lights are being lit, an unforgettable view over London. I have climbed this tower on several occasions to visit Big Ben, which, I should add, is not the clock, but the great hour bell, named after Sir Benjamin Hall, who was Chief Commissioner of Works when the bell was hung.

The wireless has given Big Ben world-wide fame. His peculiar deep and resonant boom, said to be due to a crack, penetrates into every corner of the world.

The way up is a hard, spiral climb. There are three hundred and seventy-four steps, and as you ascend the shallow stone tube is suddenly filled with a shattering series of reverberations as the bells above strike a quarter. You arrive eventually in a room in which you could drive a small car, and here are the works of the clock. Four long steel tubes, bearing the immense clock-hands, radiate to the four clock-faces. The clock-dials, which from ground level might appear to be white enamel, like the face of an ordinary watch, are made of opal glass so that they may be illuminated at night; and this is done by electric lights reflected from white walls built five feet behind them. The Roman numerals are two feet high, and the space between the minute divisions round the dials is one foot. The most interesting object is the pendulum, thirteen feet long, with a bob on the end which weighs four hundredweight. When I was last there I noticed a halfpenny lying on the bob, and I thought that it had been left by a former visitor; but I was told it had been put there to regulate the pendulum. When the clock was first installed two men, stripped to the waist, used to wind it every week; now it is wound by electricity.

Above the clock, in a maze of surrounding staircases, hangs Big Ben himself and four Little Bens. When I tell you that Big Ben weighs thirteen and a half tons, it may convey something of his size, and just as impressive is the giant sledge-hammer, weighing four hundredweight, which rests threateningly against his rim, ready to crash out the hour. Everybody knows the chimes of Big Ben, but how many know that they are playing:

So hour by hour be Thou my Guide,
That by Thy power, no step may slide.

When you hear this crashed out from a distance of a few feet, it sounds more like an artillery barrage than a hymn.

On a balcony outside is the lantern which, when lit, is always a sign to London that the House is sitting. And it was from this gallery that I looked over London one evening and saw street after street spring into twin lines of light. The blue mists of evening lay over them, and above the mist Nelson stood upon his column, outlined in the last moments of twilight. But the maximum time for peaceful reflection up there is exactly fifteen minutes. At the end of that time the battering-rams hit the bells and pandemonium follows, to shake and reverberate over London and, indeed, the world.

§ 4

When I stood in Westminster Hall, I looked up at the roof and remembered having read somewhere that the colossal oak-trees from which it is made were acorns not later than the Sixth Century. If this is true, it is one of the most notable and venerable objects in London and, indeed, in the world. The acorns sprouted in an England shrouded in the mist of the Dark Ages. It was the time of Celtic saints, of little stone monasteries like Iona and Lindisfarne, of Viking bands breaking their way through brambles towards the ruins of dead Roman towns; an England in which the gentle sound of the mass bell and the cry of the sea-gull were so often drowned by the shouts of the wild men in the horned helmets who came to murder and to plunder, and then, having loaded their beaked war-boats, to go off into the sunset.

Centuries of Saxons and Normans hunted the deer, the wild boar and the wolf beneath what is now the roof of Westminster Hall; they made love beneath it, had picnics beneath it, and all the time, as the great trees cast a wider shade and grew to greater bulk, the world was changing, and the Middle Ages arrived, and with them the foresters of King Richard II in 1397, who were looking for the oldest oak-trees in Sussex to remake the roof of the great hall in Westminster. So the oak-trees came crashing down, the trees that were already old when Alfred was king.

Not having a mechanical mind, I confess that the thought of the antiquity of these trees was more impressive than the thought, which I have also read somewhere, that as a feat of engineering this roof is as great an achievement as the Forth Bridge. It is the glory of Westminster Hall; and there is nothing of the kind as fine, or as beautiful, anywhere else. I was interested to see that several specimens of the roof which were badly attacked by the death-watch beetle have been preserved and are to be seen in the Hall. The whole roof was found to be so badly infested soon after the first War that a major operation was performed upon it, and I was told that now there is no reason why it should not last for another ten centuries.

In Westminster Hall poor Richard II was deposed—his first State appearance in the hall which he had rebuilt—here Walter Raleigh was condemned to die; here, as a plate let into the floor tells you, Charles I stood his trial. Here also Warren Hastings was tried for his administration in India, and the Duchess of Kingston for committing bigamy.

In our own time a scene took place in Westminster Hall which will go down in history to join all the other famous scenes. It was when King George V was lying in state under the great roof, with lights burning round his catafalque and the Imperial Crown sparkling upon the flag which draped his coffin. Crowds were passing in two endless lines, in at one door, and past the coffin, and then out at the other door into Palace Yard. When the Guards officers, who stood with bowed heads at the four corners of the dais, were changed one night, four young men in uniform silently stepped up and took their places. They were the present King, the Duke of Windsor, the Duke of Gloucester and the late Duke of Kent. Whether they were recognised by the crowds I do not know, but I remember reading of it and thinking that it was a scene that would live.

I remember seeing the coffin of King George V in the little village church at Sandringham, with a Union Jack over it, in a chancel so small that when anyone entered, the gamekeepers, who stood at the four corners of the coffin, had to move away and stand near the altar. Then in a few days time I saw the same coffin lifted up in Westminster Hall amid all the pomp and pageantry of a royal death. I wonder which scene gave one a greater sense of the solitude of kingship.

§ 5

It was Saturday morning, the sun was shining, and I went to see the changing of the guard at Buckingham Palace. The man who stood next to me on the steps of the Victoria Memorial had a solemn north-country face under a north-country bowler. I put him down as Huddersfield.

Europe's greatest free show was about to begin. All the provincial and foreign visitors to London had brought their cameras to it and were busily taking pictures of railings, people's backs, the helmets of policemen and the legs of police horses, in the hope that somewhere in the far distance a drum major might have been captured as well.

The Coldstream Guards and the Scots Guards were changing guard. The Royal banner hung limply from its pole, so the King was in London. The band played one of those good old pom-pomming waltzes which are served out with the rations to military bandmasters, and the parade stood at ease, furtively blowing bearskin out of its eyes and wishing it were on week-end leave. The two Ensigns, like a couple of cock-sparrows, walked together across the courtyard in the background, the two captains walked together, the two majors walked together. And the parade continued to stand at ease.

" Mucking about," said my north-countryman to no one in particular, but with that contempt in his voice possible only to keen students of Association football.

" The Army's just the same," I said, throwing some heartiness into my voice.

" Aye," he said. " That's reet."

Then his sombre eye followed a sergeant-major who strode briskly across the forecourt with his stick beneath his arm, came to a halt, stamped like a stag and saluted an officer.

" Mucking about," said my companion again, this time with unutterable bitterness.

Had he come all the way from Huddersfield, or wherever he came from, just to make these depressing comments? What, I wondered, was he doing in London? Was he on business or pleasure?

" Seeing the sights? " I asked him.

" Noa," he replied. " I was on parade for an hour yesterday, just mucking about. I'm from th' north-country, see? I coom from Barnsley " (I wasn't far out!). " I came down with our St John's Ambulance team for the annual tests."

He then told me that every year the St John Ambulance Association stages a series of horrible accidents in an hotel. The teams are let in one by one without instruments or bandages, and have to tackle the casualties with whatever may be at hand.

I wondered what problem my gloomy friend had been asked to solve, and I asked him to tell me more.

" All I heard," he said, " was a titled gent talking to his butler; then—wallop! down he came. Crash! He was a film actor engaged for it, see? so he didn't hurt himself. Those chaps know how to fall, see? Well, I went up to him. From the way he was lying I knew he had a fractured thigh. No splints or anything, so I looked round, and saw that the hall was decorated with crossed swords, and there were scarves and things on a table. I pulled 'em down and trussed him up a fair treat."

"But did the titled gentleman fall downstairs for every team?" I asked.

"Aye, that's reet," he replied sadly.

His next test was even more dramatic. He was told that a man had tried to commit suicide in a railway waiting-room. (I love the realism the St John Ambulance Association puts into these examinations.) He went in, and found a man lying with a large razor-gash painted on his wrist.

"So I bound him up," said my companion. "Then I propped him up and talked to him, stern like, about suicide. 'But he doesn't answer you,' said the judge. That gave me a clue. I smelt his breath! Yes, poison! It smelt funny, like peppermint. I did artificial respiration; but it was no good. I lost two marks!"

A sad look came into his face.

"Why did you lose two marks?" I asked.

"Disinfectant," he said mournfully. "There was disinfectant in the waiting-room—but I didn't see it. That's how they catch you out, see?"

At this point two policemen swung wide the gates of Buckingham Palace. The band moved up in a blaze of scarlet and gold facings. There was a noise like seals at feeding time as the sergeant major snarled, barked and stamped about. The little drummer-boys, with a simultaneous click, raised their arms and stood with crossed sticks. The brass section, removing stray wisps of bearskin from its eyes with the mouthpieces of instruments, stood with puffed cheeks ready to give a good blow. The drum major, looking as though he had swallowed his sixth poker, swung his right arm across his golden breast and waited, his wand held close to his body. Then somebody barked. The Guard presented arms. The Guard sloped arms. The Guard slow marched.

The drum-sticks descended, the band slow-stepped into the roadway, ceremoniously, pompously, playing slow, ponderous regimental music, the toe-cap of each regulation boot gracefully pointed earthwards, like the toe of a ballet-dancer. Out came the Colour, before and behind it a shining fence of bayonets; then the band broke from slow into quick time, and the Guard swung off to barracks.

The crowd split, some to follow the band, some—the more knowing ones—in the opposite direction to meet a troop of Life Guards which was jingling up the Mall from Whitehall. They blazed as Arthur's knights never blazed except in the imagination. Their white plumes lay like snow upon their shining helmets. They grasped the reins in white-gauntleted hands. Their swords shone. When they approached the Palace they rode to attention, each man sitting well down in his saddle, his sword at the carry, rising straight up, drawing a line from his knee-cap to the heavens. And the Palace sentries presented arms.

So a summer morning in London begins with pomp and pageantry. The visitors are thrilled. This is the splendid London of legend. It is impossible to remain unmoved, with a bright sun over the Mall, the geraniums in the flower-beds, the green leaves, the sun on scarlet and gold and burnished steel, flags, bayonets, swords, the jingle and creak of harness, drum-taps, the squeal of fifes and the Royal Standard of England above the Palace.

I looked round for my north-countryman. He was lighting his pipe.

"Aye," he said, "London's champion an' all; but—I ought to have seen that disinfectant. . . ."

He waved me farewell and moved off unhappily into the crowds. Unless I break my neck in Barnsley some day, we shall never meet again.

§ 6

The failure of the English people to provide their King with a London palace suitable to his dignity and power has often struck the foreigner as a strange and singular fact, and as recently as 1828 the Duke of Wellington said in the House of Lords that "no sovereign in Europe, I may even add, perhaps, no private gentleman is so ill lodged as the King of this country".

The Kings of England, however, have been repeatedly

housed on paper in the most splendid fashion. Any monarch during the last two centuries who, feeling "ill lodged", and wishing to console himself with the many fine schemes devised from time to time, has had only to take down a volume in the Royal Library at Windsor Castle, in which plans of at least twenty magnificent palaces are to be seen, any one of which would have altered beyond recognition the part of London in which it had been erected.

Why, it might be asked, were none of these palaces built? I suppose lack of money was one reason, and also, more subtly, maybe there was a feeling that a Louvre or a Versailles was not a suitable home for the British Monarchy. It is, nevertheless, interesting to glance at some of the unborn British palaces, beginning with the tremendous scheme for a new Whitehall Palace devised by that great architect of the still-born, Inigo Jones. His stupendous scheme for a sort of regal township extended from Charing Cross almost to the Abbey, taking in all Whitehall and St James's Park. So vast was this conception that Buckingham Palace (then Buckingham House), was to be merely a "royal lodge, observatory and Chamber of Rarities", and Marlborough House a "greenhouse for Exotick Plants". Both Houses of Parliament, the Law and the whole of the Civil Service, were to be housed in this palace, after the ancient pattern, and in the centre, or, more accurately, on the river frontage, the Sovereign was to inhabit a gigantic building like a couple of streets in Rome, one on top of the other.

Then came Sir Christopher Wren, who would have dearly liked the chance to transform Whitehall, but was obliged to be content to leave at Greenwich some idea of the magnificence which he would have created at Westminster. William Kent, who gave us the Horse Guards, designed a fine Palladian palace for George II, which he desired to erect in Hyde Park; for George III, Sir William Chambers drew plans and made a model of another Whitehall; and in 1766 yet another great castle in Spain was created by George Wright, with an eye on St James's Park. Soane and Nash increased the number of these interesting propositions.

Behind all this bid for splendour one seems to sense the

feeling that the Kings of France were regally accommodated, while the Kings of England were living in ancient, unplanned and makeshift buildings, or in houses smaller and less distinguished than those of many a private person. It was felt by some to be a national disgrace that no architectural composition capable of rivalling the Louvre had been erected on the banks of the Thames. And, considering the large number of amateur architects in the aristocracy at that time, it may appear surprising that sufficient enthusiasm was never generated to carry even the more modest of these plans into reality. The fact is that the Continental conception of a royal palace would never take root in English soil.

Instead, we have Buckingham Palace, which, by a process of natural growth, has become, not the Court, which is still officially at St James's Palace, but the home of the Royal Family and, by virtue of the personal qualities of George V and Queen Mary, and the present King and Queen, has become the best known and best loved palace in the world. And it is typical of the English reluctance to create a palace in the grand manner that "Buckingham House" should have become a palace in spite of itself.

The ground it occupies appears in history as a mulberry garden planted as food for silkworms by James I, who had an idea that silk manufacture might help to "wean his people from idleness and the enormities thereof". But this scheme died a natural death, and the mulberry plantation became a superior road-house where gallants in the time of Charles II took their lady friends to eat mulberry tarts. Both Evelyn and Pepys visited the place, and so did John Dryden with his favourite actress, Madame Reeve.

Near the Mulberry Garden three houses were built in succession: Goring House, Arlington House, and, lastly, on the site of the present palace, Buckingham House. Prints of the time of Queen Anne show a charming square red-brick Dutch country house, linked to its stables and out-buildings by two semi-circular colonnades. There was a wide courtyard in front of it, a fountain, iron railings and fine gates with the Duke of Buckingham's coronet, arms, Garter and George all beautifully worked in wrought-iron. When the Duke looked out of his upper windows he saw an avenue of elms and lime-trees, which is now the Mall. In the distance rose the dome of St Paul's, surrounded by the spires of the City churches and, nearer, to the left, across meadows and parkland, were the towers of the Abbey Church. As he looked down the Mall, he could see a long canal and a duck decoy made by Charles II, which is now the lake in St James's Park. Writing to a friend about his new house, the Duke said that near his windows was a little wilderness full of blackbirds and nightingales.

Upon his death Buckingham House went to his Duchess, his third wife, who was said to be the daughter of James II and Catharine Sedley, a mistress whose charms were such that Charles II considered that she must have been bestowed upon his brother by his confessor as a penance.

When the haughty and eccentric daughter of this union died, Buckingham House was bought by George III as a dower-house for Queen Charlotte; and so began its association with the Royal Family. The delightful red-brick country house was occupied by King George and Queen Charlotte, who lived a pleasant and fruitful domestic life there while they held levees and courts at the official Court of St James's. When that great builder, the Prince Regent, came to the throne as George IV, it was natural that he should have called in the architect of Regent Street to rebuild Buckingham House, or the Queen's House as it was then called. But Nash never completed the interior, for both he and his royal patron died within a few years of each other. The new King, William IV, actively disliked Buckingham Palace, as it had finally become. He never lived there, and, indeed, thought so little of it as a residence that he offered it as a temporary shelter for Parliament when the Houses of Parliament were burned down.

It looks uncommonly as though fate had reserved Buckingham Palace for the young Victoria. Immediately she was Queen she moved in, and her first act was to order a royal throne to be installed there. But her palace looked very different from the Buckingham Palace we know to-day. It was the palace designed by George IV. The frontage was set back a considerable distance and there were two projecting wings. Strangest of all, to modern ideas, the Marble

Arch stood in front of it and formed the ceremonial entrance, with the Royal Standard on top.

The palace was twice altered, once in 1847, and again in 1914, just before the War, when the Queen Victoria Memorial Scheme, with the widening of the Mall and the erection, at one end, of the Admiralty Arch and, at the other, of the Victoria Memorial, made the old palace look extremely old-fashioned. The front of the palace, as we see it to-day, was re-fashioned, without even disturbing the glass in the windows, in the short time of three months.

Fortunately the back of Buckingham Palace was not altered. Many of those who have attended a royal garden party will recollect that there is a remarkable difference between the appearance of the front and the garden-side of the Palace. The back is the almost untouched work of Nash and Blore. It is a beautiful piece of classical architecture, and looks its best on a sunny afternoon from the edge of the artificial lake. The Royal Family live at the back of the Palace, overlooking one of the largest stretches of turf in the world.

During Queen Victoria's long widowhood Buckingham Palace was remote and withdrawn from the life of the capital, but with the 1914–18 War it suddenly became the rallying point of the nation during the sorrows and triumphs of those days. It was as if by some instinctive movement of a people towards its hereditary head that the first of those great crowds surged down the Mall on a hot August day in 1914 and called for the King. After the War, George V, aided by the radio and a perfect broadcasting voice, became the father of his people.

The present King and Queen kept the Royal Standard flying on Buckingham Palace throughout the last War, although the palace was hit by bombs and damaged by blast. From the air Buckingham Palace, pin-pointed by the Mall and lying in its large gardens, is one of the most easily identified landmarks in London. Some extraordinary stories were spread during the War that deep underground shelters, which no bomb could damage, were constructed beneath Buckingham Palace, stories which had no foundation outside the minds of those who spread them. During some of the noisiest nights London has ever known the King and Queen lived in the palace observing a fatalistic attitude to danger which, as many of their subjects learned, was the only one to adopt.

Their air-raid shelter was merely a store-room in the basement which may have been blast-proof, but could not have resisted a near miss, much less a direct hit. It was furnished with a few of those gilded chairs inseparable from palace life, which looked distinctly odd in the basement, and a large gilded Regency settee. Facing the door was a circular Victorian mahogany table, on which oil lamps, electric torches, a bottle of smelling-salts, and a number of monthly magazines were carefully laid out by the hand of an experienced footman. Axes were hanging on the walls so that should the exits become blocked the royal prisoners might break their way through the windows into the Palace gardens. I had the opportunity of visiting this shelter once during the War, and thought that, unimpressive as it was, it was historically important and deserved a commemorative tablet.

§ 7

I stood on the Horse Guards parade one morning in June and watched the Household Troops give to the King that elaborate birthday present known as Trooping the Colour. The parade, which always suggests to me a ceremonial version of some military routine that was performed in the Low Countries in the time of Marlborough, is said to be no older than the reign of George II when, it is believed, the Duke of Cumberland originated it.

The King rode down the Mall wearing the uniform of a Guard's colonel, with Princess Elizabeth beside him, and followed by a staff in brilliant full-dress uniforms. They took up their position beneath the Horse Guards Arch, while, from a window above, the Queen, with members of the Royal Family, watched the ceremony.

There was a roll of drums as the massed bands of the Brigade of Guards moved across the parade-ground to the music of a slow march. The five drum-majors in white and gold, with velvet jockey caps on their heads, white gaiters on their legs, strode majestically in front. One of the most fascinating movements is the way the massed bands turn in their own length, a follow-my-leader movement which gives them a right-about turn in the most graceful manner. I can imagine an eccentric Eighteenth Century monarch making his soldiers do this by the hour.

Then came the Troop. Every year one of the Guard's regiments provides the Colour which is to be trooped, or paraded, and on this occasion it was the Colour of the 2nd Battalion, Scots Guards. The Colour is carried at a slow march between the ranks of the assembled troops, escorted by an armed guard. First it is held by an N.C.O., on either side of whom are two sentries with fixed bayonets. The escort for the Colour marches out and comes to a halt. As the Colour is handed to the officer who will carry it, the escort presents arms, while the sergeants on the flanks turn outwards and port arms to show that they are ready to shoot anyone who would attempt to take liberties with the Colour. Then, to the tune of a march played by five bands, the Colour is slowly and solemnly borne round the parade-ground.

There is something infinitely touching about military ceremonial, and I thought that an age which has endured two wars, and is talking about a third, ought not to be enjoying, as I and all those round me were enjoying, this bright burst of militarism. But, after all, I reflected, this was not war. War is a poor old lady hiding under the stairs, holding a beloved cat, while a young man thousands of feet above her in the sky, who has no hatred for her at all, who doesn't even know she exists, is doing his best to kill her and destroy the street in which she lives.

Suddenly I heard the queer, hollow, attractive tum-tumming of cavalry drums. Then the band of the Life Guards moved out, led by the piebald drum-horse whose reins are tied to his rider's stirrup-irons. Two troops of Life Guards jingled behind, the sun on their breastplates, the wind fingering their white helmet plumes.

Then came the march past of the Foot-guards. We were reminded that the Scots Guards held the post of honour when the Colour was played on to the slow march, *The Garb of Old Gaul*, and again during the quick march to *Highland Laddie.*

The King, sitting his charger under the archway, returned the salutes as each detachment went by.

"Stand easy."

Eventually that welcome order sent an unaccustomed individual movement through the rigid scarlet lines: chin-straps were eased, bearskins were lowered, rolled great-coats were moved with a wriggle of the shoulders.

The King took the opportunity, during the minute's stand-easy, to lean forward and lift the bearskin for a moment from his forehead. Then the parade stiffened. The massed bands swung along at a quick march. The King rode out with his daughter and took his place in front of the King's Guard and led it down the Mall to Buckingham Palace.

"My," said an American girl, "that was *just swell*!"

§ 8

When May 29 comes round the Chelsea Pensioners change their navy blue frock coats for red, bestowing an added touch of colour upon the streets of London. This date is that of Oak Apple Day, once a public holiday, but forgotten now by everyone except children and the Chelsea Pensioners. It is the anniversary of the day Charles II returned to the Throne and entered London in triumph. It was also his birthday. It was called Oak Apple Day in memory of his adventures in the boughs of the oak-tree at Boscobel, where he lay hidden while Cromwell's troopers sought vainly to capture him.

Before the last War I wrote a newspaper article about Oak Apple Day, in the course of which I said that, when I was a boy in Warwickshire, we used to rise early upon the morning of May 29 and gather oak leaves with oak apples attached to them. We would then pick bunches of stinging nettles, and, with cries of "Traitor", pursue every boy who was not wearing oak leaves and whip him with the nettles across his bare knees. Sometimes these "traitors" were large and muscular boys who turned savagely upon us and stung us with our own nettles.

I was immediately overwhelmed by letters, mainly from school teachers, from all parts of the country saying that children still observe this custom. (That was in 1938.) I wonder if they still do so, or if the last War has put an end to it. The childish cries of "Traitor", and the three cheers which the old men of Chelsea give for Charles II upon the parade-ground of the Chelsea Hospital, are, so one may fancy, the last surviving shouts of the cavaliers who welcomed the return of Charles II to the Throne of his ancestors.

The Chelsea Pensioners celebrate Oak Apple Day because it was Charles II who founded the Hospital, it is said—and everyone likes to believe this to be true—at the suggestion of Nell Gwyn.* The story goes that a crowd of beggars once surrounded a coach in which she was travelling. Foremost among them was a poor old man crippled in the wars, who, as he stretched out his hands for alms, so touched the tender heart of Mistress Gwyn that she did not rest until she had persuaded Charles to found a refuge for old soldiers. The story cannot be proved, but that does not mean to say it is untrue. Nell Gwyn left money in her will for the relief of unfortunate debtors, therefore why should she not have done something to relieve the distress of poor old men who had served their country? Some considerable pressure, either of a political or perhaps of a more tender character, must have been brought to bear upon Charles in order to persuade him, at a time when he was desperately hard up, to erect a building which cost £150,000.

The ancient institution is open to the public every day, although comparatively few Londoners avail themselves of the chance to inspect it and to talk to the old men who live there. American, overseas and foreign visitors go there in considerable numbers, and you will always find an architect or two among them, because the Royal Hospital, together with Greenwich Hospital, are the finest secular buildings erected by Sir Christopher Wren.

I took an omnibus to Sloane Square and walked along the

* The idea was probably that of Sir Stephen Fox, Paymaster General.

King's Road to the Hospital, where I spent an interesting hour with the old men in the red coats. They walk slowly about the cloisters, or sit puffing their pipes and reading, with spectacles on the tips of their noses, in the great hall, which is now their recreation-room.

Contrary to all accepted belief, the Chelsea Pensioners do not spend their time re-fighting ancient battles and using match-boxes as cavalry brigades and plugs of tobacco as batteries of horse artillery. It is true that, with a pint of beer in view, some of them may rake up a possibly apocryphal reminiscence, but they suspect, and often rightly, that the queer people who encourage such memories are journalists in disguise.

I will tell you what they really do talk about—rheumatism, racing and rations. When you have reached the age of seventy, your teeth are far more important to you than the Charge of the Light Brigade. In the Infirmary, which is not usually open to visitors, are some of the oldest pensioners, and their conversation is frequently upon the subject of age. If an old man can survive the critical age of seventy, I was told, he may go on living into the nineties. After seventy, he becomes proud of his age. Each birthday is a triumph. When he reaches the age of eighty he becomes boastful and begins to add on a few years, and to challenge other old men to prove that they are his seniors.

Sometimes you will see in the Infirmary a shrunken old man whose beard lies like a fall of snow over the bright ribbons of old campaigns. He will remove a pipe from a toothless mouth and say in a childish treble: "I'm ninety-five, I am."

And he will look at you with the uncompromising bluntness of a boastful little boy of five.

He will point his pipe stem at another aged veteran.

"I'm older than what he is," he will quaver maliciously. "He's only ninety, but I'm ninety-five, I am."

"Now what's all this about?" asks the Matron briskly.

"I'm just saying that I'm older than what he is."

"Yes, I know you are," replies the Matron soothingly. "We all know you're the oldest here."

"Yes, I am."

I thought the conversation of old men of ninety-five was extraordinarily like the conversation of young men of five.

The three chief sights of Chelsea Hospital are the living quarters of the veterans, which look like the interior of an old ship with rows of mahogany " cabins ", the Chapel, and the Great Hall. The old men sit reading in the Hall, or they play games and chat together. Ancient flags hang from the walls; at one end is the table upon which the coffin of the Duke of Wellington lay in state. In a glass case is the sabre of Sergeant Ewart of the Scots Greys, " the Swordsman of Waterloo ", and above hangs the Eagle of the 45th Regiment of Foot which he captured in the heat of a cavalry charge.

Nearby is a case in which are to be seen medals which no one claimed when their owners died. Many of them show the head of a young and slender queen called Victoria. They not only tell a story of hardship on many a distant battlefield, they tell also of a lonely old age in Chelsea, and no one at the end to come forward and claim the shining trophy.

The Chapel is almost as Wren left it two and a half centuries ago. Ghostly cobweb flags, whose poles terminate in Napoleonic eagles, hang near the roof. The old men who captured them have one by one departed this life.

An old man with one tooth told me that he was in charge of the gold plate. He unlocked the safe and took out a pair of superb golden candlesticks, golden ewers, a chalice and a plate, of the time of James II.

He told me that the Queen had recently visited the Chapel, and, after admiring the gold plate, had praised its condition, and had asked the name of the polish with which he cleaned it.

" And I said to Her Majesty, ' Ma'am, have you ever heard of that mythical mixture known as soldier's breath and elbow grease? ' "

It might have been thought that a veteran aged a hundred and one, who had survived many a dangerous campaign, would have been fairly safe from the King's enemies in Chelsea Hospital, but this is an unusually dangerous world, and when a parachute mine floated down in 1941 it killed thirteen veterans, including one who had been born in 1840, the year of Queen Victoria's marriage.

§ 9

Once in Chelsea, I decided to spend the day there, which is always a pleasant thing to do.

I had not been inside Carlyle's house in Cheyne Row since the War, and indeed did not know whether it had been damaged or not. I was glad to find it open and undamaged, and all the Carlyle relics beautifully displayed.

I think this house has a place to itself among the literary shrines of London. Writers, and artists in general, are, I believe, usually restless people who move about a great deal, either with their success or failure, or just because they suddenly become bored with a house and want a change of scene. Dr Johnson was a great mover. He had about sixteen different London addresses in his time. Both Thackeray and Dickens moved house frequently. Carlyle, on the other hand, lived in the same house in Cheyne Row for almost half a century. I cannot remember any other literary man who took root in one spot in the same way. All his books, except *Sartor Resartus*, were written in this house.

The place is naturally soaked in Carlyle's personality. If you like Carlyle, you will not be disappointed. To me, he is not an attractive person. I think of him as a mixture of Bernard Shaw and John Knox, and I have an idea that I would not have liked him as I would have liked Boswell, Johnson, Lamb, Leigh Hunt, Dickens, and a hundred more. He had, so far as I know, no appealing human frailties. He did not drink like Boswell, he was not afraid of death like Johnson, he did not idealise women, as so many writers have done. Yet there must have been something attractive about him. A man who could fill a churchwarden's pipe and put it out on the doorstep, filled with tobacco, for any poor passer-by to smoke must have had some loopholes of likeability in him. But he was so often irritable and arrogant.

It is a charming little Georgian house with a narrow back garden, and, as a commentary on the change of values during the past century, it is interesting to reflect that Carlyle rented it for only £35 a year. The rooms are, of course, full of the things you find in such museums: furniture used by the

Carlyles, pens, letters, the piano upon which Chopin played, to the delight of Mrs Carlyle, pictures, busts and—what a devastating snort of contempt Carlyle would have given—the great man's dressing-gown and shawl, in cellophane wrappers.

At the top of the house is the sound-proof room which Carlyle added in a vain attempt to cut out the river and street noises, and the sound of the crowing and cackling of the " demon fowls " in the next door garden. His married life with Jane Welsh Carlyle was one of mutual bickering and irritation, although I suppose they were really deeply attached to one another. Possibly a child might have made all the difference to Jane and have given her an escape from the loneliness of life with an egoist. When Carlyle was seventy-one and Jane was sixty-five, she went for a drive with a little dog. She stopped to let it have a run and another carriage came along and knocked it down. She sprang out and gently picked it up and took her place in the carriage, which continued on its way. But Jane had died of heart failure, and was found seated in the carriage with folded hands, the little dog upon her lap.

In the house in Cheyne Row her husband began to torture himself with remorse, and to regret that he had not been kinder to her while she was alive. He was now the acknowledged head of English literature, as Johnson had been in the previous century, but it meant very little to the sad old man who, in the course of the next fifteen years, sank into a lonely senility, becoming frailer and more languid. Visitors who called upon him in these last years saw a poor old man in a dressing-gown, a man with a shaggy white beard, his blue eyes filmed with age, a nightcap upon his head, and carpet slippers on his feet. He would be sitting near the fire in an arm-chair, propped up with pillows. " I am near the end of my course," he said to one visitor, " and the sooner the better is my own feeling." He was carried down from his bedroom to the drawing-room on the first floor on a February day in 1881. He was then eighty-six. The day before he died, he was heard to say to himself, " So this is Death: well——"

While I was thinking of this, for the whole house reeked to me of Carlyle's old age, the caretaker came in and apologised for having neglected me.

"The plumbers are in," she said, which xplained the hammering and knocking that echoed through the building. "You see, we're having inside sanitation and a bath-room put in. It's being put into the powder-room. I've been here forty-five years and I just can't believe it. I have to keep on going up to look at the bath and make quite sure it isn't a dream."

"So Carlyle had no bath or lavatory?"

"He had a hip bath, and the lavatory was in the garden."

I said good-bye to Cheyne Row, glad to have arrived there upon such an historic occasion.

§ 10

Two other men of genius, Turner and Whistler, sank into unhappy old age not far away. A tablet upon the wall of 119, Cheyne Walk, notes that J. M. W. Turner died there in 1851. The little house was the scene of the great painter's extraordinary "disappearance" when he was at the height of his fame, or perhaps on the reverse slope of it.

Turner was a queer character. He was the son of a London barber. He had a lobster-red face and a piercing grey eye. His manner could be rough and uncouth or, with his friends, light-hearted and merry, but he was essentially suspicious and secretive and, strange to say, this superb impressionist could not express himself in words.

When he was seventy-two, he decided to disappear. He had a fine but neglected house in the West End of London, which he abandoned, although it was kept open and the housekeeper retained in residence. For four years no one knew where he was living.

He would appear unexpectedly at a public function and then vanish again. He cleverly foiled the attempts of all his friends to discover his secret.

Just before he died, it was found that he had been living for four years at 119, Cheyne Walk, under the name of Admiral, or "Puggy", Booth. His companion was a huge, coarse Scotswoman of about fifty, named Sophia Caroline Booth, whom he had known in his youth. He used to call her " old'un " and she called him " dear ". On the roof of the house he put up a railing upon which he used to lean at daybreak, wrapped in an old dressing-gown, as he watched dawn over the Thames. Those who accepted him as Admiral Booth probably imagined that he was some old sea dog who had come down in the world, for although Turner was a rich man, he lived for the last few years of his life as if he did not possess a shilling. The house, which has now been altered and enlarged, was so small when Turner died that the undertakers could not get his coffin upstairs, but had to carry his body down to it.

Whistler lived in several houses in Cheyne Walk. As a young man, in fantastic and eccentric clothes, with a rapier-like gift of repartee and a brilliant wit, he was a notable figure in Chelsea long before he was recognised as a great painter. At 96, Cheyne Walk, which he rented when he was in the thirties, he gave a housewarming. It was attended by a crowd of friends, including the two Rossettis. For some unknown reason, Whistler had delayed the decoration of the drawing-room until the morning of the party. Two young men, who were called in to help, protested that the paint would not be dry in time.

" What matter," cried Whistler enthusiastically. " It will be beautiful! "

By the evening the room was an attractive flesh colour, with pale yellow doors, a colour scheme which the guests took home with them on their clothes.

In this house Carlyle sat for the portrait which has become so famous. Whistler asked for three sittings, but obtained many more. Carlyle was not a good sitter. He ordered Whistler to " fire away," and when he became restless, the artist would shout, " For God's sake, don't move! ", until finally Carlyle rebelled and confessed that Whistler was " the most absurd creature on the face of the earth ".

The painter left Chelsea, returned, left again, and returned at last to die there. At the age of fifty-three he married a widow, Beatrix Godwin, whose death nine years later left him shattered and lonely. He drifted about for years, living with friends or in lodgings until, a sick man of sixty-eight, he found his way back to Cheyne Walk, this time to No. 74.

Those who knew him in his gay, laughing youth and middle-age saw a pathetically changed being.

" When we saw Whistler in his big shabby overcoat, shuffling about the huge studio," wrote E. R. and J. Pennell in their *Life of James McNeil Whistler*, " he struck us as so old, so feeble and fragile, that we could imagine no sadder or more tragic figure. It was the more tragic because he had always been such a dandy, a word he would have been the first to use in reference to himself. . . . No one would have suspected the dandy in this forlorn little old man, wrapped in a worn overcoat, hardly able to walk."

He grew more feeble, and in about a year collapsed and died. So in Cheyne Walk two great painters who immortalised the river Thames were denied by fate the dignity and the consolations of old age, and left this world, to which they had given so much beauty, sad, lonely and piteous.

§ 11

With thoughts of Turner and Whistler in my mind, I stopped on my way back at the Tate Gallery, whose correct name is the National Gallery of British Art. But no one ever calls it by that name: it is always the Tate Gallery, or simply " the Tate ".

While every Londoner knows the Tate, how many could tell you anything about Henry Tate, the founder? He was a man who owed his fame and fortune to an absurdly simple device. He invented lump sugar! Starting life as a grocer's boy in the north of England, he entered the sugar business in Liverpool, where he quickly perceived that a lot of trouble would be saved were sugar sold not as loaf sugar but in uniform lumps. " Tate's sugar cubes " soon became known all over the world. No one had ever thought of this before.

Tate with his lump sugar, Lipton with his tea, and Leverhulme with his soap, belong to a definite little Edwardian period of yachts, country houses, art collections and munificent benefactions. Henry Tate collected pictures, which were hung in a gallery in his home at Streatham. He had bought the finest works by Millais—the drowned Ophelia floating in a lily pond, the *North-West Passage* and the *Vale of Rest*. These, with other pictures by contemporary artists, Tate wished to give to the National Gallery, but there were certain difficulties and it was eventually decided that, if the Government would find a site, Tate would build a gallery of modern art and place the foundation in the hands of the Trustees of the National Gallery. The site chosen was that of Millbank Prison, then being pulled down, a huge fortress-like building designed like a cart-wheel, with the Governor's house as the hub.

The relation of the Tate Gallery to the National Gallery is similar to that of the Louvre to the Luxembourg. The student who wishes to study modern British masters, who are represented perhaps by only a few pictures in Trafalgar Square, will find the rest of their work in the Tate. Turner is a good case in point. Probably his best pictures, *The Fighting Téméraire*, *Rain, Steam and Speed*, and his imaginative classical pictures, are in the National Gallery, but there are rooms of Turners at the Tate which anyone must see who is interested in his work.

I went there to look at the Turners, but I regret to say that I did not see them. I was sidetracked by the Sargents. What a painter he was! Like Van Dyck and Velasquez, he perpetuated a period in history. If you would see the Edwardians as they wished posterity to see them, you must go to the Tate and look at the Sargents—the Wertheimers', father, mother, sons and daughters, Lord Ribblesdale, as Master of the Buckhounds, Mrs Carl Meyer, the Misses Hunter, and the rest.

In a theatre sometimes you are suddenly aware of the machinery of illusion. You think that behind the exquisite scene are men in shirt sleeves, electricians, scene shifters and others, all hidden, all waiting to change the scene, all invisible, but all so important because, without them, there would be no scene at all. While I admired these Sargents, I was conscious of so much that was "off stage". Surely Sargent never painted a portrait in which a butler, a valet or a lady's maid was not implied. You never see them, but an age which has to clean its own shoes and wash up, knows that they were there.

Behind all Sargent's portraits is a rich, cigar-laden atmosphere of Edwardian prosperity. There are yachts in the atmosphere, grouse moors, huge country houses, the Stock Exchange, and a portly personage with a beard who for most of his life was the Prince of Wales.

I think Sir Osbert Sitwell has brilliantly analysed Sargent and his art in his *Left Hand Right Hand*.

" In order to make a living in England during the late-Victorian and Edwardian ages," he writes, " every portrait painter had, to a certain extent, to become a faker of old masters, because the clients who could afford to patronise him demanded ' Give me the sort of Gainsborough that my grandfather had '—or, more usually, that somebody else's grandfather had, and which the grandson had sold—' but not so old-fashioned ! ' was the clamant cry. Sargent, by supplying old masters, to which was added the skin-thin glint of the French Impressionists, novel to the English public, precisely met this demand."

It is this grand manner in Sargent which one admires. But he could do other things. It is childish that *Gassed*, the result of a visit to the Western Front during the War of 1914–18, should be in the Imperial War Museum just because it is a war subject. It should be removed and hung in the Tate, as near as possible to *Lord Ribblesdale*.

I confess I was delighted by the Sargents. I felt that he was a great artist. I felt also that I had left this servantless age behind and was back in a world where money at least had value. Sargent never married, and he died in Chelsea in Whistler's old studio in Tite Street, at the age of sixty-nine. It was typical of Sargent, his art, and the age in which he lived, that the contents of his studio, the drawings and paintings and all the débris of his life, should have fetched £175,260 at Christie's. It was the last Golden Age and Sargent was its mirror.

CHAPTER NINE

I go to St James's Palace and remember the day when it was a refuge for female lepers. I walk in St James's Park, the Green Park and Hyde Park and recall the history of these ancient hunting grounds. I visit Kensington Palace and see the room where the young Victoria was sleeping when she became queen.

§ 1

AS I was walking down St James's Street one morning I glanced with pleasure at the old red Holbein Gateway to the Palace which Hogarth introduced into plate four of *The Rake's Progress*. It looks the same now as it did then. Two sentries were pacing up and down, and the gate was, as usual, open.

I saw a timid little group of visitors trying to pluck up sufficient courage to take a peep inside. Gaining confidence from a fishmonger's van, which sped casually in, they waited until the sentry was at the end of his beat, and then hastily entered, to discover that St James's Palace is the most accessible, the most friendly and the most public royal building in London.

If it be true that the English are masters of under-statement, perhaps St James's Palace might be called the architectural equivalent. Can this modest, low-pitched building, into whose windows any passer-by may peep, be " our Court of St James's ", to which for so many centuries emperors, kings, sultans and presidents have despatched their ambassadors? The very name of " palace " sits strangely upon it. Could anything look less like the official Court of England?

Yet that is the very charm of St James's Palace. It is small, it is intimate, and it has no railings. It is so much part of London that the King, when he lived there, was less remote from his subjects than he would have been in Berkeley Square.

And Pepys hit this off well when he wrote in his *Diary* for October 19, 1663:

> "Coming to St James's I hear that the Queen did sleep five hours pretty well to-night, and that she washed and gargled her mouth, and so to sleep again."

How perfect that is! How admirably it describes the atmosphere of this little nursery-rhyme palace. You feel that it might be possible, opening any one of the many little doors, to find the King in his counting-house counting out his money or the Queen in her parlour eating bread and honey. It is actually on record that during the time of George II a visitor to the palace tripped and fell headlong downstairs and through a door at the bottom, where he lay stunned. When he regained consciousness a stern little man with white eyebrows and a red face was bending over him and sticking plaster on his skull. He had fallen into the King's sanctum. What could be more intimate and friendly? What could be more delightfully like *Alice in Wonderland*?

Even to this day you can walk through the gatehouse, which bears the monogram of Henry VIII, and wander into the little courtyard beyond, where some of the lamps wear crowns. Here you may watch the butcher's boy delivering the meat to York House or the grocer's boy delivering the rations at any one of the many doors or windows. The domestic details of palace life, usually so carefully hidden from the public, are at "our Court of St James's" displayed to the whole of London. You can tell where the various residents of the palace buy their meat, poultry, vegetables and groceries by reading the names on the vans that drive into Ambassadors' Court.

The palace itself is usually seen only on the morning when the King holds a levee, and then those summoned to attend see more of each other than of the palace. I went there one morning with an official from the Lord Chamberlain's office, who first took me through a door into the Colour Court. I recognised this as one of the unknown beauties of London. It is like one of the finest courts in the Temple, but it is even more attractive, and more human, because women are to be seen there instead of barristers. It is surrounded by the houses of Court officials. In the centre of the flagstones rises an incredibly decayed wooden post with a socket perhaps five inches deep on top of it. This is the staff in which two centuries ago the Colour was fixed during the changing of the guard.

But what charmed me about the Colour Court was its domestic life. How often have I watched the butcher's boy cycle mysteriously out of Ambassador's Court to some unknown region beyond. I now discovered that he goes to Colour Court; and there he finds women cooking and bustling about in kitchens. Instead of ringing the bell, he pops his parcel through the palace windows. This surely must be an old tradition. I fancy this was the method o. delivery when Charles II lived there, and no doubt his sardonic majesty often looked from a window above, especially if there were any good-looking milkmaids about!

The Lord Chamberlain's official took a key from his pocket and unlocked " our Court of St James's ". We were in a little hall facing a delicate staircase which the King mounts when he holds a levee. This led us to the State apartments. I was surprised to find that we were alone in the Palace. The State rooms are shut off from the residential quarters and are opened only on royal occasions.

As usual in palaces, room opened into room, and from the walls of these rooms gazed the faces of Stuarts and Hanoverians. The first Georges curvetted upon white horses, innumerable forgotten princesses looked down towards us, their shoulders slipping out of white satin gowns, and the Stuarts gazed politely at the Hanoverians, and the Hanoverians gazed politely at the Stuarts. Now and again my companion flipped a blind-cord and let a little more light into the empty palace where these great ones live among dust-sheets and silence.

So we passed from room to room, while I wondered what a courtier of other days, who was familiar with the Louvre, Versailles and Fontainebleu, would have said of this modest little English palace. To us to-day it may seem grand enough, but in times when even a private mansion was designed to impress the beholder with the wealth and social position of its owner, St James's Palace must have struck its visitors, as it did Sir John Fielding in 1776, as a place which " reflects no honour on the kingdom, and is the jest of foreigners ". Peter the Great told George III that were he King of England he would turn Greenwich Hospital into a palace and St James's Palace into a hospital.

Yet, I reflected, the mighty monarchs who inhabited the great palaces of the world have vanished from their kingdoms, while ambassadors are still credited to " our Court of St James's ".

The most interesting room we entered was one of the early apartments, where a Tudor fireplace bears the initials of Henry VIII and Anne Boleyn united by a true lovers' knot. What a relic of dead love; what a thing to find in the heart of London. It appears likely that Henry intended to live in this place with his fascinating young queen, and it was a habit of his to immortalise his love on chimney-pieces. How strange it is that his later queens did not persuade him to send a stone-mason with a chisel to obliterate these memories of Anne Boleyn.

We came to the Throne Room, where we lifted the sheeting which covered the throne to see the rich red velvet beneath and the Royal Arms worked in jewels. I noticed that beneath the throne, under the carpet—a feature never seen normally—was a large square of match-boarding. I was told that George V disliked standing for a long time on a soft carpet, and that during a levee, when he stood for perhaps an hour and a half, he discovered it much less tiring if a sheet of match-boarding were placed between the carpet and the floor. Near the Throne Room is a window overlooking Friary Court, where the heralds proclaim a new sovereign upon his accession; and it was at this window the young Victoria burst into tears when she heard the crowds cheering her as queen.

In the long sweep of English history St James's Palace is almost a newcomer as a royal Court. The Plantagenets held court at Westminster, the Tudors and most of the Stuarts at Whitehall, and it was only with the Hanoverian Georges that St James's became a royal residence for any length of time. Its true role in life seems to have been that of a royal maternity home. The number of princes and princesses born there is remarkable, beginning with the children of Henrietta Maria. This Queen loved St James's Palace, and chose to bear her children there. It was the birthplace of Charles II and James II. Mary II was also born there, so was Anne. The Palace was the scene of that fantastic Protestant story that James Edward, the father of Bonnie Prince Charlie, was not his mother's child but had been smuggled into the palace in a warming-pan.

Another role of the Palace was to be the lodging of certain royal favourites. At one time there lived at St James's two women who must have had a lot in common, Madame de Beauclair, a mistress of James II, and the once formidable beauty, Hortense Mancini, Duchess of Mazarin, a mistress of Charles II. Both these ladies were retired to St James's, where they became close friends, and, becoming interested in spiritualism, entered into a pact that the one who died first would appear to the other. Some years after the Duchess had died she appeared in St James's Palace to her friend, who promptly expired a few hours later. This story was widely credited at the time, and provides the palace with, I think, its only ghost story.

It is not certainly known in which room Charles I spent the last three nights of his life. We seem to be foreseeing the French Revolution more than a century before its time when we read of the unfeeling brutality which surrounded the King's last hours. Clarendon, in one of the suppressed passages of his history, described how a guard of Cromwellian soldiers was forced upon the King, and how they jested, smoked and drank in his presence as if they were among their own comrades in the guard room.

§ 2

Long before the West End was dreamt of, when there was nothing but an occasional cottage or a cowshed between what is now St James's and Charing Cross, fourteen "leprous maidens" were isolated in the meadows in a leper-house dedicated to St James-the-Less. This pious foundation was supported by wealthy merchants in distant London, whose spires could be seen by the afflicted maidens as they looked from their windows eastward across the intervening meadows. Stow says that these poor creatures spent their lives "chastely and honestly in divine service".

In order to support the funds of this foundation, Edward I, in the year 1290, granted to the leper-house the profits of a fair which was to be held once a year outside the gates for several days, beginning on the eve of St James's Day, July 24. This event, known as St James's Fair, became one of the famous carnivals of mediæval London. Every summer booths and stalls, mountebanks and jugglers, pedlars, musicians, bear-wards, strong men and fat women, and all the immortal and changeless characters of fairs the world over, established themselves round the leper-house and gave the poor, unfortunate inmates a rich taste of the great gay world.

As anyone will know who has studied the street markets of London, and such ancient institutions as Barnet Fair, there is nothing in life more tenacious and more jealous of its privileges than the ancient right to buy and sell and get drunk at a certain place at a given time each year. You can pull down palaces, you can even, in these days of the bulldozer, move mountains, but it is impossible, without going to Parliament and calling in the police, to alter a right of way or abolish an ancient market. So St James's Fair continued to turn the meadows of Westminster into a brightly coloured pandemonium for centuries, and so it was when Henry VIII cast his eyes upon the leper-house and thought what a suitable hunting-box it would make. At his request, Eton College, to whom it then belonged, exchanged it for other property, and Henry acquired the old place and the "leprous maidens". The leper-house he pulled down and the lepers he pensioned. That is how "our Court of St James's" began.

The history of the Fair is also interesting. Henry VIII apparently made no attempt to stop the rabble which assembled every summer round the gates of his hunting-box, but when the hunting-box became a royal palace its occupants found the fair an unpleasant annual infliction. During the Plague year Charles II managed to have it moved to St James's Market Place, a turning off the Haymarket. This area was becoming built up, and so in the course of the next few years the Fair was obliged to migrate farther west to a large piece of waste ground, north of Piccadilly, called Brookfield because the waters of the Tyburn ran across it. Under the Great Seal of England in 1688 James II gave sanction for a fair to be held in that place on the first of May annually and for ever.

And the name of this event was Mayfair.

§ 3

The English people have always cherished an uncomplicated love for the country. Whether the trials of war, which have inflicted upon the landowner the painful duties once performed by servants, such as the feeding of hens, or whether the experience of living in the basement of a large country house, or even in the gardener's cottage or lodge, have moderated this passion, time alone will show. The townsman, however, continues to revel in the sentimental and scenic aspects of rural life as did his mediæval forefathers before him, and seeks every opportunity of visiting the country.

Is it therefore surprising that these fundamental national traits and instincts are reflected in London? What is the London square but a little bit of country, captured, as it were, and enclosed by the town? What is the London flower-box but a square in miniature, a little slice of country on the window-sill: an attempt to enliven and refresh the drab streets with some memory of the countryside?

Of course the most spectacular rural feature is the park. London's parks are as different from the planned parks of the Continent as Berkeley Square is different from the Piazza di Spagna. Our parks are just pieces of the English countryside preserved in London. They are the largest squares of all; the most extensive reminder London possesses of the beloved English countryside. No matter that generations of landscape gardeners have skilfully given to our parks that air of natural beauty which has now reached maturity. That is how the Londoner would have it; and any attempt to formalise the parks of London would be violently and indignantly resisted.

The most famous and popular of all the open spaces are the royal parks, three in number—the Green Park, St James's Park, Hyde Park and Kensington Gardens—an area of about nine hundred acres. The intelligent foreigner, whom I have mentioned before, might, as he studied London and the Londoner, think it peculiar that the parks which are called "royal" appear to belong more than any other part of London to the general public. And they have done so since the Restoration. Earlier kings may have thought of the royal parks as their own personal property, but no monarch since the time of Charles II would have dreamed of doing so. The reply of Sir Robert Walpole to Queen Caroline is well known. When the Queen asked how much it would cost to incorporate a portion of a park with the palace gardens, Sir Robert replied, "Only three crowns, madam."

The royal parks are all that is left of the hunting-grounds of the early kings. Henry VIII could hunt the stag, course the hare and fly his falcons from Westminster to Hampstead Heath; and it is a curious, and not unpleasant, reflection that while His Grace was hunting or hawking over this carefully protected area he was securing for future Londoners the right to picnic beneath oak-trees, to play cricket on green grass and to swim in, or boat on, the Serpentine. Cromwell's Government sold the royal parks to private individuals, but when Charles II was restored to the throne these persons were dispossessed and the parks were returned to the Crown. And it was under Charles II that the royal parks assumed their modern character as recreation grounds. Coaches and hackney carriages were then numerous, and it was almost as easy for city-dwelling folk, like Samuel Pepys, as it was for West-End courtiers, to drive out to St James's or Hyde Park to see the crowds or just to sit on the grass, as Londoners have always loved to do.

To anyone who has lived in London the characters of the three royal parks are separate and distinct. Hyde Park is a microcosm of an English county, like a scale model in an estate agent's window; St James's Park is a garden, and the Green Park, the smallest of the three, is a grass verge to Piccadilly. It is the most natural of the three parks, and looks like the home park of Buckingham Palace. It offers the quickest escape from the streets of the West End, and it provides the millions of people who speed past it every day on omnibuses a pleasant glimpse through trees of grassy hummocks and knolls. If you took a census, I think you would find that nine Londoners out of ten would prefer to sit on the Green Park side of an omnibus than on the Piccadilly side.

Many people must have wondered why it is called the Green Park, for it is no greener than Hyde Park or Kensington Gardens. The explanation is that in the old days a deer enclosure was made of the upper park, which at that time was almost treeless. The deer cropped the grass so closely that, to our ancestors of the Stuart and Georgian ages, this park was a great sweep of short green turf. If you stand on the high ground near the top of Constitution Hill and look towards the Mall, you have a good idea of the appearance of this park in the old days. I think this is still one of the most attractive sweeps of grassland in any of the London parks.

Small as it is, the Green Park has a strong and unique character. Its northern boundary is one of the busiest and most famous streets in the world. What visitor to London has not carried away with him a memory of sitting on a summer's morning in the Green Park watching through the trees the traffic speeding left and right along Piccadilly? I remember once falling into conversation with a foreigner in the Green Park who turned out to be a Pole. He told me that, to him, this park was the most extraordinary sight in London.

"Why?" I asked.

"Look," he said. "Sheep are grazing all round us, here right in the middle of Piccadilly! It is something that no one could have imagined or believed. Don't you call that extraordinary?"

And I had to agree that it was.

Characteristic of the Green Park are the people who go there to fall asleep on the grass. I fancy that this habit is not as usual as it once was. Between the wars the Green Park was the dormitory of every idle and destitute person in the city. Many of them were tramps, a race that appears to be dying out, some were hard-luck cases, but the majority were known to the park keepers as " regulars ".

" I know them all," a keeper once told me, " and I have known them for years. Now and then you get someone who has come down in the world through no fault of his own; but you can take it from me that most of them have never done a day's work in their lives. There's no reason to-day why anyone should sleep out in London, but some of these people would rather die than go to a casual ward or a shelter. I think the idea of having a bath frightens a lot of them. They drift about the streets all night, sometimes snatching forty winks on a bench, then as soon as we open in the morning they come in and go to the Sheep Pen, which we park keepers call ' the dosser's bit '. Sometimes an old regular disappears perhaps for a year, and you wonder whether he's dead or doing a stretch, then some morning you see him full length on the grass with a newspaper over his face, same as usual. If you say to him, ' Hullo, back again? ', all you get is a grunt or silence."

On summer afternoons and evenings the life of the Green Park centres round the bandstand and the eastern end of the park near the gravel path which leads from Piccadilly to the Mall. The name of this path, although few Londoners probably know it, is the Queen's Walk; and the Queen was Caroline, wife of George II, who loved the London parks and was the creator of the Serpentine.

Unlike the other two royal parks, the history of the Green Park is fairly tame, except for a series of robberies and a number of duels, and for a period during the Eighteenth Century when Fashion, suddenly deserting Hyde Park and St James's Park, transferred itself to the Green Park. It then became " the thing " to promenade there every evening before dinner, which at that period was from 4 until 5 p.m., so that in summer time the parade took place in broad daylight. During this time it was possible to see all the wealth, nobility and beauty of London dressed for dinner elegantly strolling up and down and indulging in small talk. Society in those days was a small, rigid caste; everybody knew everybody else, and the general public was as much interested in the aristocrats and their beautiful ladies as a modern crowd in the film stars who attend a first night. I suppose the Royal Enclosure at Ascot is the last relic left to us of a great parade of rank and fashion, but the Green Park parade lasted for nearly half a century! The mind recoils in amazement at the thought of the precious hours of life that must have been occupied in dressing up for this parade: the washing and the stretching of gloves, the tying of cravats, the dressing of wigs, the laundering, the dress-making, the powdering, the turning this way and that before the mirror; and all to peacock for an hour or so in the Park! One can imagine the beau's lodgings scattered with rejected cravats and the lady's bedroom in disarray, a country maid in tears clearing up the stockings, the petticoats and the gowns which madame, now smiling so sweetly over her fan in the Park, had rejected only a moment before with the fury of a virago; and one can smile at the thought of the pains taken to launch a new waistcoat, a new hat or a new gown. But so seriously was this parade of fashion considered at the time, and so popular was it, that the balconied houses in Arlington Street, which provided a grandstand view of the promenade, were let at the astonishing sum in those days of £4,000 a year!

Then suddenly this river of satin and brocade ceased to flow. The affected laugh, the carefully-thought-out epigram and compliment were no longer uttered in that place, the fans were no longer flicked and flirted, the ebony canes no longer tapped the gravel; for it became fashionable to have dinner from 8 to 9 p.m. That change in the dinner hour killed the Green Park parade stone dead. To be seen there after that was to proclaim oneself out of touch with what Continental people still refer to as " high life ".

Do the sleepers on the grass, I wonder, who are such a strange feature of London's parks, ever dream that red-heeled shoes are passing by? Do they ever awaken, having fancied themselves to have been the centre of a crowd in satin and brocade, a crowd that quizzed them through glasses and prodded them with ivory canes and passed on laughing to think that a creature so strange and so uncouth could have invaded the Green Park?

"Blimey," one can hear such a sleeper exclaim, "I must have been dreaming of that there film!"

§ 4

When I was very young I wrote a novel about two London lovers. They were poor, romantic and they worked in the City. They must have been more misanthropic than the real thing, for they were always trying unsuccessfully to be alone. In one chapter, I remember, they even climbed the Monument in order to kiss in solitude. I obviously did not know enough about love, or about London, in those days to know, as any London lover could have told me, that two people in love are alone even at a football match.

However, I remembered this youthful indiscretion early one morning when I was taking a walk through St James's Park. It was that time in the morning when the park is full of young men, the most junior members of the Civil Service, lingering about, sitting on seats and reading newspapers while they wait for their offices to open. As I looked at them I became aware that many had got there early in order to exchange with a girl a greeting so brief that it was, at the same time, a parting. Lovers of an almost appalling simplicity and youthfulness were shyly holding hands, or attempting not to hold hands, as they sat for a moment under the trees before he went off to H.M. This or That and she went off to her Underwood or the gowns department.

I watched a young man say good-bye to a girl as if she were about to travel alone and on foot through the Congo, instead of to Piccadilly. It was a terrible parting. Even I, so remote and disinterested, was distressed by it. Eventually they managed to conclude it, and she went off with many a backward wave to some adjacent office, while he took his aching heart to Whitehall. There is a stage in love-sickness when the patient imagines that if a chimney-pot happened to fall anywhere in London it would descend in a straight line upon the cranium of the adored one. He was in that stage. It is true that probably this couple would meet to eat their sandwiches at lunch time, but what an appalling desert separated them until the joyous clock struck one! It is commonly believed that Whitehall is staffed by men in whose veins the usual red corpuscles have been transformed into red tape, but a walk in St James's Park in the early morning suggests that many a letter is written by Pelleas and posted by Melisande.

Promptly at nine o'clock the character of the park changes. The few remaining nursemaids in the neighbourhood appear with perambulators, and the varied crowd of people who have a day off in London select their chairs beside the lake. So upon a summer's morning the ping of the ticket man's punch is heard from the Horse Guards to Buckingham Palace.

This park is the most artificial and formal of all the royal parks. While the Green Park does not possess one flower-bed, St James's Park is full of them: it is a gardener's park. In spring the flowers trumpet forth the season with a massed band of tulips; and in autumn their dahlias are one of the sights of London. Another feature of St James's Park, which adds greatly to its charm, is the lake. In the centre of London we have a garden planted round a lake, and upon the lake are all kinds of wild fowl; and the king of the birds is the famous pelican, whose remote predecessor was placed there by Charles II.

This park is really a memorial to Charles II; and what finer legacy could any king leave to his people than a park full of flowers and a lake full of ducks? No sooner had he returned to the Throne than he decided to make something of St James's Park. During his exile on the Continent he had seen some of the best landscape-gardening of the time, and he had admired the magnificent parks and gardens with which the King of France was surrounded. It must have been a shock to him to return to Whitehall and to find St James's Park not only without shape or design but also untidy and neglected. He decided to plant flowers, make walks, create water for wild-fowl and build an aviary along that side of the park which is still called Birdcage Walk.

What a pity, and how unfair, that Charles's fondness for women should be the only aspect of his character that is still remembered. How rarely anyone mentions his great personal influence upon the re-designing of London after the Fire and upon the growth of the West End, and who remembers his deep interest and knowledge of shipbuilding and naval affairs? Two pleasant traits of his character were his fondness for walking and his love of dogs and birds.

It is believed that in the year he was restored to the Throne he sent over to Paris for Le Notre, the designer of the Tuileries Gardens, who, having examined St James's Park, is said to have declined to submit a design for such a lovely piece of natural English scenery. If that is true, Charles was left to his own devices, and he did very well. His first improvement was to join up the various wells and pools in the park to form a long strip of water, the fashionable Dutch canal of the period, which was the forerunner of the present lake. This canal stretched from the back of the Horse Guards almost to Buckingham Palace. To one side of it was a series of smaller canals which formed a duck decoy.

Nothing endeared Charles to the ordinary folk of his time more than his habit of walking in St James's Park with his dogs, and the hours he spent playing with the birds in his aviary in Birdcage Walk or in feeding the ducks on the canal. He was completely unselfconscious, and did not mind who saw him. It is said that he was sometimes to be seen bathing and swimming in the canal. The pelicans of St James's Park are among the best-known sights of London, but it is not generally realised that they are a living link with the age of Charles, Nell Gwyn, Pepys and Wren. The first pelican was presented to Charles by the Russian Ambassador, and Evelyn, who went to see it in February 1664, wrote:

> "I went to St James's Park where I saw various animals and examined the throat of the Onocrotylus, or pelican, a fowl between a stork and a swan, a melancholy waterfowl, brought from Astrachan by the Russian Ambassador. It was diverting to see how he would turn a flat fish, plaice or flounder, to get it right into his gullet

at its lower beak which being filmy stretches to a prodigious wideness when it devours a great fish."

Charles often lost his pets in the park—like all spoilt dogs, they probably refused to obey the royal command to come to heel—and the newspapers of the time contain many advertisements for them. In the *London Gazette* for November 1671 is the following appeal :

" Lost four or five days since in St James's Park, a dog of His Majesty, full of blue spots, with a white cross on his forehead, and about the bigness of a tumbler."

A bitter advertisement, which has always been considered to have been written by Charles himself, runs :

" We must call upon you again for a black dog, between a Greyhound and a Spaniel, no white about him, only a streak on his Brest, and Tayl a little bobbed. It is His Majesty's own Dog, and doubtless was stolen, for the Dog was not born or bred in England and would never forsake his Master. Whosoever findes him may acquaint any at Whitehall, for the Dog was better known at Court than those who stole him. Will they never leave robbing His Majesty? Must he not keep a Dog? This dog's place (though better than some imagine) is the only place which nobody offers to beg."

History is silent about this theft, and we do not know whether Charles and his dog ever came together again. But the advertisement remains, expressing in every sentence the sardonic humour of a man who was not always the Merry Monarch.

At the same time that St James's Park was transformed, a new pall-mall—the present Mall—was taking shape. Most European cities possessed these long avenues shaded by trees where a game like croquet, called *palamaglio* by the Italians and *paille maille* by the French, was played with four-feet-long mallets of lance-wood and balls of box-wood. This game is older than some writers on London appear to think. Mary Queen of Scots played it, and also golf, as early as 1568, when, as the *Calendar of Scottish Papers* says, she was playing at Seaton " richt oppinlie at the fieldis with the palmall and goif ". Scotland caught the craze from France quite half a century before England took to it. Writing in 1598, Dallington in his *Travels* mentions having seen the game played in France, and marvels that " we have not brought this sport also into England ". Probably it came south from Scotland with James I, from whose reign we can probably date Pall Mall. The game was certainly played there in the time of Charles I.

When the West End began to grow, buildings interfered with the game in Pall Mall, so it was necessary to lay down another alley nearby in what is now the Mall. The trees which line the Mall to-day were not planted as an approach to Buckingham Palace: they are the successors of the usual trees which were always planted on either side of a pall-mall.

Pepys once had a chat with the man whose task it was to keep the new Mall in order.

" I walked in the Park," he wrote, " discoursing with the keeper of the pall-mall, who was sweeping it, and told me that the earth is mixed that do floor the mall, and that over all there is cockleshells powdered and spread to keep it fast, which, however, in dry weather turns to dust and deads the ball."

The official who performed this task was known as " the King's cockle-strewer ".

There were also other attractions for Charles II near St James's Park, as we learn from Evelyn, who one day in March 1671 walked through the park with the King as far as the Mall where, he writes:

> " I both saw and heard a very familiar discourse between the King and Mrs Nelly, as they called an impudent comedian, she looking out of her garden on a terrace at the top of the wall and the King standing on the green walk under it. I was heartily sorry at this scene."

Skaters may be interested to know that skating with steel skates was first seen in England upon the frozen surface of the St James's Park canal in December 1662, when cavaliers who had been in exile in Holland brought out their skates, to the wonder and delight of the Londoners. Both Evelyn and Pepys were there, and were charmed by the sight. " Having seen the strange and wonderful dexterity of the sliders on the new canal in St James's Park, performed before their Majesties by divers gentlemen and others after the manner of the Hollanders, with what swiftness they pass, how suddenly they stop in full career upon the ice," wrote Evelyn, " I went home by water, but not without exceeding difficulty, the Thames being frozen, great flakes of ice encompassing our boat."

This and suchlike scenes, so marvellously preserved for us in the pages of the diarists, one would dearly love to have witnessed in that distant, exciting and naughty London of the Restoration. How interesting it would have been, for instance, to have seen Charles rowing in a boat alone on the Thames, as he occasionally did. Now and again, of course, there was an object in his sculling, such as that on an evening in May 1668 when he suddenly cancelled his coach and his Life Guards and decided instead to pay a visit to the Duchess of Richmond at Somerset House.

" He did on a sudden," says Pepys, " take a pair of oars or sculler, and all alone, or but one with him, go to Somerset House, and there, the garden door not being open, himself clamber over the walls to make a visit to her, which is a horrid shame."

It may have been a " horrid shame " to Pepys, but to us it is an appealing picture: Charles, a great wig framing his sombre dark face, lace ruffles falling over his wrists as he took the oars, then a flash of satin breeches and embroidered waistcoat as His Majesty climbed the wall! And what did a lady say when visited by such a burglar?

§ 5

I walked through Hyde Park one afternoon picking my way between men who were lying as if dead near the public footpaths. This, unless I am much mistaken, is a type of sleeper peculiar to London, for I do not remember to have seen in Paris, Rome or any other great European city, so many citizens so publicly " lost in the arms of morphia ", as a Mrs Malaprop known to me would express it. I wonder if these men are sleeping off a debauch, or are they, like Napoleon, just good sound sleepers who can slip into unconsciousness anywhere and at any time?

If I wished to go to sleep in Hyde Park, I would seek out with the greatest care the most secluded spot I could find, not only because I should hate to be seen in the pathetic helplessness of slumber, but also an atavistic cautiousness would make it impossible for me to sleep in the open, just as I cannot bear to sit with my back to an unlocked door. Possibly the sleepers of Hyde Park are somnambulistic exhibitionists.

Many a time, so defunct do they look as they lie in crumpled attitudes, I saw the tender-hearted or the hospital-minded linger doubtfully near, or, having passed, they would return and take a careful look to make sure that life was not extinct. The men sleep like dogs and, like dogs, they suddenly awaken, shake themselves, glance round, rise and walk away.

Another notable sight in Hyde Park are the lovers who lie in each other's arms. Visitors from the licentious Continent turn pale and pass them with shocked, averted eyes. Can this really be the England they have been told about, the nation of reserved and modest people? How, by the way, did the English get their reputation for taciturnity and reserve? If it ever existed, it has certainly broken down now, as anyone who falls into conversation with a Londoner about the Blitz will agree!

I thought, as I walked on into the park, that those who enjoy what is said to be the true study of mankind should find Hyde Park the best spot in London. I suppose one would have to be a foreigner to appreciate how very English it is: the thousands of people spread out over the grass, lying beneath the trees, the family parties, the children, the dogs, the cricket matches with rolled-up coats for wickets, and all round, pervading the air as the sound of insects fills a lazy summer's day, the noise of distant London.

I came to a bandstand where a Guards' band was playing a selection from Gilbert and Sullivan. The canvas chairs stretched round in a great half-circle, thousands of them, and when there was a sudden pause in the music, the chairmen's punches rang like little bells. In a few yards of vacant grass near the bandstand an entirely adult little woman, who could not have been more than five years of age, was dancing by herself. Everyone in the vicinity was watching her, and she knew this very well. Every now and then she would pause in her pirouettes to make certain that her audience was with her. Her plump, miniature woman's legs would twinkle in the sunlight, she would point a little foot in a pink kid shoe. Indulgent smiles rewarded her everywhere.

"Isn't she sweet?"

And upon the faces of her parents was an expression of fulsome satisfaction. Little boys of the same age would be mere grubs, but here was a fully fledged butterfly.

I watched a blind man who had the profile of a Cæsar. He sat in a chair side by side with a woman of almost repellent ugliness, who was reading a newspaper to him. When she paused or turned the page he would give her a smile of grateful adoration. The blind live in a world of sound and touch, and his hand would go out and pat her on the shoulder as if his fingers were eyes. And she sat there hideous and certain of his love. A contented warmth wrapped these two people together, and her unlovely face softened when he touched her, but she did not smile as he did. She knew he could not see, and she continued to read.

I walked on and looked at the Serpentine with its shrimp-pink fringe of sun-bathers. And I came at length to the Ring Tea House, a place that perpetuates a most interesting name. I went in, and managed to find a table. The sparrows hopped about picking up the crumbs round my feet like tame mice.

The Ring Tea House is not only the most comfortable but the best place to consider the long and interesting history of Hyde Park. When William the Conqueror parcelled out estates among his followers, the Manor of Hyde fell to a knight named Geoffrey de Mandeville, or Manneville, the ancestor of the Mandeville family, Earls of Essex. It was then rolling open country broken by slight hills which are now the Haymarket and Piccadilly. The lark sang above a solitude where deer grazed, wild cattle and wild pig haunted its dense thickets, and in the winter, when far-away London huddled white-roofed behind her walls, wolves howled in Hyde Park and hunted their prey from Hampstead to the village of Charing.

If Geoffrey de Mandeville stood on the highest part of his manor of Hyde he could see the grassland falling away towards the Thames, and in the marshes of Thorney Island stood the Norman abbey, the Minster in the West, which Edward the Confessor had built. When his wife Athelais died, she was buried by the Benedictine monks of Westminster, and when Geoffrey followed her to the grave he left the Manor of Hyde to the Abbey.

So Hyde Park belonged to the monks of Westminster for nearly four and a half centuries. The abbots had a pleasure-house there. The monks fished, no doubt, on the banks of many streams, like the Westbourne, which flowed from Hampstead, and, traversing Hyde Park, found their way into the Thames. When Henry VIII decided to make his great hunting-ground, he persuaded the monks to exchange the Manor of Hyde for the dissolved priory of Hurley in Berkshire, just as he had persuaded Eton College to exchange the leper-house which became St James's Palace. Few of those who visit the old priory in Berkshire, whose gatehouse is now the Bell Inn, perhaps know that it was the price of the transfer of Hyde Park to the Crown.

As soon as Henry possessed himself of Hyde Park, he enclosed it for the preservation of game, and he issued a proclamation in 1536 forbidding his subjects, on pain of imprisonment, to hunt or hawk " from the Palace of Westminster to St Giles's in the Fields and from thence to Islington, to our Lady of the Oak, to Highgate, to Hornsey Park and to Hampstead Heath ".

What a picture this suggests of Tudor London: a city on its hill, with miles of country all about it, and the sound of the hunting-horn ringing from dells and thickets from Hyde Park to Hampstead.

For over a century Henry VIII, Elizabeth, Edward VI and James I, all in their time, hunted this great stretch of country, and whenever a visiting prince came to England, or a new ambassador was welcomed to the Court, it was the fashion to arrange in his honour a hunt in Hyde Park.

Charles I was more interested in collecting pictures than in hunting. He it was who threw Hyde Park open to the public, and, in opening it, he created a new chapter in the social life of London. The City had by that time burst its bounds, and the first houses were rising in the fields round St James's and Piccadilly. Noble families developed the habit of taking coach from their native shires to spend a few months in the neighbourhood of the Court.

The focus of their outdoor activities was a racecourse in Hyde Park called the Ring, the name preserved in the Ring Tea House. It was just a circle of railed-off turf, and it looked, no doubt, much like any modern fair ground in the country. In 1632 James Shirley wrote a play called *Hide Parke*, in which bookmakers cried the odds very much as they do on a modern course. Most of the characters in the play wagered extravagantly, and some of the women bet " a paire of scarlet silke stockings " against " a paire of perfumed gloves ". Years afterwards Samuel Pepys saw this play produced on the stage with live horses.

In addition to the horse-racing, there were coach-races and races between running footmen. These men, who were sometimes known by the ancient and odd name of " whifflers ", were kept by the grandees of the time to run ahead of the coaches with silver-headed canes. Such races roused considerable enthusiasm, and sometimes the footmen, becoming even more excited than the onlookers, stripped off their clothing and ran naked.

So, with Hyde Park and the Ring, we can see the first stirring of fashion in the West End. Gone were the days, as in Elizabethan times, when the gallant in search of amusement would turn naturally to the play or the bear-pit in Southwark. It was the beginning of that cleavage between the City and the West End which was made complete in Georgian times. It was the first sign of that movement which created a fashionable and aristocratic community centred round the Court; and so popular did this infant West End become, and so many were the families who forsook their estates for the joys and follies of London, that the Star Chamber was obliged to order them to leave the capital and to return to their estates. In days when the local lord, knight and squire were unpaid administrators, they could not be allowed to frivol their time away in Hyde Park and Whitehall. Thus West End fashion, after its false dawn, had to wait for the time of Charles II before it really topped the horizon. But in the meantime the Civil War took place, and Hyde Park, no longer the scene of gay race-meetings, became a grazing-ground for Cromwell's cavalry. The King was executed. England became a republic for eleven years. During this time Hyde Park was sold by auction, and the Journals of the House of Commons contain this brief but expressive entry for November 27, 1652: " Resolved that Hyde Park be sold for ready money." It was put up to auction in three lots, and fetched £17,068 2*s*. 8*d*. There is not an estate agent in London who will not turn green at the thought.

The three men who had the unique experience of buying Hyde Park were Richard Wilcox of Kensington, John Tracey, a merchant, and Anthony Deane of St Martin-in-the-Fields, a shipbuilder. I know nothing about the first two, but Deane was the friend of Pepys, and the man who, together with Samuel, was committed to the Tower on the evidence of many infamous witnesses of giving information to the French.

Deane made himself unpopular by charging an entrance fee at the park gates. " I went to take the aire in Hide Park ", wrote Evelyn in April 1653, " where every coach was made to pay a shilling and every horse sixpence, by these sordid fellows who purchas'd it of the State." It seems that Deane soon sub-let his portion of the park to a farmer as pasturage, and this man increased the entrance fee, so that an outing in Hyde Park under the Commonwealth was hardly a democratic pleasure.

Cromwell frequently rode and drove his coach in the park, and the same kind of crowds which formerly had gathered to catch a glimpse of Charles I assembled to see the Lord Protector. Although the Puritans tried to damp down the gaiety of Hyde Park, cheerfulness continued to break through, especially upon May Day, when it was the fashion to be seen in the park wearing new clothes. One of the sanctimonious newspapers of the time reported that May Day in 1654 "was more observed by people going a-Maying than for divers years past, and, indeed, much sin committed by wicked meetings with fiddlers, drunkenness, ribaldry and the like. Great resorts came to Hyde Park, many hundreds of coaches and gallants in attire, but most shameful powder'd-hair men, and painted and spotted women. Some played with a silver ball, and some took other recreation."

Cromwell was once very nearly killed in Hyde Park. He had received from the Duke of Holstein a gift of six grey Friesland coach-horses and, driving them one day in the park, he used the whip too freely. The high-spirited horses, unaccustomed to such treatment, bolted. The postilion was helpless, and Cromwell was flung from the driver's seat to the pole, where he clung for some time, until he fell to the ground. The coach passed safely over him, but his foot caught in the harness, and he was dragged for some distance, during which a pistol went off in his pocket.

When Charles II was restored to the throne, one of the first acts of the Royalist Parliament was to declare the sale of the Crown lands to have been illegal, and as soon as Charles made it clear that he wanted his subjects to enjoy Hyde Park free of cost, the change was greeted with enthusiasm. Now began the most brilliant period in the history of the park. The West End was growing up. Noble families were acquiring London houses. People of all ranks flocked to London to see the King enjoy his own again; and Hyde Park focused the gaiety of the capital.

Pepys has preserved for us a perfect picture of Hyde Park in those days. One can hear the laughter and see, almost as if one had been there, the light-hearted, scandalous, good-looking crowd that fluttered round the court of Charles II. And what a day it must have been, that May Day in 1669, when Pepys and his patient wife drove round the park for the first time in their own coach! She was wearing her two-years-old flowered tabby gown, but Samuel was dressed in a magnificent new suit with gold-laced sleeves. The horses' manes were plaited with red ribbon and the reins were green.

Sometimes Charles himself, with his long-suffering queen, drove out in a coach drawn by six piebald horses; but more often His Majesty rode alone round the Ring, encountering everywhere the smiles of his ladies. Now and then the coaches and the horsemen paused in astonishment as the Moorish Ambassador and his suite would enter the park and, casting their spears up into the air, would catch them at the gallop.

It is from this fashionable assembly round the place where you can now have tea under a striped umbrella that we may date West End folly, West End fashion; in fact, the West End itself.

§ 6

I have found that a walk round the Serpentine in the afternoon or early evening is an excellent thing if you are tired or depressed. You can be sure of seeing children, dogs and ducks all happily absorbed in their own actions, and unconscious of the world and its cares.

The children are generally small boys with shrill voices, armed with sticks and jam-jars. Their concentration is so complete that if by any mischance they should fall into the water, I am sure they would go on fishing for minnows just the same. There is something about the capture of a minnow which rouses these children to the wildest pitch of excitement, and every fisherman will look at them with envy and understanding.

This stretch of water which gives such pleasure to children, dogs, ducks, bathers and oarsmen was at one time an untidy marsh formed by eleven pools through which the Westbourne flowed. Queen Caroline—perhaps, with the exception of Queen Mary, our keenest gardening queen—decided to make something of the marsh, and, with the connivance of Sir Robert Walpole and the Treasury, dammed the Westbourne in the autumn of 1730 and excavated the bed of the lake. It was a novelty in those days, when the straight Dutch canal was popular with gardeners, to make an ornamental water that produced artificially the effect of a natural lake, and that the name Serpentine could be bestowed on what is, after all, only a gentle bend shows what an innovation it was.

The lake continued to be fed by the Westbourne for a century, but by that time the increase of houses in Paddington had fouled the stream, so the Westbourne, like the Fleet and the Walbrook, became a sewer, and for a time the Serpentine was fed by water pumped from the Thames. At the present time the water supply is most complicated. It comes from a deep well at the head of the lake, from underground springs, from a series of wells in St James's Park and from the ordinary water-mains. The Round Pond in Kensington Gardens, the Serpentine, the lake in the gardens of Buckingham Palace and the lake in St James's Park are all connected, and water can be made to flow from one to the other in the above order.

The Royal Humane Society's station on the banks of the north bank of the lake has a long history. It is the third life-saving station to stand on the spot since the first was erected somewhere about 1774 in a room in an old farmhouse, probably the Cheesecake House which Pepys mentioned. The present building was erected in 1837, and the foundation stone was laid by the Duke of Wellington. The institution has guarded bathers for over a century and a half, and now keeps its eagle eye on the " Lido ". It began with experiments in artificial respiration carried out in 1773 by a Londoner, Dr William Hawes. He maintained, in the face of considerable scepticism, that it was possible to restore life to people who appeared to have been drowned, and he offered a reward for every apparently dead body taken from the Thames if brought to him within a reasonable time. For two years he paid the rewards out of his own pocket, whether his attempts at artificial respiration were successful or not. He made friends with a Dr Thomas Cogan, who had lived in Holland and was familiar with the work of a society in Amsterdam which had been formed as early as 1767 to restore the apparently drowned to life. These two doctors joined forces, and formed the Royal Humane Society. In the old days, when skating frequently took place on the Serpentine, the Institution's boatmen were as much on their toes as they are nowadays during the bathing season.

The usual place for duels in the park was a spot near the Humane Society's station. The popular time for these old-fashioned substitutes for our less dignified libel action was from six to nine o'clock in the evening. One of the most famous duels was fought in 1712 by the Duke of Hamilton and Lord Mohun, described by Thackeray in *Henry Esmond*. Both duellists were killed. The most unusual encounter was that of Lieut. Redmond McGrath, who in 1765 fought four opponents at the same time, disarmed them all and broke their swords.

So many people fought duels in the park in the Eighteenth Century, so many highwaymen lurked beneath the trees, so many suicides took place in unfrequented glades and dells, and so many notorious characters were hanged at Tyburn nearby, that the park gained the reputation of being haunted. The two most famous of its ghosts—although I do not think they have been seen in our time—were Dick Turpin mounted on Black Bess, and Jack the Ripper with the girl he murdered in the Serpentine.

Those in whom the rare virtue of gratitude is present will not leave Hyde Park without a thought for the architect who designed the many perfect little lodges, which I think are among the unnoticed and unappreciated beauties of London. There is one at Grosvenor Gate, two at Stanhope Gate, Cumberland Lodge, the entrance lodge itself and the Guards Magazine near the Serpentine. They are all exquisite little essays in the Greek idiom, so fashionable during the Regency. Decimus Burton was only twenty-five years of age when he designed these lodges and the lovely Greek entrance screen at Hyde Park Corner. Not only was he the youngest architect who has helped to change the face of London, but he was also one of the most fortunate, for he was able to build against the changeless background of trees and grass.

Burton lived to be eighty-one, so he spent a life-time with the delightful and mature work of his youth. Whatever satisfaction he may have enjoyed as he contemplated his lodges must have been cancelled when he looked across at the triumphal arch, now at the top of Constitution Hill, which he designed to lie on the same axis as the park entrance and to form an introduction to it.

But, alas! London has never had any luck with triumphal arches, and has never known where to place them to the best advantage. We have only three, if we accept that pedantically Doric introduction to Glasgow in front of Euston Station, the only arch that has not been literally pulled to pieces and moved about London as if it were a bit of unwanted furniture. The Marble Arch began its career as the triumphal entrance to Buckingham Palace; now it is the entrance to nothing; the Constitution Hill arch—or the Green Park or Wellington or Pimlico arch, as it is also variously called—is just as pointless. Poor Burton's life was made miserable for years by the crowning of his arch with a statue of the Duke of Wellington on horseback, so huge that before it left the studio twelve men sat inside the horse and drank the sculptor's health!

It is said that a French officer gazing up at the arch so absurdly captured by Wellington remarked acidly: "*Nous sommes vengés!*"; and if anyone wishes to see this statue now, he will find it more suitably commanding Cæsar's Camp at Aldershot.

§ 6

When I had finished watching with amusement the great variety of character unconsciously displayed by the young yachtsmen on the Round Pond, I walked across to Kensington Palace. This building is not a lovely place, neither is it an exciting one. Incendiary bombs damaged it in 1940, it escaped several near misses in 1943 and in 1944 it was hit by a flying-bomb.

Several members of the public were drifting through the acres of pine-panelled rooms, while the ghosts of Wllliam III, wheezing with asthma, Queen Anne, sitting dumb behind her fan wondering what was for dinner, George II in one of his furious rages, the poor blind princess, Sophia, daughter of George III, the Duchess of Kent and the young Victoria peeped at them from the shadows.

I thought the only interesting room in the palace is the bedroom where the young Victoria was sleeping that night in June when she was awakened and told that she was a queen.

It is a very ordinary, heavy-looking room, papered with a floral wallpaper, and containing a number of objects which were there at the time. The most extraordinary, I thought, was a pair of Indian clubs on a ledge above a hideous fire-place. The thought of Victoria in youth or age twirling Indian clubs is fantastic!

We may imagine the girl of eighteen snuggled into the pillows on that June morning, the birds singing outside in Kensington Gardens, the sun up and the palace echoing to the knocking of two men who had driven all night from Windsor to tell Victoria that William IV was dead.

As so often happens when one has anything desperately urgent to say, everything conspired to frustrate the messengers. Exalted as they were—one the Archbishop of Canterbury, the other Lord Conyngham, the Lord Chamberlain—they were kept waiting at the gate, unable to rouse the porter. At last he came and, as if they were suspicious characters, let them into the courtyard and vanished. In the silent palace at last, they found themselves alone in a room; and still no one came. They rang a bell. A sleepy servant appeared. They asked that the attendant of the Princess Victoria be told that they desired an urgent audience. There was more delay. They rang again. The attendant said that the Princess was sleeping so sweetly that she could not be aroused. Then the drama that the Archbishop and the Lord Chamberlain had been bottling up during this period of anti-climax broke out, and they cried:

"We are come to the *Queen* on business of state, and even her sleep must give way to that!"

In a few moments they were kneeling before a young girl who came into the room wearing a white dressing-gown and a shawl, her hair loose on her shoulders, her bare feet in carpet slippers. That was history's first sight of Queen Victoria. She herself described the scene in her Diary:

> "Tuesday June 20th. I was awoke at 6 o'clock by Mamma, who told me that the Archbishop of Canterbury and Lord Conyngham were below and wished to see me. I got out of bed and went into my sitting-room

(only in my dressing-gown) and *alone* saw them and they acquainted me that my poor Uncle the King was no more, and expired at 12 minutes p. 2. this morning and consequently I am *Queen*. . . .

"Since it has pleased Providence to place me in this station I shall do my utmost to fulfil my duty towards my country; I am young, and perhaps in many things, though not in all, inexperienced, but I am sure that very few have more real good will and more real desire to do what is fit and right than I have . . ."

In two hours time the young Queen held her first Privy Council.

"Five feet high, but she not only filled her chair but the room," was the comment of the Duke of Wellington.

Yes, it is an interesting room, this room in which the great, fearless Victorian Age began; and we who live in this shabby twilight of fear and indecision cannot look on it unmoved. But I still think that the two most interesting objects in it are the Indian clubs.

§ 7

The Three Fountains, outside Rome, where St Paul is said to have been beheaded, was once a notoriously malarial spot. There came to it one day over eight hundred years ago a pious pilgrim called Rahere, a Norman from far-off London, a man who, having been a gay courtier in the reign of William Rufus, had entered the Church in the following reign, that of Henry I.

While he was visiting the Three Fountains, he contracted what was evidently a severe attack of malaria. During his illness, St Bartholomew appeared to him in a vision and Rahere took a vow that, if he recovered and arrived home safely, he would erect in London a great Priory and a hospital for poor men. Thus it might be said that long ago a mosquito held within it not only the germ of malaria but of St Bartholomew-the-Great, Smithfield, and St Bartholomew's Hospital, always known affectionately as "Bart's", the oldest hospital in the English-speaking world.

One Sunday morning I took an omnibus to Newgate Street, and, after admiring the clear view of St Paul's above the hoarding of blitzed buildings, I walked down towards Smithfield. It is difficult to imagine this featureless district of offices, warehouses and meat markets as the place, as once it was, of jousts and tournaments and the place where witches and martyrs were burned at the stake.

A highly educated young policeman, with whom I fell into conversation, told me that Smithfield was a depressingly quiet spot these days.

"There's no crime and there's no meat," he said—"in fact Smithfield nowadays has the charm of a graveyard."

He pointed to his helmet.

"And in spite of the change in the type of criminal today," he said, "we have to walk around as if we were about to be hit on the head by Bill Sikes. Helmets are now ridiculous. The chance of being hit by a bludgeon is one in a million. The modern crook is far more likely to pull a gun on you."

I walked on to Smithfield, while the educated policeman strolled on in the calm of a Sunday morning gazing discontentedly along the empty streets and trying a door now and then.

I came to "Bart's" Hospital, and to a Tudor gateway nearby which led to the porch of the church of St Bartholomew-the-Great. I looked at hospital and church and thought of the mosquito of the Three Fountains and was amazed by the inscrutable ways of destiny.

I can never enter this church without a feeling of astonishment and pleasure. There is nothing else like it in London except the little Chapel in the Tower. They are the two oldest churches in London, and the only places in which a man may stand and say to himself, "I am in the London of the early Norman kings." The Chapel in the Tower is more complete. It is brown and new-looking; St Bartholomew's is black with age. There is no other building in London which looks so heavy with time. It is a massive piece of Norman London, a tremendous and dignified fragment of those consecrated fortresses which the Normans erected to the glory of God.

Morning service was just beginning. I watched the choir in its red surplices—for St Bartholomew's is a Royal foundation—walk towards the Sanctuary. Christian worship began in this church about the year 1123, and that it continues to-day is due to those who have reclaimed the church from the squalor and ruin into which it fell after the Dissolution of the Monasteries. There was a time when the Lady Chapel was a printer's office in which Benjamin Franklin worked for a year, the north transept was a blacksmith's forge, the crypt was a wine and coal cellar, the cloisters were used as stables. The history of the church during the past century has been the gradual reclamation of such features from degrading purposes and the reincorporation of them within the church.

I sat beside a tremendous column, and thought that when it was so firmly planted in Smithfield, Henry I was on the throne, the king who succeeded Rufus, who " never smiled again " when the White Ship went down with his son and heir, the king who, as every schoolboy knows, died of " a surfeit of lampreys ". The London, of which this church is the most massive surviving fragment, was a bi-lingual city of Norman and Saxon, the Tower of London was still a new building, Westminster Hall was newer still, St Paul's Cathedral was also a new Norman cathedral and Westminster Abbey was the Norman church built by the Confessor. All over London Norman churches, larger or smaller, were replacing the little thatched, wooden churches of Saxon London, most of which were fated to be swept away in the fire of the year 1136.

When the service ended I walked round the church and came to the tomb of Rahere to the north of the sanctuary. Beneath a carved stone canopy, I saw the painted figure of the man who founded St Bartholomew's church and hospital so many centuries ago lying in a black Augustinian habit, a little angel kneeling at his feet.

I walked to Holborn Viaduct to see a very different but equally interesting church.

Ely Place, Holborn, is a curious little backwater, a cul-de-sac with a lodge and gates at one end of it. It is just a short street of Georgian houses tenanted now mostly by solicitors and business firms. Until recent times Ely Place was technically speaking not in London, but in Cambridgeshire. It did not pay London rates and taxes, neither did its one public-house observe London times of opening.

This happy state of affairs seems to have ended in the last century, when someone left an abandoned infant on a doorstep in Ely Place. When the child was taken to a foundling hospital the authorities said that, as foundlings were supported by the rates, Ely Place must be taxed accordingly; and this was done.

The only remaining signs of the Freedom of Ely Place are that the City police have no right of entry and the lodge gates are closed each night by watchmen who until the outbreak of the last War were in the habit of calling the hours of night. Another lingering memory reposes in the Post Office, which will, I believe, deliver in Holborn a letter addressed to Ely Place, Holborn Circus, Cambridgeshire.

The peculiar status of Ely Place dates from the days when it was the London palace of the Bishops of Ely. Not a trace of the palace remains except the little Catholic church of St Etheldreda's at the end of the cul-de-sac, once the chapel of Ely House. It was purchased by the Fathers of Charity in 1874 and is the only pre-Reformation church in London in which the Mass is still celebrated.

I descended the steps into the ancient crypt, the only part of the church now in use, for the chapel above was badly damaged when a bomb exploded on one of the seven-hundred year old chestnut beams of the roof. A priest told me that money is already being collected to restore the church, which one day will be among the most beautiful Gothic churches in Europe.

Every Sunday after Mass members of the choir and a few of the parishioners look in at the old *Mitre Tavern* at the other end of Ely Place. It is an old-fashioned little tavern which is reached by way of a narrow alley. The original *Mitre* was built in 1546 by Bishop Goodrich for the use of Palace officials, and there was a time when it received its licence from Cambridgeshire.

The strangest of the relics in the public bar is the trunk of a cherry tree enclosed in glass, a tree, I was told, that once marked the boundary of the Bishop's garden. Although long since dead it is presumably still rooted in the same spot, although why it should have been considered so significant, I cannot say and neither could anyone in the *Mitre* tell me.

§ 8

Two features of London street life disappeared with the 1914–18 War: one was the man with the dancing bear—the bear-ward, a character as old as the Middle Ages—the other was the German band. I remember them both when I was a child. Another extinct character is the Italian organ-grinder, a swarthy individual with greasy ringlets, ear-rings and, upon his shoulder, a monkey dressed in a red-flannel petticoat. And it seems ages since I heard a Scots piper in the streets of London.

While we now patiently endure any kind of mechanical noise, even the maniac chatter of the pneumatic road drill, we are quite intolerant when it comes to the more pleasant sounds produced by human beings. Street cries and street music are no longer popular. It is many a long year since I threw down a penny to a London organ-grinder, and how typical of London a few years ago were the barrel organs and a band of dancing children.

There is, or used to be, a shoeblack at Charing Cross, who wore a red jacket, and the other day I was delighted to see a man sitting on the kerb in a street off Sloane Street mending cane-bottomed chairs. He told me that his father and grandfather had done this work, and that they had taught him. The knife-grinder is still with us, but I think the muffin man may have gone because muffins without butter are impossible. I remember him between the wars on a Sunday afternoon as he passed along ringing his bell, a plate of crumpets and muffins on his head wrapped in a white napkin. In those days butter was 1*s.* 8*d.* a pound and margarine was a social solecism.

The Punch-and-Judy show is now almost a curiosity, and

the hawkers who once lined Ludgate Hill, and let loose mechanical toys under the feet of passers-by, have long since vanished. But the sweep is still with us. He can be seen cycling along or driving a small car. Some Londoners still believe it lucky to touch him as he goes by.

The old-clothes man, though not so common as he once was, still exists. Recently I saw an old character I had not seen for years. He is a little old man with a bushy grey beard who pushes a barrow round the West End, calling for old bottles and any old clothes and iron. He always wears, one on top of the other, two grey Ascot " toppers ".

CHAPTER TEN

How Piccadilly became the heart of the West End and the story of the growth of West London in the time of Charles II. A walk down Bond Street and a visit to the Wallace Collection. I go to Shepherd Market and have something to say about the London taxi-cab driver.

§ 1

BETWEEN the wars, in days which now seem so remote, the flower "girls" of Piccadilly presided over a West End which, in retrospect, was gay, amusing, well dressed and cheap—a Savile Row suit cost twelve guineas, a fillet steak half a crown and a dozen oysters five shillings.

Grouped round the Fountain of Eros with their baskets of flowers, the "girls" (for they were endowed with eternal youth, and even the great-grandmothers among them were never called flower "women") sat all day long merrily ironic, bringing to the core of the West End a hearty breath of the good old Cockney East. In the very heart of fashion, and great critics as they were of the current mode, for it was always passing before their eyes, they were preposterously unfashionable. They might, indeed, have been in fancy dress. They wore what was then the normal attire of the East End female: a straw hat, or a man's cap, transfixed by a hat-pin, a shawl and an apron. They might have been placed there by Cruickshank as models for one of the illustrations of *Life in London.*

If you were sufficiently smart, or if you looked like the sort of person who would wear a buttonhole, they would call you "captain" or "lovey", probably the last endearment of the Eighteenth Century. Though you might be hurrying to some sordid business appointment, the greeting caused you to walk more slowly and to feel like a man about town.

The Fountain of Eros belonged to them, and to them alone.

They would mount its steps and refresh their carnations and roses in its waters, and above the roar of Piccadilly the sound of their voices ripped the air like handsaws:

"Vi'lets, luvley vi'lets, lidy . . . pennig-a-bunch. . . ."

"G'mornin', captain. What about a nice carnation, dearie?"

It was a Metropolitan commendation coming down to this age of bowler hats from who knows what regions of be-ribboned gallantry, and the man so addressed passed on thinking that his blue serge should be scarlet and his umbrella a sword.

Secure in the occupation of the most central spot in the world, approved by all and loved by many, the flower "girls" of Piccadilly were Cockney vestal virgins, and it is only now, when they have vanished, leaving behind them one last priestess of Flora, that we realise how much poorer London is without them. Why, one wonders, have they gone? Is it because the age of buttonholes appears to be over? Is it because the Westminster City Council has banned street-trading in Piccadilly? I expect so.

But what a hideous exchange has been made for the delightful flower "girls" of Piccadilly! During and since the War the steps of the Fountain have been occupied by an untidy fringe of foreigners, provincials, soldiers, sailors and their lady friends; and they sit hour after hour watching the traffic and at night gazing at the lights, which, as G. K. Chesterton said, must be a wonderful sight if you can't read! The centre of Piccadilly Circus, which used to look so lovely with its baskets of primroses and violets in spring, its roses in summer and its dahlias in autumn, is now, in my opinion, one of the most depressing and regrettable spectacles in the capital. I have an idea that the habit of sitting round Eros began during the War with the Americans, who chewed their gum there and mournfully smoked their cheroots, wondering why the heck they were in London.

The popularity of the statue of Eros—a work that drove its creator, Sir Alfred Gilbert, into exile—is one of the inexplicable things about London. Why should this little winged figure have become so famous in our time? It is not loved for its grace and its beauty, or not solely for these, but perhaps more for the fact that somehow it expresses the lightness and the gaiety which are traditionally supposed to be centred around Piccadilly. I remember once during a recent ocean voyage defeating a well-informed quiz team with the question: "What is the statue of Eros made of?", the answer being aluminium. I believe it was the first statue ever to be made of that metal. It is, of course, a pun in aluminium. When asked to design a memorial to the philanthropic seventh Lord Shaftesbury, after whom Shaftesbury Avenue is named, Gilbert thought it would be a happy idea to create an archer in the act of preparing to bury a shaft in the Avenue. But someone in the old Board of Works, who evidently disliked puns, turned Eros round, so that Gilbert's playful idea is now pointless. Poor Gilbert, who was extremely temperamental and was always destroying his own work, was so exasperated by officialdom that when Eros was ready he told the Board of Works to melt it down, sell it and give the money to the poor; then he shook the dust of England from his feet and lived abroad for twenty years, returning only at the personal request of King George V.

How I wish scientists, instead of promising flights to the moon, would perfect the Time Machine and offer us an occasional week-end in the past! For instance, I would like to put back the clock and take a walk along Piccadilly in the time of James I, say about 1603. I should then be in a position to tell you whether all the things written by London topographers about the origin of this strange name are nonsense or not.

There were no buildings at all along what is now Piccadilly in the year 1600, and it was then known as "the Way to Reading". The wild buglosse, or ox-tongue, grew in the dry ditch banks, says Gerard in his *Herbal*, and a district which now bears such a heavy weight of stone and concrete was a place of hedges, streams and green pastures. In 1623 the Middlesex records mention "William Cable, yeoman, dwelling near Pickadilly Hall"; and that is the first time the famous name is mentioned. If we could have walked down Piccadilly in that year, 1623, when James I was King and Shakespeare had been dead only seven years, we should have seen no more than five or six little cottages on the high ground at the top of the Haymarket and one handsome house near what is now Great Windmill Street, called " Pickadilly Hall ", the country home of a Strand tailor named Robert Baker.

I suspect a familiar ring of Cockney irony about the name of this house, as if Baker's contemporaries had concluded that he had become a little too grand in trying to ape the country gentleman, in other words, getting " a bit above himself ". Perhaps some wit, knowing that his shop in the Strand was full of *pickadils*, or *pickadillos*, and that he had made a fortune out of these objects, laughingly nicknamed his house " Pickadilly Hall ", and so unwittingly gave to the world one of its most celebrated place-names.

The *pickadil* was the stiff, starched ruff and collar, sometimes stretched on a wire framework, which became fashionable at the beginning of the Seventeenth Century, and by the middle of the century had become a broad lace collar that covered the shoulders, as so often seen in portraits by Van Dyck. The fashion expired in the time of Charles II, when the immense periwigs worn by men made the *pickadil* an impossible thing to wear, and was followed by the cravat or neckcloth.

Another building in Piccadilly touched by the same irony was " Shaver's Hall ", one of the famous gaming-houses of the time, kept by the Earl of Pembroke's barber, Simon Osbaldston. It possessed two bowling-greens, a tennis-court, shady gravelled walks, dining-rooms and four rooms on the top floor for cards and dice.

Several street names still link themselves with Piccadilly's remote rural past: Windmill Street commemorates a mill that used to stand opposite what is now the Windmill Theatre; hay was sold for centuries in the Haymarket, and Vine Street's appropriate association with wine is believed to have begun long before the Boat Race when the Benedictine monks of Westminster had a vineyard there. But Piccadilly did not really begin to take shape until the great nobles began to move there in the time of Charles II. The old mediæval palaces of the Strand, more like an Oxford college than the Seventeenth Century idea of a nobleman's house, had become hopelessly out-of-date, and the Strand as a residential area was not what it had been. So these palaces were sold, and streets of houses took their place, but retained the names of their owners.

The growth of London beyond the City Wall began with the Dissolution of the Monasteries in the reign of Henry VIII and, despite repressive legislation, continued during the reigns of Elizabeth and the first Stuarts. London could not possibly grow before this time because it was completely hemmed in by monasteries and nunneries—the Carmelites at Whitefriars, the Preaching Friars in Holborn, the Priory of St John of Jerusalem, and also the Benedictine nunnery, in Clerkenwell, the Charterhouse in Smithfield, to mention only a few.

When this enormous area of land was taken from the Church and became private property London began to extend in every direction except in that of the Crown lands to the west. Neither Acts of Parliament nor royal proclamations could stop the spreading of an overcrowded city across the now available Church properties towards the villages that lay beyond.

This was a natural growth that nothing could stop. The West End was something rather different. It was an aristocratic speculation. It was already beginning in the time of Charles I, was stopped during the Civil War and received its real impetus with the restoration of Charles II to the Throne. And in this reign the great West End property boom was assisted by the Fire of London. The cavaliers who had shared the King's exile reaped their reward in gifts of land, and the West End began to grow up round the Court with the erection of stately town houses, squares and building estates.

" Speculative building is a very old way of making money," wrote Mr John Summerson in *Georgian London*. " It must go far back into the Middle Ages and have grown up almost simultaneously with the notion of a rent-roll as a source of wealth. It was a familiar practice in Tudor times. As the aristocrats shifted out of the walled cities, their palaces were taken over or demolished or subdivided to provide accommodation for humbler people whose rents brought an income to the new landlord. It was the poorer classes—the hands flocking to the towns from an impoverished countryside—who were the speculator's first quarry; they were served with the minimum of accommodation for the trifling rents which could be extracted from them. But in course of time the speculator aimed higher. As urban life became richer and more elaborate, as the professional classes expanded, as the Court and the Civil Service drew more men into their proximity, the 'town house' which was neither a great mansion nor a hovel became an important need."

The fourth Earl of Bedford showed the way with the development of Covent Garden in the reign of Charles I, but the difficulty of obtaining building licences, and the years of civil war, made it impossible for other noble imitators to follow suit. However, no time was lost once Charles II was established on the throne. The two first great speculators were the fourth Earl of Southampton, in Bloomsbury, and Henry Jermyn, Earl of St Albans, in St James's. Southampton's scheme was significant. He set out to cater for the less spectacular ranks of the nobility, the gentry and the new professional classes, and thus were created those extremely sensible, well-designed houses, more or less alike, which, modified in Georgian and Victorian times, have become the well-to-do standard London home.

Jermyn's scheme was slightly different, and it was frustrated by events. He was a great courtier and a great gambler, and his influence with Henrietta Maria was so powerful that some people suspected a love affair. Like many another cavalier who returned from exile with Charles II, he was richly rewarded for his loyalty, and, no longer young, and "more a Frenchman than an Englishman", as Charles once described him, he decided to create in the open fields round St James's a great aristocratic square, after the French fashion. It was to contain a few splendid and sumptuous mansions—only four a side—which would be inhabited by great families, but before the square was built the Plague devastated London, to be followed by the Fire; and the whole housing situation was changed. Half the City lay in ruins. There was a rush to the West End. Jermyn, who was extremely lucky not to have built his original St James's Square, was able to modify his scheme, and so to provide more houses in the square, and to lease them, not to a few great families but to a larger number of equally profitable aristocrats.

Even before the rush to the West End was accelerated by the Fire, a great deal of building was going on there. St James's Square had been begun, and an entirely different type of building was being erected in Piccadilly. That was the great West End mansion, the Seventeenth and Eighteenth Century successor to the mediæval Strand palace.

It must have been interesting to take a coach into the fields of Piccadilly at that time, as both Pepys and Evelyn did, and to see the meadows piled with bricks, lime and timber. Three of the great Piccadilly palaces were Clarendon House at the top of St James's Street (the site of Bond Street, Dover Street, Albemarle Street and Stafford Street), Burlington House and Berkeley House, afterwards Devonshire House. All these great mansions were erected between 1664 and 1668. Each one was a country house erected in London. They all had huge gardens which stretched back and were divided from the open country by high brick walls. Burlington Gardens commemorates the gardens of old Burlington House. Berkeley Square was a part of the gardens of Berkeley House. And although the first West End streets soon began to stretch across the fields towards Oxford Street, those great mansions were still countrified fifty years later; for when Handel stayed with Lord Burlington in 1715 he was given rooms at the back of Burlington House because he liked the sight of fields and trees.

Clarendon House was one of the most beautiful, as it was one of the most ill-fated, of London's mansions. It was built by Edward Hyde, Earl of Clarendon and Lord Chancellor under Charles II, a great and brilliant statesman who might perhaps have flourished in Elizabeth's time, but under Charles he was fated to fall. He could not be shaken, and he would not pay court to the royal mistresses. Charles found him a virtuous bore, but, when the Dutch War broke out and life became dangerous, Clarendon was an admirable scapegoat, and Charles dropped him like a hot coal. The London mob detested Clarendon, and blamed him for all the disasters of the age. When the old man was driven into exile in France, where he wrote his classic *History of the Rebellion*, he attributed his downfall, not so much to his political life as to his " weakness and vanity " in building Clarendon House and to the " gust of envy " which his great palace directed upon him.

Both Pepys and Evelyn saw the house being built, and nineteen years later they saw it being pulled down. Pepys called it " the finest pile I ever did see ", and Evelyn said, " It is without hyperbole the best contrived, the most useful, graceful and magnificent house in England ". It was only just finished when Evelyn called there one day in 1667 to find old Lord Clarendon suffering from gout and sitting in a wheel chair while he watched his garden gates being put up. The old man appeared to be depressed, and the next day Evelyn heard that he had bidden farewell to all his greatness and had gone into exile in France. Sixteen years later Evelyn again stood in Piccadilly, where " after dinner I walked to survey the sad demolition of Clarendon House ".

Upon the site of this splendid mansion a group of speculators, headed by Sir Thomas Bond, built Bond Street, Dover Street, Albemarle Street and Stafford Street. Bond, who has given his name to one of the most fashionable streets in the world, was, like Jermyn, a cavalier who went into exile with Henrietta Maria and returned to London with Charles II to reap the rewards of the Restoration. He lived at Peckham, where Evelyn visited him in a house which had " a fine garden and prospect through the meadows to London ". I am sure that few of the thousands of people who see these four streets every day know that their cellars are firmly planted in the London of Charles II. I remember during the last war—and during an air raid—having to go to a building at the Piccadilly end of Dover Street, now split up into dozens of separate shops and businesses, and on the way up my hand fell upon the magnificent broad handrail of the original staircase, standing there still, complete with its fat, twisted, typically

Stuart balusters. It was an unexpected treasure to find in a building that gave no hint from the outside that its stairs had been trodden by men who had lived in the London of Charles and Nell Gwyn, Pepys, Evelyn and Wren; and the idea so delighted me that I stood there examining the balusters by the flame of a cigarette-lighter until brought to my senses by the sound of an approaching V.1.

§ 2

The men who built the first houses and streets in the West End of London wore silk and satin coats and gold-laced waistcoats. Great periwigs fell to their shoulders, and in their huge hats ostrich and other feathers were sewn. They wore ribbons at their knees. Swords slanted from the long skirts of their embroidered coats, and they carried canes of ebony and ivory. The romanticist sees them always in the act of bowing and making a leg to pretty ladies in the Mall, fighting duels, writing delightful little poems, for it was the age when every gentleman could write a poem, and while he often sees them making love, he rarely thinks that they were probably more interested in making money. When you contemplate the group of cavaliers and others who laid the foundation o the West End of London, it is clear that you observe a gang of get-rich-quicks as tough and as efficient as any similar gang to-day in London, New York or Johannesburg. The financial instincts which we erroneously associate only with this age of stock exchanges and telephones were highly developed in the age of swords and satin. Beneath the mighty periwigs of that time lived brains as acute as those of any " city slicker ". I imagine, for instance, that Dr Nicholas Barbon, or Barebones, the son of that dreary old Puritan Praisegod Barebones, could show the City of London a thing or two even to-day.

Barbon, who was born in 1640, when Velazquez, Cromwell, Charles I, Milton, Lely and Bunyan were alive, was a fully fledged modern business man, and one much above the average intelligence. He wrote several treatises on finance (one of which was quoted by Karl Marx!), and after the Fire of London he originated the idea of house insurance. But his main activity was the buying up of old properties and the erection of new squares and streets. Long before the age of 'isms and 'ologies, he knew all that was necessary to know about psychology, and he was extremely skilful in applying it. How perfect, how modern, how reminiscent of many another great financier is the following description of Dr Barbon from the *Autobiography* of a man who knew him, Roger North. The scene is a meeting in the London of Charles II between Dr Barbon and a number of men who were ready to oppose him. Says North:

> "They would certainly be early at the place, and confirm and hearten one another to stand it out, for the Doctor must come to their terms. So they would walk about and pass their time expecting the Doctor, and enquiring if he were come. At last word was brought that he was come. Then they began to get towards the long table, for the Doctor was come! The Doctor was come! Then he would make his entry, as fine and as richly dressed as a lord of the bedchamber on a birthday. And I must own that I have often seen him so dressed, not knowing his design, and thought him a coxcomb for so doing. Then these hard headed fellows that had prepared to give him all the affronts and opposition that their brutal way suggested, truly seeing such a brave man, pulled off their hats and knew not what to think of it. And the Doctor, also being (forsooth) much of a gentleman, then with a mountebank speech to these gentlemen he proposed his terms, which, as I said, were ever plausible, and terminated in their interest. Perhaps they were, at this, all converted in a moment, or perhaps a sour clown or two did not understand his tricks, or would not trust him, or would take counsel, or some blundering opposition they gave; while the rest gaped and stared, he was all honey, and a real friend; which not doing he quarrelled or bought off, as I said, and then at the next meeting some came over, and the rest followed. It mattered not a litigious knave or two, if any such did stand out, for the first thing he did was to pull down their houses about their

> ears and build upon their ground, and stand it out at law till their hearts ached, and at last they would truckle and take any terms for peace and a quiet life."

How often have we met Dr Nicholas Barbon, not in silk and satin, but in a Savile Row suit, descending majestically from a Rolls Royce or seated behind a vast mahogany desk, a cigar in his manicured fingers, telephones at his elbow, his face shining with well-being, his whole personality carefully calculated to create confidence and to dispel opposition.

I suppose if anyone may be said to have invented mass production Barbon was the originator. His staircases, which we now think so beautiful, his mantelpieces, his window-frames and his cornices were turned out by the thousand. Beyond the beribboned coxcombry of this contemporary of Milton we seem to catch a glimpse of the assembly line and—Henry Ford!

And Barbon was only one of many such speculators who ranged in rank from the peer to the mechanic. There was Colonel Panton (Panton Street), a professional gambler; there was Abraham Storey (Storey's Gate), one of Christopher Wren's master masons; there was Sir Thomas Clarges (Clarges Street), a politician; there was Gregory King (King Square, now Soho Square), a political pamphleteer. They were all interested in money. And behind them, ready to build the houses, were first-rate craftsmen who had served years of apprenticeship to their various trades. As the West End grew up so rapidly under their skilful hands, the City became greatly concerned and alarmed. Some few years after the Fire whole streets in the City were standing empty, so powerful were the attractions of the new suburbs beyond Charing Cross, and so steady was that westward drift that has been in progress ever since.

So if we do think of Cavaliers charging against Roundheads, or toasting the King over the water, or flirting with ladies in the Mall, we may also think of them standing among brick-yards and lime-kilns and gazing at the fields round Piccadilly with acute, speculative eyes.

§ 3

The street that Sir Thomas Bond built over two and a half centuries ago is a short street that for many years ended in fields until, in 1721, New Bond Street carried it north to the Tyburn Road, or Oxford Street. It is a street of lovely and costly things: pictures, prints, jewellery, books, gold and silver, women's clothes; and the name Bond Street stamps even the most ordinary article with a peculiar cachet.

The art dealers who do business there are, generally speaking, so wise and full of experience that to be able to drop in and talk to them and look at their pictures, their prints, their porcelain, their gold and silver is part of a collector's education. When I was young I used to think how wonderful it would be to be rich enough to buy any of the exquisite things in Bond Street that took my fancy, but I have reached an age when I do not believe the possession of such objects would give me half the pleasure I have had in talking with those who buy and sell them.

I remember Bond Street between the wars, when it was still touched, so it seemed, by the last lingering elegancies of the Eighteenth Century. One saw exquisitely dressed women there. There was an air of leisure about the street. The Bond Street "lounger" had not yet become extinct. And while the shop windows of Bond Street seem hardly to have changed at all, the people who glance into them appear vastly different to me. War, taxation, post-war hardship, the servantless age have banished leisure, and while it must be—or Bond Street would become insolvent—that many people can still buy diamond bracelets and old masters, few of them look as if they can afford to do so.

The collector with sufficient money is forced sometimes reluctantly to admit that, when all is said and done, some of the best things are to be found in Bond Street and the little streets that lead from it. The collector of moderate means may pretend to despise the rich collector who merely has to take his cheque-book to Bond Street to be offered treasures for which others seek in vain; but, after all, Bond Street is a treasure cave; and if you asked me to lead you quickly to a clock or a watch by Tompion, an authenticated Constable or a mediæval monstrance, it is to Bond Street that I should inevitably take you. The average passer-by has no idea what strange and lovely things repose in the safes of Bond Street, even in this shabby age.

Some people prefer Bond Street on a morning when the sun is almost warm and the air is spiced with spring, but I like to think of it just as it is getting dark on an evening in autumn. The lamps have just been lit, the homeward traffic is beginning to fill the narrow roadway from kerb to kerb, and every window is a brilliantly lit frame for a glimpse of something good. It may be a set of Hepplewhite chairs, a pearl necklace, a piece of jade, a clock by Knibb or Quare, a mink coat, a row of books bound in red or green levant morocco. But each object is as good as it is possible for it to be. One may not be able to afford to buy it, but it is a privilege to be able to look at it and to learn from it.

And in the dusk, with a faint blue mist coming down over London and the chill of winter already in the air, how good it is to have walked down Bond Street having been defeated in a sale-room, having seen something which you longed to possess vanish from your grasp; how good it is for the soul to have walked down Bond Street telling yourself that it doesn't really matter a bit, that you're just as happy without it and that, anyhow, you could never have afforded it. But how much better to have walked down Bond Street radiant with triumph, with something you have longed for and dreamt about clutched in the secrecy of your overcoat pocket, something that was knocked down to you for so much less than you were willing to pay, something so lovely that you can't believe it is yours, a treasure which you furtively bring out by the light of a lamp to assure yourself that this is not another of life's many dreams.

When I have been bored in London—which was never often or for long—I have dropped in to Christie's or Sotheby's during a sale. Whence comes this endless stream of treasure? It is one of England's mysteries. It has been in circulation for centuries. The rich men of the Georgian age attended sale-rooms just as we do to bid for the Italian masters just as we now bid for the Georgians; only they paid much less for them! The cellars of Christie's and Sotheby's suggest that somewhere in Great Britain is an inexhaustible Ali Baba's cave that throughout the sale season disgorges a rich supply of Queen Anne tea-services, Chippendale chairs, tapestries, old masters, bronzes and china. Some of these things have a sale-room pedigree. They are bought by one generation and sold by another. They have been changing hands for centuries, and they return to Bond Street and St James's Street even from America. Others appear for the first time, and are listed in the deliciously snobbish terms of the catalogue as " the property of a gentleman ". It is an incomplete sentence: it should run on: " who would do anything for five hundred pounds ".

But let us peep into the sale-room. The auctioneer sits in his pulpit facing the most mixed crowd in London. There stand Lord and Lady X, who have been literally living on their ancestors for years, slipping the fifth earl into Christie's one year and the state bed into Sotheby's the next. It is strange and interesting to think that a man who fought at Blenheim and Ramillies can pay his descendant's income tax in 1951! Then there is the great American collector, nothing to look at, but what a powerful cheque-book. There are several elderly women of the type known as " gentlewomen in reduced circumstances ", and a pack of dealers and agents, some of whom look well groomed and prosperous, others who pick their teeth horribly with tram tickets as they scornfully inspect a Gainsborough.

" And now," says the auctioneer in a creamy voice, " how much for Lot eighty-four, ' The Portrait of a Lady ' ? "

Two men who wear green baize aprons lift upon an easel a beauty of three centuries ago. She looks down upon the mixed crowd with faint contempt. She is young, her breasts are pushed upward into the bodice of her gown, her lovely neck is encircled with immense pearls, two pearls drop from her ears, there are more pearls in her hair, and she wears that air of smothered naughtiness which was fashionable at the Court of the second Charles.

She had never been rung up on a telephone, she had never

drunk a cocktail, driven a car, been in an aeroplane, yet, being a woman, she was completely modern, and I felt that I could have taken her to luncheon at Claridges or the Berkeley with the greatest ease and pleasure.

" Three hundred guineas," says a shaggy man who does not look as though he could afford five shillings.

The bidding goes on.

" Five hundred," offers a collector.

" Six hundred," says an American voice.

All the time the battle of winks and nods is closely watched by a young woman who bears a faint far-off resemblance to the picture. Put her auburn hair in ringlets, hang pearls in her ears, dress her in a low-necked brown dress and pose her hand artificially before her, and she might indeed pass for her ancestress.

" Six hundred guineas . . . going at six hundred guineas," cries the auctioneer, rolling his tongue round that unctuous and greedy word.

He brings down the hammer.

As the men in baize aprons remove the canvas, it seems to me that for one brief second the eyes of the girl in the picture meet the eyes of the girl in the room, and the glance says:

" Well, my dear, I have paid for your wedding. My bones were dust two centuries ago; but, darling, my face is your fortune."

And the girl goes out into Bond Street thinking about her trousseau.

The next picture is closely watched by a little old woman in black. Her famous Murillo is being sold at last.

There are thousands of people who possess an " old master " which they believe will step in and save them during a critical moment in life. Their faith in the value of these works is so sublime that even when their treasures have been valued, and are declared to be fakes, they refuse to believe it. They think the valuer is deceiving them deliberately in order to buy the picture for a song.

The old lady watches her Velazquez go up, thinking that if it fetches only £3,000 she will be able to get a little cottage in the country, while if it fetches £20,000, as the admiral always said it would—and he was always right about everything—she could even end her days in luxury and help those who were once her dependants. She remembers how proudly the admiral used to show off the picture after dinner.

"Only gave five hundred for it, my boy, and it's worth fifty thousand if it's worth a penny!" (She does not know that it was planted on him by a crook dealer when the Fleet was in Barcelona.)

"Now," says the auctioneer, "how much for this. Lot eighty-five. School of Velazquez."

There is an unpleasant silence, then a coarse voice says:

"Five guineas."

There is another unhealthy pause.

A seedy man walks up to the picture, sucks his teeth and shakes his head rudely.

"Five guineas . . . six . . . six ten . . . six guineas . . . going at six guineas . . ."

The "gentlewoman in reduced circumstances" sits there numb with pain and incredulity. But what a blessing the admiral cannot know! What would he have done? What would he have said? She can imagine his tall, lean figure rising in that room, his blue eyes taking fire, and his voice:

"Look here, sir, this is damned roguery . . ."

What a blessing the admiral cannot know!

"Eight guineas, nine, ten, eleven, twelve, twelve, twelve . . . any advance on twelve . . . going . . . going." Bang!

And the old lady goes out into Bond Street having sold her last dream for twelve guineas.

§ 4

Upon the edge of that district whose frontier is Oxford Street, among the long streets and squares full of doctors, and shops which display the latest thing in operating tables, is to be found Hertford House and the Wallace Collection.

It is a notable experience in these days, when to possess anything is a social sin, to go to Hertford House and see what treasures a rich family was able to accumulate a century or so ago. There is nothing else in London like the Wallace

Collection: it is a little Louvre Museum. There is probably in the world no more surprising display of the acquisitive abilities of a few wealthy and cultivated aristocrats. It is also the most splendid gift ever made to the nation by an individual.

The fourth Lord Hertford, who began the collection, was considered by his contemporaries to be an eccentric recluse. He was born in the year 1800 and he died in 1870. He spent most of his life in Paris. It is said that he left England because of a dispute with the authorities about the drains of his house in Piccadilly. Rather than give way, he left the staircase unfinished, closed the shutters and declared the place uninhabitable in order to avoid paying the rates, and left for France.

His income was more than £240,000 a year. He had no interest in the social world or in people. His main object in life was to find and buy beautiful things. Pictures, clocks, furniture, bronzes, marbles, porcelain, all attracted him as long as they were first-rate. He rarely went to the sale rooms, but all the dealers in Paris knew the English *milord* who offered fantastic prices, and they were only too glad to take treasures to him before they reached the auction room. He was always delighted to snatch a work of art from beneath the nose of a rival, especially of an emperor, a king or a prince.

When he died at the age of seventy he owned the most magnificent private collection of art treasures in the world. His companion and fellow collector was his natural son, Richard Jackson, who later took the name of Richard Wallace. There was not much difference in age between father and son, Jackson, or Wallace, having been born when Lord Hertford was eighteen. It was not until the morning of Lord Hertford's funeral that Richard Wallace knew he had inherited the collection.

When Wallace decided to move the treasures to London an extraordinary experience awaited him. Hertford House had been vacant for thirty-five years. Old and devoted servants had been maintained there, had died and their sons and daughters had succeeded them, and for thirty-five years they had cleaned the house and kept it ready for the absent owner. When Sir Richard Wallace entered, a friend who was with him said that " notwithstanding that everything was in readiness for the invisible owners, a solemn silence reigned everywhere. On the walls of the drawing-rooms the lovely visions of Reynolds and Gainsborough were displayed side by side with the elegant types of Van Dyck, the superb paintings of Titian, and the glowing canvases of Rubens, represented by the latter's masterpiece, the famous *Rainbow*; but all these living and radiant works had, by the slow action of time, become covered with a thick coating of bloom through which, as through a veil, their beauty was but dimly revealed, clothed as it were with a kind of mysterious and melancholy grace."

Sir Richard and his French wife lived as quietly in London as Lord Hertford had lived in Paris. They rarely went out and saw few friends. Apparently the acquisitive instinct may be inherited, for, like his father before him, Wallace went on adding to the already enormous collection. When he died, he left the collection to his wife; at her death, and at her wish, it passed to the nation.

I have often come away from the Wallace Collection wondering whether the possession of so many superb things brought happiness with it, and, if so, was such happiness due to the objects themselves or to the sense of possession, which can be a powerful emotion almost akin to love, pity and hate.

I have also wondered whether life with so much gilt French furniture, so many Bouchers, Lancrets and Fragonards, to say nothing of Gainsborough, Reynold and Romney, would make it difficult to spend a few days in a railway hotel bedroom in Manchester. It is of course conceivable that the owner of so much richness might well be discovered in a state of utter happiness in the almost criminal bareness of such a room, gazing blissfully at a fumed oak wardrobe and an engraving by Marcus Stone. While it must have been wonderful to have had the knowledge, and the means, to collect all these works of art, surely there must have come moments when it was necessary to get away from them.

My abiding memories of the Wallace Collection include those almost edible ladies whose rosy curves were so decoratively, and so indecorously, painted by Boucher. Nowhere can you see so many fine Bouchers, and among them the elegant and exquisite portrait of that remarkable woman, the painter's patroness, the Marquise de Pompadour. She stands in her garden at Bellevue, one arm resting lightly upon the plinth of Pigalle's statue of Love and Friendship, which is now in the Louvre. Her lap-dog, Inès, sits beside her on a marble seat. She wears the tight, low bodice of the time, the front laced with bows, the wide skirt spread out over a pannier, and she looks at you with the smooth small face of an arrogant page-boy.

She was one of the great cold-blooded mistresses of history and Boucher's portrait, painted when she was thirty-seven, and five years before her death, is probably flattering, otherwise she would not have kept it. It was intended to mark an interesting phase in her relationship with Louis XV, the moment when their love had definitely turned the corner into friendship.

Boucher seems to have ministered to the royal love affair with considerable effect. In the same gallery are four large fleshy panels, *The Visit of Venus to Vulcan*, painted five years before the portrait, when the Pompadour believed that the King's passion was on the wane. These panels adorned her boudoir and were much admired by the King, but his son, Louis XVI, considered them improper and had them taken away. They went to Germany during the French Revolution, returned to France and were bought by Lord Hertford, who set them up in the form of a screen in his bedroom in the rue Laffitte. When they came to London Sir Richard Wallace hung them in his wife's boudoir. What a strange story it is, beginning with a royal mistress two centuries ago and ending in a quiet London square.

Another provoking woman at Hertford House is Mrs "Perdita" Robinson, whose Christian name was Mary, a great beauty seen in three portraits painted by Gainsborough, Romney and Reynolds. Each of these great painters seized upon a different aspect of her so that one appears to be looking at three different women. The best picture, though possibly not the best likeness, is Gainsborough's full-length portrait in the grand manner, which shows Mary Robinson seated against a rural background and expressing an overwhelming sweetness and gentleness.

When she was in the twenties she achieved success on the stage in such parts as Rosalind, which displayed her admirable figure, and Perdita, in which role she captivated the accessible heart of the Prince Regent.

She received a bond sealed with the royal arms for £20,000, which was never paid, and the prince soon tired of her, for it would seem that, in spite of her great beauty, she lacked refinement, was vain and difficult. It is however to her credit that she also tired of her royal lover and fell genuinely in love for some years with a veteran of the American War of Independence, Colonel Banastre Tarleton. He was responsible for the tragedy of her life. In order to save him from his creditors she made a long journey in a post-chaise and caught a chill which left her paralysed at the age of twenty-four, and she remained a cripple for the rest of her days. She then became a professional authoress and wrote her memoirs and a number of songs and verses, and died, aged forty or forty-two, poor, forlorn and crippled. No one seeing this lovely girl, as painted by Gainsborough, would dream that fate had so much humiliation in store for her.

I always leave the Wallace Collection bewildered by the variety of perfect things I have seen there: pictures, snuff-boxes, furniture, statues, bronzes, china and porcelain, medals and miniatures, but the predominating memory is that of Eighteenth Century France and of the courts of Louis XV and XVI, the rosy beauties of Boucher, the pastoral revels of Lancret and the two exquisite, and well-known, Fragonards, *The Swing* and *The Souvenir*. This last is the picture of a lady in silhouette carving a love message on a tree while a little dog watches her. The catalogue aptly compares it with a *nocturne* by Chopin.

And I wonder how many people have wondered, as I have done, why the cavalier by Frans Hals is called the *Laughing Cavalier*. Were he called the Contemptuous Cavalier or the Disdainful Cavalier it would, I think, be a little nearer the truth.

§ 5

I turned down Whitehorse Street and soon found myself in Shepherd Market. This queer little Georgian–Victorian backwater might have been lifted into the middle of the West End from any old market town in England. Beneath its surface it is intensely sophisticated, but you would never suspect this by daylight as you wander round looking into the windows of greengrocers, butchers and grocers, all of them small friendly shops.

I know nobody who lives in Shepherd Market, and I have always intended to read the one or two, I am told, good books that have been recently inspired by it. The people who live in the flats above the shops must be one of the last village communities in London. I should imagine that everybody knows what everybody else has done, is doing and is about to do; for village communities are like that everywhere.

After dark, when the lamplight falls upon archways and the buildings rise up half in shadow, Shepherd Market is Hollywood's idea of London as it ought to be. All it needs is a hansom cab permanently on duty. But it has something even more antiquated: it has a sedan chair.

I went one night into a pinkly lit and fashionable bar in the market which was so crowded with people of the same social class that it almost had the air of a refugee camp. The words " my dear old boy " and " darling " peppered the conversation so monotonously that I wondered whether this might not be the remains of Mr Michael Arlen's Mayfair. Leaning against a sedan chair, in which there was a telephone, stood an enormous black man. He was the personification of assurance. He was expensively, almost foppishly, dressed in American clothes, rings sparkled on his fingers, he rolled a cigar round his mouth, tilted his hat at an angle and continued to survey the crowd with unblinking interest. And all the time, as I say, he was casually leaning against a sedan chair; a strange sight. I thought of the negro slaves, the pampered little black boys in turbans, the negro coachmen and footmen who ministered to the vanity of the Eighteenth Century, and the picture made by this sophisticated negro was indeed a provoking one. But no one paid any attention to him. He might not have been there at all. I had a strong urge to go into the sedan chair and ring up Peter Cheyney.

The man who has given his name to this little corner of London was a builder-architect, Edward Shepherd, who had a hand in the building of Grosvenor and Cavendish squares. He obtained permission to build a cattle market in May Fair in 1738, and every May the merchants, the pedlars, the jugglers, the actors, the tightrope walkers, the men with dancing bears and performing monkeys congregated round the market and held the annual fair that has been going on for centuries, first outside St James's Leper House, then outside St James's Palace, then in the Haymarket and finally in Mayfair.

This once almost fabulously exclusive district, whose swan song was so prettily rendered by Mr Arlen, is that nest of streets between Berkeley Square and Park Lane. The Fair was held on what is now Hertford Street, Curzon Street and Shepherd Market. It seems to have been a turbulent and rowdy occasion which continued for over a fortnight. There were drinking-booths, raffles, lotteries, side-shows, plays, races, merry-go-rounds and bull-baiting. At one time it was frequented " by all the nobility in town ", and it was probably the most disreputable gathering in the West End. The great attraction in 1701 was a tightrope walker known as Lady Mary. She was said to be the daughter of an Italian nobleman who had eloped with Finlay, the showman. The following year Queen Anne opened a purity campaign and issued a proclamation which was read in all the churches for the encouragement of virtue. May Fair that year was visited by constables who arrested certain well-known women who, with the help of their friends, drove the constables into the sheep-pens, where they were bombarded with brickbats. When the battle was over one of the constables, John Cooper, lay dying. A Gloucestershire butcher was charged with the crime and was hanged at Tyburn. The business caused a great uproar and ended in the suppression of May Fair as a " publick nuisance " and a " nursery of Vice and Atheism ", but the fair seems to have been revived and to have continued with all its old-time " drunkenness, fornication, gaming and lewdness " until about 1750, when the influential people who now lived in the surrounding streets rose in their wrath and had it abolished.

It was Sydney Smith who said that the parallelogram between Oxford Street, Piccadilly, Regent Street and Hyde Park " enclosed more intelligence and ability, to say nothing of wealth and beauty, than the world had ever collected into such a space before ".

And that, I think, is probably true of Mayfair as it was in the late Eighteenth Century.

§ 6

The London taxi-cab, so often the jest of visiting Americans, has achieved by the rigidity of its design a certain old-world dignity, almost as if it were a mechanical four-wheeler. It is as typical of modern London as the hansom-cab of Victorian London. To see it stranded upon Epsom Downs during Derby Week is as though one of the minor landmarks of London, say the Griffin, were taking a trip into the country. Wherever the London taxi-cab goes—and it sometimes goes as far away as Brighton—it takes along with it the shadow of the capital.

The men who drive the taxi-cabs of London are naturally a race apart. I have known them, and have admired many of them, for years. Some of the old stagers used to drive horse-cabs, but that generation is now rapidly vanishing. The tempo of life, and the war, of course, the lack of petrol, the horrible habit of hanging a glove over the meter and speeding contemptuously past a fare, have improved neither the manners nor the prestige of the London taxi-driver.

The other day I struck an old driver who might have been a thin relative of Bairnsfather's " Old Bill ". I sat looking at the nape of his aged neck, his greying hair, admiring the way he dodged in and out of the traffic and wondering what his age really was. When we parted I gave him an unusually large tip because I liked him and because he was old. He looked at the money in the palm of his hand, smiled and winked at me and said:

" Thank yer, Guv'nor. Don't often meet a toff these days, and that's a fact! "

What a strange conversational throw-back to a dead age! He remembered the age of " toffs ", " swells " and " nobs ".

" You see this 'ere," he said, still gazing at the money. " Do you know what I'd rather 'ave than this 'ere? I'll tell yer . . . a blinkin' fat rump steak and a pint o' porter."

He then leaned towards me and deplored the age in which we live. He was an old snob. He loved toffs. He liked " a gentleman ". You could always tell a " *real* gentleman " from the other kind. Not 'arf you couldn't! But nowadays, driving a " keb " in London, blimey, what a queer collection of odds and ends you met. Not 'arf you didn't! But in the old days . . . Ah, the old days, when you could get a rump steak and a pint o' porter. . . . Them was the days, guv'nor, them was the days, and we shan't see them again. Not 'arf we shan't. . . .

And away he went.

Do you ever wonder how the taxi-driver knows London? Do you ever wonder why his fares so seldom puzzle or surprise him? There are six hundred and ninety-nine square miles in the Metropolitan Police area, and he is supposed to know his way in and out of all of them. Before he is allowed to drive a cab in London he must pass one of the stiffest topographical examinations imaginable. It takes place in the Public Carriage Office at Lambeth, where would-be taxi-drivers are examined by the police. Until a man gets sixty-six per cent of marks in this examination he is not given a licence. In some years before the War twenty thousand men were examined, but perhaps only five hundred would pass. Unless a man is hopeless he can try to pass this test as long as the police will endure him. One would-be taxi-driver I have heard of has been trying to pass the examination for three years.

" Knowledge of London " is the inscription on the door. Inside are a number of small rooms where police officials sit talking to unhappy-looking men. The chief examiner is a police superintendent. This man is a terror. He has the whole map of London in his head. He knows every street.

He knows every public building, club, theatre, monument, park. I once asked him how he gained his encyclopædic knowledge of London.

"When I was a lad," he said, "my father was so interested in London that we used to walk miles every week-end. That is the only way to know London. You cannot do it in a car. You *must* walk. I have often walked forty miles in a day over hard pavements, and that takes some doing, learning street names and getting the map of London into my head."

"Has any man ever passed your examination the first time?"

"Never. There was once a man who passed the second time. But that is quite exceptional. We have a man who has been up ninety-eight times, and he is still trying! We have hopes of him. Would you like to hear some of the examinations? Right . . ."

He pressed a bell. A policeman entered and sprang to attention.

"Send up John Jones," said the superintendent.

A nervous and earnest young man entered and timidly sat down. This was his eleventh attempt to pass the "Knowledge of London" examination.

"Now suppose," said the Superintendent, "you were at Harrod's and I asked you to take me to the Royal Oak railway station . . ."

John Jones half closed his eyes and gazed at the ceiling like a small boy at school.

"Well, sir, I leave Harrod's on the right—Brompton Road—cross to Hill Street—Montpelier Square, right and left, and into Montpelier Street. . . ."

The Superintendent bristled, and the back of his neck looked indignant.

"Surely Montpelier Street is first?" he asked.

"Yes, sir," replied John Jones abjectly.

"Well?" said the Superintendent.

"Then," continued John Jones, "I turn left for Knightsbridge, turn left at Alexandra Gate—Hyde Park—Victoria Gate; turn left, Bayswater Road; turn right, Westbourne Street; then Westbourne Crescent . . . crescent . . . crescent . . . crescent . . ."

" Well, go on," said the Superintendent.

Poor John Jones saw his taxi-cab receding from him. He panicked. He looked rapidly all over the ceiling and found there no answer to his problem.

" Gloucester Terrace," he said desperately. " Then Porchester Place . . ."

" Does Gloucester Terrace run into Westbourne Grove? " asked the Superintendent sternly.

John Jones suddenly gave it up. He collapsed.

" I can't remember," he said miserably.

" Come back in fourteen days," said the Superintendent. " Take your map and study London. Walk about London. It's the only way."

In a dozen little rooms in the building other imaginary taxi-cab journeys were being made.

" Suppose," said a police inspector to his victim, " I picked you up at the Royal Thames Yacht Club. How would you take me to Fulham Cemetery? "

In the next room an even more melancholy journey was being outlined.

" How would you take me from Brompton Cemetery to Wormwood Scrubs Prison? "

In a third room a more or less cheerful trip was suggested.

" If you picked me up at the Savage Club, how would you take me to Fulham Town Hall? "

In a fourth room a gay, but improbable ride was proposed.

" How would you take me from the Lying-in Hospital for Women to the Finsbury Park Empire? "

And the would-be drivers stood unhappily twirling their caps or hats, gazing at the ceiling as if it might suddenly become a magnificent crib on which they might read the answers.

" If I could only take you there, sir," pleaded one applicant, " I would be able to take all the short cuts, but I can't remember the names of them here! "

" That's all very well," replied the examiner. " The public expects you to know the nearest way. If you can't tell me the nearest way, I can't give you a licence."

" But sir, if I was only on the road . . ."

" Nonsense! Come back in a week."

And the would-be drivers walk out into the Lambeth Road, saddened and dejected.

Now and again, of course, a taxi-driver really does pass the examination. He then gets a licence and turns up with his cab to take a driving test. A plain-clothes police inspector—the only man in London entitled to sit beside a taxi-driver—puts him through his paces. He has to reverse a cab between a difficult line of posts. If he touches a post, he is ploughed. If he succeeds, he is taken out into London. I was offered a trip with a new driver.

The inspector, placing a little stool next to the driver, sat down. He watched every movement.

" Go on, get cracking! " he said.

The driver asked me in a most unprofessional voice:

" Where shall I take you, please? "

The inspector smiled wearily.

" Say, 'Where to, sir?' " he growled. " Don't be such a cissy."

" London Library," I replied.

We sped off. The inspector stopped the driver three times and made him reverse into back streets in three movements.

When we got to St James's Square the taximeter registered nothing—the first time in my life that this had ever happened!

" Am I your first fare? "

" Yes."

I gave him five shillings for luck.

" I hope," said the inspector primly, " all your transactions with the public will be as fortunate. Spit on it for luck. Now take me to New Scotland Yard. . . ."

The taxi-driver and the bus-driver have a long and varied ancestry. The first men to move members of the public from here to there were the Thames watermen, who, in days when the roads were narrow and fit only for packhorses and foot-passengers, were to be seen in their thousands on the river. Stow says that in Tudor times there were forty thousand watermen working on the Thames, but this surely must be an exaggeration. However, the Thames was alive with them, and the wherries were as numerous as gondolas upon the canals of Venice; indeed, the pictures which Canaletto painted when he came to London in the Eighteenth Century look so like Venice that it is surprising to see the dome of St Paul's or the Abbey in such an Italian setting.

The Thames waterman wore a livery of sorts, although there seems to have been great variety in their dress, and they wore a brassard like the modern taxi-driver. The old-time equivalent of the cry of " Taxi " was " Oars! " or " Sculls! " which the fare shouted to attract attention when he reached the top of the water-stairs. But more often than not he was mobbed by watermen at a slack period of the day. The sculler rowed a small boat, and two oarsmen manned the wherry, which was faster and cost twice as much. The watermen always felt themselves a threatened community, and set up wails of despair throughout history at every change in the habits of the capital.

That the theatres in Shakespeare's day were on the south bank of the river naturally meant a profitable business for the watermen; accordingly when Drury Lane and Covent Garden replaced the theatres of Bankside a cry of despair rose from the boatmen, who saw stark ruin staring them in the face. Even worse was the arrival of the coach and the hackney-carriage.

The first coach made in England seems to have been built for Lord Rutland in 1555. Queen Mary had one, and so did Elizabeth, a splendid but uncomfortable, springless wagon drawn by six grey Hungarian horses, whose long tails were dyed orange colour! Like the sedan chair and the umbrella, coaches when first seen were considered effeminate, and no proper vehicle for an able-bodied man. By 1634 there were twenty hackney carriages plying for hire in the Strand, and in the time of Charles II there were six thousand coaches in London and a hundred and twenty-seven hackney carriages. The traffic blocks were probably worse then they are to-day.

John Taylor, the water poet, voiced the despair of his calling when he wrote, " This is a rattling rowling and rumbling age," and then broke into verse:

Carroaches, coaches, Jades and Flanders mares
Do rob us of our shares, our wares, our fares ;
Against the ground we stand and knock our heeles,
Whilst all our profit runns away on wheels.

A curious feature of life on the Thames in the old days was the violent and ribald abuse known as water-language from which no one, no matter how exalted, was immune. The moment anyone entered a boat on the Thames he was liable to be insulted in the most revolting manner by any passing waterman, and also by his passengers, and it was the custom to repay abuse with abuse. Malcolm, writing in 1810, said that " the Thames seems to have a charter for rudeness; and the sons of Triton and Neptune have not only a freedom of, but a licence for, any sort of speech."

Unpopular monarchs, queens as well as kings, were verbally attacked while the royal barge made its way on the river. Poor Catherine of Braganza was often taunted with her husband's mistresses and her inability to provide an heir. Remarks which on land would have been treasonable were regarded as a joke on the Thames. Earlier monarchs seem to have taken water-language in good part, but the Hanoverians disliked it and attempted to put a stop to it. I have read somewhere that Handel's lovely *Water Music* was composed in order to drown the torrent of abuse that would have greeted the new king, George I, during his first river progress.

There are many instances in literature of water-language, but the classic retort was that of Dr Johnson, who, as reported by Boswell, replied to a passing waterman, who had made unpleasant remarks about his appearance, " Sir, under pretence of keeping a bawdy-house, your wife is a receiver of stolen goods."

The sedan chairman was another feature of London's transport, often a hefty Irishman, frequently drunk and sometimes, like the link-boy, in league with footpads and highwaymen. Those who say that the first sedan chairs came to London in 1634 are forgetting the wife of the French Ambassador, who in 1603 travelled all the way from Edinburgh to London in a chair in the train of James I. She was borne by eight men, who took it in turns to carry her in relays of four.

The chair had probably nothing at all to do with Sedan, but more with the verb *sedere*, to sit, although even the *Oxford English Dictionary* cannot answer this. The chair was apparently Italian in origin, and became popular in the time of Charles I, when Sir Sanders Duncomb was given a monopoly to hire them for fourteen years. That it was effeminate, that it was disgraceful to degrade fellow-men into beasts of burden were criticisms which did not interfere with the popularity of the chair; and it must indeed have been convenient, in times when roads were filthy, for anyone wearing a new velvet suit or a white satin dress to be able to step into a chair in the house, and be carried to dinner or theatre.

We come a step nearer the modern taxi-driver with the horse cabmen and the drivers of the Victorian hansom. Like the sedan chair, which was typical of the Eighteenth Century, the hansom was typical of Victorian London; " the gondola of London ", the romantics of that time called it! It was the invention of Joseph Aloysius Hansom, the architect, who was born at York in 1803. He should have made a fortune out of his " safety cab ", as he called it, but something went wrong, and the only money he ever received for it was £300. It was a delightful vehicle, a sedan chair on wheels, convenient, intimate and much faster than the four-wheeler or " growler ".

When the motor-car appeared on the streets of London in Edwardian times—it became popular about 1907—it was driven by a new type, the motor mechanic, a calling that received many recruits from the ranks of the younger, more adventurous cab-drivers. Like most new things, at first rather a joke, the taxi became a serious rival, and eventually the extinguisher, of the four-wheeler and the hansom. The taximeter, which was at first spelt " taxameter ", was a German invention fitted to horse-cabs in Germany as early as 1890, but the London cabmen would have nothing to do with it. Many hansom-cab drivers, presumably more dashing and modern than the cabmen, consented to them, but it was left to the driver of the motor-cab to make them an everyday feature of life in London.

And now, with the coming of the aeroplane, the word taxi has even become a verb.

§ 7

A friend of mine, who writes thrillers and was in search of atmosphere, arranged to visit the Piccadilly tube station after the last train had run, and asked me to go with him.

It was one o'clock in the morning. London was, or should have been, asleep. Piccadilly wore a tired, furtive air. There was a lot of lamplight but few people. Eros aimed his shaft at someone to whom love was probably a mockery, and a policeman moved in the direction of Vine Street arm in arm with a small hatless man who evidently believed himself to be Hercules.

We whistled at the closed gates of the Tube station, and were admitted to that exotic sub-circus. But it was empty. Wax women displayed their pyjamas, their nightdresses, their stockings, and their most intimate under-garments to a small, critical band of men who carried bags from which large hammers protruded. They lit their pipes.

" Blimey, I'd like to see my old woman in that . . ."

" Not 'arf, you would! "

" Not 'arf, I wouldn't! I'd give 'er a clip on the ear."

And the wax woman returned the gaze of the disapproving males with an expression designed to arouse the envy of her own sex.

We descended a staircase that no longer moved, and found ourselves in one of the most uncanny places in London—a dead tube station.

" This is exactly what I want," said my friend. " You see, my heroine, escaping from a gang that is trying to kidnap her, jumps out of the last train at Piccadilly. . . ."

Possibly because tube stations are always associated with a frantic crowd, with movement, the roar and light of a train, with cries of " Move down the car, please! " and the banging of doors, the silence of a station into which no train will come seems weird and abnormal. I looked into the round black circle of the tunnel and listened for the train that would not come. Normally there is generally a hint of an approaching train, but now there was nothing but a dead and hollow silence.

Advertisements at 1 a.m. are nauseating. The idea of drinking whisky or, even worse, vermouth, of going to Scotland, keeping a schoolgirl complexion, asking for a Bass or a Guinness, visiting the Zoo, buying a wedding-ring or subscribing to *Punch* was not only fantastic at that time in the morning but it was also impossible. The most impressionable and easily influenced person could do none of these things at that time. The only advertisements that could appeal to one would extol the virtues of blankets, mattresses, pillows, hot-water bottles and the danger of night starvation.

We walked along the platform noting all these things and watching a melancholy cleaner sweep up the appalling debris left behind by the public. Two bill-posters arrived with a ladder, a bucket and a roll of paper.

"Juice off, Bill?" said one.

"Try it," suggested the melancholy sweeper.

"Sez you," said the bill-posters, lighting cigarettes.

Every night when the last train has taken its tired cargo to bed a small army of men descend on the hundred and seventy-one miles of track and examine every lamp, disc, wire, signal, bolt, screw and sleeper. Their four hours' inspection while London is asleep is probably the most important activity of the night. They gather on the dead stations with their leather bags, and, standing upon the edge of the platforms, look down at the rails with an intent expression as they wait for the "juice" to be cut off. It is cut off in sections, but sometimes the gangs, becoming impatient, take a little walk with death.

A foreman climbed down and fixed a small metal shoe to one rail and an object like a small doll's house to the other. Instantly twelve electric lights shone in the doll's house—a sign that the juice was not yet off.

"As long as you don't fall across the conductor rails you're all right," explained the foreman. "It'll soon be off."

The gang jumped into the danger zone, and we followed them. It is so easy, but so unpleasant, to be brave in public.

"Where are we going?" I asked.

" Leicester Square," was the fantastic reply, as we set off between the line of shining rails.

A shout came suddenly down the tunnel. " Juice off! "

We began to walk boldly. The gang swarmed over the rails, hitting and tapping.

A walk underground from Piccadilly to Leicester Square is the most nightmarish journey you can imagine. Green lights shone in the tunnels, and the gangs went slowly, like explorers in an Egyptian tomb. I was told that mosquitoes live underground all the year because of the even mild temperature. Sometimes a ganger who falls asleep is bitten in mid-winter!

Suddenly we arrived at Leicester Square. The station stood in lamplight, but not a soul on it. The tunnels, always so ominous with the threat of an approaching train, were dead and cold. The gangs looked like rats as they bent over the tracks with their hammers.

So we climbed up on the dead platform.

" What an experience! " my friend was saying, " what atmosphere! "

And I was thinking that perhaps in a thousand years' time some archæologists, digging their way into the ruins o. Leicester Square tube station, will write a learned book about a race whose abiding interests were drink, soap, face-powder and corsets.

§ 8

Booksellers Row migrated from the Strand long ago, and now it exists in a magnificent chain of second-hand shops which begins almost at the Tottenham Court Road and extends on both sides of the street to Leicester Square, where there is the largest collection of second-hand books in English in the world.

These shops have a selection of their cheaper copies on shelves outside on the pavement, from which the passer-by may pick and choose for as long as he likes. Inside are books by the ton. The shops possess the cold, pathetic, orphanage smell of ownerless books, of books waiting to be bought, read and treasured and placed upon shelves with others of their kind. They begin in the cellars, which extend in some places under the street. They mount, by way of rickety stairs, to floor after floor, ending in the attics, until you wonder how these floors, ceilings and walls can bear the dead weight of them.

The man who has never in his life become lost to all thoughts of time and food in the Charing Cross Road, and at the end of the day has not found himself hugging beneath his arm some book, or books, which he is proud and happy to possess, does not know one of the purest joys which London can afford. The road is a busy one. The traffic rushes one way to Oxford Street and the other to Trafalgar Square. The pavements are always filled with hurrying crowds, and the bookmen stand with their backs to the world, the book readers, the book hunters, the book tasters, the book maniacs—for books, like drink, can affect the brain—completely oblivious that they are not standing in an empty street.

I have known the Charing Cross Road for thirty years, and I think I know every shop and bookseller in it. To me all the shops are different and each has its own peculiar personality. There is the shop that I would enter only as a last resort. There is the shop I would choose if I wanted a foreign book, and one I would make for if I wanted a book on Boucher or Van Steen, or any artist old or new. There is the shop I would go to if I wanted an Eighteenth Century book in contemporary calf, and one I would go to if I wanted anything from *Pears Cyclopædia* to a first edition of Boswell.

While I know all the booksellers, and remember some of them before they became grey and put on weight, and though I have spent countless hours discussing books with them, I cannot remember one occasion when I have spoken to a fellow bookman; for we are a silent, misanthropic and lonely crowd. Also I have never met a book-woman. I suppose these exist, but it so happens not to have been my good, or bad, fortune to have met one. Women come into a second-hand bookshop with a definite request and are out again in a flash. They do not moon about all day in search of they know not what. In fact, after all, I am inclined to think that probably book-women do not exist; for one cannot count girl students and young females turning over books on the ballet. If they do exist, they are probably young and sprightly, for it is inconceivable that the female sex should produce the equivalent to the ancient, dusty bookworm, with his spectacles on the end of his nose, who is such a constant feature of the Charing Cross Road. No elderly woman would surely spend a whole day looking for nothing.

Book-collectors will probably bear me out that no woman, and few men, are the perfect companions on a book hunt. If women are in love with a book-hunter they will begin with maddeningly helpful enthusiasm, coming up with some unsuitable volume and the remark, "I've found something which will interest you, darling," then as the hours pass they will pout and pine, and if unable to distract the seeker, will sink with injured reproachfulness into the nearest chair and dip into several novels. The only possible companion is a man who is as keen on butterflies or Byzantium as you are on something else.

I believe it to be true that a man once walked into a bookshop and said: "Have you got a book called *The Rise and Fall of the Holborn Empire*?" and I know it to be true that a man wearing a riding-jacket picked out a book I wrote on the Holy Land, called *In the Steps of the Master*, and asked, "Have you got any more about hunting?"

Most second-hand booksellers could write an amusing book about their customers. They all know the bibliomaniac, the man to whom the amassing of books is a compulsive neurosis. Buried away among the memories of booksellers are extraordinary stories of ordinary shabby little men who for years hover like hawks over the bookshelves, interested in everything, and then one day are found dead in Balham or Brixton in a tall old house so crammed with books from cellars to roof that the police have to squeeze in sideways. Only bachelors can become real bibliomaniacs; most wives cure the victim when books start to invade bedrooms and bathroom. But it does happen now and again that a wily collector manages to carry on an affair with the Charing Cross Road without the knowledge of his wife.

I remember once noticing an eager little hunchback who was turning over the books with the avidity of a collector. I met him in shop after shop, and all the booksellers knew him. At last I asked one to tell me who this hunchback was.

" He lives in the country," I was told, " and he comes up to London once in about six months. Before he leaves home he has to promise his wife that he won't buy any books. But, you see, he can't help it, for he's been a collector for years. As soon as he gets to town he makes straight for the Charing Cross Road, and before he goes home one of us has to fix him up so that his wife won't think he's carrying a parcel. So he steps into the office and takes off his coat, and we pack the books on each side of his hump. Many a time I've helped to load the poor little chap up like a pack-mule; and it's amazing how much stuff he can carry on his back. Of course he can't buy any folios . . ."

I have often thought that many of the best things in London are free: the National Gallery and the British Museum, Hyde Park and Kensington Gardens, the Changing of the Guard, the Thames bridges and the Embankment, a walk down Bond Street and, of course, the Charing Cross Road. Lost to the world that touches their elbows as they stand there, the bookmen pry and pore into the books, looking and seeking, and sometimes even finding. I love to remember the hours I have spent there, perhaps on spring mornings, sometimes in winter, oblivious of cold feet, when the shop doors open to the warning ping of a little bell, and often in the evening when the lamps have been lighted and the titles shine out splendidly in gold behind the plate-glass windows.

§ 9

The dance floor in the Tottenham Court Road throbbed and rocked with the latest disharmony known as " Bebop ". It was an enormous dance floor. I suppose there were four hundred African natives dancing with wild abandon, and a high proportion of them with white girls. I could pick out the sleek Jamaican, the dark Tanga native, the lighter coloured Bantu. Some were extravagantly over-dressed in square-shouldered American suits, brown shoes and chromatic ties, others were dressed poorly and some were wild, bewildered-looking and shaggy, as if they had been dropped into the Tottenham Court Road straight from the bush. But they all knew how to dance to the jungle rhythm. They would suddenly hold their partners at arms' length, twirl round, execute some fantastic foot-work and, clasping their partners again, go off stamping and writhing.

This African invasion of London is something new. Chinatown has ceased to exist, but this black London extends from the Charing Cross Road to Euston. It is not considered polite to refer to these natives as black men or negroes. The phrase used is " coloured gentlemen ".

A police inspector, whom I met in the street as I left the dance hall, told me that the black population of London appears to be increasing. Many of the men are students brought to England under the auspices of the Colonial Office. Some remain good, some go bad. There are also many stowaways, notably from the West Indies, and these, after a brief imprisonment, are released to find their own level, which is generally the underworld.

The inspector agreed with me that this black London is something hitherto unknown. It is inaccurate to compare it with New York's Harlem, because the men have no women of their own race, and there is no family life. London's African population, which now numbers many thousands, is composed of students and men who are technically students, and of stray men from all the African colonies and dependencies.

I noticed in the dance hall certain flashy, cigar-smoking individuals, obviously the social leaders of the community, who on several subsequent occasions I spotted in Hyde Park holding forth on the injustice of being black in a white world. But they seem to be able to throw off their sense of injustice in the evening.

I asked the inspector to tell me about the African invasion of the underworld, and his comments were brief and lurid.

" Is the Colonial Office aware of the by-products of self-government ? " I asked.

The inspector smiled. " Ask me another," he said.

CHAPTER ELEVEN

I see Regent's Park, visit the Zoo and Madame Tussaud's. I remember the old Caledonian Market and wish it still existed. I go to the British Museum, where I see the Mildenhall Treasure and the Sutton Hoo Ship Burial. I attend an operation in a London hospital.

§ 1

ADMIRERS of the Prince Regent—and I suppose there are many of them now that "Regency" furniture has become fashionable—will probably admit that one of his outstanding achievements was Regent Street. It is the most handsome street in London, and to think of London without it is to imagine a cramped and undistinguished West End. It was therefore a good day for London when the Regent decided to build himself a palace in Marylebone Park Fields and to link it by a long processional avenue with his London palace, Carlton House—something like the wonderful streets Napoleon was making in Paris at that time.

Regent Street was driven through a dreary district of slums and market-gardens, of old inns where highwaymen concealed their loot, and through marshland where only a generation before sportsmen like General Oglethorpe had shot woodcock. The Regent's palace was never built, but I believe the site was to have been what is now Queen Mary's Rose Garden in Regent's Park. Carlton House, the palace where "Prinny" entertained his friends and his varied mistresses, has completely disappeared except for a few columns which uphold the portico of the National Gallery and the private chapel of Buckingham Palace.

The curve of Regent Street, where it leaves Piccadilly Circus on its way to Oxford Circus, is one of the fine things about London. Even the rebuilding of the street cannot quite take away the beauty of that graceful line. It was forced on Nash, the architect, by practical problems connected with the difficulty of buying up certain properties which stood to the east of his new road. Very cleverly making a virtue out of a necessity, he just triumphantly by-passed them with a curve. Nash was a Welshman from Cardigan, and no doubt the Principality is proud of the son who made such a mighty change in the appearance of the capital; for Regent Street must be considered as the royal mile leading to all the classical terraces of Regent's Park.

It is the only park in this, and perhaps any other country, that was designed side by side with a unified architectural scheme. Regent's Park was the first magnificent garden suburb. When we talk about Regent's Park we think of the houses as well as of the park. When someone tells us that he lives in Regent's Park, we do not imagine that he is living in a tent or under a tree; whereas if someone told us that he was living in Hyde Park we should not readily believe him, or think his address was an affected euphemism for Knightsbridge or Bayswater.

Nash built the houses and terraces of Regent's Park to a single harmonious design, and though they have often been criticised, and very harshly, this last burst of classicism is most impressive, and I can never go to Regent's Park without thinking how brilliantly Nash ransacked the ancient world and adapted it to the requirements of the English butler.

There is something exquisitely well-bred about the appearance of Regent's Park, almost as if Nash had sent Athens to Eton. Bath is a city that was built by men who could read Greek and Latin, but Regent's Park always seems to me like a magnificent translation. I have known quite a number of people who have lived there, and I have had luncheon, tea and dinner in Regent's Park on many pleasant occasions. But I have often thought, having penetrated the magnificent façade, and coming upon some old lady living there in a flat behind tremendous columns, that it was as surprising as to discover someone who had made a cosy little dwelling in the corner of a film studio during the filming of *The Last Days of Pompeii*.

Still, in this age of the common man, I suppose we should be grateful for anything as uncommon and well-bred as Regent's

Park. It is so clearly the swan song of the " first gentleman in Europe ".

When I went to Regent's Park the other day I saw a vast field on which young and old were playing cricket. How many matches were in progress at the same time, I have no idea: the field was covered with them. There was a lake upon whose waters small yachts were sailing. There was a playground where children were letting off their astounding superfluous energy on swings and in sand-pits.

I saw an open-air theatre where a graceful girl in a black veil was dancing all alone to the sound of a piano. She was rehearsing a dance for a Shakespearean play. I saw Queen Mary's Rose Garden. It is really a museum of roses, but different from all other museums because if you fall in love with an exhibit you can write down its name—all the trees and bushes are carefully labelled—and go to the nursery and buy a specimen to plant in your own garden. I defy even the most casual of gardeners to walk through this place uninspired, while to the rosarian it must be paradise.

Like all the other parks in London, Regent's Park reflects what is apparently a national characteristic. I refer to the complete lack of interest in statuary. This art in London is purely a personal art, and the person immortalised must have done something, preferably something violent. You often hear people, when faced by an unknown statue, ask, " What did he *do*? " Is it therefore surprising that our streets contain so many men sitting on horses, so many senators?

Regent's Park deserves a few good statues. There is Hylas and the Nymph in the St John's Lodge Gardens, and the charming boy-and-toad fountain near the Rose Garden, but nothing else worth notice. The boy and the toad is delightful. The little naked boy sits on the ground near the toad, from whose mouth a stream of water shoots and hits the outspread palm of the child's hand. It has something of the charm of the Fontana Tartarughe in Rome.

And I went to the Zoo. The Zoo is a wonderful place. It is beautifully arranged, and, as one would expect in a country which loves animals, the captives are obviously as happy there as they can be, and a good deal safer than they would be in their native lands. If you asked me to name my favourite corner of the Zoo, I should say the Aquarium. The colour of the submarine landscapes, the incredible things that inhabit them, the strange miniature armoured monsters on whose survival Nature has expended such infinite pains, the exquisite frilly soles that flutter up and down in the water tremulously, the baleful eye of an octopus behind a stone, the little sea-horses like submerged chessmen—all these things are unforgettable, interesting and exciting.

Every time I go to the Zoo I look in vain for a strange man whom I met there during the War. He was an animal-painter. But he was also an animal-eater. I met him in the Reptile House, where some dangerous snakes had been " put down " because it was feared that an air raid might release them into Regent's Park. This man's hobby had been for many years the cooking and eating of unusual meats. Whenever an alligator or a giraffe died, he would go to the Zoo and ask for a portion of the body, which he would take home and cook.

He told me that flamingo tastes like pheasant; the Coypu Rat, or nutria, is like hare; python, which he had eaten only once, tastes rather like veal, and crocodile, he said, was exactly like veal. Giraffe tastes like horse, and ostrich reminded him of something between pheasant and beef—an appalling mixture, I should have thought.

Bear he thought was excellent. It was just like a prime cut of Scotch beef. He once made a first-rate steak-and-kidney pie when a Malayan sun-bear died. Two friends shared this dish with him, and said that it was the best steak-and-kidney pie they had ever tasted. When he told them it was made of Malayan sun-bear they were both sick, "Which shows you what a strange thing prejudice is," was his comment.

One of his remarks will always please me. After a moment's silence, during which he glanced hungrily at an alligator, he remarked sadly, " I've never had the chance to eat an iguana."

During the War it became the fashion for members and friends of the Zoological Society to make themselves responsible for the rations of various animals by paying a weekly sum and " adopting " them, an idea which was so popular that it still continues. To become the godparent of a humming-bird costs a shilling a week, and this is the cheapest form of guardianship, while the most expensive, as might be imagined, is to make yourself responsible for an elephant, which costs twenty shillings a week. Perhaps in no other country but one full of animal-lovers would it be necessary to preface the official list of adoptable animals with the warning: "It must be pointed out that adopted animals cannot be taken away from the Gardens."

§ 2

One of the earliest memories I have of London as a small boy is that of the wax figures in Madame Tussaud's exhibition. Those figures made such an impression upon me that even when I grew up I could never bring myself to revisit the place.

One night—it was March 18, 1925—an excited news editor rushed me out of a newspaper office with the information that a serious fire was to be found somewhere in the Marylebone Road. I arrived in time to watch one of the most violent fires I have ever seen. The hundreds of wax figures in Madame Tussaud's exhibition were going up in tongues and streamers of vermilion flame. The fire would appear to die down for a moment, only to revive again with fearful enthusiasm as a couple of queens, a president and a few poets were added to the flames. In the morning, when the Salvage Corps allowed me to walk at my own risk in the still-hot ruins, there seemed not a thing left.

Everyone thought that Madame Tussaud's was finished, but fortunately the moulds from which the historic collection had been made were not destroyed. A new and a much grander Madame Tussaud's eventually took its place among the sights of London; and this was the waxwork show I visited the other day.

Most reference books lead one to believe that waxworks only became popular in this country when Madame Tussaud sought refuge in London after her exciting experiences during the French Revolution. But it is not so. Waxworks have always been popular in England. Wax effigies of the dead were carried in funeral processions, and were afterwards exhibited to great crowds in Westminster Abbey. About a hundred years before Madame Tussaud came to England there were at least three waxwork shows open in London. Perhaps the most famous was Mrs Salmon's exhibition at the Horn Tavern in Fleet Street. Another was Mrs Goldsmith's in Green Court, Old Jewry, and the third was that of Mrs Mills in the Inner Walk of Exeter Change in the Strand. Mrs Mills not only exhibited the great ones of the age, but also stated in her handbills that "persons may have their effigies made, or their deceas'd friends on reasonable terms". It is interesting to note that even before the arrival of the great queen of waxworks the business was in the hands of women. I wonder why?

I have an idea that many people who go to Madame Tussaud's are unaware that the extraordinary little woman who founded the show led an infinitely more exciting life than most of the characters on view in her exhibition. Marie Gresholtz was born at Berne, Switzerland, in 1760, and at the age of six went to live in Paris with her uncle, Dr John Christopher Curtius, who ran a fashionable wax museum there. His studio was the resort of members of the French aristocracy and of men like Voltaire, Diderot, Rousseau and Mirabeau. Young Marie began to outshine her uncle as a wax modeller. "There was witchery in the tips of her subtle fingers", one writer said of her.

Why or how the art of wax modelling became a fashionable craze at this time, I do not know. Just as Nero is said to have fiddled while Rome burned, so the French aristocracy made wax apples and pears while the guillotine was being sharpened. Young Marie was invited to live at Versailles in order to help Madame Elizabeth, sister of Louis XVI, to become proficient in the art. She spent nine years in the tragic Court upon which the fury of the French Revolution was about to descend. One of the first warnings was the angry mob that surged round the studio of Curtius on July 12, 1789, demanding models to carry in a street demonstration. In this way they obtained the busts of Necker and the Duc d'Orleans, which they bore in riotous procession through Paris. On that fateful Sunday the first blood of the Revolution was shed when the mob bearing these wax figures came into conflict with a detachment of the Royal German Regiment. Two days later the Bastille was stormed.

Curtius, accurately forecasting the temper of the time, withdrew his niece from Court and installed her for safety in his studio. The Revolution developed into the Reign of Terror. The wax museum suddenly achieved a new and sinister fame. Who could more ably model the victims of the guillotine than Curtius and his niece? Bloodstained heads were delivered to them straight from the guillotine with orders that they must be cast and copied, and it is said that young Marie often worked with tears in her eyes as she took a death-mask from the face of many a gentle, harmless creature who had been her friend.

When the Terror turned and destroyed those who had provoked it, Marie Gresholtz was forced to take the death-mask of Marat, the " Friend of the People ", of Charlotte Corday, and of Robespierre, whose head was delivered to her within an hour of his death. One cannot help wondering whether the Chamber of Horrors, which has been a feature of the Tussaud exhibition for over a century and a quarter, may not owe something to the experiences which Marie Gresholtz endured at this time. It is commonly said that this gruesome side show was inspired by a Cave of Criminals which was a feature of her uncle's exhibition in Paris, but surely its gory character may have a deeper psychological origin?

Marie's republican sympathies were at one time questioned, and she was flung into prison. Among her companions at this time was Josephine, afterwards the wife of Napoleon. When she was released, Marie found the wax museum in a bad way. Her uncle had died, or was poisoned by his political enemies, and had left behind a mass of debt. Marie struggled for years to make a living. At the age of thirty-five she married François Tussaud, who is described as a wine-grower, or an engineer, and they managed, by working together, to pull the show back into shape. But in a few years time Marie's marriage went on the rocks and she decided to leave France.

She arrived in the London of George III with two small sons and a collection of wax figures. She was then forty-two years of age, and her first exhibition was opened in the Strand.

She was a courageous woman and, like so many small people, brim full of energy. She toured her show all over England and Scotland, and when within sight of the Irish coast the ship containing her waxworks was wrecked with the partial loss of its cargo. There has never been a more distinguished wreck off the Irish coast. For days the bodies of kings, queens, celebrated beauties, criminals, artists, dramatists and writers were washed up on the shores of County Cork. Madame built up the collection again and turned a disaster into a triumph.

When she returned to London she found a barn-like structure in Baker Street which had served at one time as a mess room for the Brigade of Guards. Although the building has been reconstructed, burnt down and reconstructed a second time, the exhibition is still housed on the same site.

When she was eighty-one Madame decided to retire, and she handed the business over to her two sons, Francis and Joseph. She died in 1850, aged ninety. Francis and Joseph bequeathed the business to Joseph II, the grandson of Madame. He left it to his son, John, her great-grandson, who had a long and prosperous reign. He it was who placed Tussaud's among the chief sights of London. He died aged eighty-four in 1946, having seen the exhibition destroyed by fire in 1925 and seriously damaged during the Blitz in 1940. The present Tussaud—his son, and Madame's great-great grandson—is Bernard Tussaud, who most days may be found in Baker Street modelling the features of a king, a film star or a criminal.

I asked Mr Tussaud to tell me what happens when he decides to include some well-known character in his exhibition.

" First of all I get an interview with the person," he said. " I take a chart of measurements. I also have with me a photographer, who takes snapshots of the sitter from all sorts of unusual angles. Look, this is the sort of thing . . ."

He opened a filing cabinet and drew out pictures of the

tops of heads and the napes of necks, pictures of hands and feet, pictures of chins and noses. It is the most unconventional gallery of celebrities in the world. If you wished to know what the nape of Mr Churchill's neck is like, or if you wished to look at the top of the Aga Khan's head, they would turn up such details in a second in Baker Street.

"While I model the head and neck in clay, the sitter's tailor or dressmaker has given measurements from which we construct a plaster body," continued Mr Tussaud. "Only the face and hands are made of wax. When the clay head is completed it is cast in plaster of paris. The mould thus made is then filled with molten wax which, when cold, reproduces the original clay."

The next difficulty is the eyes. Glass eyes of the right size and shape are skilfully placed in the sockets, a process which Mr Tussaud says can make or ruin a likeness. Incredibly difficult, to an onlooker, is the method of putting on the hair and eyebrows.

I watched a deft young woman in a room next to the studio giving a luxuriant head of hair to the bald wax skull of a popular actress. The head had been gently warmed, and each hair was pressed separately into position to a depth of a quarter of an inch. I was told it takes two weeks to put hair and eyebrows on a normal head.

The sitter is asked to give a plaster cast of his hands; if this is not possible, someone with similar hands is used instead. When the figure is complete it is sent to the wardrobe mistress to be clothed, and here we come to one of those delightful bits of useless information of which London is so full—all the waxworks wear undergarments or, I am told, their clothes would not hang properly! The perfect clothing for a Tussaud figure is, of course, a suit or a dress belonging to the sitter, and these are frequently given. The figure of President Truman wears a suit, collar and tie belonging to the President, which were flown to London by Mr Attlee after a Washington Conference. Marshal Tito sent from Belgrade the elegant uniform, complete with ribbons, and the riding-boots which clothe his figure.

The real Chamber of Horrors is, I think, the storeroom in

which the heads cast by Madame during the French Revolution are casually flung together on shelves. Most of them bear scars at the neck, and all of them are steeped in authentic horror which no sculptor could achieve. Robespierre's head is a ghastly death-mask. The cheek and jaw are clearly pocked by the shot-marks inflicted the day before his death either by himself or a gendarme.

Walking round this exhibition again for the first time since I was a child, I thought how like, yet how unlike, a wax figure can be to the original. The very striving after such intense realism, the clothing of figures, real spectacles and handkerchiefs, seems now and again to defeat itself. Some people make good waxworks, some do not. I discovered that for some reason the wax effigy of a dead person is more convincing than that of a living one. Defunct statesmen and remote American Presidents are extraordinarily life-like, while those of living statesmen are oddly unreal. And nearly everyone looks younger in wax than in life, probably because most wax figures possess a more or less uniform complexion.

I think the most life-like figure in the show is the Chelsea Pensioner who stands in the dark looking at the death of Gordon. A girl who found herself standing next to him trod on his foot or knocked against him, said " Sorry " and, realising that she had spoken to a wax figure, gave a little cry of horror and moved away!

The most realistic tableau—and one I remember from long ago—is the " Murder of the Princes in the Tower ". The illusion, if you get the lantern carried by one of the warders hidden against Brackenbury, is almost perfect. The " Death of Harold at Hastings ", with an arrow sticking out of a blood-stained eye-socket, is just as ghastly as I thought it was when I was eight years of age.

But I realised that the Chamber of Horrors has now no terrors for me. I thought that the dreary-looking collection of men and women and the various bric-à-brac of the condemned cell were more sordid than horrible. The widespread belief that a reward waits for anyone who will spend a night in that place is a London legend, but there is no truth in it at all. People write from all parts of the world asking to be allowed to spend the night there. The watchmen who patrol the exhibition tell me that the Chamber of Horrors is not a pleasant place after hours, even when you are used to it. The Metropolitan Railway runs directly beneath it, and the building trembles, and a murderer often seems to be waving a hand, as an occasional late train shakes the building.

The work which to my mind lifts the exhibition out of the region of waxworks into that of art is the handiwork of Madame Tussaud herself. The fineness and the quality of her work have rarely been equalled, and never surpassed, by any of her descendants. A really important figure is her portrait of Napoleon; indeed, it is an object of the greatest historical interest, for Madame took it from life. She had met Josephine when she was in prison, and the Empress no doubt arranged the sitting. The story that has come down in the Tussaud family is that the cast of Napoleon's face was taken at six-thirty in the morning, and that Madame, before covering his face with plaster, protected his nose and ears and remarked, "I beg you not to be frightened, sire." Napoleon is said to have replied, "Madame, if you surrounded my head with a dozen pistols and every one loaded I should still not be frightened."

She also modelled Wellington from life. It is strange that Wellington, it is said, was a frequent visitor to the tableau of Napoleon lying in state. They say in the Tussaud family that he used to appear early in the day, before the rooms were crowded, and stand silently gazing at the effigy of his opponent. I wonder why. He must have had a liking for the macabre, for he also used to visit the Chamber of Horrors. Once when Madame Tussaud expressed surprise that he should be interested in such things, Wellington is said to have replied, "Why not, Madame; it's life?"

Two more fascinating figures modelled from life by Madame Tussaud are those of Byron and Scott. When she went to Abbotsford to model Scott in 1828 he gave her a suit of his clothes, a corduroy waistcoat and gaiters, and his effigy wears these garments to-day against a sporting background which includes a retriever and a grouse. One of the most interesting of all her portraits is herself. She made this when she was over seventy. We see a little bird-like woman with a large intelligent nose, a thin mouth and two observant eyes behind steel spectacles. She wears a huge Salvation Army type bonnet over a white mob-cap. She was an astonishing little woman, especially in an age when so few women were careerists, and she deserves a full-length biography. Her life covers a remarkable span of history. In youth she handled heads fresh from the guillotine, and in old age she travelled about Victorian England in railway trains!

I was interested in the principle which determines the arrival of a new character in the waxwork show and the disappearance of an old one; for wax celebrities in Baker Street are always being removed to the melting-pot to make way for new arrivals. Public interest is said to be the one and only justification for inclusion in the exhibition. Observers are always on duty watching the crowds, noting the figures which interest them and those which are silently passed by. When a wax figure is consistently neglected by the public he is eliminated, and this ignominious process of being " sent down " from Madame Tussaud's is a constant one! There is a room upstairs stacked with the heads of people who are still alive, well-known characters in public life and on the stage or the screen—I charitably forbear to give any names—in whom the public are said no longer to be interested.

The members of the Royal Family are still, I am told, the most popular figures in the show. Film actors are, strangely enough, slumping in popularity. The life of a star on the screen is short enough, but in Baker Street it is even shorter. Actors and actresses, as waxworks, have been in decline for years, and the public interest has been transferred to radio commentators and other broadcasters. This is understandable. Until television is common these people are merely voices, and people wish to know what their owners look like. Before the days of photography, in the Seventeenth and Eighteenth Centuries, people used to go to waxwork shows impelled by precisely the same curiosity to find out what the great ones of the earth looked like.

Once a week, I was told, the kings and queens, soldiers and sailors, film stars, tennis champions, actors, writers and murderers are undressed and clothed in clean lace and linen. Every wax figure in the exhibition has two sets of underwear! Every figure is valeted in the morning before the doors are opened. Hair is brushed, beards and moustaches are trimmed, boots are cleaned, buttons are polished. Many of the women are shampooed every week and their hair waved and re-set.

I must say that I enjoyed myself enormously at Baker Street. I enjoyed the unsophisticated "ooh's" and "aah's" of horror which occasionally broke from the lips of my fellow-visitors. When one realises the thousands of London sights which have enjoyed popularity in their time, and have vanished leaving nothing behind but maybe a stray reference in a diary or a letter, the vigour of Madame Tussaud's show, a genuine relic of the Eighteenth Century, is profoundly interesting.

§ 3

One of the sights of London which has vanished during the War years is the Friday junk fair in the Caledonian Market. I wish this could be revived. It was a wonderful occasion, which gave much innocent pleasure to thousands of people.

The dream of finding hidden treasure is one that lives in the heart of youth and age. The hope of discovering in some dusty shop a blackened canvas which, after the application of a little linseed oil and methylated spirit, might be revealed as a lost Rembrandt is a dream that inspires the minds of rich and poor. And thousands of people who have never discovered anything in their lives go on searching in the belief that one day something *must* turn up. A goodly proportion of these treasure-hunters used to go to Islington every Friday to prowl among the most comprehensive spreading forth upon the ground of every conceivable thing that has ever been made and owned by Man. In many ways it was a pathetic and shameless parade of all kinds of worn-out and distressed objects.

I used to arrive there early, in time to watch the thousands of pedlars, hucksters, higglers, hawkers, costers and cheap-jacks appear with their treasures and rush eagerly to their pitches. Some would arrive grandly by car; others came more painfully, pushing barrows containing their goods; still more, with their patient wives, arrived on foot, bearing upon their backs mysterious and provoking bundles tied up in sacking and brown paper.

In a remarkably short time the thousands of salesmen had sorted themselves out and the market, its stalls and rails now hidden beneath a dun-coloured covering of humanity, was ready to do business. The stall-holders were ranked in long rows, and those who had not aspired to the dignity of a stall would spread their treasures on the cobble-stones. The procedure of the visitor was to make a slow progress up one row and down another, like a general inspecting the kits of an enormous ragged army.

A feature of the market was its attraction for those who normally patronise shops. Hundreds of hunters of the antique, collectors of silver, jade, pictures, books and furniture descended every week on this market to make a slow and hopeful progress; for the atmosphere of that colossal junk fair was such that hope was perpetually kindled and renewed every Friday.

The Americans were another feature. They were to be encountered at almost every stall. Their voices were everywhere.

" Say, how much for this? "

" Five quid."

" I guess that's too much."

" It's the biggest bargain you ever got in yer life, lady. . . . Well, say four pun' ten? "

After the American woman had drifted away it was good fun to pick up the same silver tea-caddy and ask the price.

" Three quid," would be the reply to an English accent.

Then, later on, it was amusing to assume a husky voice and say:

" Whatcher want fer this? "

" A quid."

" Ten bob."

"A quid, I tell you."

"Give yer twelve and six . . ."

"No—a quid."

"Come on, be a sport, eighteen bob?"

"Right you are—it's a gift."

That was the way it was done. The original price in the Caledonian Market, with a large proportion of the salesmen, was based on the appearance and accent of the customer.

Where, I often wondered, did all this stuff come from? Where in the world was there to be seen a more amazing rubbish-heap? Buried away among it must be something worth having, or surely collectors would not have gone there every week with such regularity. But that was always so difficult to believe.

In the course of ten minutes I would be offered a policeman's helmet, a hunting-flask in a leather case, a glass full of huge alien butterflies, six Indian miniatures, a silver champagne cooler, a ruined vapour bath, a bag full of stage jewels, a Chinese teapot, a pair of dangerous-looking roller skates, an enormous meerschaum pipe and a porcelain bath. Sometimes I used to stand puzzled and amazed before such an assortment of things. By what strange destiny, or lack of it, had these varied and unrelated objects found themselves spread out within a few yards of each other on the flags of the Caledonian Market?

The philosopher, for whom the market must have had an even greater attraction than it had for the connoisseur, was forced gloomily to meditate on the pitiful tragedy of decay, and the humiliation of it. Why, for instance, could the bridal dress, with the dusty spray of orange-blossom still upon it, not have mouldered into dust, and so have saved itself from the contemptuous probing fingers of some dealer in old clothes?

Those who passed up and down before the stalls were rather like beachcombers at work after a gale. And the weird assortment of objects all jumbled together in fantastic disarray reminded one more than anything else of the driftwood washed up by the sea. The tides that washed their debris up every Friday were the tides of Neglect, Decay and Poverty.

Behind the astonishing choice of useless things one seemed to see thousands of death-beds, thousands of homes breaking up, thousands of once-treasured things falling on the scrap-heap, thousands of pointless hideous things being driven from the lumber-room into the cruel light of day.

Some of the objects offered for sale with such crazy hope, or such cynicism, were obviously far too old and useless ever to find a buyer. Who could make anything of the odd bits of iron, the dead internals of long-vanished machines, the fractured cog-wheels, the rusty piston-rods all spread out so carefully to catch the passing eye?

I used to notice with amusement how often a seeker passed on his way looking for nothing, or anything, picking up an old boot here, gazing intently at a pair of debauched dance slippers there, handling a disembowelled clock, flirting a moment with an antique kitchen sink, passing on, ever hopeful, ever watchful, towards disillusioned iron bedsteads until, with a sudden air of discovery, he would slowly remove an ancient black bonnet and reveal the headless torso of a bronze Apollo.

No sight in the market fascinated me more than the thousands of old shoes and boots. There they stood in long, miserable rows stamped with the personalities, and often the bunions, of those who had once worn them. Some looked as though they had limped every yard of the road to ruin, others had drifted jauntily through life, some, like the dusty satin dance-slippers, had known gaiety and laughter, some, like the pair of mosquito boots, had experienced the perils of imperialism. Except a hat, nothing is so clearly branded with personality as a shoe. Why the extremities of the human body should absorb character so plainly I do not know. Gloves, oddly enough, record little or nothing—which is strange, because the human hand is a miraculous thing. Stepping into dead men's shoes is a terrifying phrase. I used to wonder who would have the nerve to buy these old shoes and boots which so obviously belonged to someone else. It was grotesque and positively ghoulish to see a pair change hands, or rather feet.

And no doubt I was just as grotesque and ghoulish myself; indeed, I think few people have been more ghoulish, for once, in the fervour of my youth, I found myself the owner of a mummy. She—for of course she was the usual priestess of Isis—cost me ten shillings.

But at least twenty years must have passed since I walked the cobble-stones of the Caledonian Market, interested more in the remarkable types to be seen there than in the possibility of a Georgian salt-cellar.

The market was known all over the world, especially I think in the United States, for American visitors were among its most ardent seekers. Some months ago I dined in South Africa with a number of English people who are living at the Cape, and the conversation became nostalgic. Some remembered Bond Street on a summer's morning, some Piccadilly, some the City, the river, the parks, the bridges, and, safe in a warm climate, someone even became lyrical about the London winter. To my delight, the woman next to me at the dinner table, an actress once well known upon the musical comedy stage, said that in moments of home-sickness she sometimes recalled among her memories of London the Caledonian Market.

" How I loved it," she said. " It was—well it was just London, wasn't it ? "

She was introduced to the market by a dresser called Rosie.

" One day," she continued, " Rosie, a dear old Cockney, turned up at the theatre wearing an appalling fur coat. If it was fur, it was the fur of some unknown animal. ' Rosie,' I cried in astonishment, ' how grand you look ! Where did you get it ? ' "

" ' Off the stones, miss,' " replied Rosie, revolving slowly before the mirror.

" ' Off the stones, whatever do you mean ? ' "

" ' Come off it, miss, do you really mean to tell me you don't know the Calley ? ' "

What a grand Cockney expression it is—" off the stones."

To anyone who saw the Caledonian Market in its prime it recreates the scene so vividly that you can positively see the seekers slowly passing up one aisle of decay and down another, pausing here, bargaining there, some of them looking for a lost Rembrandt and some of them for Rosie's appalling fur coat.

§ 4

The sight of the British Museum with its escort of pigeons always awakens in my mind the happiest of memories. That vast black treasure-house with its solemn air, as of some gigantic and mysterious temple of antiquity, has occupied so many of my Saturday afternoons and so many luncheon hours in days when I was a young man working in London. I suppose I have hastily eaten sandwiches in every public-house round about Great Russell Street, gulping them down in order to have as much of the time as possible at my disposal in the Egyptian and Greek rooms.

I cannot remember how or when I managed to make friends with Sir Ernest Wallis Budge, the Egyptologist. He was in some ways a terrifying old man, and he had a reputation for rudeness which I could never understand because I met nothing but kindness from him. And this was remarkable, for I must, without knowing it, have tried his patience often when I burst upon him in the little room off the mummy room where he wrote so many of his learned books. Yet he went out of his way to be kind and helpful to me. I remember once, when I had written something or done something which annoyed a woman then influential in London, he wagged a plump finger at me and said solemnly:

" Remember, my boy, that a young man with his way to make in the world can have no more dangerous enemy than a rich woman with a good cook."

He was grey and rotund, with a certain resemblance to Tweedledum or Tweedledee, and although he generally wore a frock coat, and always a silk hat, the coat was rarely brushed, and the hat often resembled an old and mangy black cat. I loved to see him in the morning on his way to tackle some translation from the Coptic or the *Book of the Dead*, standing in the forecourt of the Museum with a bag of peas in his hand while the pigeons swooped round him and often settled on his shoulders. He was also devoted to the museum cat.

Wallis Budge was completely of the Nineteenth Century, and so indeed was the Museum during his reign. There was no attempt at selection: everything was in the window. Of recent years the British Museum has adopted a more critical attitude, and has shown only the best things, placing the second-rate in the basement for the use and instruction of students.

The Museum's war record is a matter for pride. A year before the war thousands of folding crates were made, and all the nation's treasures were classified either as perishable or non-perishable. The moment war came the enormous collection was packed up and sent away, some of it to the country, and a lot of it to the deep tunnels of the Chancery Lane tube, eighty feet below the pavements of London. I saw it there, an uncanny sight, in the early days of the war, in charge of two men who lived, cooked and slept there—probably the two safest individuals in London! I remember one of them, who was cooking something on an electric stove, surrounded by the crated heads of Pharaohs and Cæsars, said to me when I happened to remark how nice and cosy it was down there, " Yes, but it's a long way up if you forget a pinch of salt! "

Sir John Forsdyke, then head of the Museum and organiser of its air-raid defences, gave me the impression that he enjoyed every moment of the Blitz. The Museum's bomb story is, I think, the best and least credible I have ever heard. During one raid a bomb fell through the Edward VII Gallery, made a hole in the floor and failed to explode in the premises beneath. Some time afterwards, during another raid, a second bomb fell through the *same hole*, and also failed to explode! What millionth of a chance came off that night I have no idea, but what a lucky chance it was! The Reading Room was kept open throughout the War, a great achievement.

I thought the post-war museum better than ever when I visited it recently. The things are displayed better than ever before. The Elgin Marbles in their new gallery have never been seen to such advantage, and most of them are at eye level. But the two things that interested me most were the objects from the two romantic discoveries made, both in Suffolk, one during the War and the other the year before the War. Chemists and restorers have been busy with them for years, and they are at last visible to the public. The Mildenhall Treasure is a huge collection of Roman silver which was buried about 400 A.D. by some Roman who hoped to save it from a Saxon raiding party. He hid it so well that he saved it for fifteen centuries for a day when, once again, men in England were burying treasure with the same object! The hoard was turned up in 1942 by two men when they were ploughing a field at West Row, near Mildenhall, Suffolk, on the edge of the Fens. There are silver plates, goblets, spoons, bowls, ladles, and, the loveliest object of all, a silver dish two feet in diameter called the Neptune Bowl. It is richly and exquisitely decorated in raised relief. In the centre is the head of Neptune with matted hair and beard, a face very similar to that of the stone Neptune in the Pump Room Museum at Bath. Round this head in a small circle nereids are riding sea-monsters; in a larger outer circle maenads and satyrs are dancing wildly round Hercules, who, as the catalogue notes, is "plainly drunk". He is supported by two satyrs, and his lion-skin and club have fallen from his hands to the ground. I think this dish is the most beautiful relic of Roman Britain that has come down to us.

The second discovery was made on a sandy heath not far from the sea about ten miles from Ipswich, at a place called Sutton Hoo. The owner of an estate there, Mrs E. M. Pretty, decided to solve the mystery of three great mounds, or tumuli, which stood on her land. One was empty, the second bore traces of a ship and the third contained the Sutton Hoo Ship Burial. When the diggers had opened the mound, they saw printed in the earth the timbers of a huge war galley eighty feet long. All the wood had rotted away, and only the rusted nails were left. In this boat were found all kinds of extraordinary things: gold, jewellery, silver-plate, weapons, bowls, the remains of cauldrons, buckets, bronze dishes, drinking-horns and a purse full of money.

At first some people thought that this was a Viking burial. Sometimes when a Viking chief died he was strapped to his war-boat and pushed out to sea; or he might have been buried in his boat on land. And this discovery looked very like such a burial. The boat had been hauled half a mile overland and pushed on rollers up an escarpment, where it was dug into the soil, the dead man's possessions were placed inside it and the whole boat was covered with earth. The chief's sword was found, blade and scabbard rusted together into a solid mass. Most remarkable of all was the dead man's helmet, made of iron and in parts plated with silver. There were two hinged ear-flaps to it and a hinged portion to protect the nape of the neck. A hinged visor covered the face from the bridge of the nose to the chin, with three openings in it, for the eyes and the mouth. The nose and mouth of this visor are moulded in gilded bronze, and above the mouth is a neatly clipped, extremely modern-looking moustache.

But where was the man for whose comfort in Eternity all these preparations had been made? Not a trace of him could be found. Perhaps he had been cremated nearby, perhaps he had been buried elsewhere and is yet to be discovered. The archæologists say that the burial may be that of the East Anglian King, Aethelhere, who was buried about 655 A.D.

While the Roman silver from Mildenhall is much the more beautiful, the ship burial is more romantic, more provoking and more unusual; indeed, nothing like it has ever been found in England before.

§ 5

I was having lunch in my club one day with a friend who is a distinguished surgeon. He mentioned that he was operating that afternoon in a London hospital, and upon the spur of the moment I asked if I could go with him and watch him?

We were soon on the way. He entered the hospital like royalty. Everyone bowed down before him. Watching him closely, I was aware that he was putting on an act. He was being the great and famous surgeon. He was deliberately radiating confidence. It was expected of him, and it was the atmosphere in which he worked. The younger doctors were gratified when he spoke to them; the nurses, with whom he cracked a few diminutive flirtatious jests, clearly adored him.

We were dressed in white overalls, white caps were placed upon our heads, and a white pad across our mouths. We entered the operating-theatre, which was large, domed and white, like something out of a futuristic play. The surgeon glanced at some X-ray films, said, " Ha; that's it, is it? " and walked over to a nurse, who almost curtsied as she held out a pair of rubber gloves, into which the great man placed his hands.

I was conscious of drama. The overture had been played. The curtain was just going up. I forgot about London and the throb of life all round us in the streets below: all the drama of the world seemed concentrated within the white walls of this theatre.

The door opened. A noiseless stretcher glided into the room; and I saw him for the first time. He was a poor little elderly Londoner, who looked, as he lay in the sleep of anæsthesia, as though Fate had been kicking him about the world, waiting for him to get up and then kicking him flat again. How that poor little man had suffered. It seemed impossible that he was ever well and healthy, that he had ever sat in some suburb surrounded by a family and had carved a Sunday joint; that he had ever loved a woman or kissed a child. He looked like some thin alabaster Christ taken down from the cross.

The bright overhead lights poured on his pitiful chest. A group of white figures surrounded him. My friend walked up, his eyes above the gauze confident, cold, almost casual. His hands, red-brown in thin rubber, appeared filled with an uncanny vitality. A woman's hand in rubber gave him a little shining knife.

My desire to look away was so great that I would not permit myself to do so. He took the knife and, with a gesture as strong, as sure and as beautiful as that of a great violinist moving his bow, began the operation.

Of all the things that happen in London every day, this is surely the most awe-inspiring and the most wonderful. Here was a life poised on the point of a knife; a few moments in which everything is to be yes or no; a white room at whose windows the wings of Death are beating. I was astonished, as I watched, to realise that this was not horrible as Rembrandt's *Anatomist* is horrible.

There was no sound but the tinkle of metal against glass

and a hiss of steam from another room. Yes, there was another sound. The surgeon was talking to himself. I knew from the tenseness of his assistants, from the way they watched his hands, that this muttering was a sign that he was dealing with life or death. And it was a tremendously encouraging sound, because it was full of affirmatives.

"Yes . . ." I heard him mutter, "that's all right. . . . Yes, now here we are. . . . Yes, yes. . . . Good . . . yes."

Nothing surprised him. The poor little body had not puzzled him. He was like a man who had opened a deed-box to find everything as he had expected it. And now his hands were most interesting. They had altered. No longer were they the hands which held the X-ray film and put on the white cap. They had a life of their own. They were not ordinary hands. They were more like mechanical hands. They never moved an unnecessary inch. If they wanted something they just opened for a second and a woman's hand offered a little shining thing. The hands grasped it and continued. When they had finished with the little shining thing they dropped it because it was the quickest way to get rid of it, and waited open for something else to be placed in them.

The theatre sister who fed the surgeon's hands was almost as interesting as the surgeon himself. She knew every stage of the operation and anticipated every move and every need. She never made a mistake as she stood picking one by one the little gleaming instruments from a glass-topped table.

"You can come near," said the surgeon to me.

I summoned up enough courage to approach.

"That was killing this man," he said, and I looked at the little breathing body and saw a thing taken from it no larger than a few hay seeds.

The surgeon stood back. A nurse took glass tubes, wrapped them in linen, cracked them, dipped sterilised gut in disinfectant and handed them to the surgeon. Length after length went into the eager hands. And it was over.

The surgeon retired to the ante-room. He removed his cap and mouth-pad.

"Have you saved his life?"

"Yes, I think so."

And the hands that had played with life and death above the roofs of London fished clumsily in a waistcoat pocket for a cigarette-case. They were now ordinary hands doing ordinary things. He picked out a cigarette and snapped a cigarette lighter. It refused to work! Those marvellous hands could do nothing with it. I gave him a match.

"Thanks," he said.

A young doctor came in with a blue paper. It was the next fight.

§ 6

Charles Dickens has done more than any writer to create and perpetuate a picture of early Victorian London with its fogs, its filth and squalor, its narrow alleys, its lamplit courtyards, its prosperous, self-satisfied inhabitants and its poverty-stricken masses. Admirers of the novelist, who come from all parts of the world, go to 48 Doughty Street as Johnsonians go to Gough Square.

This neat, prim little house in Bloomsbury was the first real home possessed by Dickens. He signed a three-year lease when he was twenty-five and moved in with his wife, a few weeks old infant, his wife's sister, Mary, aged seventeen, to whom he was devoted, and his younger brother, Fred. The books written in Doughty Street include the *Pickwick Papers*, *Oliver Twist*, *Nicholas Nickleby* and a part of *Barnaby Rudge*.

When the Dickens family had been in occupation seven or eight weeks an event occurred which affected Dickens, in moments of depression, all his life. He had taken his wife and her sister to the theatre. They returned brimming over with high spirits and went up to bed. Hearing a cry from Mary's room, Dickens entered and found the girl fighting for breath. She died in his arms. Dickens was shattered by his sorrow. He took a ring from Mary's hand and wore it on his little finger for the rest of his life.

He could not write a word for months and was obliged to interrupt the publication of both *Pickwick* and *Oliver Twist*, which were appearing serially. Instead of the usual instalment which his readers were eagerly expecting, they saw an announcement that " since the appearance of the last number of this work the editor has to mourn the sudden death of a very dear young relative to whom he was most affectionately attached and whose society has been for a long time the chief solace of his labours."

But grief for the death of Mary alternated, when he got down to work again, with delight at the success of *Pickwick*, so that " one stands back astonished at both the depth and the elasticity of the temperament displayed," writes Dame Una Pope-Hennessy in *Charles Dickens*. " The same man," she continues, " who could sit immobile in his study in front of Mary's picture mourning as if he could not be comforted, would in a few hours preside over a book-banquet or dance delightedly at a party. . . . His temperament cannot be accounted for; it is only possible to state how it operated."

The caretaker of the Dickens House told me that before the property was bought by the Dickens Fellowship in 1924 it was a boarding house and there seemed every likelihood that it might have been altered out of all recognition or pulled down. Now it has been preserved and is more or less as Dickens knew it in 1837. The rooms are full of manuscripts, letters, autographs, pictures, busts of Dickens and the usual odds and ends of an author's life.

The room where the work was done is the little back room on the first floor. In cases elsewhere are the first editions of every book written by Dickens. The basement has been transformed into a replica of Dingley Dell kitchen where Mr Pickwick played games at Christmas-time with the servants. Extraordinary to see such a solid manifestation of something that was merely an idea in the room above.

Dickensians come from all parts of the world, I was told, to walk about this house, to read letters written by Dickens, to look into his mirror, to see his chair, his walking stick, his toddy glass and to stand in the little room where several of the novels were written.

Dickens moved from Doughty Street to a much grander house, 1 Devonshire Terrace, Marylebone Road, which seems to be much the same as it was in his time, although I have only looked at it over the garden wall. A blue L.C.C. memorial tablet has been placed on this building, and the prowling Dickensian may care to know that in this house the novelist concluded *Barnaby Rudge*, and wrote *Martin Chuzzlewit*, *A Christmas Carol*, the *Cricket on the Hearth*, and most of *David Copperfield*.

§ 7

There is no sound in the early morning but the shrill chirping of the sparrows in the London square. The sun is up and, although this is the best time of the day, a hush lies upon London. The first omnibuses are slowly bowling along the empty streets past the closed shops in the early sunlight.

There is a grinding of wheels in the square and the sound of milk-bottles being dumped hastily on York stone. The milkman's pony is probably standing with its forefeet on the pavement, ready to straighten up and move on as his master proceeds down the square. There is sure to be a cat in the garden watching the sparrows, and several more crossing the road; for London cats believe that the whole metropolitan area belongs to them from midnight until seven in the morning.

There is an air of washed clean innocence about London in the early morning. It seems that all human vanity, frailty and malice have been forgotten in the night. Every London dawn looks like New Year's Day, and the bright matins of the sparrows, sounding from every tree, roof-top and eave, is a hopeful, cheerful chorus that lifts up the heart, bringing courage, humour and faith, the three most important gifts which any fairy godmother can take to any cradle.

CHAPTER TWELVE

A few words about the treasure houses of South Kensington, a visit to the Royal Naval College at Greenwich and the Maritime Museum. I go to Hampton Court Palace to walk through its galleries and to sit in its gardens. I go to Broadcasting House, and say good-night to London on Westminster Bridge as Big Ben strikes twelve.

§ 1

BOOKS could be, and have been, written about Soho, Bloomsbury and South Kensington.

Soho is largely decayed Georgian. The Huguenots settled there long ago and foreigners have been attracted to the place ever since. King Theodore of Corsica lived there in the Eighteenth Century, Karl Marx in the Nineteenth. To-day the restaurants and the film trade dominate Soho, and the crowds that fill the streets are alien crowds as different from a typical London crowd as the exotic grocers' shops of Soho, with their flasks of Chianti, their parmesan cheese, their tunny fish and cloves of garlic, differ from the shops of the ordinary English grocer.

Soho is pervaded by a melancholy air of exile. When Jacques, who was in the Maquis, and his Italian wife, whose brother was an anti-Fascist, have made enough money they will sell their little restaurant and go to live in France. When Nicholas, the Cypriot, has served long enough and his already shiny evening suit no longer possesses even a fifth-hand value, he will pack his bags and go home to Larnaca. And so it is all over Soho. Men and women are working there and dreaming of somewhere else. There are Greek exiles, Turkish exiles, even Chinese exiles, and the recent war has still further increased the nationalities to be found there.

The streets of Soho are filled with a kind of damped down vitality. Maybe people are a trifle swarthier there than elsewhere, they gesticulate more, they form groups on the pavement and argue, they buy old and incredible newspapers written in many languages. Just as stray whiffs of foreign cooking drift out from the basements and the ventilators of Soho, so a gesticulating group in the street will bring a whiff of the Piazza del Popolo, in Rome, Constitution Square, Athens, or the Puerta del Sol, in Madrid, and a chance phrase spoken under a London lamp-post will recall for a moment a glimpse of Vienna or Warsaw.

Yet several centuries of foreign occupation have failed to make Soho look Continental. It is just a rather shabby old part of Georgian London. The lower storeys of the buildings may have been modernised and may display saxophones and cinema projectors, or they may have been fitted with plate glass doors which open to chromium-plated cocktail bars, but the upper storeys are still the dingy red-brick houses which stood there in the days of Boswell and Johnson.

Bloomsbury, like Soho, is mostly Georgian in period. It is dominated by the British Museum and London University on one boundary, and by the restless world of the terminal railway stations on another. It is a district that has adapted itself to modern times with many a lingering backward glance to the days of its grandeur, days when the fine squares and the great houses were occupied by rich merchants and by distinguished members of the professions.

The great squares of Bloomsbury are still the glory of this district, although there is hardly a house that has not been split up into offices and flats or converted into a boarding house. Whenever I think of Bloomsbury I see the pigeons wheeling in the forecourt of the British Museum, I hear the chirping of sparrows in the trees, I see iron railings curving round a square, enclosing a few tall plane trees. A group of foreign students with books beneath their arms saunter from a boarding house, which is three or four houses made into one, and the archaeologist and the orientalist pass slowly from shop to shop in Great Russell Street where the booksellers know almost all that is to be known about the East and its literature. In moments when the triumphs of research have seemed more attractive than the toil of writing, I have felt that a flat in Bloomsbury within sight of the British Museum might possibly be the height of felicity.

The great ones of Bloomsbury are almost too numerous to mention. Gray, Shelley, Cowper, Coleridge, William Morris, Swinburne, and Christina Rossetti were among its poets, Dickens, Thackeray, Macaulay, Hazlitt, Lamb, Isaac d'Israeli and Darwin among its writers, Constable, Burne-Jones and Millais among its painters. More recent residents have linked the name of Bloomsbury with intellect and communism. The "Bloomsbury intellectual" and the "Bloomsbury Bolshie" suggest to the modern Londoner, no matter how unjustly, a talkative young pipe-smoker with a beard and a coloured shirt who flourished between the wars.

The parents of South Kensington were the Prince Consort and the Great Exhibition of 1851. This district is the gift of Albert the Good to the, on the whole, ungrateful nation over whose intellectual shortcomings he earnestly presided. His name is commemorated by the Albert Memorial, the Albert Hall and the Victoria and Albert Museum. Kensington is as rich as Bloomsbury in boarding houses and hotels. If Bloomsbury may be said to specialise in foreign students, Kensington might be said to specialise in old ladies. But it is difficult to generalise on such matters.

When the Great Exhibition in Hyde Park was over and it had been decided to move the Crystal Palace to Sydenham, a certain number of objects were considered to be worth preservation, and these formed the nucleus of the enormous treasure house later to develop into the "Victoria and Albert." At first its object was purely to instruct and to show how art might be applied to industry, and this intention is still indicated by the classification of objects under such headings as "Woodwork", "Metal work" and "Ceramics". The Victorian founders of the exhibition knew that the age of machines needed the inspiration of the age of craftsmanship. As museum space is always scarce, and there was quite a lot of it in South Kensington, the "Victoria and Albert" has become filled with treasures, many of which now obscure its utilitarian intentions.

It is difficult to describe this museum, which is still reorganising itself after the War. All one can say is that a more wonderful collection of beautiful things does not exist elsewhere in the world. There is hardly a lovely object made by the hands of man which is not represented in the collection: furniture, tapestries, carpets, lacquer work, sculpture, ivories, glass, clocks and watches, gold and silver work, iron and brass work, lace and fabrics, paintings, silhouettes and miniatures.

There are rooms removed from old houses and furnished with period furniture, there is a gallery which illustrates the story of male and female costume for three centuries. To know the whole collection is hardly possible, to visit it and fail to learn something is impossible.

Many a strenuous day may be spent by the visitor to South Kensington in tramping the galleries of the " Victoria and Albert ". And if he has any energy left he may walk across Exhibition Road to penetrate still further into this world of museums. He can step from the " Victoria and Albert " into the Natural History Museum where he will see many of the strange creatures which share the earth with us. This Gothic building gives the visitor who is sensitive to his surroundings the impression that the Zoo has escaped from Regent's Park and has taken refuge in a cathedral.

The Science Museum, which is nearby, stresses the importance of science, just as the " Victoria and Albert " stresses the importance of art to industry. Here you can see *Puffing Billy*, the *Rocket*, and other early locomotives. Hanging suspended from the roof, you will find the biplane which Colonel Cody flew in 1912, and the Vickers-Vimy machine in which Alcock and Brown made the first direct Transatlantic crossing in 1919. An eloquent commentary upon Man's conquest of the air is the V.1, or " doodle-bug ", seen in section.

The Children's Gallery in the basement is perhaps the most popular part of the museum. Here is to be seen an artificial rainbow and a door that is mysteriously opened by an invisible ray. I expect modern children, to whom the possibilities of the atomic age are the topic of everyday conversation, are perhaps less thrilled by these wonders than a former generation.

Should the visitor still be able to walk after seeing these

museums, there is still the Museum of Practical Geology, which is a good deal more interesting than it sounds. The hall is enlivened by a revolving replica of the earth with all the geological formations indicated in coloured relief. Even more spectacular is a model of Vesuvius which breaks into eruption with the utmost regularity.

The geological specimens known as precious stones, upon which Man, because of Woman, has placed so high and fictitious a value, have a place all to themselves in the centre of the hall. Here replicas of the most notorious diamonds in the world may be seen, as well as every kind of jewel.

Probably no part of London can compete with South Kensington in the wide variety of interest which it offers to vastly different mentalities. There is something there for everybody. The enormous buildings, which look so forbidding from the outside, are crammed with beauty and with interest. It would be good to believe that the Exhibition of 1951 would leave to posterity one fraction of the legacy which has in the course of time assembled itself round the relics of the Great Exhibition of 1851.

§ 2

I was standing in a queue at Westminster waiting for a boat to Greenwich. There were all sorts of people in the queue, mostly, I think, from the Provinces, but in these days, when everyone looks alike, it is difficult to say. I found myself next to a neat grey-haired little man who was fanning himself with a panama hat.

The Houses of Parliament rose above us, hot and yellow; Big Ben boomed the hour, and the tram-cars swept past, sucking the warm air after them.

" My word, sir, it's a real scorcher, don'tcher think? ", said the little man.

He wore a grey alpaca coat and a pair of dark trousers. His good manners were perfectly assumed, and his accent, with just a trace of Edwardian " howdedo " about it, had been carefully acquired, but in what trade or profession I could not imagine. We stood together, moving up a yard at a time as the queues, like animals waiting for the ark, dispersed, some for the Richmond, Kew and Hampton Court boats and some for the down-river boats to Greenwich.

The tide was high. Tugs with a following of barges were speeding up-stream, causing a wash in which the pleasure-boats rocked and danced, to the amusement of the passengers.

" I love my London, sir," said the little man, " and I flatter myself I know it well."

" You've lived here a long time? "

" All my life, sir. And how old would you say I am? "

He looked about seventy-five, but, to please him and make him feel happy, I said sixty.

" Ah, you're far out, sir," he said, highly gratified. " I'm seventy-three."

A large blowsy woman ahead of us turned and said in a peevish voice:

" You're nothink of the kind, Alfred. Don't put it on so. You'll be seventy-one next birthday, and not a day older."

The little man was confused by this rebuke, for he could see that he had made an impression on me, and he was now wondering what I was thinking of his companion, obviously his wife, whose manner and voice had let him down socially. As a matter of fact, I was wondering if he had been a valet, if that rather precise, precious manner of his were a reflection of some distant master; that spinsterish neatness would fit quite well some old Edwardian swell living alone in St James's Street. His wife, immense and formidable as she now was, had been no doubt a pretty buxom parlourmaid forty years ago. I had quite settled this in my mind when we descended the ramp to the floating pier and embarked on the boat.

We were too late to sit under the awning, and so settled ourselves amidships, with our backs to the river. A man in a yachting cap lit a cigarette, started the engine, took the wheel and we were off. Some of the women took out their knitting, a few ardent photographers got busy, and a young man with a microphone began to instruct us.

" Now, ladies and gentlemen," he said, " on our right is County Hall and the Exhibition Buildings, and we are approaching Hungerford Railway Bridge, with Charing Cross Station on our left. . . ."

We looked about at these well-known scenes, which somehow appeared brighter and more exciting from the river.

" On our left," continued the Voice, " is Cleopatra's Needle, and we are now approaching new Waterloo Bridge. . . ."

What a lovely flight of white arches it is, spanning the river so effortlessly. We passed into its shadow, experienced a second of comparative coolness and emerged into the sunlight.

" On our left is Somerset House, and the ship moored opposite is Captain Scott's *Discovery*. . . . On our left also is Shell Mex House, and next to it the Savoy Hotel. . . . Those trees and lawns are the famous Temple. Ahead of us, ladies and gentlemen, is Blackfriars Bridge."

The little man sitting beside me dropped his voice to a whisper and said to his wife, " 'Ere, Emma, move up a bit, will yer? I'm perishin' well crushed to death." His lapse into the vernacular after his conversation with me was surprising. I supposed that was his natural accent. What could he be? I put out various feelers, but he responded to none of them.

The splendid roof-line of the city, with the dome of St Paul's, escorted by all the City spires and steeples, took up my attention. London that morning looked strangely like a Canaletto with a blue sky above, the river, the boats and the bridges. We passed under London Bridge, we saw Billingsgate Market on our left, then we came to the Tower of London, standing grey and silver-grey behind the wharf with its row of cannon. And ahead was Tower Bridge, a line of traffic running across it like mechanical toys.

" Do you know the City? " I asked the little man, thinking that possibly he was a retired clerk.

" Oh, no, sir, not at all. But I know the West End."

Perhaps he had been a waiter. But why should I worry myself about him on this hot day? I asked myself. The reason was, of course, that I felt instinctively that he was interesting.

We passed down into the Lower Pool with its maze of docks, its grim-looking wharves and warehouses. We passed Wapping, we turned the acute bend into Limehouse Reach and—then the microphone went wrong! The little man sprang into action. He blew into it. He tested the wires.

He took a screw-driver from the pocket of his alpaca coat, he did something and, behold, the thing worked again!

"That was clever of you," I said. "You are evidently a wireless expert?"

"Oh no, sir, not an expert by any means," he replied. "But I understand electricity."

"Is it your business?" I asked.

"It was, sir, it was. Nearly sixty years ago, sir, I was apprenticed to a Bond Street electrician. In those days electricity was a dangerous novelty. The firm was a fashionable one, and it served the aristocracy; yes, sir, it served the highest in the land. It was a great thing to be employed by this firm. All the employees when they were sent out to mend a fuse, or to see a duchess about switching over from gas to electricity, had to wear frock coats and bowler hats. And we always had to wear gloves. Funny, isn't it, sir, to think of those days now, when an electrician will go into any house in Park Lane wearing blue overalls! But when I was a young man we were inspected by the head of the firm before we went out on a job. And we were never allowed to carry a tool-kit. They were carried by small boys. And we always had to go out in a four-wheeler."

"An electrician's life must have been a very gentlemanly one in those days."

"Ah yes, sir, that was the policy of the firm. As I say, sir, electricity was a novelty, and the aristocracy were very proud of their wonderful new electric light. But, looking back on it, how very primitive it was! I have often been ordered to sit until two in the morning beside the switch-board when a dance was being given in the West End, in case the lights fused. And one had to be properly dressed for that, too."

I was delighted with the little man. I had been right about him. He was interesting. His manner, his voice, his spurious gentility were all a reflection of the dead-and-gone Edwardian era, when even Bond Street electricians had to dress up and wear gloves when they served the aristocracy.

"And there was another rule of the firm," said the little man. "If you went into a lady's bedroom and saw jewels lying about—and by God, sir, you did see some sparklers in those days, for you know what the aristocracy were like coming home three sheets to the wind and flinging everything all over the place; well, it was a rule of the firm that you had to call the butler and ask him to see that the jewels were locked up. It wasn't that the firm distrusted its employees. Oh no, sir. As the head of the firm used to say to us, ' It isn't *you* we mistrust, but suppose her ladyship lost her pearls one night, she might blame it on the electrician! ' "

And as we chugged down the Thames on that hot summer day the little man in the alpaca coat managed to build up for me a life-like picture of a dead world: " toffs " in silk hats handing out tips of golden sovereigns to young electricians, great ladies in low decolletage moving towards dressing-tables in a haze of champagne, butlers guiding the young man from Bond Street round the house, and the young man from Bond Street carefully drawing on a pair of silk gloves (provided by the firm) so that the delicate paint-work should not be damaged.

" It was a very different London, sir," said the little man.

" Do you think it was a happier London? " I asked.

" Oh, undoubtedly, sir," he replied. " People were not spiteful in those days. And, say what you like, the aristocracy were the cream of the earth, sir. And in those days, sir, a sovereign went as far as ten pounds go to-day. But to-day, sir, *nobody* is happy."

And with these depressing words we arrived at Greenwich.

§ 3

I had not been to Greenwich since the War, and the first thing I noticed when I stepped ashore was that the *Ship* Hotel has been bombed. I suppose I have sat at those windows, eating whitebait and watching the Thames, not more than three times in my life, yet so happy were those occasions that I saw with a feeling of personal bereavement the old place split asunder and open to the sky.

Whitebait cooked by all hotels and restaurants known to me are brown, but the ancient recipe used by the *Ship* turned them white. I remembered that the waitress—I even remember she was a North-Country girl—told me the last time I was there it had taken the chef two years to learn how to cook whitebait, but she said the very sight of them made her feel sick. How people could eat them, heads, tails, eyes and all, she couldn't think!

I have always liked Greenwich. It has quality and atmosphere. The Royal Naval College is the most impressive building on the Thames, with the exception of Hampton Court. And there is nothing between London Bridge and Westminster to approach it. The town, the park and Blackheath all breathe the spirit of the Eighteenth Century, and even the mass of ugliness—the gasometers, the tall chimneys, and the squalid riverside settlements which creep up close to Greenwich on all sides, and on both banks of the river—have not yet robbed it of its last lingering beauties.

Books on London written about eighty years ago describe the naval pensioners who used to haunt the slopes of Greenwich Park and sit watching the passing ships through brass telescopes. Those old men, many of them veterans of Trafalgar, lived in what is now the Royal Naval College and was then Greenwich Hospital, the naval counterpart of Chelsea Hospital.

The Greenwich pensioners seem to have borne a strong family resemblance to the Chelsea pensioners except that, as old drawings and engravings prove, they were much more knocked about in the wars. Artists of the time nearly always drew them with a black patch over one eye, or showed them with a peg leg like John Silver, or an iron hand like Captain Hook.

In one of its paternal moments, the Admiralty gave these old men the choice of out-pensions, and naturally most of them, having been cooped up all their lives in wooden ships, decided that they would rather end their days in individual retirement than in an institution which, after all, was more or less like a ship. So Greenwich Hospital ceased to house pensioners about 1873, and became the Royal Naval College.

As I walked up from the landing-stage I thought that the atmosphere of the old sea-dogs still clings to Greenwich. That is probably because the background has not greatly altered. The Thames looks much the same as it did then, the splendid—but that is too tame a word—the noble and unforgettable buildings, now the Naval College, are the same, and so are the green slopes of Greenwich Park where the old men used to sit with their spy-glasses. It would not be strange, I thought, to meet John Silver stumping along the roads of Greenwich with his peg leg.

And, sure enough, no sooner had I turned into the main street than I saw a peg leg! Those primitive false limbs are rapidly vanishing, in fact I cannot remember when I last saw one. This wooden leg was worn by no old sea-dog, but by a young boy of about fourteen years of age. The poor little fellow limped along, laughing gallantly at his efforts, which were like those of a bird with a broken wing. A young man who was with him picked him up and carried him, but the boy protested, and used his wooden leg as a weapon to force his friend to put him down again. So he went tapping along the streets of Greenwich, making a sound which must have reminded those grey stones of the heroes of Trafalgar.

I walked up to Greenwich Park, which is one of the most beautiful of the Royal parks. It is on a sloping hill which affords a stupendous view of London and the Thames. From the terrace by the Wolfe Memorial I saw London lying to the west, the dome of St Paul's standing up immediately above Tower Bridge. And the foreground is that historic curve of the Thames known as Greenwich Reach, where the ships pass, some on their way to the Pool, others outward bound for foreign parts. This is a view of London which wayfarers saw century after century as they approached the capital along the Dover Road, and I do not know a finer one.

There are some splendid avenues of chestnut-trees in the park, many of them, I believe, planted at the command of James I; and there are probably no older trees anywhere in London. A curious relic is "Queen Elizabeth's Oak", now just a hollow cavern covered with ivy, but it lived, so an inscription informs us, until 1875. I entered an unexpectedly lovely garden where some enormous cedar-trees were growing, an extraordinary sight amid this typically English parkland. An old gardener told me that before the War hundreds of

Japanese visitors used to go to Greenwich just to see the cedars.

" Some of them," he said, " used to bow down and make the sign they make in their temples as soon as they set foot in the garden. It was strange to see them in ordinary clothes bowing and scraping in front of the trees."

More exotic to my eye than any grove of cedars is the Royal Observatory on the top of the hill. The onion-shaped domes, that sometimes in the old days could be seen slowly parting and opening like ripe fruit cracking in the sun, used to conceal powerful telescopes by whose aid, so one always imagined, that mysterious official, the Astronomer Royal, surveyed the terrifying wastes of space. But the Royal Observatory and the astronomers have now moved to Hurstmonceux, Sussex.

But of course they have not been able to take the zero meridian of longitude with them! This is well worth looking at and, for a line of such importance, I must say it is singularly unassuming. It is just a line, drawn across a path from some point inside the Observatory, which disappears furtively into a shrubbery. Greenwich Mean Time is slightly more impressive. There is a time-ball on the east turret. The instant Greenwich says it is 1 p.m. the ball drops from the mast in a definite manner which forbids all argument. It is a pity, I think, that the astronomers have had to desert Greenwich after all these years (and after putting Greenwich so literally on the map), but no doubt they will preserve the strange little building in which they have studied the Universe since the time of Charles II.

§ 4

The present superb Greenwich Palace began its career as a hospital for old sailors, and it is now the Royal Naval College. Steen Rasmussen, the Danish architect who wrote one of the best books on London written by a foreigner, thought that, considered as a hospital, it was " absolutely fantastic ". And of course it is. No King of England has ever inhabited a palace half so splendid. One can imagine the amazement of foreigners in the old days as they came up the Thames to be told that Greenwich Hospital was not a royal palace, but a refuge for worn-out mariners.

Yet, fantastic though it may be, what a wonderful gesture of affection and gratitude it is on the part of a nation whose power was born at sea. I do not think if you searched England from Land's End to the Border you could discover a more beautiful tribute to the love and esteem in which seamen have always been held in this country. That it was designed and built and handed over to the old men centuries before Democracy was believed to be the fount whence all generous actions flow is at least a provoking thought.

The group of buildings are in two sections, separated by a highroad. The group on the water-side is the Naval College, a mass of Italianate grandeur which shows Wren at his best, and behind, and on higher ground, is the exquisite Queen's House, built for Anne of Denmark by Inigo Jones. Wren, who was not allowed to pull it down, built the Naval College in front of it, but in such a way that from the river the Queen's House is seen at the back, and the later buildings form a kind of immense frame for it.

Only the chapel and the Painted Hall in the College are open to the public, but on the high ground at the back is a building with the Queen's House in the centre which contains one of the most interesting and also one of the best displayed museums in the country. It is the National Maritime Museum, which was founded by Act of Parliament before the last War to illustrate the story of the Royal Navy, the Merchant Navy and the Fishing Fleet.

I walked through halls, each one devoted to some aspect of seafaring life in ancient or modern times. Mounting a staircase, I heard the time sounded on a ship's bell as if we were at sea, and upon the landing I saw a custodian striking a bell which he told me was the old bell of H.M.S. *Vanguard*. The staircase, made of teak from old battleships, led to a magnificent picture-gallery where admirals in velvet suits, vast periwigs framing their faces, gazed from marine landscapes where men-o'-war rode the waves in the background.

When George V opened the Museum he presented to it the

Journal of Captain Cook's second voyage, written in the navigator's handwriting. I noticed a fine portrait of Cook by Nathaniel Dance and a vivid picture by Zoffany of Cook's tragic death. He was clubbed to death by angry natives at Hawaii in 1779.

Of course the presiding deity of the Museum is Nelson. How does one explain the magic of Nelson in days when all that the average person knows about him is "England expects", that he was in love with Emma Hamilton and that he died in the moment of victory? Yet the Nelson touch is still potent. Round every case which contained a Nelson relic, I saw twenty people for every one in other parts of the Museum. They gazed at his pictures—and how often Nelson, in spite of his long absences, found time to have his portrait painted—and they examined with hushed interest every object which might have been hallowed by his use. The most sought-for of all the relics is, of course, the undress uniform coat which Nelson was wearing at Trafalgar when he was picked off by a sniper concealed in the mizzen top of the French ship *Redoubtable*. The bullet-hole high up on the left shoulder is plain to see. And the coat refutes an absurd story that Nelson was so vain that, before he came on deck, he put on all his orders so that, blazing with stars, he was an inevitable mark for the enemy. This coat and two others belonging to Nelson in the same case have replicas of his four orders not pinned but permanently sewn to them; for that was the custom at the time. So it was not vanity that attracted the fatal musket-ball, but fashion.

While there is not a single room in this museum which does not contain something of note, I was particularly interested in Neptune's Hall, where the best of all models, those of ships, can be seen by the hundred. There are old galleons, ships of the line, frigates, brigs and so on down to the sleek modern battleship and the graceful liner, and looking upon this great fleet from the walls are experienced figureheads salted by the seven seas. The most provoking contrast are two large-scale models, one of the Battle of Trafalgar and the other of the Atlantic Battle of the last War. In the first, warships are seen within grappling distance of one another, they are firing broadsides from a few yards distance, and men can jump from deck to deck, but in the second there is a colossal expanse of ocean where ships which cannot see each other are yet within gunshot range.

The Queen's House, which is linked to the Museum by two classical colonnades, might be called the most interesting and significant house in England. It was built for Anne of Denmark, the wife of James I, and had she lived it might have been ready for occupation about 1620. It was the first "modern" house erected in England. Inigo Jones, the architect who startled London with his Italian piazza in Covent Garden, built it in the Italian style which became the pattern for all the great houses of England in succeeding ages.

The crowds who wander through it to-day see nothing revolutionary about it. It is just another of those marble halls with tall windows and doorways designed for giants; indeed, it is necessary to have a feeling for buildings and for beautiful rooms (above all, it is perhaps necessary to have lived in a rambling Tudor house) to notice how noble and yet how simple it is. It was the first fine house in England designed not for a pack of mediæval retainers, but for a family. The great hall, which had been the general living room in England for as long as men could remember, was now merely a vestibule with the other rooms leading from it. An age in which the great glazed and gabled piles of Burghley, Hatfield, Knole, Hardwick and Audley End were still new must have seen the Queen's House with astonishment. It had stepped out of Italy into Greenwich Park. The thousands of people in England now who can roam through so many great houses whose owners can no longer afford to live in them should make a point of going to Greenwich, if only to see the house which inaugurated the fashion in building that led to such exercises in stone as Blenheim, Wentworth Woodhouse and Seaton Delaval, to mention only three of the more gigantic constructions built in the style which has influenced the appearance of every nook and corner of the land. The new buildings which Inigo Jones planted at Greenwich and in Whitehall were the first signs of a change in taste which in time led, not only to the stately classic palaces, but to the exquisite red-brick vicarages and mansions, to the sensible squares and terraces of London, down to the last little Regency artisan's dwelling that had any pretensions to style.

Two Stuart queens lived in this house: Henrietta Maria, queen of Charles I, and Mary of Modena, queen of James II. When Mary, wife of Dutch William, ascended the throne she could not bring herself to live in a place which was so full of youthful memories of the father whose throne she had been obliged reluctantly to occupy. The strength of her feeling for the house can be judged not only by her refusal to live in it, but also by the fight she put up for its survival. But for this it would have been pulled down when Greenwich Palace was rebuilt. She it was who suggested that the new Palace should be built in two sections, with a space through which the old house could look down towards the river and the ships.

It was Mary also who turned the new Greenwich Palace into a naval hospital. For a long time she had wished to found for seamen a haven similar to that of Chelsea Hospital. Having expressed these admirable wishes, she died suddenly of smallpox, aged thirty-two, and her broken-hearted William saw that her desires were fulfilled.

§ 5

I walked down the hill towards the Royal Naval College. The tide had turned. The motor-boats were still arriving with their crowds of day-trippers and, remembering what I had seen and what remained to be seen, I thought that a trip to Greenwich is probably the best value London can offer on a hot summer's day.

It was said as recently as a century and a half ago, when Greenwich was still countrified, that it was one of the most lovely sights round London; but no one, alas, could put in such a claim for it to-day. Gasworks, grain elevators and tall chimneys deform the banks of the river, and the Thames is grey and oily. Upon a little patch of mud and shingle I saw with mingled alarm and admiration two little boys in bathing-dresses step slowly into this filthy water, while their mother sat near and actually watched them do it.

When I entered the gates of the Royal Naval College I saw that Greenwich is now as full of young marine technicians (for it seems absurd to apply the word sailors to those who go down to the sea in electrical power-stations) as it was once full of old seamen broken in the French wars. I read in the excellent guide sold at the College that at one time, out of two thousand-odd Greenwich pensioners, ninety-six were over eighty, sixteen over ninety and one claimed to be a hundred and two! The ages of a group of a hundred of these old toughs amounted to eight thousand two hundred and fifty-two years!

The old men lived chiefly on broth, with pease pudding on fast days. Meat was generally beyond their powers, and upon those occasions when it was issued they called it bull's meat, and were furious. They were given a shilling a week for tobacco, and had nothing to do but to be of good behaviour. Bad old men were made to wear a yellow coat with red sleeves as a badge of disgrace and were told to sweep the square. This was the worst that could befall them. Unlike old soldiers, who, so I seem to remember, never fade away, old sailors actually do and did, and with the long peace after Trafalgar, combined with an increased demand for old sailors in the merchant service and the possibility of getting light employment, the Royal Naval Hospital found its inmates decreasing, and eventually they were given out-pensions and the Hospital ceased to exist.

I wonder what the old men who fought at the Nile and Trafalgar would have made of the young men of to-day who know all about radar and are taught to shoot ships over the skyline? What would they make of a naval air pilot? What would they have said, as they tottered up the slopes of Greenwich Park with their telescopes, if an aircraft carrier or a modern battleship had steamed past? Can you imagine how crutches, sticks and peg legs would have shivered with amazement and how telescopes would have gone up to every sound eye?

To-day the black-and-silver masses of Portland stone look down no longer upon the brave old sailor-men, but upon hundreds of mathematically minded young officers who pour out of lecture-rooms with books beneath their arms and march smartly off to another lecture, their heads full of the abstruse and complex problems of modern seamanship. Among them are men from various parts of the world, for Greenwich is now the naval university of the Commonwealth. Its president is an admiral, its commander is a captain. Some of its students spend three years learning naval architecture or electrical engineering. Some take a course in history or languages, others go in for metallurgy and chemistry, physics, and applied mechanics. (And they are still called sailors!) There is also a staff college where, incredible to relate, even admirals may be seen, with note-books in front of them, assimilating the higher technicalities of war at sea.

Naturally the sightseer is not permitted to disturb such studies, and I found myself politely shepherded to the only two public sights of the College: the Chapel, which is large, dark and impressive, and the Painted Hall, which is the most wonderful mess-room in the world.

I knew the Painted Hall was magnificent, but, having seen it before cluttered up with paintings and other things, I had no idea how splendid it would be when restored, as it now is, to its original condition as Wren built it and as Thornhill painted it. Four hundred officers can dine at its long, polished tables set beneath the great swirling ceiling-scapes of Thornhill. Silver candlesticks copied from old silver in the possession of the Admiralty shine upon the tables, and the scene is one of magnificence and grandeur that it would be difficult to equal anywhere in the world.

When you mount the steps into this hall you see a group of impressed spectators standing with their heads back gazing up at the ceiling upon which Thornhill expended nineteen years of hard work. Much of his work in country houses has perished, and his frescoes round the dome of St Paul's have been touched up and restored, but this ceiling shows what a fine, vigorous painter he was. You see William and Mary surrounded by a great cloud of flying allegory, Queen Anne and Prince George of Denmark, similarly accompanied, the landing of William of Orange at Torbay and of George I at Greenwich, and in a corner the painter, as he often did, introduced his own portrait.

Thornhill was only fifty-nine when he died, yet he had been born in the reign of Charles II and had lived through the reigns of James II, William and Mary, Queen Anne, George I and the first seven years of George II. What an enormously crowded and varied period this was! It included a restoration, a rebellion, an invasion and the peaceful landing of George I. The varied imagery of Thornhill's ceiling is somehow symbolic of the crowded restless age of change in which he lived. The task of painting a ceiling must be the most trying and exhausting form of the art, and Thornhill evidently considered it three times as difficult as painting on an upright surface, for he agreed to paint the walls of the hall for £1 the square yard, while he charged £3 a square yard for the ceiling. At the end of nineteen years the hard-hearted Commissioners refused to meet him in any way, and paid him on the basis of his estimate, which worked out at only about £300 a year.

The custodian pointed out a little room at the upper end of the hall, now part of the domestic arrangements.

"When Nelson lay in state here," he said, "his body was removed to that little room every night. We call it the Nelson Room."

Nelson again. All the necks straightened up and a whisper of real interest passed round the visitors. But the custodian did not tell us that the crowd which came to see the lying-in-state was so large that sailors armed with boarding-pikes were on duty to keep order. And when the people filed into the hall they saw unbleached candles in sconces and a coffin upon which rested a viscount's coronet; and there was a clergyman who stayed by the body all day long, growing more weary and haggard as the days passed. He was the Rev. Alexander Scott, chaplain to the *Victory*, who had been unnerved and shattered when the ship went into action—"like a butcher's shop," he had called it but, regaining control of himself, he went down into the red cockpit and knelt by the dying Nelson until the last. The poor man was unable to leave the body and, having watched it day and night for two weeks, was seen upon the morning of the funeral half crazed with fatigue and grief. He wrote to Lady Hamilton: "When

I think, setting aside his heroism, what an affectionate, fascinating little fellow he was, how dignified and pure his mind, how kind and condescending his manners, I become stupid with grief for what I have lost." He might surely have written " we " to Emma Hamilton.

And a visit to Greenwich proves that to-day, nearly a hundred and fifty years after, a " fascinating little fellow " Nelson still remains.

While I waited for the boat to take me back to London, I walked the pier and thought of the first Greenwich Palace which was swept out of existence to make way for the present buildings. It had its golden age in the time of Henry VIII and Elizabeth. It must have looked rather like Hampton Court Palace, though the site must have been finer, the river broader and the view glorious across the meadows upstream to the spire of St Paul's.

Henry VIII was born at Greenwich, and he loved the place. Old prints of Placentia, as the palace was called, show a straggling mass of low brick buildings, turreted walls, towers, gateways, courtyards and gardens on the bank of the river. German armourers had their forges and workshops at the back of the palace where they made Henry's tilting armour. There was a tilt yard overlooked by a gatehouse, on the site of the present Queen's House, where the Queen and her ladies watched tournaments and joustings.

The palace was the scene of Henry's obsession with Anne Boleyn and of his divorce from Catherine of Aragon. While Catherine was still at Greenwich, the King installed his mistress there, as he also did at Hampton Court, and when the poor Queen was eventually driven out and the divorce was arranged it was from Greenwich that Anne Boleyn, hated by the Londoners, went gaily by barge to the Tower to spend the night there before her coronation.

" How like you the look of my city, sweetheart ? " asked Henry as he helped her from her splendid litter at the Abbey on the following day.

" The City is well enough," she said, " but I saw a great many caps on heads."

Four months afterwards, the future Queen Elizabeth was born at Greenwich, to the disappointment of her parents, who were so sure of a son that the royal printer had already set up the announcement of the birth of a prince, and was obliged to add a couple of s's to the word. Three years afterwards, while Anne was watching a joust at Greenwich, she dropped her handkerchief in the lists; a knight took it up, placed it to his forehead and returned it to her on the point of his lance. The King saw it, and, to the dismay of the Court, rose suddenly and left the tilting. That night Anne spent in the Tower in the same rooms she had occupied before her coronation, and in a few weeks time she had died on Tower Green.

With Elizabeth the old Palace learned to laugh again as it had done in the days when her father was young. It was the scene of her gay Courts, of revels and dancing, and upon May mornings the meadows and woods rang with laughter as the Queen with her ladies and the whole court went out a-Maying to the hedges of Lewisham. There are many glimpses of Elizabeth at Greenwich. Perhaps less familiar than the account by Paul Hentzner is that of another German, Lupold von Wedel of Kremzow, who came to England in 1585. His spelling of London names was peculiar. Whitehall was "Weithol" and Hampton Court was "Hempenkort", so that it is not surprising to find him going down the Thames to see the Queen at "Grunewitz".

Elizabeth at this time was fifty-two. Wedel waited in the dining-hall for her to return from church. She entered dressed "in black velvet sumptuously embroidered with silver and pearls. Over her robe she had a silver shawl, that was full of meshes and diaphanous like a piece of gossamer tissue. . . . While she was at church a long table was made ready in the room previously described, under the canopy of cloth of gold. On her return from church there were served at this table forty large and silver dishes, all of gilt silver with various meats. She alone took her seat at the table. . . . After the queen had sat down, a table was set up at the end of the room near the door, and at this table five countesses took their seats. A young nobleman habited in black carved the meats for the Queen, and a gentleman of about the same age, arrayed in green, served her beverages. This gentleman had to remain kneeling as long as she was drinking; when she had finished, he rose and removed the goblet. At the table to her right stood gentlemen of rank, as, for instance, my Lord Hower (Lord Howard of Effingham). He is styled Chamberlain, but has the rank of a Lord High Steward in Germany. There stood further Mylord Lester, the Master of the Horse. He is said to have had a love-affair with the Queen for a long time. Now he has a wife."

The writer describes how every course was carried in by knights and nobles led by officers of state bearing white wands. Musicians played, and the Queen, who spoke continuously, summoned various people to her, who knelt until commanded to rise. When the Queen had finished eating the five countesses rose and, after twice making a deep curtsey, walked over to the other side of the room and stood waiting. Elizabeth then rose and turned her back upon the table, while two bishops stepped forward and said grace. Three earls with a large silver gilt basin, and with two noblemen bearing a towel, knelt before the Queen. She drew a ring from her finger and handed it to the Lord Chamberlain. Water was then poured over her hands, and she replaced her ring.

The Queen seated herself on a cushion on the floor, and a dance was begun. At first only the most distinguished courtiers danced, and then the young men laid aside their cloaks and rapiers and asked the young women to dance. All the time the Queen, seated on her cushion, summoned men and women to her and talked all the time.

"She chatted and jested most amiably with them, and pointing with her finger at the face of one, Master or Captain Rall (Raleigh), told him that there was a smut on it. She also offered to wipe it off with her handkerchief, but he anticipating her removed it himself. They say that she now loves him above all others, and this one may easily credit, for but a year ago he could scarcely keep one servant, whereas now owing to her bounty he can afford to keep five hundred."

Raleigh's rise to fame occurred at Greenwich, and it is said that the famous incident of the cloak took place at the gate-house which once stood where the Queen's House is now. Upon a window in Greenwich Raleigh is said to have scratched, "Fain would I climb but that I fear to fall", to which Elizabeth added, "If thy heart fail thee, climb not at all."

It was a great day at Greenwich when Drake, the first Englishman to sail round the world, brought the *Golden Hind* up the Thames to Deptford, and as he passed the Palace he fired a salute to the Queen. Elizabeth went to Deptford and knighted him upon the deck of his ship. It was at Greenwich that Elizabeth signed the death-warrant of Mary Queen of Scots, and the old palace was the scene of the Council which met to make plans to resist the Armada.

A wonderful glimpse of the great Queen at Greenwich in her old age has been preserved. She kept the Scots Ambassador waiting in a room where the corner of a tapestry had been purposely lifted. He was able to see into the next room, where the aged Queen was dancing to the sound of a small fiddle, and, being a diplomat, he probably understood that he was intended to see this and that he was expected to return to Scotland and tell his master, James, that Elizabeth was young and sprightly and that he had better put thoughts of succeeding her out of his mind.

The little boat came in, and we packed ourselves into it. As we went towards London, I thought that I had spent a happy day, and one that I should remember for a long time to come.

§ 6

I arrived at Hampton Court as a summer's day was in full swing. The Thames was covered with rowing-boats, the banks of the river with picnic parties; day trippers were arriving at intervals by steamer from London and the swans cruised up and down with the air of having strayed out of a fairy-tale. As I was having lunch in the bow window of the *Mitre*, I glanced across at the Palace opposite, reflecting that the last time I had seen it was during a snow-storm.

It was on a Sunday in midwinter when, with impetuous generosity, I had offered to collect a boy from a preparatory school at Ascot and take him out for the afternoon. It had occurred to me that it would be adventurous, exciting, and probably against the rules, if we made a sudden dash at London, had tea at my club and returned in time for prayers. That was the kind of outing that would have delighted me when I was young. But when I suggested it to an elderly boy of twelve I was firmly snubbed, and so came to the conclusion that the young people to-day are either better, or maybe more timid, than I was.

"It's out of bounds, sir," I was told, with pained condescension. "Mr Warner would be in a most frightful bait."

"Well, where would you like to go?" I asked, depressed by the thought of Ascot on a freezing Sunday afternoon.

"Could we go to Hampton Court, sir?" asked the boy, and, although I could not have imagined a less suitable day for this expedition, we were soon on our way. We stopped at Staines and, walking out on a floating landing-stage, watched the Thames sweeping past in ice-green floods. It was raining and the sky was blue with unshed snow.

When we came to Hampton Court the snow was lying thinly on the palace roofs, and the old building rose in the greyness of a winter afternoon, withdrawn and lonely; for the boy and I were the only visible explorers. I reflected that, like most people, I had been there only on fine summer days or on days that promised to be fine. Here was another Hampton Court, and one well worth seeing. It suggested hunting-parties in the woods, log fires and hot drinks. It called to mind, not Charles II and ladies with satin gowns falling from white shoulders, but Wolsey and Henry VIII in fur pelisses, the icy wind whistling through corridors and up flights of stone stairs while, snug behind doors, king and courtier, in low panelled rooms hung with tapestries, watched the flames fly up the chimney.

The boy, who had told me how interested he was in history, could not have been more casual and bored once we found ourselves in the palace, which was disappointing, for I did my utmost to rouse his interest. There seemed to be something on his mind. It took me several galleries and presence chambers to realise that he had come to Hampton Court with one object only: to see the Haunted Gallery, so we cut short everything and went straight to this spot, which was living up to its name that afternoon in the thin winter light.

"You see, sir, Hodges has got a book called *Haunted Houses*, which we read in the dorm at night. And this book says how the ghost of Catherine Howard . . ."

There came towards us the sound of footsteps, and the boy's face became pale with delicious apprehension. It was, of course, a custodian, but one who knew what we wanted. The ghosts, he said, are many, but the three most famous are Jane Seymour, Catherine Howard and Mistress Sibell Penn, nurse of Edward VI. He told us how Jane Seymour has been seen on dark nights with a lighted taper in the gallery, and how poor young Catherine Howard—she was only twenty at the time of her execution—has been heard shrieking on her way to the chapel where Henry was hearing Mass when her doom was sealed. Sibell Penn's ghost is linked with the sound of a spinning-wheel which was heard years ago and noted, apparently, by many people. It is an unmistakable sound, and no one could account for it. At length, during renovations to the Haunted Gallery by the Office of Works, a doorway was found leading to a small, hitherto unknown room, where those who knew of the mysterious sounds saw, with astonishment, an antique spinning-wheel whose treadle had worn a groove in the old floor.

It may be an argument in favour of ghosts that the obvious spectres do not haunt Hampton Court. I should have expected Wolsey, Henry, perhaps Catherine of Aragon and certainly Anne Boleyn.

People who take schoolboys out for the afternoon will perhaps agree that it is never possible to predict what may happen. The most unlikely people may find themselves riding an elephant or writing down the numbers of locomotives at Paddington. The end of my day was barely credible. I found myself, chilled to the bone, wandering round the Maze in Hampton Court. When I forgot how ridiculous was the situation I almost enjoyed it. The Maze was dusted with snow, the earthy paths were ice-hard and, of course, we were the only inmates. The boy, like all children, found his way through with ease and was waiting for me flushed and exultant.

" It's quite easy, really, sir," he explained. " I worked Smith Minor's system, which is turn to the right as soon as you can and then again to the right, and then always turn to the left."

Someday I must go back and put Smith Minor's system to the test. When we returned to the school the headmaster gave me a glass of sherry in his study and hoped we had had an interesting day.

" I'm sure you have improved his mind," he said, with more than a hint of sarcasm. " I had no idea the boy was so interested in history. His work certainly does not reflect it."

Now upon this warm day I walked the broad avenue to the palace again, this time in company with the crowd of visitors which London sends out to Hampton Court on a summer's day, some wheeling perambulators, some carrying children and picnic baskets. Who, I wondered, can estimate the effect of such buildings upon the imagination of the general public? They are part of an English heritage, and are impressed upon the minds of millions. Some wander through them dull of eye and mind, yet perhaps aware subconsciously that they are in the presence of something important and significant. Some go there, no doubt, just to indulge the English love of sitting on the grass, and others to stand impressed, and maybe a little puzzled, amid the grandeurs of the past, conscious at the same time that they are in some obscure way connected with them.

To me, Hampton Court is the place above all others where it is easy to imagine Henry VIII and his great daughter living their everyday life, sitting in front of the fire in winter-time, playing tennis, gardening, riding out to hunt the stag, dancing and entertaining their friends. But the emphasis is placed upon the Stuart State apartments, and one comes last of all to the older Tudor rooms and the great hall where Henry VIII feasted and revelled and where possibly Shakespeare may have acted.

I wish visitors might see Hampton Court in the right sequence. Instead of entering the Stuart State apartments, I should prefer to enter by way of the Great Hall and go through the few remaining Tudor rooms, which in a perfect world would be sumptuously furnished with tapestries, oak chairs, tables, sideboards and clocks. It would then be possible to see the kind of rooms in which Wolsey and Henry VIII lived four centuries ago.

Cardinal Wolsey chose Hampton as his country home because the doctors told him that it was the healthiest place within twenty miles of London. Like many another large and possibly robust man, Wolsey was terrified of illness, and his country palace was a safe retreat from the crowded streets of London during times of plague. One of his first acts was to bring a good water supply from Coombe Hill, three miles away, and the lead pipes passed beneath the Thames above Kingston bridge.

The Cardinal had good taste, a love of pomp and splendour and enormous revenues, so that his palace soon became the most magnificent in the realm. Henry VIII was at first enchanted and then envious. The scale of Wolsey's establishment would have been surprising in any age, and incredible in this servantless age of ours. Presiding over two kitchens, one of them the Cardinal's privy kitchen, was a master cook, who dressed in velvet and wore a chain of office; they show you the little room in which he used to draw up his menus. Under him were eighty assistant cooks, yeomen and scullions. About a hundred servants were at work in the wardrobe, the laundry, the woodyard, to say nothing of the stables where the master of the horse controlled a great number of grooms and stable-boys. Apart from the domestic establishment there were sixty priests and officers of the chapel, the choir and a crowd of personal attendants and functionaries. As Lord Chancellor, Wolsey maintained a second establishment which included heralds, serjeants-at-arms, minstrels, clerks, armourers and running footmen.

It is said that upon one occasion Henry VIII asked why a

private subject should have created such a regal home, and Wolsey, who was evidently well prepared for the question, answered tactfully, " In order to present it to his Sovereign." He may have said this as the Spaniard says " My house is yours ", or as the Arab offers a guest anything that he admires; but both Spaniard and Arab would be sadly disconcerted were they to be taken literally! Nevertheless, Henry chose to take Wolsey at his word, and eventually became the owner of Hampton Court.

The Palace then became the background to all Henry's matrimonial adventures. Every one of his six queens walked the red-brick courtyards, the galleries, the gardens, the park, each one tasted brief happiness there, one queen bore his only son there. One was married in the Chapel of the Palace. It was, of course, the scene of several of his honeymoons. The palace saw him first, in Wolsey's time, as a gay young man of twenty-five married to thirty-one-year-old Catherine of Aragon, the widow of his dead brother, Arthur. They were happy for some years, until Henry's roving eye settled upon Anne Boleyn. He installed her in the same palace with his Queen at Hampton Court. After she had become Queen, Anne Boleyn detected in a room at Hampton Court her husband's flirtation with her successor, Jane Seymour, and it was at Hampton Court that Jane died of puerpural fever after having given birth to the son who became Edward VI.

After her death Henry awaited apprehensively at Hampton Court the arrival from Dover of his " great Flanders mare ", Anne of Cleves. He had been betrayed into marriage, it is said, by an optimistic portrait by Holbein. Unable to bear the anxiety, Henry went off to meet her in disguise, and came up with her in a house at Rochester. Anne was looking out of a window at a bull-baiting. Henry, who must have been an advanced sentimentalist, approached incognito, and presented her with a token from himself. She thanked him briefly, but was evidently much more interested in the bull-baiting. Henry then retired to another apartment and donned a suit of purple velvet in which he returned to introduce himself.

It is probably not true that Henry was immediately repelled by her appearance, for he said to Cromwell the next day that although she was " nothing so fair as had been reported ", she was " well and seemly ". Before the marriage, however, the bridegroom became so reluctant that he asked the Council if " I must needs put my neck in the yoke ". On his marriage morning he said grimly, " If it were not to satisfy the world and my realm, I would not do that which I must do this day for none earthly thing." He even referred to his bride as a " Dutch cow ".

The royal sacrifice for England was not, however, of long duration, and at Hampton Court some few months later Anne waited complacently for the news that she had been divorced and given the title of " royal sister ", which suited her quite well. Against the leafy background of Hampton Court, Henry was captivated by the youthful charm of Catherine Howard, and two years later he rode away from the palace broken-hearted by the knowledge that his rose was not without a thorn. The old palace, which must by that time have become rather cynical, was the place of Henry's sixth and last honeymoon. If experience counts in matrimony, Henry and Catherine Parr should have had the recipe for success. They were married in the Queen's Closet at Hampton Court, Henry vast, unwieldy and almost a cripple, she a small fair-haired woman of thirty-one who had been twice widowed. She would have been known in the Eighteenth Century as a bluestocking. She was a Greek and Latin scholar, and could argue theology with any doctor of divinity, but she also possessed a fund of feminine sympathy which was spent upon the ailing King and upon his three neglected children. No doubt Henry admired her at times as much as he resented her in moments when his ulcerated leg was giving him pain. It is on record that once, when she had dared to correct him upon a point of theology, he broke out with a touch of the old Henry. " It is good hearing," he cried, " when women become such clerks; and a thing much to my comfort in mine old days to be taught by my wife! " Ill and irritable as he was, and in need of nursing, it is too much to believe that he might have concluded his domestic experiences by becoming a hen-pecked husband. But, of course, stranger things have happened.

It would be fascinating to know what this intelligent woman thought of Henry VIII. Something possibly may be inferred from the fact that a few months after his death she married her fourth husband, Lord Seymour of Sudeley. He is said to have been in love with her before she became Queen, and their reunion might have been a romantic one were it not known that this scheming, ambitious man, who ended his life on the scaffold, had made advances to Mary, Elizabeth and even to Anne of Cleves!

§ 7

In Elizabeth's time Hampton Court became a holiday palace in which the Queen sought escape from the affairs of State. Anyone of the time who glanced through the windows overlooking the Privy Garden on a sharp winter morning might have seen the unusual spectacle of the Virgin Queen taking a brisk walk " to catch her a heate ", which she did regularly while at Hampton Court, though when in public she was never guilty of the vulgarity of quick walking, but " went slowly and marched with leisure ". She loved the Privy Gardens, whose walls were overhung with rosemary and whose hedges and trees were clipped to resemble men, beasts and birds. In these surroundings she talked with Melville, the Scots Ambassador, who has left an account of Elizabeth's attempt to make him admit that she was more beautiful and more accomplished than Mary Queen of Scots; and Melville, although a highly competent flatterer, escaped from the ordeal only with difficulty and with his loyalty to his mistress barely intact.

Like her father, Elizabeth loved the chase, but, being Elizabeth, she liked to introduce a touch of pageantry into it. Among the extraordinary ghosts which might rise up from the floors of little red-brick villas round Hampton Court is that of Elizabeth attired for the hunt and attended by ladies dressed in white satin and mounted upon ambling palfreys. When she came within bowshot of the stag she encountered fifty archers dressed in green, with scarlet boots and gilt bows, who presented her with a silver arrow winged with peacock's feathers. After the royal shaft had been discharged the party rode on to some shady bower where minstrels were playing and luncheon stood ready beneath the oak-trees.

Elizabeth's projected marriage, which became England's foreign policy for so many years, was first discussed at Hampton Court when Cecil produced the Earl of Arran for her inspection, the first of her many suitors. But she did not like him. He had no brains, was nothing to look at and, as she said to the Spanish Ambassador, " she would never have a husband who would sit all day by the fireside ". She would only marry a man who could ride and hunt and fight. Possibly remembering her father's disastrous marriage with Anne of Cleves, whom he had espoused as the custom was in those days on the strength of a portrait, Elizabeth would have nothing to do with the miniatures and pictures, but obliged all the young men who desired to marry her to travel across Europe before she flirted with them and turned them down. I suppose the modern psychologist would trace to her father's many unsuccessful marriages Elizabeth's refusal to take a husband. So Hampton Court was the scene of Henry's many honeymoons, as it was of the beginning of his daughter's long resistance to the state of matrimony.

At Christmas time the Great Hall, where one stands in another world and age, was the centre of the Court's merry-making. Wires were stretched across it from which hung hundreds of oil-lamps. This early theatre was the scene of masques and plays from Christmas Eve until Twelfth Night. To see the hall now, beautifully tidy, polished and empty, is to have no idea of the scene it must have presented in Tudor times when the carpenters were putting up the stage and erecting elaborate scenery, introducing trees from the park to represent a forest and painting canvas houses; when the actors were rehearsing in the Great Watching Chamber and the tailors, dressmakers and sempstresses were busy making and adapting costumes for the players. What would we not give to have a film of those events? If only the cinema camera had been invented four centuries ago and one placed in the hands of Leicester, what a scene would have been preserved of Hampton Court at Christmas time: of the Queen and her ladies watching the play, of the Queen dancing a coranto or a galliard, or possibly even the daring volto, which was banned in many European Courts, but was danced by Elizabeth, as we can see from a picture at Penshurst which shows her being lifted into the air by her partner like a ballet-dancer.

Hampton Court knew Elizabeth first as a high-spirited young Queen with natural red hair, and it saw her for the last time as a high-spirited old lady of nearly seventy whose wig was red. Upon this last occasion, four years before her death, someone glancing through a palace window saw the old Queen dancing a Spanish dance to the sound of pipe and tabor. The morning of her departure was wet and stormy. The saddle-horses were waiting in the courtyard. Lord Hunsdon said that " it was not meet for one of her Majesty's years to ride in such a storm ". Elizabeth was furious. " *My* years ! " she cried. " Maids, to your horses quickly ! ", and, although hardly able to sit upright, she disappeared into the storm; and Hampton Court never saw her again. For two days she refused to speak to Lord Hunsdon!

§ 8

The State Apartments, which are the chief sight of Hampton Court, were built by Christopher Wren for William and Mary, who considered the old royal quarters antique and inconvenient. They form a colossal royal flat through which the visitor wanders, pausing to admire the splendid pictures, the tall state beds, a superb clock by Tompion and a gorgeous barometer by Daniel Quare.

The presence upon the walls of these rooms of the spoilt-looking and monotonous court beauties of the time of Charles II may give some visitors the impression that they are walking through the halls where the Merry Monarch held Court. But of course they are not. Charles when at Hampton Court lived in the old Tudor apartments which Wren pulled down. These rooms must have felt that the bad old days were back, for the age of honeymoons began again with Charles. He brought to Hampton Court his young bride, Catherine of Braganza, whose arrival coincided with the birth of a son to Charles by Barbara Castlemaine. Among the instructions given to Catherine by her mother before she left Lisbon was that on no account was she to tolerate, or receive, Lady Castlemaine. But as Anne Boleyn had been determined to humiliate Catherine of Aragon in the same palace, so Lady Castlemaine forced the King to present her to the Queen. Charles did this suddenly and boldly in the face of the whole Court. He advanced holding the beautiful Barbara by the hand and led her to the throne, where Catherine of Braganza, who had not heard her name clearly, was at first most gracious, then, suddenly realising what had happened, burst into tears and was carried fainting from the throne-room with a bleeding nose.

After the reign of Charles II nothing spectacular happened at Hampton Court except a mole. Into the earth made by this mole a horse called Sorrel stumbled one day in the year 1702, and William III, who was in the saddle, was flung to the ground and received injuries from which he died. The Jacobites of that time, rejoicing at the death of Dutch William, raised their glasses to the mole of Hampton Court "the little gentleman in the black velvet coat".

As I explored the State apartments I thought that, much as I should like to have seen the palace in the time of Henry VIII, it would have been seen best in the time of Charles I, before the art treasures had been put up for auction. Few people realise the enormous number of treasures lost to England, and now dispersed throughout Europe and many of them lost for ever, when the Commonwealth Parliament sold the contents of the royal palaces after the execution of Charles I.

The Hampton Court sale, to say nothing of the sale of the Whitehall pictures, is enough to turn the modern connoisseur and art collector pale with envy. Treasures which only a millionaire could buy to-day were sold for a few hundred pounds. Titian's *Venus*, now in the Prado at Madrid, fetched £600; Van Dyck's great portrait of Charles I, bare-headed and in armour on a brown horse, now in the National Gallery, was valued at £200, and Raphael's Cartoons, the designs for the tapestries of the Sistine Chapel, now in the Victoria and Albert Museum, at £300!

The sale, which was one of the longest upon record, lasted at intervals for three years. The Palace was packed with every kind of treasure and antiquity accumulated first by Wolsey, then by Henry VIII, Elizabeth and later monarchs. It must have been a museum of English furniture, for there were chairs and beds that had belonged to Wolsey, canopies, vestments, musical instruments, tables, cabinets and all kinds of curiosities. How much, I wonder, would Henry VIII's walking-stick fetch at Christie's to-day? In 1649 it fetched 5*s.*! Cardinal Wolsey's mirror surmounted by his arms fetched £5, and a pair of gloves belonging to Henry VIII went for 1*s.*!

The sale of the Whitehall Palace pictures was an equally disastrous event. Charles housed this splendid collection in a special gallery. It included twenty-eight canvases by Titian, nine by Raphael, four by Corregio and seven by Rubens. The Puritans destroyed pictures of Christ or the Virgin Mary and are said to have burnt three by Raphael and four by Leonardo da Vinci. Any pictures which were considered immodest were hidden away until it was decided what to do with them, and in this way some were forgotten and preserved. That is the strange history behind *Adam and Eve* by Mabuse, which hangs to-day at Hampton Court.

§ 9

I sat in the gardens and watched children playing ball, I admired the fountains and the ducks and I saw the Great Vine. I then saw the old Tennis Court, built in 1529 by Henry VIII, where members of the Royal Tennis Court Club still play—surely the oldest athletic association in the country.

Henry, who was a good player, was perhaps the first person in England to wear tennis-shorts. Nothing half as spectacular was ever seen at Wimbledon, for his shorts were silk or velvet drawers slashed with "cuttes" and the edges sewn with gold cord. The King began his tennis career without a racquet, using a padded glove instead, and a hard ball stuffed with compressed wool. The tennis " net " was merely a fringed cord drawn across the court.

I returned again to the gardens to sit on a seat and watch the life around me. A man and a woman painfully in love were sitting under a great tree, and when I grew tired of contemplating them, and of wondering what will happen to them and for how long they will remain in that condition, I began to think about gardens and the history of gardens. The gardens of Hampton Court are England's most attractive essay in the manner of Versailles. They are also, I suppose, the last surviving princely garden in this style in England. I thought of the change of garden fashion and what an interesting subject this is. The mediæval garden was, I fancy, an offshoot from the monastery garden. It often nestled timidly on the other side of the castle moat beneath my lady's tower. It was a walled place of bowers, flowers and fountains where, in days when the Great Hall was really a lounge hall and was always full of men and dogs, lovers, as in the *Romance of the Rose*, could find a quiet retreat. The crusaders returned from the East, having seen the gardens of Constantinople and Syria, bringing with them new fruits, flowers and herbs; the Elizabethan navigators returned from the New World with more novelties, and the English garden went on changing from age to age as these strangers from far countries became naturalised in our beds and borders. (Who nowadays thinks of the potato as an American or the geranium as a South African?)

As life became more secure the castle moat was filled in and was made into a garden. It became larger and more elaborate, but it was always a piece of land which man had trained, clipped, formalised and separated from the surrounding wildness of the natural landscape. The Elizabethan garden was a place of box hedges, formal beds and topiary. It was a place to enchant the eye and the sense of smell, with its sweet williams, its stocks and its pinks, a place to sit in and to play in—in other words, it was an outdoor extension of the house. The most magnificent example of formal garden architecture was at Versailles under Louis XIV, splendours which are reflected beside the Thames at Hampton Court. This kind of garden was well suited to an age of corsets and satin, of high-backed chairs and courtly manners, and as I looked at the gardens of Hampton Court all the modern people seemed to fade away, and I saw, in imagination, men and women in the elaborate clothes of another day walking in dignity towards some carefully calculated vista.

When Charles II was restored to the throne the gardens of England were in a deplorable condition. Great estates had been confiscated, many of their owners had died during the Civil War and others had been in exile. Anyone who has neglected a garden for two summers can readily imagine what the gardens of England looked like after eleven years; for the Puritans cared only for vegetables, and considered elaborate gardens an unnecessary, perhaps even a wicked, luxury. When the cavaliers came back there was a tremendous burst of gardening, led by the King, who, it is said, got André le Nôtre, the designer of the Versailles gardens, to help him.

But a great change of gardening fashion was on the way. Politics and æsthetics both had a part in it. During the French wars of the next century Englishmen turned away from the French garden much as some people refused to listen to Wagner during the 1914 War. The English upper classes, nurtured on the classics and inspired by the Grand Tour, found in the overgrown gardens of the Italian Renaissance the perfect contrast to the clipped formalism which then seemed to them like a version, in vegetation, of French absolutism. Noblemen, returning from Italy, swept their enclosed formal gardens out of existence. They put down turf, dammed up rivers to make picturesque little Alban lakes, set skilfully placed trees, built classical ruins in groves and made grottoes and caverns. At great expense they bullied the shaggy English landscape into obedient tidiness, and were then able to walk or ride out from their Palladian houses into a countryside designed to awaken in their minds the same romantic associations that came as their coaches rolled down from the Alps into Italy and as they stood, meditating pleasantly upon the fall of greatness, in the ruins of the

Colosseum. Horace Walpole, writing of one of these gardening revolutionaries, said, " He leaped the fence and found all Nature was a garden."

It was the end of such gardens as those of Hampton Court. They were no longer in good taste. The carefully tended naturalness of a Hyde Park was the new ideal, with a little classical lodge-gate or a temple or a stray statue to give the right touch. And it was interesting to sit in the formalism of Hampton Court and to see the logical conclusion of the love of natural scenery personified by a party of young cyclists, girls and men, in the shortest of shorts. One maid, who was wearing rather superior shorts of blue linen, would indeed have been welcomed as a charming " nymph " by Lord Burlington, and other connoisseurs of the Eighteenth Century, and have been considered well worth incorporating in any of the new landscapes. But how out of place she looked with her, I must say very beautiful, legs in a garden designed for stately ladies in sweeping skirts of gold brocade.

§ 10

I was walking up Bond Street one evening on my way to Broadcasting House where I had to speak to Africa on the General Overseas Programme. As I walked on, I muttered to myself as much as I could remember of my script, thinking how odd and magical it was that in a short while my voice would be heard thousands of miles away in lonely farms and homesteads, in mission stations and traders' posts, in towns and cities all over Africa.

I wondered whether my old friend Freddie would hear me on his farm near Oldeani, in Tanganyika, whether Joan would hear me in Uganda, whether Charles and Mabel, surrounded by their tobacco, would hear me in Rhodesia, whether James would be sitting on his verandah in Kenya drinking a sundowner and listening with the evening wind rasping through the trees and the crickets snapping. But it would be too late for a sundowner! It would be 8 p.m. in London, 9 p.m. in Nigeria and 10 p.m. in East and South Africa. (He would probably be having a night-cap!)

Lots of people would hear me in Johannesburg and Cape Town, and I should no doubt get letters and postcards from friends in Somerset West in the shadow of the Helderberg. I could already see these letters clearly. "We heard you beautifully. You might have been in the room." "Isn't it funny, Jimmy switched on the wireless by chance and the first thing we heard was your voice." And the inevitable friend: "We thought you sounded rather depressed". Meanwhile none of these things had yet happened, and I was walking up Bond Street in the evening.

Of all the modern buildings in London Broadcasting House is perhaps the most remarkable and the most important. It is also strange to remember that this immense organisation functioning from its impressive stronghold in Portland Place began only in the nineteen-twenties in humble little offices in Savoy Hill, off the Strand. I wonder what we should have said in those days, when we were delighted and surprised to receive letters from listeners as far off as Cornwall, could we have been granted a vision of Broadcasting House to-day, and could we have known that this strange new toy of ours would in our time help to keep alive the flame of freedom in Europe and make known the chimes of Big Ben in every corner of the world.

Broadcasting House expresses the spirit of the Twentieth Century as completely as the Tower of London expresses that of the Eleventh. And the two buildings have something in common. They are both constructed round a central keep. The core of Broadcasting House is a huge tower of immensely thick brickwork, windowless, airless and insulated from outside sounds. The air is pumped into it over water sprays that filter the dust and soot. If the electric light and power failed elsewhere, the emergency batteries of the tower would come into action instantly. In this strange fortress—the best built in London since the White Tower—you will find all the B.B.C. studios.

I was shot up into one of them and left there with a microphone. When the red light came on I began to speak, and when I had finished the red light went off. The programme organiser came in and said that everything was fine and would

I like a cup of coffee? We walked together to the lifts through this fantastic world of aerial instruction and entertainment, where, on the other side of plate glass windows, we could see men and women earnestly speaking into microphones, orchestras noiselessly crashing into symphonies, comedians laughing at jokes which we, a few yards away, could not hear, although listeners were probably laughing at them in Canada, and actors engaged in some inaudible drama. And all this varied talk and sound was being silently shot into the ether to be translated into sound again thousands of miles away.

The café where the B.B.C refreshes itself and its guests is a curious and unusual place because its clients are so varied. Many of them are known to the world only as voices. Some are known as voices with names attached to them. Few are known by sight. The unimpressive little man drinking a cup of tea was an announcer whose voice suggests a man at least six feet high who could take charge of the Foreign Office and be Home Secretary in his spare time. It is a mistake for anyone to see a favourite author or broadcaster. When television becomes more accessible it will destroy as many illusions as a book luncheon.

At the next table sat a popular actress, a test pilot, a rural dean and an Oxford don, their host the question master of a Brains Trust. The composed individual in fancy dress behind them was a native chief who was paying his first visit to London. The door opened and in came a minor member of the Cabinet, his script, which I felt sure he would be certain to rustle crisply, protruding from his pocket. Uncle Mac, who has instructed and amused more children than any living man, was sitting there with a person whom I seemed to recognise as a popular funny man whose voice, to me, is instantly the signal to switch off.

What a curious life it is, this day and night effort to send news, instruction and amusement over the air. It resembles in no way a newspaper, which is born to-day and is dead to-morrow. A newspaper is a masterpiece of extemporisation. It is made by men who haven't the slightest idea what they are going to do when they arrive on duty. But the work of the B.B.C. is planned ahead for months. It is a cold-blooded, deliberate organisation and the master of the whole show is a clock with a large red seconds hand.

On my way out my host took me to see the dedication stone of the building, upon which are written these fine words:

> This Temple of the Arts and Muses is dedicated to Almighty God by the first Governors of Broadcasting in the year 1931, Sir John Reith being Director-General. It is their prayer that good seed sown may bring forth a good harvest, that all things hostile to peace or purity may be banished from this house, and that the people, inclining their ear to whatsoever things are beautiful and honest and of good report, may tread the path of wisdom and uprightness.

And there came to mind Dr Goebbels and the horrible voice of "Haw-haw"—"Jairmany calling"—and I reflected that in the battle between good and evil, which now appears to have reached its climax, broadcasting, like every other great invention, has created its demon.

Feeling unpleasantly wide awake, for it was just past eleven o'clock, and wondering what Africa had thought of my broadcast, I walked down Regent Street to Piccadilly Circus. The theatres were emptying and the streets were crowded. Every taxi was either occupied or disinterested. One driver stopped and asked if I were going towards Paddington, but when I said "no" he sped on without a word. How incredible this would have been some years ago.

Walking on down Lower Regent Street, I saw the lovely sight of Trafalgar Square empty in the light of arc lamps, the lions guarding the thin black column that rose up to lose itself in the dark. Whitehall was empty except for a few people turned out from the public-houses. The Cenotaph, just another monument now, stood cold and forlorn in the middle of the road. No one nowadays bares his head to it as we all did thirty years ago. The men who kept the home fires burning, who walked the long, long trail and saw roses blooming in Picardy, are incredibly far away from us now. Even their photographs in civvies or in breeches and puttees begin to look archaic. To the modern schoolchild Ypres and Neuve Chapelle are as remote as Sebastapol; and why not? Yet I remember, as if it were yesterday, the day the Cenotaph was unveiled in 1920, the warm flood of emotion, the rawness of our memories, the crowds of young women in black, and the feeling that our friends and comrades were still with us; for we could still remember how they looked and how they spoke. Now we, who were once their contemporaries, are old enough to be their fathers.

When I came to Parliament Square I saw the lantern burning in the Clock Tower, a sign that the House was still sitting. Big Ben struck eleven-thirty. A half moon slipped out of a cloud and shone for a moment upon the Abbey. I crossed over to Westminster Bridge and saw a golden chain of tramcars spinning along the Embankment full of people going home to Kennington, Camberwell, Brixton and the southern suburbs. The tide was high, and when a tramcar was not grinding round the curve to the bridge I could hear the water lapping against the stones.

The Thames. . . . Everything begins and ends with that river whose ebb and flood is the pulse of London. I saw its waters below me, dark, oily and swift, and I began to think of its nineteen centuries of history, a long time for men to have lived in the same place, striving, loving, hating, building and pulling down, failing and succeeding, dull men, inspired men, good, bad and indifferent, century after century from Roman times until to-day. To each generation, the Thames, coming freshly from the sea and returning again to the sea, might be said to symbolise life itself.

It is easy to be lonely in London but not so easy to be alone, and every Londoner knows the magic of those rare moments in the early morning, or late at night, when the busy scene is deserted and he looks at London as he might look at an empty stage.

There are cities which, by virtue of the contribution made by their inhabitants to the story of Mankind, are immortal, and London, with Athens and Rome, is among them. The Thames and the Tiber will flow together in history, Westminster Abbey and the Parthenon, strange as it may seem, are not unrelated; and we who have lived and loved, suffered and struggled in London know that in this place upon a river bank, where so many millions of men and women have lived, there is a spirit or soul. Together with so much that is ignoble and sordid, this thing persists at the heart of London, this continuity of human effort with all its glories and all its shames, which touches those who are conscious of it with pride and with something almost like happiness and, difficult as it may be at times, with faith.

Big Ben struck twelve. The lantern still burned above the House of Commons. A taxi most surprisingly drew up, and an old Cockney voice, so unusual in these days, asked:

" Keb, guv'nor ? "

Not a taxi, but a cab! The question, like so much that is attractive in London, came out of the past.

I looked round at the dark river and the lights curving along the Embankment, at the Gothic mass of Parliament and the shape of the Abbey beyond.

" Good-night. . . . Good-night, London."

BIBLIOGRAPHY

I would like to express my gratitude to the following authors:

Bell, Walter G.: *The Great Fire of London.*
Davey, Richard: *The Pageant of London.*
The Tower of London.
Evelyn, John: *Diary.*
Fitter, R. S. R.: *London's Natural History.*
Kent, William: *An Encyclopaedia of London.*
London for Everyman.
The Lost Treasures of London.
Larwood, Jacob: *The Story of the London Parks.*
Law, Ernest: *A Short History of Hampton Court.*
London Museum Catalogues: *London in Roman Times.*
Malcolm, James Peller: *Anecdotes of the Manners and Customs of London during the Eighteenth Century.*
Muirhead: *London and its Environs* (Blue Guides).
Pepys, Samuel: *Diary.*
Royal Commission on Historical Monuments: *London.* Five volumes.
Sheppard, Edgar: *The Old Royal Palace of Whitehall.*
Stanley, Arthur Penrhyn: *Historical Memorials of Westminster Abbey.*
Summerson, John: *Georgian London.*
Thornbury, Walter: *Old and New London.*
Walpole, Horace: *Letters.*
Wheatley and Cunningham: *London Past and Present.*
Younghusband, Sir George: *The Tower of London from Within.*

INDEX

N.B.—*Churches* and *Inns and Taverns* are grouped under those headings.